Communication Theory & Research

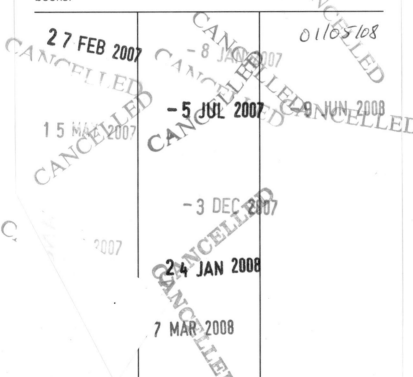

Communication Theory & Research

An *EJC Anthology*

Edited by
Denis McQuail, Peter Golding and Els de Bens

$ SAGE Publications
London ● Thousand Oaks ● New Delhi

SAGE Publications Ltd
1 Oliver's Yard
55 City Road
London EC1Y 1SP

SAGE Publications Inc.
2455 Teller Road
Thousand Oaks, California 91320

SAGE Publications India Pvt Ltd
B-42, Panchsheel Enclave
Post Box 4109
New Delhi 110 017

British Library Cataloguing in Publication data

A catalogue record for this book is available
from the British Library

ISBN 1-4129-1832-4
ISBN 1-4129-1833-2 (pbk)

Library of Congress Control Number available

Typeset by C&M Digitals (P) Ltd., Chennai, India
Printed and bound in India by Gopsons Papers, Noida

Contents

Notes on Contributors

Jo Bardoel is Professor in the Department of Communication, Radboud University, Nijmegen and a Senior Research Fellow in the School of Communication Research, University of Amsterdam.

Inbal Barzel graduated in Psychology from Bar Ilan University.

Els de Bens is Professor in the Department of Communication, University of Ghent.

Daniel Biltereyst is Professor in the Department of Communication, University of Ghent.

Mutlu Binark is in the Faculty of Communication, Gazi University, Ankara.

Jay G. Blumer is Professor Emeritus, University of Leeds and the University of Maryland.

Kees Brants is Professor of Political Communication, University of Leiden and Senior Research Fellow in the School of Communication Research, University of Amsterdam.

Thorbjörn Broddason is Professor of Sociology and Director of Media Studies at the University of Iceland.

Marjorie Ferguson was Professor in the School of Journalism, University of Maryland.

Peter Golding is Professor and Head, Department of Social Sciences, Loughborough University.

Klaus Bruhn Jensen is Professor of Film and Communication, University of Copenhagen.

Bariş Kiliçbay is at the Faculty of Communication, Gazi University, Ankara.

Jeffrey Klaehn is Professor in the Department of Sociology and Anthropology, Wifred Laurier University, Ontario.

Olessia Koltsova is Associate Professor in Mass Communications, Department of Sociology, University of St. Petersburg.

Tiina Laitila graduated from the University of Tampere and works as a freelance journalists in Stockholm.

Tamar Liebes is Professor in the Department of Communication, Hebrew University, Jerusalem.

Dafna Lemish is Professor and Chair, Department of Communication, University of Tel Aviv.

Sonia Livingstone is Professor of Social Psychology at the London School of Economics.

Denis McQuail is Professor Emeritus, School of Communication Research, University of Amsterdam.

Karl Erik Rosengren is Professor Emeritus, Department of Sociology, University of Lund.

Rossella Savarese is Professor in the Sociology of Media and Cultural Processes at University Federico II, Naples.

Preben Sepstrup is Ekstern Lektor, Department of Information and Media Studies, University of Ärhus.

Hedwig de Smaele is Associate Professor in the Department of Communication, University of Ghent.

Patrick Vyncke is Professor in the Department of Communication, University of Ghent.

Liesbet van Zoonen is Professor of Media and Popular Culture, University of Amsterdam.

Preface

The *European Journal of Communication* was founded in 1985 and its first issue appeared in the Spring of 1986. The chief architect of and driving force behind the foundation of the Journal was Jay G. Blumler, of the University of Leeds, strongly backed by our publishers, Sage. The first editors were Jay Blumler, Karl Erik Rosengren (University of Lund) and Denis McQuail (University of Amsterdam), supported by an active Editorial Board and a larger number of corresponding editors drawn from most of the countries of Europe. It is now edited by the undersigned and based at Loughborough University and the University of Ghent.

The publication of this anthology marks the twentieth anniversary of the Journal's inception at a time when Europe was experiencing an acceleration in communication research and an expansion in the number and size of teaching programmes in higher education devoted to media and communication. The then aim of the Journal was to expand the opportunities for publication of theory and research and to make a contribution to the definition and identity of the field. Its particular role, as reflected in the chosen title, was to reflect the range of different traditions of communication research (and issues for research) on the European continent and to contribute to a greater interconnection and dialogue between the different schools of work. It would also serve to make research in Europe more widely known to an international audience.

The field of communication was then, as now, open to alternative definitions and the editors of the first issue identified the central phenomena to be dealt with as 'processes of public communication within and between societies and thus primarily to do with mass media and mass communications'. At the time it could be argued that the study of communication in Europe was more united by way of an imported North American heritage than by a shared approach to issues of public communication. There was, of course, much in the way of shared experience in the history of media development and similarities of media systems. It was already very clear twenty years ago that European media as well as social and political life were undergoing similar changes in response to the same technological and economic challenges. In the first issue of the Journal, the editors argued that 'Europe has provided the cradle for many of the prevailing forms and practices of mass communication and is also distinguished by a shared history, traditions of scholarship and, to a degree, social and economic circumstances'.

Although 'Europeanness', as we rather loosely identified it, was important to the aims and profile of the *EJC* it was not the primary defining criterion for editorial selection. This was and remains the scholarly quality of research, thinking and writing. But there were subsidiary criteria, especially those to do with the need to cover a very diverse field of topics and to try to represent the perspectives of different countries and regions. The ambition was to be equally interested in theory and empirical research (especially when combined) and normative as well as social-scientific theory. The doors were to be open to younger as well as established scholars and to 'thoughtful professionals in communication as well as academics' (to quote the opening editorial again). One of the most ambitious aims of the original *EJC* was to address questions of intellectual or social significance.

The content of the Journal has inevitably changed to reflect developments in society, culture and media, plus intellectual responses to these. The field of communication has become more specialized and there are many more journals published in Europe, but there still seems to be a need for a generalist publication that deals with core issues. The broad aims of the *EJC* have not changed greatly and it should be possible to recognize much the same lines of thinking in the selections reproduced here, even though they are mainly drawn from issues of the last few years. We are still committed to an open and diverse policy of selection, still concerned with potential intellectual and social significance, still focused primarily on public communication, but recognizing that sharp lines between public and private can no longer be drawn.

The existence of this book and the success of the Journal in its ambitions reflect the efforts of innumerable authors, reviewers, advisers and helpers. On an anniversary occasion it is appropriate to name a succession of dedicated Book Review Editors and Associate Editors. Klaus Schönback, Robin Cheesman and Michael Pickering have served in the former capacity. The latter have included Holli Semetko, Robert Buinett, Margaret Scammell, Tudor Oltean, Wendy Monk, Hilde Jansseus, Liz Sutton, Heather Owen, Dieder van Landuyt, Sarah Rawson and Annelore Deprez. We are much indebted for their collective efforts over the years. In a more immediate sense, we are very grateful to Julia Hall for encouragement and support in the whole enterprise and to Jamilah Ahmed and Fabienne Pedroletti for organizing out the task of production so efficiently.

Denis McQuail
Peter Golding
Els de Bens
March 2005

Introduction and Overview

Denis McQuail

Origins and development of the field in Europe

Communications and media as a field of research in Europe scarcely predates the Second World War, apart from the case of Germany where a press science (*Zeitungswissenschaft*) was quite well established in some German universities. Much of this work was historical or practical, but theory about the links between the press and society had also been developed by German sociologists (Hardt, 2003). For understandable reasons, this tradition did not have much influence on post-war development although a number of those engaged in the study of mass media and society were part of the 1930s' diaspora, mainly to the United States (Averbeck, 2001), giving rise to an indirect effect. Early French sociologists, notably Gabriel Tarde, had attached great importance to the press and other means of publicity as influences on collective behaviour, the formation of opinion and the transmission to modernity. Pre-Second World War and immediate post-war British sociology, however, was focused on social problems, among which the contemporary mass media did not really figure. In general, the task of post-war reconstruction in Europe was too large to allow much attention to be directed to the media. All in all, at the mid-twentieth century it seemed that the field was largely open for the 'invasion' of American ideas about mass media and methods of enquiry. As Tunstall (1977) observed, not only were the media American, so was media science.

These remarks should not be read as indicating any lack of early awareness in Europe of the immense potential significance of the mass press, film and radio from political, cultural and social perspectives. There was clear evidence of the close involvement of mass media in the unfolding events driven by nationalism, war and totalitarianism. However, social science was under-developed and the field was largely left to speculation and amateur investigation. An exception to this judgement is the pre-war engagement by the BBC in systematic radio audience research. Post-war American influence showed up in a predilection for sample survey enquiries into 'media use' and studies of media effects carried out by statistical methods. It took the arrival of the new mass medium of television to really stimulate media research, especially as it was not only credited with potency and viewed by many as problematic, but also held out a new promise of enlightenment, education and cultural development. In the 1950s and 1960s, the study of media was largely framed according to topics that lent themselves to enquiry within the frames of leisure-time use, effectiveness in political persuasion, protecting and meeting the needs of children and youth and the merits or demerits of 'mass culture'. Apart from this, a central and growing concern of media industry and others was the measurement of audiences for the various competing media.

From the later 1960s onwards, a new wind was blowing in European social science, perhaps especially from Britain. The dominant paradigm of study of media uses and effects was challenged by critical theory that interpreted the tendencies of media content, especially in news, as a form of hidden ideology designed to maintain hegemonic control on behalf of state bureaucracies or big business. Attention also turned from messages, audiences and effects to include the political economic supports for the media system. Another strand in the new movement was the development, more or less simultaneous in North America and Europe, of sociological enquiries into the media production process, especially of news. The results shed light on the reasons for dominant tendencies of content and supported the view that media tend to maintain rather than challenge the status quo. In addition, a major change had occurred in the study of popular and mass culture, involving a revaluation of the significance of popular forms (particularly in music and fiction) and a rejection of what were perceived as elitist and hierarchical perspectives. Along with this came a break with quantitative methods of enquiry and a turn towards ethnography and qualitative methods in general.

Although European media research has sometimes been claimed as distinctively more 'critical' than American research, in line with Merton's (1957) contrast between American empiricism and European *wissensociologie,* by the time of general upheaval post-1968, there was not much to choose between America and Europe in this respect. The distinctiveness of the European field of media enquiry was not clear at the end of the 1970s, except perhaps in the area of popular culture (in the UK at least), which has been mentioned, and also in a preference for qualitative methodological alternatives to surveys, experiments and statistical analysis. One form this preference took was in the greater use of ethnographic methods, especially for studying audiences, or 'interpretative communities'. Another was to be found in the attraction exerted by semiological theory and methods in the study of media content, largely following the guidance of French theorists, especially Barthes and Grémas.

The institutionalization of teaching programmes

Until this time, the field of media and communication differed markedly from the situation in the USA in that there were very few programmes of media study at any level or for any purpose, whether academic or professional. The study of media was mainly an individual research pursuit or organized in a handful of under-funded research centres. Occasional courses were given within the framework of study of politics, sociology, psychology or education. In some countries there were separate institutions for the professional training of journalists, but these were practical in orientation and made little contribution to research and theory. The main exception was Germany where several universities had established programmes in communication science and the same was true of Belgium and the Netherlands. However, from the early 1980s onwards more or less the whole of Europe saw a rapid introduction and expansion of undergraduate and graduate programmes in media and communication under various names, responding to demand from growing student numbers and the decisions of educational authorities.

The precise reasons are hard to pin down, but a general explanation can be found in the belief that an 'information society' was being born, in which skills relating to communication of all kinds would be in demand. There was a practical correlate in the expansion of media industries and the growth of professionalization, leading to new work opportunities in the field of communications and media. The enthusiasm for opening courses was not much restrained by the fact that the background of most existing communication research (focusing on media effects on society) was not very suitable or practical for meeting the needs of an information society. Nevertheless, the study of mass media provided the available core that could be expanded to deal with more relevant matters such as organizational communication, understanding new technology and developing practical skills of communication, advertising, public relations and journalism. Particularly important and difficult was the need to bridge the gap between the public communication functions of mass media and the private (person-to-person) communication networks carried largely by telecommunications and subsequently the Internet. Despite the difficulties, a new field of media and communication teaching and research has been forged in Europe that marks a break with its founding period.

European 'exceptionalism'?

Despite the debt owed to the United States for founding principles of 'communication science' and the continuing influence wielded through literature and the dominance of international scientific publication, a distinctively European approach to media and communication has developed. This is not, as is sometimes caricatured, more qualitative or more critical (or more amateur), but different in its agenda of issues and in the relative salience of different themes. The distinctiveness stems ultimately from the fact that European media systems and circumstances are different in many, although not all, respects. Virtually every communication 'problem' takes on a somewhat different definition.

There is no space or need to delve too deeply into the characteristics of media systems in Europe, but they are different because of the history and geography of the region (see Hallin and Mancini, 2004). The first characteristic is that they are very diverse in forms of organization and regulation, despite shared legal and normative principles, especially in respect of freedom and regulation. Media systems are surprisingly varied in terms of habits of use, despite similar social and economic conditions. This opens the way for fruitful and even necessary cross-national comparative analysis that is not really possible in North America.

Second, national history accounts for the fact that, despite a commitment to basic freedoms of the press, each media system has a significant relationship to the state and the political system that seems unusual, even sometimes undesirable, through American eyes. At least these relations are more transparent than they are in the United States. There is no standard model for arranging these relationships, but it means that politics does tend to have some acknowledged interest in media performance and some means of influence. At the same time there are mechanisms in place for managing this relationship to ensure either a degree of independence or of transparency in the arrangements for linking politics with media.

The conditions described have also resulted in persistent concerns about political diversity and balance in the media. This has been a legitimate object of policy making in many European countries. Various forms of economic intervention have been instituted, with particular reference to the newspaper press (broadcasting being separately regulated in this respect) and in some cases limits have been set to the degree of concentration of ownership. With varying degrees of effectiveness, many countries also have adopted self-regulatory mechanisms such as press councils and ombudsmen (see Bertrand, 2003). There have also been safeguards in some cases for the rights of journalists within their employing organization.

In most European media systems, the most distinctive feature, as seen from outside is the existence of a large publicly financed broadcasting service alongside offerings by private channels (although the ratio of public to private is now being reversed). The origins of public control of broadcasting (formerly often under monopoly control) are political as well as technical. Public broadcasting was and remains an important means of linking the political system with the media system. However powers of control have mainly been used to ensure that broadcasting does not upset the balance of advantage between established political interests. Public broadcasting has been an object of more or less continuing and equally balanced praise and criticism and is continually under review, especially now that it offends against reigning neo-liberal principles and requires new justification in an age of abundance and freedom of consumer choice. The most basic form of justification is that it ensures that one media sector at least is accountable to the public and that some public space is preserved for cultural and informational policies that the market cannot achieve. Whatever the balance of argument, there is no doubt that the taken-for-granted presence of a public media sector has left its mark on the agenda of European communication research.

The particular geography of Europe has consequences other than those mentioned. The boundaries set by nation states and often by language create divisions but also provide some natural protection against international competition and incursion, except where small countries are overshadowed by a large same-language neighbour as in the examples of Ireland, Switzerland, Austria and French-speaking Belgium. Within a number of countries, differences of language and historic region have persisted and are either reflected in the media structure or give rise to pressure for recognition. For many countries, it is hard and sometimes impossible to maintain a viable audio-visual sector without heavy reliance on imports. The winds of globalization have blown rather coldly across Europe for at least twenty years in the age of satellite, cable and Internet, although it is remarkable how little the actual balance of content of what is offered and consumed has changed in that time, leaving aside the greater volume. In any case, it is clear that the discourse of globalization has been widely heard across Europe, although with less resonance in countries such as the UK and Germany that are big enough to manage the challenges.

One of the characteristics of communication research (whether for good or ill) everywhere is that it tends to respond to the circumstances and events in the 'real world'. There is pressure for it to do so because a central feature of the media is the continuous reporting back to society about 'reality' and because news media frequently become implicated in the events they report. Even in the spheres of entertainment and culture, the media are characterized by continuously changing and evolving formats, styles and fashions, requiring a similar response from those who study media culture. In respect of historical events, the general consequence of this time- and space-bound feature of the field is that attention focuses differentially on what is 'locally' most significant (local here referring to Europe). In the period of development of communication science in Europe there have been major themes that are somewhat particular to the region. These include: the Cold War and the 'Iron Curtain' actually dividing Europe; the tensions in relations with America over foreign policy and in the cultural sphere; the gradual movement towards a more united Europe by way of the EC and later the EU; ideological conflicts between left and right; various internal insurgencies and terrorist movements that have afflicted several major European countries, including the UK, Spain, Germany and Italy; varied response to the Balkan wars of the 1990s; the response to immigration into Europe, especially in the later phase of large-scale asylum seeking. These and other matters have often provided the stimulus to research and shaped the pattern of topics.

After the 'communications revolution' of the early 1980s public communication policy increasingly took an economic and liberal turn (Van Cuilenburg and McQuail, 2003). A well developed and flexible media and communication system was seen as a necessary condition of national prosperity in the Information Age. While the rhetoric of the Information Age was heard in the United States, in practice it was left to a narrowly focused and inflexible market system to promote innovation. In Europe, both national governments and the European Community directly subsidized new media and used projects of law to open up new sectors based on the new forms of communication technology. The very fact that there are two levels of communication policy, at national and European level, makes for a distinctive pattern of governance and ensures that a variety of principles of the public interest – economic, social and cultural – are continually in play. Latterly the trend in European countries has been towards setting up a single national agency for the regulation of communication issues affecting different media, ranging from broadcasting and telecommunications in particular, to television and even the press in some respects.

Against this background, we can better understand the evolution of the main themes of European communication research and their particular focus. These themes are dealt with under the following headings, with a few explanatory remarks added.

News research

In fact the study of news content and news use has not differed greatly in priority or shape from its American and other international counterparts. It has been concerned with the staple issues of the reflection (or not) of reality; with the routine newsroom forces that influence selection policy; with many forms of bias (usually unintended) that characterize patterns of news; with the nature of news values; with the process and consequences of 'framing'; with 'learning' from the news, agenda-setting, etc. (see Renckstorf et al., 2001). The diffusion of news has also been studied in Europe. However certain distinctive 'angles' can be observed. To begin with, the obligation of public broadcasting to be informative and objective, as judged not only by traditional journalistic norms, but by reference to regulatory norms, has given a distinctive thrust to news research. Public broadcasting is often compared with the 'private' competition. There has also generally been more recognition in Europe of the fact that 'objective' news' is shaped by implicit ideologies. In an earlier, critical, phase, public broadcast news was often accused of supporting the status quo. In the more recent era of expansion and privatization referred to above, the new, competing, news services of private television have been suspected of departing from the former high standards of television news.

As noted above, news research has continued to be stimulated by successive conflicts and divisions in which the role of news as the informer of society is often put to a severe test. Most recently, the Iraq War and before that military action in Afghanistan and Kosovo have highlighted the pressures on television to meet divided public expectations of fairness and accuracy and also meet expectations of governments committed to controversial policies. The socially contentious topic of immigration and asylum seeking has tested the capacity of a press caught between strong popular prejudice amongst the audience (quite commonly) and the dual wish to be sympathetic and objective.

The study of news has also been influenced by the European traditions of audience reception research and textual analysis. From the audience point of view, the 'news' has to be made sense of from the point of view of the individual and the particular national perspective on events. The interpretation and remembering of news is influenced by many peripheral or seemingly irrelevant thought processes. It is not a rational linear process of learning. The occasion of news use is also very much ritualized in the home, linked to domestic routines and events.

European television fiction

Research into fiction in Europe has been influenced by a number of the features mentioned earlier. The primary issue has been the extent to which Europe can and does develop its own production capacity for the most popular category of television, that of fiction and drama. For the most part this refers to various series and serials dealing with settings related to crime, health and various other social contexts, plus the general type known as the 'soap opera'. In the earlier period of enquiry, starting in the 1970s, the great appeal of the glossy American serial typified by *Dallas*, proved an object of great interest. The question most asked was why this unrealistic and foreign product could have such a powerful pull on audiences, especially those composed of women. Was it some underlying intrinsic and universal factor of the stories told or simply the high production values and comparability to glossy Hollywood films? More prosaically was it due in part to the relatively low cost of such material to many European broadcasters? While statistically, foreign (especially American) fiction has continued to retain its seemingly dominant position, much has changed in twenty-five years and the same questions are no longer being asked. The great expansion of European television in terms of channels and hours of broadcasting has sustained the demand for the American product but, leaving films aside, there has been a shift in popularity to domestically produced content, where it is available. There is much more home-made basic 'soap opera' in Europe, and this has been shown to reflect both different values and audience interests than the original US model and also to reflect something of the differences between European national cultures.

Journalistic roles and ethics

There is a normative tradition in European communication theory that involves stronger claims on behalf of 'society' than is typical of the United States. Theory is directed against the failings of journalism in terms of accuracy and fairness in reporting as well as against the familiar evils of sensationalism, offences against privacy and personal dignity. Latterly critical attention has crystalized around the allegation of 'tabloidization', meaning a shift to style and content that courts popularity as an end in itself. Depending on the country concerned, and leaving public broadcasting aside, we are likely to find expectations of service to society and to the political and justice system. Sometimes these expectations are reciprocated by professionals within the journalistic profession. In some countries, elements of the press allow themselves to be accountable on essential matters and in some cases law and regulation set demands. However, it cannot be said in general that private media, whether press or television, are especially inclined to put ethics and public duty before commercial considerations. There is little inclination to do so and the development of more open markets in Europe and of policies at European level to develop a single market have made it difficult if not impossible for any large-scale media enterprise to ignore the imperatives of the global market. Even so, there are some bridges between external criticism and internal professionalism.

Audience and reception research

The adoption of critical theory, the re-evaluation of popular culture and the critique of empiricism in audience studies between them exerted a strong influence on European audience research from the 1970s onwards (Jensen and Rosengren, 1990; Alasuutari, 1999). Attention turned away from surveys of media use and formal studies of gratifications and towards the sub-cultural context of reception and the in-depth study of personal responses to particular media experiences. The move represented rejection of manipulative applications of research in the interests of media providers or would-be communicators, even where these were public broadcasters. The results generally shed light on the numerous interconnections between features of everyday life and media experience, indicating quite a strong degree of audience determination, contrary to the traditional dominant model. Some of the studies carried out showed the apparent anomaly of the attraction of distant and unrealistic content (especially American), showing a capacity for audiences to maintain a critical distance from the values of imported content, while appreciating storylines and features of production. The general proposition that content could be 'decoded' in ways different from the seeming overt message was supported in many studies. Even so, the extent to which audiences could be considered to be 'in control of' their own media experience has remained more or less a matter of belief rather than demonstration.

Content and textual research

There is an inconsistency between the tenets of reception research and the basic assumptions of the semiological tradition that held sway in Europe from the early 1970s. The appeal of the latter had originally been its counterweight to the counting and statistical analysis of the content analysis tradition offered as part of the dominant paradigm. Content analysis treated the 'meaning' of media texts as relatively unproblematic, at least where it concerned the origin, intention and likely effect of messages. Semiology offered the means of uncovering latent or hidden meanings, especially in respect of implicit ideology and 'meta-themes' of content. Elements of Marxist or Freudian theory were also engaged in the interpretation of content (Williamson, 1978). Work of this kind failed, however, to make contact with the emerging ethnographic and reception schools and was gradually marginalized. In its place, various forms of 'discourse analysis' were developed that sought to combine systematic text analysis with alternative modes of interpretation, taking account of the nature of 'texts', context of production and use, etc.

The political economic versus the popular cultural perspective

The development of critical theory in Europe was affected at some point in time by a growing gap between those who emphasized the determination of media ownership on media structures and therefore eventually content and those who focused more directly on the ideological tendencies in content that favoured the status quo and the potential for popular resistance. In the end, the 'culturalist' branch of critical enquiry largely parted company from the political economic school, leading to separate publications and a cessation of dialogue across the divide. It also moved to a position where popularity (variously defined) became a criterion of merit and a guide to understanding. The political economic school was to some extent vindicated by the large changes to media systems referred to above that were driven by technology, economics and politics more or less in that order. The major shift towards privatization of 'broadcasting' and of the telecommunications sector required a sophisticated understanding of the economics of the case as well as the technology. For the cultural school, there was at least the relative novelty in Europe of popularly driven abundance of media culture. The Internet has opened a large range of opportunities for both 'schools', although it is probably more relevant to note that it has stimulated its own branch of enquiry, with new ideas and models, that is not rooted either in the political economic or the popular cultural tradition.

The public sphere

The notion of a 'public sphere' was widely seized on during the 1990s, especially following the translation of Habermas' seminal study (1962) into English (1989). It offered something of an escape route from the seemingly hopeless pursuit of the goal of more 'democratic media'. Commercial media were flourishing and expanding and the one main sector of the media that was democratically accountable (public broadcasting) was either declining or failing in its perceived public duties. A wider concept of a sphere of free publication, discussion and debate within a larger 'civil society' seemed a more realistic and still worthwhile goal, despite its somewhat mythic origins and its elevation of rational discourse above emotion and popular feeling (Dahlgren, 1995). It was essentially an old-fashioned notion, but it was seen as having a potential for renewal and to provide some solid ground for societal claims against the media and for erecting new structures (for instance in cyberspace). The notion also appealed to those emerging from the stern grip of communist regimes and into the embrace of commerce. For a mixture of reasons, but especially a general response to 'commercialization' of media, the public sphere notion has remained in play as a viable basis for a theory of media–society relations.

Communication policy

The various technological and system changes that have been mentioned as taking place in Europe during the last twenty-five years have to some extent been the result of new policies on the part of national governments and of the European Union (especially in its search for an integrated market in media as in other sectors). Where not policy-led, it has been aided and legitimated by policy, opening up an expanding field of enquiry. Previously, communication policy was largely confined to regulation of public broadcasting and rather marginal and ineffective efforts at limiting press concentration. In the new era, communication policy topics multiplied to cover: the regulation of private satellite and cable television; many matters of cross-border transmission; rules for ownership and cross-ownership; new copyright issues; regulation of privatized telecommunications; boundaries of operation between the various competing electronic media; rules if any, for the Internet; cultural issues arising from transnationalization; varied plans to stimulate coherent technological change, for instance in relation to digital television; issues arising from the convergence of modes of media transmission and; harmonization of the expanding number of regulatory bodies.

Not least important has been the public demand for governments to respond to some traditional problems associated with new media, especially where they concern the welfare of young people in particular and moral standards in general. The expansion of electronic media has far outpaced the capacity of existing regulatory regimes to deal with questions of potential social or individual harm. The somewhat dormant issue of public service broadcasting has also come back into play, especially because of renewed assaults on its legitimacy, problems of public funding and a general sense that its role in the contemporary world is not always clear. In any case all this has provided the stuff of much conflict and debate and also new and varied thinking and research.

Political communication

The US tradition of election research was initially transported to Europe and the basic model still serves some of the same purposes, especially where it comes to estimating the effect of one or other influence on a campaign outcome and testing certain widely applicable hypotheses, such as those of agenda-setting and framing. The correspondence of European and American research was promoted by the apparent similarity of campaigning trends (more professionalization, political marketing, etc.) and also of media behaviour in relation to politics (negativity, focus on conflict and personality, neglect of fundamental issues, etc.). Over time, European electoral behaviour and attitudes to politics seemed to be converging on an assumed American model (lower turnout and activism, more cynical attitudes).

Even so, there have been differences in the focus of theory and research that can be attributed to features of European politics, especially the greater prominence of political parties and partisanship, the key role of regulated broadcasting in campaigning and the greater politicization of private media, especially the newspaper press. These features allow comparisons to be made between the content and maybe effect of 'neutral' broadcasting and partisan press, and between the various partisan elements of the media system. The typically more concentrated European election campaigns and the limited number of major broadcast channels (in some countries) allow more scope for panel studies and experiments about effects. Comparative research in political communication has been fruitful, despite the 'local' nature of each election event; and the institution of the European Parliament in the 1970s provided a unique object of study, in that campaigns were fought at the same time in several countries for seats in the same body (Blumler et al., 1983).

In conclusion

This account of some of the prominent themes in European communication research is not and cannot be complete. There is a great deal going on elsewhere under other headings, although a distinctively European perspective may be harder to discern. This applies, for instance, to much research on popular culture, although that has largely found its own alternative home. It applies to feminist theory and research and also to research on many aspects of children and media, both of which have developed within a common international frame of reference. Much the same could be said of research into 'new media', including the Internet, computer games and various uses of new technology. Here too, there is little distinctive about the European situation, although the region offers good opportunities for comparative research.

References

Alasuutari. P. (ed.) (1999) *Rethinking the Media Audience*. London: Sage.

Averbeck, S. (2001) 'The post-1933 emigration of communication researchers from Germany', *European Journal of Communication*, 16(4): 451–77.

Bertrand, J.C. (2003) *An Arsenal for Democracy: Media Accountability Systems*. Creskill NJ: Hampton Press.

Blumler, J.G. et al. (eds) (1983) *Communicating Politics: the Role of Television in the European Elections*. London: Sage.

Dahlgren, P. (1995) *Television and the Public Sphere*. London: Sage.

Habermas, J. (1962/1989) *The Structural Transformation of the Public Sphere*. Cambridge MA: MIT Press.

Hallin, D. and Mancini, P. (2004) *Comparing Media Systems*. Cambridge: Cambridge University Press.

Hardt, H. (2003) *Critical Communication Studies*, Second edition. Lanham MD: Rowman and Littlefield.

Jensen, K.B. and Rosengren, K.E. (1990) 'Five traditions in search of the audience', *European Journal of Communication*, 5(2/3): 207–238.

Merton, R.K. (1957) *Social Theory and Social Structure*. Second edition. New York: Free Press.

Renckstorf, K., McQuail, D. and Jankowski, N. (eds) (2001) *Television News Research: Recent European Approaches and Findings*. Berlin: Quintessence Books.

Tunstall, J. (1977) *The Media are American*. London: Constable.

Van Cuilenburg, J.J. and McQuail, D. (2003) 'Media policy paradigm shifts', *European Journal of Communication*, 18(2): 181–208.

Williamson, J. (1978) *Decoding Advertisements*. London: Marion Boyars.

Section One

International Communication

2

Research into International Television Flows: A Methodological Contribution

Preben Sepstrup

Earlier Research: a Critical Note

Most research on international communication flows is related to a (more or less explicit) discussion of the 'media imperialism thesis' as introduced by Schiller (1969, 1976) and developed and discussed by, among others, Nordenstreng and Varis (1974); Read (1976); Boyd-Barret (1977); Tunstall (1977); Lee (1980); Mattelart et al. (1984); and Lealand (1984).

The essence of the much debated media imperialism thesis is that a few countries – and especially the USA – dominate both international and national media structures and impose their cultures, values and ideologies on the receiving countries. Depending on the specific standpoint, more or less emphasis is given to the 'conspiracy' or 'intentionality' version, that is, that this dominance is consciously aimed at by large, powerful countries (USA) and multinational corporations, not only for the sake of economic profit but also for ideological reasons such as disseminating cultural and political values, business norms, consumption orientation, life styles, etc. The basic media imperialism thesis thus comprises a hypothesis about imbalances in international television trade, a hypothesis about the cultural effects on specific groups as a consequence of these imbalances, and a hypothesis about the reasons for such lack of balance.

The crudest versions of the media imperialism thesis have been criticized, modified and developed by both conservative and radical researchers. Interesting theoretical contributions have come from Nordenstreng and Varis (1974), Tunstall (1977), Mattelart et al. (1984), and Garnham (1977, 1979). Pragnell (1985)

Source: *EJC* (1989), vol. 4: 393–407.

and Tracey (1985) are recent examples of a rigorous rejection of the conspiratorial version of the thesis.

Without going into details of the twenty-year debate about the shape of international television flows and their determinants, it is fair to conclude that the position of West European countries in the media imperialism framework remains uncertain; no authors explicitly exclude Western Europe from the media imperialism thesis. It also seems that empirical evidence about international television flows, and particularly about their effects, is scarce. Until recently the empirical 'evidence' in both major and minor studies of international communication flows has mainly comprised compilations of examples at a 'trade press level' referred to above, plus routine reference to the classic systematic empirical work by Nordenstreng and Varis. More recently, reference has normally been made to Varis (1985), but this has not changed the dominant understanding since the conclusions of this study are similar to that of the earlier joint work (Nordenstreng and Varis, 1974). [...]

Proposal for a Conceptual Framework

There is an obvious need for a framework to guide descriptions and analyses in the field of research on international communication flows. Such a framework is suggested in this section. Television is used as an example but the basic elements of the framework apply to all kinds of media content.

The general purpose of all studies on international television flows has been to establish knowledge about the movement of programmes between countries on the assumption that these have cultural and economic effects in specific countries or regions or among specific groups of viewers. Some of the most frequently used concepts in the publications based on these studies are 'international', 'transnational', 'internationalization' and 'transnationalization'. The references listed at the end of this article convey the impression that these concepts are normally used without reference to commonsense definitions to describe both the flows (the independent variable) and their effects (the dependent variable).

An investigation of the application of these notions in a number of central contributions to the literature on international communication flows does not add to conceptual clarity (see Nordenstreng and Varis, 1974; Read, 1976; Tunstall, 1977; Lee, 1980; *Many Voices*, 1980; Janus, 1981; Janus and Roncagliolo, 1979; Hamelink, 1983; Anderson, 1984; Mattelart et al., 1984; Mowlana, 1986; Varis, 1985).[1]

In these publications 'internationalization', and the now more frequently used 'transnationalization', are employed to describe several phenomena: the expansion of something transnational, the global penetration of, for example, advertising, the transcending of borders, the growth of transnational companies or even growth of co-productions, and sundry effects like the homogenization of cultures, the creation of new non-indigenous cultures and cultural synchronization.

All the above mentioned publications are interesting contributions to the study of international communication flows, but none of them offers a general

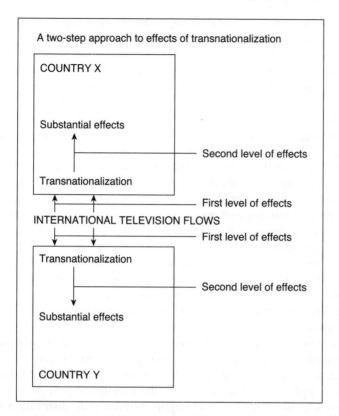

FIGURE 2.1   A TWO-STEP APPROACH TO EFFECTS OF TRANSNATIONALIZATION

At the first level transnationalization is a dependent variable and at the second level an independent variable.
The independent variable at the first level is 'television flows'. At the second level the dependent variable is 'substantial effects'.

systematic approach which is clearly related to communication theory, or a consistent vocabulary which could be used by other researchers – and which might have improved the accumulated results of this research by preventing the fragmentation of approaches and reported findings.

As a modest beginning towards a general, systematic approach I suggest a two-level understanding of international television flows. First, the flows as defined by Mowlana (1986: 4, see note 1) should be considered as an independent variable influencing or determining the dependent variable, transnationalization, which will be defined in detail below when the basic framework is developed. This means that transnationalization is understood as a 'first-level' effect of international flows.

The second level conceives transnationalization as an independent variable creating or determining the dependent variable, that is, the (substantial) effects which actually can be perceived from a cultural, economic or consumer point of view, such as the formation of values, the contents of television, conditions for national public service broadcasters or patterns of programme consumption (see Figure 2.1).

The first level – transnationalization as an effect of international television flows – must be thoroughly and systematically described before the second and more interesting level of aggregated substantial effects can be examined. In some ways this is not a very exciting exercise – which may be why there are so many attempts to jump from some kind of description of flows to the second-level effects. However, the first step is necessary in order to establish a properly conceived context for approaching the 'second-level effects'.

Concentrating now on the 'first-level' effects, I suggest that the transnationalization variable is related to a specific 'area' like a country, a group of countries or delimited groups of TV viewers.[2] Transnationalization, therefore, is basically perceived as a national phenomenon, which is a consequence of international flows as defined above. Transnationalization of supply therefore is the transnationalization of nationally offered supply which means certain television signals using standard technology that are available to a given country (or group of countries or groups of viewers).

The next step in a systematic approach is to specify the object of 'transnationalization'. The objects normally dealt with in existing research are 'ownership', 'supply' and, to some extent, 'consumption'. I will concentrate here on 'transnationalization of television supply' and 'transnationalization of television consumption'.

In order to define and operationalize 'transnationalization of national supply' and 'transnationalization of national consumption' more precisely, I suggest a distinction between three 'sources' or 'dimensions' of supply and consumption. Television supply may be divided into the national supply of multilaterally distributed television, the national supply of bilaterally distributed television and the national supply of nationally distributed television. These divisions are reflected in the concept of transnationalization and taken together they constitute the total 'transnationalization of supply and consumption'.

The national dimension of national supply and consumption relates to television distributed by the domestic media (e.g. by national public service broadcasters). This is referred to as 'nationally distributed television'.

The bilateral dimension of national supply and consumption relates to television which originates in the domestic media of another country and reaches the nation under consideration (through normal transmission, or by satellite, etc.) simultaneously and unedited (e.g. West German television in neighbouring countries). This is called 'bilaterally distributed television'.

The multilateral dimension of national supply and consumption relates to television originating outside a particular country and with no single intended direction of the flow (e.g. the signals from pan-European satellites). This is called 'multilaterally distributed television'.

Every communication flow naturally has a technical point of origin. In principle the multilateral dimension could be expressed as the sum of bilateral transnationalization transmissions between the specific (technical) country of origin and the countries where the signals are available. However, the substance of the multilateral dimension is the existence of communication flows for which the 'receiving country' is (relatively) unimportant and for which a multiplicity of directions are intended. The classification of television as bilateral or multilateral therefore depends on the motives for distributing the signals. Bilateral television assumes a national anchoring of the distributor and national distribution as the predominant purpose. The distributor of multilateral television has no substantial national relationship and distribution to several countries is the major purpose of the activity.

These dimensions of transnationalization are directly related to the sources of supply created by present technology and are thus convenient for future research because they adapt the analysis of international television flows to the development of information technology in recent years in Western Europe.

Since the last UNESCO-sponsored study on international television flows in 1983 (Varis, 1985), reception from neighbour countries has continued to grow, satellite channels have been established and the numbers of West European television channels have almost doubled (Schrape, 1987; cf. 'Television Programming in Europe', No. 2, 1987). It is now more necessary than ever to keep track of the sources of, and routes for, television output in a given country and also of the distribution of output (and consumption) between the three main dimensions of transnationalization. This type of monitoring may become an important basic tool for both technologically and culturally oriented media policy decisions.[3]

The most substantial argument, however, for separating the three dimensions is the hypothesis that the important 'second-level' effects are related to the sources of transnationalization.

If the two-step approach is accepted, and bearing in mind that transnationalization is basically a national phenomenon with three dimensions, I would suggest the following set of standard transnationalization measures of the 'first-level effects' of international television flows.

Transnationalization of Supply

The Multilateral Dimension

$T(m)$-S is the supply of television in a specific country which is multilaterally distributed. (T(m)-S may be measured in hours or as a share of total supply of television hours. In principle T(m)-S also applies to a group of countries or specific group of viewers.)

$T(m)$-S/CO is the supply of television in a specific country produced in a designated country of origin which is multilaterally distributed. (T(m)-S is the sum of T(m)-S/CO measures. T(m)-S/CO may be measured in hours or as a share of total supply of television hours or as a share of multilaterally supply. In principle T(m)-S/CO also applies to a group of countries or specific groups of viewers.)

The Bilateral Dimension

T(b)-S is the supply of television in a specific country which is bilaterally distributed. (T(b)-S may be measured in hours or as a share of total supply of television hours. In principle T(b)-S also applies to a group of countries or specific groups of viewers.)

T(b)-S/CO is the supply of television in a specific country from a designated country of origin which is bilaterally distributed. (T(b)-S is the sum of T(b)-S/CO measures. T(b)-S/CO may be measured in hours, as a share of total supply of television hours or as a share of bilateral supply. In principle T(b)-S/CO also applies to a group of countries or specific groups of viewers.) Notice that T(b)-S/CO normally has two elements – domestic production from the country of origin and imported programmes to that country – which may influence a detailed calculation of an accurate T-S/CO – see next section.

The National Dimension

T(n)-S is the supply of television in a specific country which is nationally distributed and has been produced outside the country under observation. (T(n)-S may be measured in hours, as a share of total nationally distributed television supply or as a share of total supply in the country. In principle T(n)-S also applies to a group of countries of specific groups of viewers.)[4]

T(n)-S/CO is the supply of television in a specific country which is nationally distributed and has been imported from the designated country of origin. (T(n)-S is the sum of T(n)-S/CO measures. T(n)-S/CO may be measured in hours, as a share of total nationally distributed television supply, as a share of all imported, nationally distributed television hours,[5] or as a share of total supply in the country. In principle T(n)-S/CO also applies to a group of countries or specific groups of viewers.)

T(m)-S, the T(b)-S and the T(n)-S measures may be added to one T-S measure covering all transnationalization of supply of television in the country (region or group) under observation. This is also true for a parallel T-S/CO measure.

Transnationalization of Consumption

The Multilateral Dimension

T(m)-C is the consumption of television in a specific country which is multilaterally distributed. (T(m)-C may be measured in hours or as a share of total consumption of television hours. In principle T(m)-C also applies to a group of countries or specific groups of viewers.)

T(m)-C/CO is the consumption of television in a specific country produced in a designated country of origin which is multilaterally distributed. (T(m)-C is the sum of T(m)-C/CO measures. T(m)-C/CO may be measured in hours, as a share of total consumption of television hours or as a share of consumption of multilaterally distributed television.)

The Bilateral Dimension

T(b)-C is the consumption of television in a specific country which is bilaterally distributed. (T(b)-C may be measured in hours or as a share of total consumption of television hours. In principle T(b)-C also applies to a group of countries or specific groups of viewers.)

T(b)-C/CO is the consumption of television in a specific country from a designated country of origin which is bilaterally distributed.

(T(b)-C is the sum of T(b)-C/CO measures. T(b)-S/CO may be measured in hours, as a share of total consumption of television hours, or as a share of consumption of bilaterally distributed television. In principle T(b)-C/CO also applies to a group of countries or specific groups of viewers. Notice that T(b)-C/CO normally has two elements – consumption of domestic production from the country of origin and consumption of imported programmes to that country – which may influence a detailed calculation of an accurate T-C/CO – see next section.)

The National Dimension

T(n)-C is the consumption of television in a specific country which is nationally distributed and has been produced outside the country under observation. (T(n)-C may be measured in hours, as a share of total consumption of nationally distributed television or as a share of total consumption of television hours in the country. In principle T(n)-C also applies to a group of countries or specific groups of viewers.)

T(n)-C/CO is the consumption of television in a specific country which is nationally distributed and has been imported from the designated country of origin.

(T(n)-C is the sum of T(n)-S/CO measures. T(n)-C/CO may be measured in hours, as a share of total consumption of nationally distributed television, as a share of all consumption of imported, nationally distributed television hours,[6] or as a share of total consumption in the country.)

T(m)-C, the T(b)-C and the T(n)-C measures may be added to one T-C measure covering all transnationalization of consumption of television in the country (region or group) under observation. This is also true for a parallel T-C/CO measure.

A number of measures of transnationalization have been suggested above.[7] Depending on the unit of measurement most of them are addable. Some are rather fictional constructions, others are relatively easy to administer. The exact choice of measures depends on the purpose of registering transnationalization. Generally it is important (1) to realize the diversity of the (first-level) transnationalization effects of international television flows; (2) to be specific about the

		Dimension of transnationalization		
OBJECT	Total trans- nationalization in country, region, or social group	**Multilaterally** distributed television	**Bilaterally** distributed television	**Nationally** distributed television
SUPPLY	T-S	T(m)-S:1;2 T(m)-S/CO: 1;2;3	T(b)-S:1;2 T(b)-S/CO: 1;2;4	T(n)-S:1;2;5 T(n)-S/CO: 1;2;5;6
CONSUMPTION	T-C	T(m)-C:1;2 T(m)-C/CO: 1;2;3	T(b)-C:1;2 T(b)-C/CO: 1;2;4	T(n)-C:1;2;5 T(n)-C/CO: 1;2;5;6

FIGURE 2.2   SUMMARY OF MEASURES OF TRANSNATIONALIZATION

1: hours; 2: share of total; 3: share of multilateral; 4: share of bilateral; 5: share of national; 6: share of imports.

effects considered; and (3) to agree on definitions and the operationalization of the effects.

The proposed measures of transnationalization are summarized in Figure 2.2.

Future Research

It is indisputable that much more systematic empirical research is needed on the consequences of international television flows. Speculation and guesswork dominate the contemporary scene, and the practice of cross-cultural communication is far ahead of knowledge of its effects.

Future research must relate to some kind of generally accepted framework along the lines suggested here. First- and second-level effects must be clearly separated. The dimensions and subjects of transnationalization must be specified and related to programme contents, consumption, perception and gratification. Local and regional television and bilaterally and multilaterally distributed television must be incorporated and much more work must be undertaken to identify the determinants of transnationalization of supply, together with the receiver-oriented determinants of consumption, and of course the cultural, economic and social consequences of this consumption. The role of commercialization for both 'first- and second-' level effects must be given an especially high priority in research.

These general recommendations can be implemented both in public and private audience research and in individual projects. Substantial developments in research on international television flows can only be achieved by broad international approaches undertaken or sponsored by international organizations – preferably UNESCO – since studies limited in scope to individual countries are of less use. If, however, predominantly impressionistic material continues to result from the more global approach to research that is recommended here, then regional, sub-regional or even national surveys must be preferred, in order to obtain findings of a sufficiently high quality.

Notes

1. Read (1976: 18) explicitly tries to distinguish between 'international' and 'transnational'. Mowlana (1986: 4) defines what has here been called the general commonsense understanding of transnational or international: 'International flow of information is defined here as the movement of messages across national boundaries between and among two or more national and cultural systems'.
2. For the sake of convenience I primarily associate transnationalization with individual countries in the following presentation of the outline of a conceptual framework for the first level of analysis.
3. To take three examples, one can think of (1) the usefulness of being able to compare coefficients of utilization (the share of supply consumed) related to public and private investments in technical facilities for providing a supply of the categories used here; or (2) the need for (international) competing broadcasters to keep track of the sources and thus the nature of the competition; or (3) that it is easy to imagine that politicians will ascribe different 'values' ('threats' or 'promises') to the transnationalization of supply or consumption caused by nationally, bilaterally or multilaterally distributed television.
4. It appears to be primarily a question of definition whether to include co-production as adding to T(n)-S. The issue may be of some practical relevance if co-produced television hours continue to grow. Unfortunately, the solution to the problem ideally seems to depend on the country under observation and the nature of the co-production.
5. This dominant 'measure' in existing research is unsuitable and often misleading.
6. This measure is unsuitable and often misleading.
7. In research on international communication flows much attention has been given to the ownership of media capital. This aspect of transnationalization may benefit from the use of a parallel to the three dimensions of transnationalization suggested here. Besides that, it is necessary to develop a much more precise approach than has been applied so far. One of the main problems has been to establish a relationship between 'second-level' effects and the potentially multidimensional role of media capital.

References

Anderson, M.H. (1984) *Madison Avenue in Asia*. Madison, NJ: Fairleigh Dickinson.

Boyd-Barret, O. (1977) 'Media Imperialism: towards an international framework for the analysis of media systems', pp. 116–33 in Curran et al. (eds), *Mass Communication and Society*. London: Arnold.

Garnham, N. (1977) 'Towards a Political Economy of Culture', *New University Quarterly* (Summer) 340–57.

Garnham, N. (1979) 'Contribution to a Political Economy of Mass Communication'. *Media, Culture and Society* 1(1): 123–46.

Hamelink, C.J. (1977) *The Corporate Village: The Role of Transnational Corporations in International Communication*. Rome: IDOC.

Hamelink, C.J. (1983) *Cultural Autonomy in Global Communications. Planning National Information Policy*. New York: Longman.

Janus, N.Z. (1981) 'Advertising and the Mass Media: Transnational Link between Production and Consumption', *Media, Culture and Society* 3: 13–23.

Janus, N.Z. and R. Roncagliolo (1979) 'Advertising, Mass Media and Dependency', *Development Dialogue* 7: 81–147.

Katz, E. and G. Wedell (1977) *Broadcasting in the Third World*. Cambridge, MA: Harvard University Press.

Lealand, G. (1984) *American Television Programmes on British Screens*. London: Broadcasting Research Unit.

Lee, C-C. (1980) *Media Imperialism Reconsidered. The Homogenizing of Television Culture*. Beverly Hills: Sage.

Many Voices One World (1980) Paris/London/New York: UNESCO/Kogan Page/Unipub.

Mattelart, A. (1976) 'Cultural Imperialism in the Multinational's Age', *Instant Research on Peace and Violence* 6(4): 160–74.

Mattelart, A. (1979) *Multinational Corporations and the Control of Culture. The Ideological Apparatuses of Imperialism*. Sussex: Harvester Press (French edition 1976).

Mattelart, A. et al. (1984) *International Image Markets: In Search of an Alternative Perspective*. London: Comedia.

Mowlana. H. (1986) *Global Information and World Communication*. New York and London: Longman.

Nordenstreng, K. and H.I. Schiller (eds) (1979) *National Sovereignty and International Communication*. Norwood, NJ: Ablex.

Nordenstreng, K. and T. Varis (1974) 'Television Traffic – a One-way Street? A Survey and Analysis of the International Flow of Television Programme Material', Reports and Papers on Mass Communication, 70. Paris: UNESCO.

Pragnell, A. (1985) 'Television in Europe. Quality and values in a time of change', *Media Monograph*, No. 5. Manchester: The European Institute for the Media.

Read, W. (1976) *America's Mass Media Merchants*. Baltimore: Johns Hopkins University Press.

Schement, J.R. et al. (1984) 'The International Flow of Television Programmes', *Communication Research* 11(2): 163–82.

Schiller, H.I. (1969) *Mass Communication and American Empire*. New York: August M. Kelley.

Schiller, H.I. (1971) 'Madison Avenue Imperialism', *TransActions* 81 (5 and 6).

Schiller, H.I. (1976) *Communication and Cultural Dominance*. White Plains, NY: International Arts and Sciences.

Schiller, H.I. (1984) 'Informatics and Information Flows: The Underpinnings of Transnational Capitalism', *The Critical Communication Review* 2: 3–28.

Schrape, K. (1987) 'Fernsehprogammbedarf und Programmversorgung', *Media Perspektiven* 6: 345–53.

Smythe, D.W. (1981) *Dependency Road: Communications, Capitalism, Consciousness and Canada*. Norwood, NJ: Ablex.

Tarlé, A. (1986): 'Dream Factories Go International', *Intermedia* 4(4/5): 79–81.

Television Programming in Europe 2. Summary Report 1986/87 (1987). London: Horizon's Media International.

Tracey, M. (1985) 'The Poisoned Chalice? International Television and the Idea of Dominance', *Dædalus* 114(4): 17–56

Tunstall, J. (1977) *The Media are American*. New York: Columbia University Press.

Varis, T. (1974) 'Global Traffic in Television'. *Journal of Communication* 24: 102–9.

Varis, T. (1985) 'International Flow of Television Programmes', Reports and Papers on Mass Communication, No. 100. Paris: UNESCO.

3 The Mythology about Globalization

Marjorie Ferguson

From sound bites to learned texts, 'globalization' reverberates through the corridors of politics, commerce, industry, scholarship, communication, environmentalism and popular culture. In moving from prophecy to assumption about the world, globalization is invoked to signify sweeping social, cultural and institutional change, the end results of which are sometimes said to define our age. If for no other reason than pervasiveness, this notion raises interesting but problematic issues.

First, there is the problem of *meaning*. It is not clear whether the different parties invoking globalization mean the same thing or even if they are addressing the same issue. Second, there is the problem of *evidence*. Despite its frequent attribution, neither the indices, nor the extent, of its actual occurrence are always clear. Third, there is the problem of *evaluation*. To whatever extent globalization (however defined) actually is occurring (and to whom), its alleged positive benefits or negative costs are difficult to assess. The deeper questions are: 'cui bono?' and 'who is being globalized (or de-globalized), to what extent and by whom?'

This article attempts to come to grips with this problematic notion, first in a more general way, and later, more specifically, through a collection of myths that have gathered around it. Finally, it seeks to raise for discussion a larger concern: the ideological overtones of the historical inevitability which has been asserted by globalizationists.

The Problem of Meaning

Although proponents and critics may differ in their definitions, there is broad consensus that globalization denotes both a journey and a destination: it signifies an historical process of becoming, as well as an economic and cultural result; that is, arrival at the globalized state.

The idea is not new. Ever since Magellan's early sixteenth-century circumnavigation of the globe founded a material reality, this worldview has gathered substance and force. Current interpreters tend to focus on the key domains of economics, politics, culture and technology. Increased economic interdependence and worldwide corporate enterprise, decreased political sovereignty for

Source: *EJC* (1992), vol. 7: 69–73.

mmon patterns of material and cultural consumption, with
ite, computer, cable, VCR, telephone, fax, television and radio
ween them being assigned a causal role in achieving intercon-
raction in all four domains.

al scientists, structural processes of institutional change are at
reordering. Thus, the topic of globalization provides a concep-
to an evolving world order and a concept for evaluating 'a par-
developments concerning *the concrete structuration of the world as*
son, 1990: 20). More holistically and in terms of process, our
incorporation into a one-world, global society is contingent on changing value
orientations that propel us towards 'the whole earth as the physical environment, everyone living as world citizens, consumers and producers with a common interest in collective action to solve global problems' (Albrow, 1990: 8–10).

Postmodernist interpretations of globality, on the other hand, focus more on
the emergence of a common culture of consumption and style (see, for example,
Baudrillard, 1985; Jameson, 1984). Acknowledging that transsocietal processes
of cultural integration and disintegration lie outside the bounds of the nation
state, the revisionist model of postmodernist globalization is both relativist and
absolutist, allowing for cultural diversity in global unity (see, for example,
Featherstone, 1990: 1; 1991: 144–7).[1]

The divergences between the 'globalizationists' and their critics should not
obscure the extent of agreement between the parties. All locate their concerns
in the empirical reality of a more visible and powerful supranational order, a
'world system' in Wallerstein's (1990) terms, that shifts many former national
concerns to the world geopolitical stage.

The Problem of Evidence

These changing contours of political and cultural economy may be located
in space and, to a certain extent, in time. In the 1980s, the globalizing impetus
manifested itself in science, politics and economics, in technology, deregulation
and the Friedmanite free market, as new commercial imperatives oscillated
between North America, Western Europe and Japan.

Typically, economic indicators are used as the yardstick of globality: multi-
continental flows of capital, services, manufacture, goods, data, telecommunications; the large-scale privatization of publicly owned assets in countries as far
flung as Britain, Australia and Mexico; the deregulation and reregulation of
broadcasting systems, most notably in Europe; and the institutionalization of
twenty-four-hour electronic world trading and money markets. But sociodemo-
graphic indicators also point to other forms of culture and value migration: for
instance, the transborder passage of social movements, such as environmentalism;
of antisocial artefacts, such as drugs and weapons; and of people, i.e. the massive
movements of refugees, professionals, tourists and immigrants.

The centrality of media technology and artefacts to the globalizing process, as
noted above, builds on pre-existing international production and distribution

systems and markets. In the information industries, for example, Reuters Holdings plc is paradigmatic of global empire building on the back of new technologies and services. Between the 1960s and 1980s, the organization metamorphosed from being a respectably low-key, non-profit-making international news agency to high-profile market leadership. In 1990, the 'world's foremost electronic publisher' recorded revenues of £1396 million and profits of £287.9 million.[2] Similarly, in the entertainment field, Hollywood's film and television producers have been global traders almost from their inception.[3]

These data also indicate an exploding world audience for television news, spurred in part by the spread of a genre here called 'television verité: that is, the live, raw video eye as recorder of instant history and shared video experiences of 'live' television news – protests in China, revolution in Eastern Europe, war in the Middle East. All serve to reinforce political, popular and scholarly perceptions of globalization as social and media-defined reality. [...]

The Problem of Evaluation

Notwithstanding the repertoire of meanings and material indicators noted above, there is a significant aspect of globalization that goes relatively unremarked: its rhetoric is as much concerned about what *should be* as what *is*. Globalization conflates the normative and descriptive, and consequently carries ideological as well as temporal, spatial, historical and geopolitical implications.

Thus, if powerful nation states and corporate interests promote globalization as a self-fulfilling prophecy for political or profit ends, it is incumbent on us to examine not only what is being hawked by whom, but who stands to lose or gain materially, politically, culturally or militarily.

As a conceptual notion, then, 'globalization' offers mixed messages. It sounds like a relatively value-neutral descriptor of a supranational universe of media interconnectivity and material and symbolic goods exchange. But on closer examination it reveals extensive causal assumptions, normative intentions and value judgements.

What is important here are the overtones of historical inevitability embedded in inferences of globalization as a unidirectional process or a fait accompli. Such rhetoric, far from being value-free, implies reification and carries ideological baggage whereby globalization becomes the new dynamic, the motor of world change. What this suggests, and what this article argues, is that this concept has taken on a life of its own: as a sine qua non for our age, its status may be moving from that of mythology to ideology.

Globalization as Mythology

Myth, in the context of globalization, is not used here in the sense of an untruth, but rather as a way of classifying certain assumptions about the modern world found in sets of ideas (myths) about world history, politics, economics, culture, communication and ecology.

Myths, then, are stories we are told, tell to others and ourselves; tales that explain, adapt and evolve as their context changes.[4] Typically, myth has a complex relationship to social reality. It builds on what is already at work. Combining the real with the ideal, it produces something of an ideal type that stretches beyond what the evidence will show. Being both *'real* and *sacred,* the myth becomes exemplar, and consequently *repeatable,* for it serves as a model, and by the same token as a justification, for all human actions' (Eliade, 1968: 23).

By guiding decisions and justifying events, myths help to structure our sense of belonging to a particular culture, to the 'our' world that is also the 'whole world'. It is the all-inclusive spatiality and explanatory aspects of myths that make them so appropriate for this study. These are not myths *of* globalization as such but myths *about* the objectives of and relationships between the disparate interests and institutions seeking to ride on the back of the globalizing momentum.[5]

The mythology about globalization also reveals how old myths adapt and new ones arise. Some are familiar, others not. Some serve particular interests or groups. But taken together they explain and justify much about the topography of a shifting global political and cultural economy. Nothing is finite about this structuring of social reality. Like all the best mythologies, this too is fluid, as new myths emerge to explain a changing world so old ones adapt or fade away.

At this point in the globalization mythology's life history, seven myths are identified: 'Big is Better', 'More is Better', 'Time and Space Have Disappeared', 'Global Cultural Homogeneity', 'Saving Planet Earth', 'Democracy for Export via American TV' and 'The New World Order'. Individually and collectively they interact with one another; some emphasize the journey of becoming, while others focus on the destination, the globalized state; and some represent both the process and the result.

Seven Myths about Globalization

The Myth of 'Big is Better'

As political ideology, public policy or corporate strategy, 'Big is Better' serves the doctrine of market liberalism. Considered together with the 'More is Better' myth (discussed below), 'Big' is invoked to present the classic Adam Smith case for expansionist, competitive capitalism. Its spatial-economic logic has driven international trade and transnational corporate expansion ever since, and in the easy credit, deregulatory 1980s, 'Big' spurred the worldwide migration of capital, mergers and takeovers.

The business of 'going global' was notable in the media industries as print, film, broadcast, cable, satellite, music, marketing and advertising organizations made the more interrelated universe a commercial reality and a technological fact. Although less remarked upon outside communication circles (see, for example, Bagdikian, 1989; Murdock, 1990), there has also been an escalation of ownership concentration and overlording in the media global village (e.g. Time-Warner Inc., Bertelsmann AG, News Corporation Ltd) with all their consequences for public discourse and diversity.[6]

While the Japanese presence in Hollywood – Sony (formerly Columbia) Entertainment Industries and Matsushita MCA/Universal – provides further evidence of media globalism, it also testifies to widely shared corporate strategies of cross-national synergy, vertical integration and economies of scale (in this case, aligning video hardware and software ownership for future HDTV profit). Thus, 'Big is Better' in the media and culture industries provides further ammunition for critiques claiming that globalization represents nothing more than corporate transnationalization at a higher level of magnitude (see, for example, Schiller, 1991).

However, what that categorical imperative overlooks is the extent of personal hubris behind corporate media expansion as the image of the global mogul took hold (e.g. Robert Maxwell, Rupert Murdoch, the Saatchi brothers). As free marketeers pursued ever wider horizons of hyperbole and investment, a symbiosis developed: the selling of globalization to the market became a part of the phenomenon itself. Thus, the myth-makers came to believe their own overextended metaphors, until their financial bubbles burst.[7] Now as agencies and media groups juggle their debt rescheduling in the 1990s, 'Big is Better' on a global scale may be losing some of its hold on the corporate mind.

This myth is cautionary and raises questions about the preordination of 'Big' as the foundation for economic globalization. It may be that corporate expansion on a world scale is riskier for some cultural (or material) industries than for others, just as it is clearly riskier in destabilized or rapidly changing national or regional contexts.

The Myth of 'More is Better'

This myth firmly places a central tenet of free market economics, the universal benefits of competition, in the context of the 1980s' ethos of excess – excessive deregulation, investment and consumption. Thus, 'More is Better' provides the cornucopia or utilitarian justification that makes 'more' a public good in and of itself: the perfect rationale for the public policies, private practices and corruptive vanities of the 'greed decade' documented in legislation, factual and fictional accounts, television and film. 'More', then, revolves around the market forces' proposition that increased competition, unfettered by ownership or trading restrictions (e.g. in airlines, telecommunications, media or finance), equals increased benefits for all; QED, increased profits, consumer choice and satisfaction.

In the wider media policy arena this myth favoured privatization and proliferation of off-air, cable and satellite television channels (and to a lesser extent, radio) and transnational programme trade (and transcultural migration of values) to fill expanding schedules. We need only to recall how 'More' served an expansionist, deregulating broadcast industry on both sides of the Atlantic – television providers in Western Europe and cablecasters in the USA.[8]

The doctrinal impact of 'more choice' on British broadcasting policy was especially notable. Unlike Italy, where a decade of de facto non-regulation and competitive chaos preceded the de jure regulation of providers and programmes (see, for example, Mazzoleni, 1990), in Britain the Thatcher government set out to dismantle the 'cosy duopoly' of BBC and ITV public service broadcasting via legislation to ensure more and different providers with scant regard for prior policies of universal provision, quality and diversity. It remains to be seen if the consequences of the recent television franchise auction will mirror those of cable deregulation in the US: more channels, ownership concentration, subscription fees and programme duplication.

In other Western European countries, where less is more has long been the received wisdom of public broadcasting, the prospect of increased foreign (mainly American) imports to fill the gap between programme hours on the new services and Euro-production has fuelled national, EC and US debate over quotas in the EC Television Directive of 1989.[9] In the event, the new channels, such as Spain's Telecino and Antena 3, the Netherlands' RTL-4 and Greece's Mega and Antenna, have brought more US films, soaps and game show formats to Europe (*Married ... With Children* is very popular in Greece); but they have also increased opportunities (by as much as 50 percent) for local programming.[10]

However, the equation 'more providers equals more channels equals programme diversity' is a half truth that ignores the extent to which broadcasters' own choices are constrained by programming and production economics, questions about the extent of audience demand for 'more choice' and increased subscription costs for pay-per-view or cable services. (Conversely, the opponents of 'More' often overlook the apparently universal thirst for escapist visual entertainment.) [...]

The 'More' myth, then, sounds plausible. It fits with the globalization worldview of material and symbolic goods interdependence and with the technology of distribution, but fits less well with the cultural logic of particular media markets (e.g. where mixed economy public service broadcasting has flourished and defined itself as a service rather than a product).

The Myth of 'Time and Space Have Disappeared'

'Time and Space Have Disappeared' recalls nineteenth- as well as twentieth-century prophecy, hyperbole and inflated expectations about, respectively, the wonders of electricity and electronic media uniting the world. But the early oracles were not alone in linking communication technology to globalization.

Much 'information revolution' rhetoric from the 1970s onwards has dwelt on the facts and fantasies of communication abundance from converging computer, fibre optic, cellular, digital and satellite technology. This myth assumes their consequences are those of rendering distance in space and variance in time irrelevant: i.e. they have 'disappeared' as constraints on business or personal life. Thus, industrial policy based on information technology (IT) as the key to economic competitiveness has rationalized technology as the key to future national and corporate prosperity.[11]

While it is true that the structural transformation of capital, information and goods markets would not have happened as it has *without* modern telecommunications and computing, the potential of IT as a force for public and private good is inflated to say the least. Especially, much 'wired societies' euphoria overlooks problems of differential access, principally North-South, to the alleged benefits and the complexity of differential impact on time–space perceptions and social experience.

The postmodernist attention paid to temporal and spatial categories as emblematic of a more globalized, transnational culture, differentiates their meaning from an earlier modernity. Claiming that classic theorists such as Weber and Marx favoured time over space, where the road to modernization was one of becoming rather than of being, Harvey (1989: 205) sees conflict: 'beneath the veneer of common-sense and seemingly "natural" ideas about space and time lie hidden areas of ambiguity, contradiction and struggle'.

Such contradictions are based on subjective as well as objective material factors. Thus, redefinitions of time and space provide a material connection between the processes of a more global cultural and political economy and the postmodern condition. But the unknown frontiers of a postmodern world create a crisis of uncertainty for Jameson (1984) wherein the 'hyperspace' of a global culture requires new 'cognitive maps' to negotiate.

Uncertainty about where and when we are in the world is at odds with the idea that technology can confer benefits of time–distance compression for all. The mobility of commerce, organizations, information and people does *not* make time and space irrelevant, rather, it highlights the extent to which these areas of experience have become more, not less, multilayered, interrelated and complex. For the uprooted, the restless or the peripatetic, the business of 'living life' (family, friends, work) in three or four time zones requires new negotiating skills in a perceptual world of spatial indeterminacy and temporal recalculation, a world of 'time without time' and 'space without space' (Ferguson, 1990).

Neither do we know much about how shared broadcast media experience alters time–space perceptions by bringing the faraway near. Speculation, for example, as to how television may foster reproduction of political action or replication of iconic protest images from one part of the world to another, overlooks the fact that the mechanisms by which any such effects might occur remain something of a black hole in communications research.[12] To a greater extent than other myths about globalization, 'Time and Space' typifies the extension of our horizons and problematics in the communications field.

The Myth of 'Global Cultural Homogeneity'

This myth relates to McLuhan's notions of global village shared experience and to aspects of postmodernist and media imperialist interpretations of a more culturally (and economically) intertwined world. More specifically, it relates to the interconnectivity of the transnational organization of cultural production, distribution and consumption in the broadest sense, and, in the context of this article, to the export and import of media artefacts from the print, music, graphic, audiovisual and information industries.

Simply stated, then, 'Global Cultural Homogeneity' infers that the consumption of the same popular material and media products, be they Swarzenegger, *Cheers*, Pepsi, Big Macs, Disney Worlds, clothes, cars or architectural fashions, creates a metaculture whose collective identity is based on shared patterns of consumption, be these built on choice, emulation or manipulation.

Moreover, this myth has its nation-state and regional variants. Claims of 'national cultural integrity' or of 'regional cultural authenticity' (as manifest in, respectively, Canadian broadcasting policy goals or the EC Television Directive) typify attempts to protect or promote a national or regional collective identity based on notions of shared citizenship or sovereignty. (This notion, in the case of the EC, is under threat of extinction before it is ever realized owing to the rising pressure for wider membership.)

In fact, neither 'Global Cultural Homogeneity' nor its national or regional variants, fit the emerging conflict models of the nation state, or the exclusionary imperatives of ethnic or regional entities. The first evokes a seamless web of artefact and tradition that does less than justice to the rich, global patchwork that exists, while the goals of the latter two fly in the face of dramatic, and sometimes bloody, evidence of repluralization. Paradoxically, we witness an antifederalist ethos competing with a resurgent regional economic protectionism in the EC, the North American Free Trade Area (NAFTA) and the proposed South-East Asia trading bloc.

Consequently, either this myth presumes that it is possible to argue the existence of a global cultural economy that ignores the counter pull of localism and the rich traditions of variance, or it assumes, wrongly, that cultural identities are contained within political borders or are conferred on a transhistorical world society basis by an ethic of consumption (or exploitation). [...]

The Myth of 'Saving Planet Earth'

If globalization as an historical process only emerged fully formed in the 1980s, now, in the 1990s, ideas about planetary interdependence embrace an ecological dimension. The one-world, Gaia, philosophy at the heart of 'Saving Planet Earth' links culture and economy to perceptions of a world ecosystem and its protection. Not only are we enjoined to 'think globally and act locally', but also to realize that eco-crises such as 'global warming require the rise of the global politician, buttressed by a global citizenry, whose vision extends for decades' (O'Riordan, 1990).

The utopian ideas embedded in this myth are transcultural and synchronic, displaying the power of myth to reinvent itself across space and time. In fact 'Saving Planet Earth' combines ancient (and sometimes sacred) beliefs about man's intimate relation to nature with modern ideas of eco-activism. Narratives about the environmentalist project to rescue the planet from self-destruction, echo archaic myths of the 'eternal return', and such sentiments, according to

Eliade (1968), appeal to our primitive longings for cyclical regeneration and new beginnings.[13] [...]

The Myth of 'Democracy for Export via American TV'

'Democracy for Export' is an old myth that displays uniformity over space, time and sacred belief. That is to say, 'Democracy for Export via American TV' is a recycled version of seasoned ideas about the power of the mass media to influence public opinion with respect to political ends. Accordingly, it updates the technology but not the premise about direct media 'effects'.[14]

These ideas resurfaced in a US Department of Commerce inquiry into the globalization of mass media firms (Obuchowski, 1990); the document, whose economic aims are to expand US audiovisual trade competitiveness and dominance, also envisages a politico-cultural agenda. The latter surfaces in assumptions about the effectiveness of US film and television products as exporters of US values and 'democratic ideals', notions premised on assumptions that global media can play 'an increasingly significant role in promoting free speech and fostering demands for democratic reforms internationally' (Obuchowski, 1990: 7). (A view that gains popular credence everytime CNN is cited as the lingua franca of the video era by political leaders on the world stage and their media watchers.)

What this conflation of politics and economy presents, then, is 'Democracy for Export via American TV', a highly functional set of ideas for the US film and television industries (and the US President's own personal worldview, see next section). Moreover, the benign view of media products as vehicles of political enlightenment stresses their potential for political persuasion (e.g. abandoning communism for democracy) over their potential for cultural dislocation (e.g. emphasizing individualism over collectivism). [...]

The Myth of 'The New World Order'

This, the most recent addition to globalization's mythology, demonstrates how new myths arise and old ones reappear or adapt in response to changing conditions. From the US President's first call for a 'New World Order' (NWO) during the Gulf War, this myth's core ideas have offered mixed messages, few of them clear. Therefore, we may usefully distinguish between 'world order' as the creation of order *in* the world and as an ordering *of* the world (according to a particular set of ideological conditions or economic practices). Both meanings are conflated in this myth and its ongoing revision.

Also evident from the outset was that even if the purported purposes were global, the authorship was American, and that here was an unclear vision of a New Jerusalem of world political power premised on the demise of communism and the triumph of capitalism. Before the mirage was fully formed, however, a 'new' NWO unfolded with dramatic swiftness: the Moscow 'coup' of August 1991 and the rapid disintegration of the Soviet Union that followed.

Both the old and new versions mesh with an earlier triumphalism about the end of history (Fukuyama, 1989). This thesis is essayed on the premise that 'Western liberal democracy seems at its close to be returning full circle to where it started: not to an "end of ideology" or a convergence between capitalism and socialism, as earlier predicted, but to an unabashed victory of economic and political liberalism' (Fukuyama, 1989: 3).

The notion of history having ended is connected to the end of the Enlightenment in postmodernism and to our having fallen over the edge of modernity into an uncertain void (see, for example, Harvey, 1989; Gitlin, 1989), one characterized by shifting lines of political sovereignty that exceed the bounds of the nation state (see, for example, Bauman, 1990). [...]

Mythology, Ideology and Television
Verité – Towards Further Discussion

This article attempts to address the problematic notion of globalization by examining the mythology within its discourse and associated problems of meaning, evidence and evaluation. Important as it is to recognize these myths, it is also important to acknowledge the empirical reality of a more interconnected world political and cultural economy.

However, this does not infer any consequences of a hegemonic global meta-culture or a supranational boardgame controlled by powerful states or transnational corporations. Throughout I have stressed the importance of scepticism towards ideas that a 'global ecumene' is emerging on the basis of any media reductionist or technological determinist assumptions. Globalization, defined either as a journey or a destination, demands a critical approach.

Nor are any lines of cultural causality clear as to who is globalizing whom: British media barons buy New York newspapers, Hong Kong billionaires buy Vancouver's waterfront, Germans buy RCA Records and Japanese buy Radio City Music Hall. Moreover, similar kinds of questions can be posed as to who is *deglobalizing* whom, given the inconsistencies and hostilities of ethnic, religious and other forms of localism within developed and lesser developed countries alike, e.g. Spain, Canada, the former Soviet empire, Sri Lanka, India. The list is long and growing.

A more fruitful area for debate, I suggest, is examination of the resurgent economic determinism at the heart of the globalization rhetoric emanating from postmodernists, media imperialists and corporate publicists alike. Are we witnessing not only an historical process and phenomenon but also the emergence of a new determinist philosophy of world history and social change?

Although these are ultimately empirical questions, the ideological overtones are heavy with normative, determinist implications of historical inevitability. The result is that globalization is being promoted both as a means and an end. Two propositions follow from this. First, it is clear that whether the context is political, cultural or economic, this notion and its attendant myths function as a gospel of the global market. Second, and relatedly, when we explore the global worldview (as manifest in, for example, 'Big', 'More', 'Democracy' and 'NWO') we find that it is refashioning an ideological mantle of historical materialism in its own image.

What is clear is that globalization *is* a teleological doctrine that promotes, explains and justifies an interlocking system of world trade. What is *not* clear is the future evolutionary path of this form of market economy determinisn. The new Marx has yet to arrive who will periodize the globalizing phase into a stage model of human history. Given its problematic and contingent nature, therefore, globalization either as mythology or as ideology is being shaped both by the unpredictability of world events and by the tendency of economic and political theologians to revise (and re-revise) their dogmas.[15]

What is clear, also, is that the old centre–periphery models of economic and cultural imperialism no longer fit a volatile geopolitical structure that deconstructs and reconstructs 'before our very eyes', any more than they fit the crisscrossing migration of investment, jobs, people, products, communication and consumption that characterizes the late twentieth century.

It may be that lacking as we do any single (or bipolar) vantage point of observation or control, the kaleidoscope is a more apt metaphor than the panopticon for the postmodern world. It may also be as Tylor (1891: 282) averred that 'even as "truth is stranger than fiction", so myth may be more uniform than history'. Thus, the myths about globalization may prove more consistent than their future as history or ideology. On present evidence, neither the gospel of the market nor globalization as the planet's manifest destiny seem particularly uniform or universal.

Notes

Aspects of this essay were presented in papers for: Sommatie '90, Eindhoven, The Netherlands, 1990, the Communications and Culture Symposium, Yugoslavia, 1990, the 18th Telecommunications Policy Conference, Airlie House, VA, 1990 and the 4th International Television Studies Conference, London, 1991. I would like to thank particularly Jay Blumler, Denis McQuail, Philip Schlesinger and Sari Thomas for helpful comments on earlier papers or versions. A book developing these ideas is forthcoming.

1. Postmodernist emphasis on culture (defined to include theme parks and fast food restaurants as well as media artefacts) and patterns of common cultural consumption cross-nationally also features in media imperialist/cultural dominationist critiques, most notably Schiller's (1991).
2. Financial data source: University of Maryland on-line company report (Barton, 1991).
3. As early as 1925, one-third of Hollywood's gross film earnings came from foreign sales (Jowett, 1976: 125). In the 1980s exports soared as demand rose for audiovisual products from proliferating VCRs, broadcast and cable channels; by 1990 US film and television export trade reached a surplus of §3.5 billion (US Department of Commerce, Assistant Secretary Obuchowski).
4. Following Eliade (1968: 18), myth becomes fictive only when it 'becomes "decandent", obscured; it turns into tale or a legend'.
5. As such their stories continue a tradition, recurrent across two-and-a-half millennia from classical Greece to contemporary popular culture. Work on myth and communications has drawn upon early cultural anthropology and sociology (e.g. Durkheim, 1976; Malinowski, 1974),

French structuralism, semiology and sociology of religion (e.g. Lévi-Strauss, 1969; Barthes, 1973; Eliade, 1968), and McLuhan's (1968) global vision of electronic media. For recent work that builds on notions of television's mythic role in shaping cultural form and symbolic content, see, for example, Bird and Dardenne (1988), Carey (1988) and Silverstone (1988).

6. Many have a dual agenda: to maintain their press oligopolies by maintaining their power leverage over political and corporate allies whose public media images they control (Bagdikian, 1989: 811).

7. See 'The Flight of Icarus', in *The Economist* (16 March 1991: 65) with respect to the struggles of the Saatchis and WPP to extricate themselves from the global marketing debacles.

8   Legislation enshrining the doctrine of 'more choice' includes Britain's 1990 Broadcasting Act and the US 1984 Cable Communications Policy Act.

9. For the outraged response of the US government and audiovisual industry to the threat of EC television quotas, see Brown (1991). As McQuail (1991: 54) affirms, the real import–export battle is between the old public service broadcasters with strong domestic production bases in place, e.g. Britain's BBC (85 percent) and ITV (90 percent), Italy's RAH (75 percent) and ZDF's (80 percent), and the new commercial broadcasters, e.g. SAT 1, BSkyB, RTL plus, 'with ratios of homemade to imported product usually reversed'.

10. See *Variety* (15 April 1991: 228–9) article, 'Local Fare Fattens Upstart European Webs', for profiles of these and other markets.

11. A typical keystone policy document of this genre was *Instant World* (Information Canada, 1971), but similar reports reside in many trade and technology policy archives of the advanced economies.

12. Zolberg (1987: 45), for example, ponders McLuhan's global village and whether the 'prevalence of television makes it possible for an event taking place in one part of the world to have an instantaneous effect elsewhere', a notion that extends itself to investigation of the role of audiovisual media in the political deconstruction of Eastern Europe and the former USSR (aka 'Democracy for Export via American TV').

13. For example, re-enacted when we celebrate a new year, a new house, a new child; in this way myths are both historical and psychological, capturing our desire 'to enter a new History, in a world reborn' (Eliade, 1968: 33).

14. For an evaluative critique of media effects and manipulative intent, see all the entries under the latter in McQuail (1987).

15. As to the ideological status of globalization as a new form of politico-economic determinism, replacing historical materialism as the engine of world history, we may look to earlier critiques of philosophies of history or ladders of progress (see, for example, Gellner, 1964) and to cautions against forcing social reality into 'transhistorical straight jackets' from whence come prophetic visions of a promised land (Mills, 1970).

References

Albrow, M. (1990) 'Introduction', pp. 3–13 in M. Albrow and E. King (eds), *Globalization, Knowledge and Society*. London: Sage.

Bagdikian, B.H. (1989) 'Lords of the Global Village', *The Nation*, 12 June: 805–20.

Barthes, R.J. (1973) *Mythologies*. St Albans: Paladin. (Translated from the French edition, 1957.)

Barton, N. (1991) 'Reuters Holdings plc – Company Report', *Merrill Lynch Capital Markets*, on-line data, University of Maryland McKeldin Library, 24 April: 1–5.

Baudrillard, J. (1985) 'Child in the Bubble', *Impulse* 12–13 (Winter).

Bauman, Z. (1990) 'Modernity and Ambivalence', *Theory, Culture and Society*, 7(2/3): 143–69.

Bird, E.S. and R.W. Dardenne (1988) 'Myth, Chronicle, and Story: Exploring the Narrative Qualities of News', pp. 67–86 in J.W. Carey (ed.), *Media, Myths, and Narratives: Television and the Press*. London: Sage.

Brown, D. (1991) 'Citizen or Consumers: US Reactions to the European Community's Directive on Television', *Critical Studies in Mass Communication*, 8(1): 1–12.

Carey, J.W. (ed.) (1988) *Media, Myths, and Narratives: Television and the Press*. London: Sage.

Durkheim, E. (1976) *The Elementary Forms of the Religious Life*. London: Allen and Unwin. (First published in 1915.)

Eliade, M. (1968) *Myths, Dreams and Mysteries*. London: Fontana Library. (First published 1957.)

Featherstone, M. (ed.) (1990) *Global Culture, Nationalism, Globalization and Modernity*, special issue of *Theory, Culture and Society*, 7(2/3).

Ferguson, M. (1990) 'Electronic Media and the Redefining of Time and Space', pp. 152–72 in M. Ferguson (ed.), *Public Communication. The New Imperatives*. London: Sage.

Featherstone, M. (1991) *Consumer Culture and Postmodernism*. London: Sage.

Fukuyama, F. (1989) 'The End of History?', *The National Interest*, 16(Summer): 3–18.

Gellner, E. (1964) *Thought and Change*. London: Weidenfeld and Sons.

Gitlin, T. (1989) 'Postmodernism: Roots and Politics', pp. 347–60 in I. Angus and S. Jhally (eds), *Cultural Politics in Contemporary America*. New York: Routledge and Kegan Paul.

Harvey, D. (1989) *The Condition of Postmodernity: An Enquiry into the Origins of Cultural Change*. Oxford: Blackwell.

Information Canada (1971) *Instant World: A Report on Telecommunications in Canada*. Ottawa: Information Canada.

Jameson, F. (1984) 'Postmodernism, or the Cultural Logic of Late Capitalism', *New Left Review*, 146: 53–92.

Jowett, G. (1976) *Film, The Democratic Art*. Boston, MA: Little Brown.

Lévi-Strauss, C. (1969) *The Raw and the Cooked: Vol. 1. Introduction to a Science of Mythology*. London: Jonathan Cape.

Malinowski, B. (1974) *Magic, Science and Religion and Other Essays*. London: Souvenir Press. (First published 1948.)

Mazzoleni, G. (1990) 'Broadcasting in Italy: Politicians and Tycoons at War', Paper presented at the 1990 annual Conference of the International Communication Association, Dublin.

McLuhan, M. and Q. Fiore (1968) *War and Peace in the Global Village*. New York: Bantam Books.

McQuail, D. (1987) *Mass Communication Theory: An Introduction*, 2nd edn. London: Sage.

McQuail, D. (1991) 'Electronic Media Policy in Western Europe: Current Situation and Trends', Report of the Euromedia Research Group, unpublished monograph, University of Amsterdam.

Mills, C. (1970) *The Sociological Imagination*. Harmondsworth: Pelican. (First published 1959.)

Murdock, G. (1990) 'Redrawing the Map of the Communications Industries: Concentration and Ownership in the Era of Privatization', pp. 1–15 in M. Ferguson (ed.), *Public Communication: The New Imperatives*. London: Sage.

Obuchowski, J. (1990) *Comprehensive Study of the Globalization of Mass Media Firms*. Washington, DC: US Department of Commerce.

O'Riordan, T. (1990) 'Global Warning', *Marxism Today*, (July): 12–15.

Robertson, R. (1990) 'Mapping the Global Condition: Globalization as the Central Concept', *Theory, Culture and Society*, 7(2/3): 15–30.

Schiller, H. (1991) 'Not Yet the Post-Imperialist Era', *Critical Studies in Mass Communication*, 8(1): 13–28.

Silverstone, R. (1988) Television Myth and Culture', pp. 20–47 in J. Carey (ed.), *Media, Myths and Narratives. Television and the Press (Sage Annual Reviews of Communication Research, Vol. 15)*. London: Sage.

Tylor, E.B. (1891) *Primitive Culture* Vol. 1, 3rd edn. London/New York: Murray/Harper Row.

Wallerstein, I. (1990) 'Societal Development, or Development of the World-System?', pp. 157–73 in M. Albrow and E. King (eds), *Globalization, Knowledge and Society*. London: Sage.

Zolberg, A.R. (1987) 'Beyond the Nation–State: Comparative Politics in Global Perspective', pp. 42–69 in J. Berting and W. Blockmans (eds), *Beyond Progress and Development, Macro-political and Macro-societal Change*. Aldershot: Avebury Press.

4 The Inflow of American Television Fiction on European Broadcasting Channels Revisited

Els De Bens and Hedwig de Smaele

Situating the research

In the 1970s, empirical research on international programme flow consistently pointed out the dominant position of the American audiovisual industry and the asymmetric relationship between the USA and the rest of the world (Nordenstreng and Varis, 1974; Varis, 1984). The often Marxist authors such as Varis (1974), Schiller (1976), Mattelart and Dorfman (1975), Tunstall (1977), Boyd-Barrett (1977) and Hamelink (1978) drew attention to the homogenization of television content as a result of the dominant American programme industry and stirred the debate on American media imperialism and more broadly on American cultural imperialism.

In the 1980s, a new wave of empirical studies (Pragnell, 1985; Silj, 1988; Sepstrup, 1990; Blumler and Hoffman-Riem, 1992; De Bens et al., 1992; Biltereyst, 1995, 1996) confirmed the dominant position of American fiction on European television. The renewed interest was caused by the launch of many new commercial channels in the 1980s. The high launch and start-up costs of the new channels and their initial unprofitability left little for domestic production, so import became the rule. American fiction was cheaper than European, and furthermore, ensured high ratings. Hence, the commercialization of the television landscape stimulated the inflow of American television programmes, especially fiction.

The authors referred to, analysed the television content and the inflow of programmes, but not the reception. They did not go into the impact of this dominant American content on the attitudes and perceptions of the viewers. Rating analyses provided only hints about tastes and preferences. In all European countries it was found that viewers showed an outspoken preference for home-made fiction. Hence, as soon as the new commercial channels had at their disposal more revenue generated by advertising, they started to invest in

Source: *EJC* (2001), vol. 16, no. 1: 51–76.

domestic fiction. Competition caused the public channels to increase their domestic production as well. However, the overall extension of broadcasting hours forced both public and commercial channels to fall back on American imports to fill the many extra television hours.

De Bens et al. (1992) provocatively launched the term 'Dallasification' referring to the non-stop homogenizing inflow of American programmes and obviously not to the Americanizing effect of this content on the attitudes and world perceptions of the viewers. Cultural studies scholars such as Morley (1980, 1992), Fiske (1987, 1991), Featherstone (1991), Ang (1982) and Katz and Liebes (1990) did indeed study the reception of this content and they concluded that no Americanization of worldviews took place. The approach of the two lines of research is fundamentally different: the first analyses the inflow and the origin of content, the second its impact on the viewer.

This contribution joins the first line of research. In this study, the programme analysis of the Euromedia Research Group from 1991 (De Bens et al., 1992) was carried out again, on a smaller scale, in 1997. In 1991, 53 European television stations from 14 European countries were involved in the analysis.[1] In 1997, 36 stations from six countries (Belgium, the Netherlands, Germany, France, Great Britain and Italy) were examined. The survey included 16 public and 20 commercial stations, all of them national and general interest channels.[2] As in 1991, the period sampled comprised the last two weeks of January (13–26 January 1997). Similar studies also use a sample of two weeks or even one week partly because of the labour-intensive nature of a programme analysis (Nordenstreng and Varis, 1974, 1986; Sepstrup, 1989; De Bens et al., 1992; Buonanno, 1998a, 1998b). However, a period of two successive weeks of programming might be considered unrepresentative since it takes almost no account of seasonal influences on programming. Although the period examined was extremely 'normal' and free of special events influencing the programming, we want to emphasize that the results refer first of all to the period examined. The figures were processed and interpreted, and then compared to the figures of the similar investigation from 1991.[3]

In 1991, the following research questions were asked (De Bens et al., 1992: 82):

- Is the position of the American programming industry (fiction) still dominant on the European television market?
- Are there noticeable differences between the purchasing and programming strategies of public and commercial broadcasting stations?

The same research questions were used in the 1997 programme analysis. No audience analysis is made (e.g. questions of preference). Nor did we consider to what extent European fiction is 'Americanized', i.e. modelled on American examples with adoption of American formats, narrative structures, codes and recipes.[4]

Finally, and in view of our findings, we try to evaluate the sufficiency of the European Union support measures to promote the European television programme industry.

TABLE 4.1 MAIN PROGRAMME CATEGORIES (PERCENTAGE OF BROADCASTING TIME; JANUARY 1997)

	Fiction		Entertainment		Information	
	Total	Prime-time	Total	Prime-time	Total	Prime-time
Flanders						
Public	36.5	33.4	13.5	19.6	17.9	23.3
Commercial	59.7	69.3	14.3	20.4	7.0	5.0
Wallonia						
Public	18.3	19.6	15.4	14.8	14.8	20.1
Commercial	55.0	67.2	8.4	12.8	10.0	9.6
The Netherlands						
Public	16.8	25.2	20.2	29.0	14.3	14.6
Commercial	49.2	54.0	26.0	22.5	10.5	13.0
Great Britain						
Public	22.6	28.5	15.5	18.5	13.7	15.2
Commercial	30.9	47.3	19.0	17.2	7.5	17.1
Germany						
Public	25.4	36.4	13.0	13.6	15.0	30.7
Commercial	56.0	65.6	20.1	26.3	5.0	2.8
France						
Public	20.4	31.0	24.3	16.9	17.5	32.9
Commercial	41.6	31.7	13.1	19.0	11.4	25.0
Italy						
Public	23.5	32.4	10.1	17.7	18.8	27.0
Commercial	44.7	45.6	18.3	25.9	12.6	9.0
Total						
Public	22.6	29.4	15.6	19.2	16.2	22.9
Commercial	48.9	57.5	18.9	21.9	8.4	9.5
General total	**37.4**	**44.9**	**17.5**	**20.7**	**11.8**	**15.5**

Note: The total broadcasting time for all stations together is 540,246 minutes or 9004 hours.

The programme weight of fiction

With 37 percent of the overall broadcasting time, fiction is by far the most important programme category on European television. This is especially true for the commercial channels, which broadcast twice as much fiction as public channels. With regard to the category information,[5] the relation is the complete reverse. As far as entertainment is concerned, public and commercial channels score similar results (see Table 4.1). The figures for 1997 confirm the results of 1991.

The share of fiction increases in prime-time, especially among the commercial channels: up to 60 percent of broadcasting time compared to 30 percent among the public channels. In general, the three main programme categories (fiction, entertainment, information) still gain importance in prime-time while the other, smaller categories increasingly lose out (especially cultural, music and sport broadcasts as well as children's programmes). The higher share of information in prime-time (especially among the public channels) is obviously due to the fact that all major news bulletins are situated in this time-lock.

Of all broadcasting stations examined, the Flemish (public and commercial) channels show the highest fiction share: 36.5 percent of the broadcasting time among the public stations and up to 60 percent (70 percent in prime-time) among the commercial stations. In 1991, this was respectively 33.5 percent and 47 percent. The increase of fiction on the commercial stations is mainly due to the arrival of two new commercial stations, Ka2 and VT4. These newcomers are also responsible for the decrease in the share of information from 15 percent in 1991 to only 7 percent in 1997.

In absolute figures, 3368 hours of fiction were examined: 891 hours on the 16 public channels in the survey and a further 2477 hours on the 20 commercial channels. The category of fiction was further subdivided into two subcategories: films (both films made for cinema and for television) and series (including serials). Among the public channels, broadcasting time for fiction was equally divided between films and series(about 440 hours each). Among the commercial channels, series amounted for 63.4 percent of fiction time. In prime-time films have the advantage on both type of channels (about 52.3 percent).

The origin of fiction

When taking *all* programme categories into account (including news, entertainment, children's programmes, etc.) the share of home-made productions amounts to 80 percent of broadcasting time on public channels and 48 percent on the commercial channels. The share of the non-national European programmes is restricted to 5 percent of broadcasting time on the public channels and to 4.2 percent on the commercial channels. American programmes on the other hand take up 11.5 percent of broadcasting time on the public channels and 44 percent on commercial channels.

However, the ratio between home and foreign, or between European and American productions in the *overall* programming is not a very relevant parameter. If we restrict ourselves to the broadcasting time devoted to fiction (i.e. films and series) and consequently exclude all other programme categories, we no longer arrive at a majority, but at a small third of broadcasting time devoted to pro- grammes of European origin: 17.3 percent national and 13.5 percent non-national European programmes. Public channels broadcast relatively more European fiction, both national and non-national, than commercial channels. Commercial channels broadcast considerably more American fiction (72 percent) than the public channels (40 percent) (see Table 4.2).

In prime-time the share of American fiction decreases and the share of European, especially national fiction, increases. This is especially marked in Flanders where *all* home-made fiction is broadcast in prime-time. In the smaller countries (Belgium, the Netherlands), 40–45 percent of all fiction is broadcast in

TABLE 4.2 ORIGIN OF FICTION (PERCENTAGE OF BROADCASTING TIME DEVOTED TO FICTION: JANUARY 1997)

	National		Non-national European[a]		USA		Other	
	Total	Prime-time	Total	Prime-time	Total	Prime-time	Total	Prime-time
Flanders								
Public	11.6	25.0	26.2	27.2	44.4	38.2	17.8	9.6
Commercial	5.1	11.9	10.0	4.4	79.5	82.3	5.4	1.4
Wallonia								
Public	–	–	53.5	85.4	35.4	14.6	11.1	–
Commercial	–	–	21.0	37.0	75.6	63.0	3.4	–
The Netherlands								
Public	28.3	44.6	30.0	21.7	36.1	31.6	5.6	2.1
Commercial	12.6	20.2	6.4	9.0	78.8	67.6	2.2	3.2
Great Britain								
Public	27.8	60.6	2.2	–	53.7	39.4	16.9	–
Commercial	24.0	59.6	7.2	3.8	53.7	33.4	15.1	3.2
Germany								
Public	50.0	77.4	25.0	18.5	19.6	4.1	5.4	–
Commercial	11.0	21.8	9.6	7.7	76.3	69.2	3.1	1.3
France								
Public	22.0	57.7	25.1	22.1	52.9	20.2	–	–
Commercial	29.9	47.3	8.2	–	60.7	52.7	1.2	–
Italy								
Public	28.0	16.2	29.3	31.6	42.3	52.2	0.4	–
Commercial	19.8	19.0	7.5	5.3	61.9	73.0	10.8	2.7
Total								
Public	28.0	40.9	25.1	26.6	40.3	30.8	6.6	1.7
Commercial	13.4	20.6	9.4	10.1	71.7	67.5	5.5	1.8
General total	**17.3**	**26.5**	**13.5**	**14.9**	**63.4**	**56.8**	**5.8**	**1.8**

[a] Including European co-productions which means co-productions between European countries or between a European country and a non-European country.

prime-time. This is much less the case in the 'larger countries' such as Great Britain, France, Germany and Italy. In these countries only 12–27 percent of all fiction is offered in prime-time. This is obviously due to the much longer broadcasting hours, which causes fiction to be programmed in the morning, afternoon and during the night as well.

Fiction from 'other countries' (such as Latin America, Australia and others) does not receive a lot of opportunities in prime-time. Also, the non-national European category is not broadcast in prime-time on several channels (e.g. French commercial channels, British public channels) thus prime-time is showing a bipolarization of national fiction on the one hand and US fiction on the other hand.

The origin of films

All stations buy most of their feature films abroad. In the two weeks sampled, 800 films were broadcast, of which 259 in prime-time. Only 17.4 percent of them were of national origin, 82.6 percent of foreign origin (see Table 4.3). No home-made film was broadcast in Belgium (Flanders or Wallonia). In leading position with regard to programming of national films are the French channels, closely followed by the Italian. In the Netherlands and Germany the public channels score reasonably well. In Great Britain it is the commercial channel that is worth mentioning.[6] In prime-time, the national film holds its position or slightly increases.

By far the most important supplier is the USA. Commercial channels depend more on American movies (66.7 percent) than their public counterparts (40.2 percent). The difference between public and commercial channels is especially noticeable in the French-speaking part of Belgium, the Netherlands and Germany, whereas Great Britain again shows the opposite. In Italy, the difference is nearly non-existent. In prime-time the share of American films further increases (67.2 percent). The increase is especially evident among the commercial channels (77 percent), although there are important differences between the countries. Flanders turns out to be the region most dependent on American films: in prime-time they are the rule leaving aside an occasional non-US film.

Other imported movies mainly come from European countries. Public channels broadcast a greater number of non-national European films (18.4 percent) than the commercial channels (11.9 percent). In addition they also broadcast more European co-productions (7.5 percent against 3.7 percent). Generally, the share of the European film (20.1 percent) is low compared to the share of American import (57.4 percent). The public channel in Wallonia is, with 53.3 percent European productions, a remarkable exception. This share almost totally comprises French films (46.7 percent). With regard to film (and also culturally and linguistically) France functions as the 'homeland' of Wallonia and replaces the missing home market.

The French and British films are equally distributed outside their own national borders; together they represent 8 percent of the films (see Table 4.4). Flemish, Dutch and German public channels regularly broadcast French films, although less in prime-time. British films can be found foremost on the Flemish and the German public channels while the Italian channels also regularly include British films. British films are shown also in prime-time.

German film scores a presence of only 1.1 percent on average. Programming is scheduled mainly outside prime-time. It is striking that while Germany does broadcast British and French films the reverse is much less the case. On French television no German films were broadcast in the period examined. Also, on the British public channels German film was absent. British films are rarely shown on French television or French films on British television.

Films from other European countries are only broadcast sporadically. Eastern European films, for example, were found only on the German commercial and the Italian public channels. In prime-time they are largely absent.

To conclude, we consider the evolution of the origin of films between 1988, 1991 and 1997 (see Table 4.4). Between 1988 and 1991, there was a sharp decrease in

TABLE 4.3 ORIGIN OF FILMS (PERCENTAGE OF THE NUMBER OF FILMS; JANUARY 1997)

	National		USA		Europe		Co-production Europe		Others		Co-production others	
	Total	Prime-time	Total	Prime-time	Total	Prime-time	Total	Prime-time	Total	Prime-time	Total	Prime-time
Flanders												
Public	—	—	61.1	87.5	22.2	12.5	—	—	11.1	—	5.6	—
Commercial	—	—	88.0	96.3	10.0	—	—	—	2.0	3.7	—	—
Wallonia												
Public	—	—	20.0	18.2	53.3	63.6	20.0	18.2	6.7	—	—	—
Commercial	—	—	73.5	67.7	20.4	25.8	6.1	6.5	—	—	—	—
The Netherlands												
Public	31.8	50.0	22.7	30.0	18.2	10.0	13.6	—	13.7	10.0	—	—
Commercial	2.1	2.8	87.5	88.9	8.3	5.5	—	—	—	—	2.1	2.8
Great Britain												
Public	14.3	14.3	71.5	85.7	2.0	—	2.0	—	8.2	—	2.0	—
Commercial	22.9	36.4	57.1	45.4	5.7	—	7.2	9.1	5.7	9.1	1.4	—
Germany												
Public	21.4	42.9	28.6	14.3	26.8	14.2	12.5	28.6	7.1	—	3.6	—
Commercial	5.0	6.8	67.3	81.8	15.3	6.8	5.5	2.3	6.5	—	0.4	2.3
France												
Public	46.9	66.7	40.7	26.7	6.2	6.6	6.2	—	—	—	—	—
Commercial	33.3	50.0	58.4	50.0	—	—	8.3	—	—	—	—	—
Italy												
Public	40.7	21.7	34.1	60.9	19.7	8.7	5.5	8.7	—	—	—	—
Commercial	35.7	26.1	46.4	60.9	8.3	8.7	8.4	—	1.2	4.3	—	—
Total												
Public	27.6	29.6	40.2	45.7	18.4	16.1	7.5	7.4	4.9	1.2	1.4	—
Commercial	11.8	9.6	66.7	77.0	11.9	8.3	3.7	2.3	5.3	1.7	0.6	1.1
General total	**17.4**	**15.8**	**57.4**	**67.2**	**14.1**	**10.7**	**6.0**	**3.9**	**4.2**	**1.6**	**0.9**	**0.8**

Note: Number of films in total broadcasting time = 800 and in prime-time = 259.

TABLE 4.4 ORIGIN OF FILMS ON EUROPEAN TELEVISION IN 1988, 1991 AND 1997 (IN PERCENTAGES)

	1988[a]	1991[a]	1997
National	29	20	17.5
USA	46	53	57.5
Europe	19	23	20
France	6	5	4
Great Britain	4	9	4
Germany	3	4	1
Rest of Europe	6	5	5
Co-productions	–	–	6
Other	6	4	5

[a] Source: 1988 and 1991: De Bens et al. (1992: 91).

national films to the advantage of European cinema but even more so American cinema. Between 1991 and 1997 we observe a further decrease of national films, though it is less marked. European films do not increase, but slightly decrease. The only category that remains on the increase is American cinema.

To gain a full insight into the shifts within the European films a spot check of two weeks is not sufficient. It does look, however, as if the European co-productions replace the separate French, German and British productions.

The origin of series

Here again the share of foreign productions is significant: 79.8 percent of the series are imported whereas 20.2 percent are of national origin. This share is still higher than the share of national films (17.4 percent). Public channels broadcast more national series (29.9 percent) than the commercial ones (17.3 percent). In prime-time the share of national series doubles (!) (see Table 4.5). Only Wallonia has no home-produced series. Germany shows a remarkably high share of national series. The German public channels ARD and ZDF broadcast respectively 87.5 percent and 71.4 percent national series and up to 90 percent in prime-time. This is a substantial progress compared to 1991 when the public channels reached a share of 45 percent and the commercial channels registered only 1 percent. Germany cannot look back on a long tradition of soaps and series. According to Mohr and O'Donnell (1996: 34–5) home-produced series only started in 1992, with the launch on RTL of the daily soap *Gute Zeiten, Schlechte Zeiten*. Flanders and the Netherlands also have a limited tradition of home-produced series. Great Britain, on the other hand, is the pre-eminent European country for traditions, and also proves it in the field of home-produced soaps. The British public channels BBC1 and BBC2 have a significant share of home-produced series (44 percent). However, compared to 1991 this represents a decline: down from 52 percent among the public channels and 55 percent among the commercial channels.

TABLE 4.5   ORIGIN OF SERIES (PERCENTAGE OF THE NUMBER OF SERIES; JANUARY 1997)

	National		USA		Europe		Australia		Others		Co-productions	
	Total	Prime-time	Total	Prime-time	Total	Prime-time	Total	Prime-time	Total	Prime-time	Total	Prime-time
Flanders												
Public	17.2	43.2	40.9	10.8	20.4	24.3	15.0	10.8	6.5	10.8	–	–
Commercial	7.3	23.9	73.5	65.2	12.6	10.9	6.6	–	–	–	–	–
Wallonia												
Public	–	–	42.9	–	33.3	100.0	23.8	–	–	–	–	–
Commercial	–	–	75.0	41.0	19.1	59.0	3.3	–	2.6	–	–	–
The Netherlands												
Public	30.2	46.5	46.2	27.9	14.2	25.6	1.9	–	–	–	7.5	–
Commercial	20.0	53.1	73.9	34.6	4.0	9.8	0.5	2.5	1.1	–	0.5	–
Great Britain												
Public	44.1	84.6	28.4	15.4	–	–	25.5	–	2.0	–	–	–
Commercial	29.6	80.8	40.8	19.2	–	–	23.9	–	5.7	–	–	–
Germany												
Public	78.8	90.0	10.6	–	1.9	6.7	–	–	–	–	8.7	3.3
Commercial	18.4	40.8	78.5	52.1	1.9	5.1	0.8	–	–	–	0.4	2.0
France												
Public	10.6	16.7	67.3	–	22.1	83.3	–	–	–	–	–	–
Commercial	42.3	33.3	52.4	66.7	4.1	–	–	–	1.2	–	–	–
Italy												
Public	9.6	–	58.6	36.4	30.8	63.6	–	–	1.0	–	–	–
Commercial	11.4	9.4	67.7	90.6	3.5	–	–	–	17.4	–	–	–
Total												
Public	29.9	57.7	42.1	15.5	16.1	21.5	7.9	2.4	1.4	2.4	2.6	0.6
Commercial	17.3	38.0	70.6	49.5	5.2	11.5	3.2	0.5	3.5	–	0.2	0.5
General total	**20.2**	**43.8**	**64.2**	**39.4**	**7.5**	**14.4**	**4.2**	**1.1**	**3.1**	**0.7**	**0.8**	**0.5**

Note: The number of series in total broadcasting time = 2904 and in prime-time = 568.

TABLE 4.6   ORIGIN OF SERIES ON EUROPEAN TELEVISION IN 1988, 1991 AND 1997
(IN PERCENTAGES)

	1988[a]	1991[a]	1997
National	37	17	20
USA	36	56	64
Europe	14	16	8.5
France	2	1	2
Great Britain	7	10	2
Germany	3	3	2
Rest of Europe	3	2	1.5
Co-productions	–	–	1
Other	13	11	7.5

[a]Source: 1988 and 1991: De Bens et al. (1992: 94).

As with films, series come for the most part from the USA (64.2 percent). The commercial channels programme more American series (70.6 percent) than their public counterparts (42.1 percent). It is striking, however, that American series are programmed mainly outside prime-time, among public as well as among private broadcasters. Among the German channels the distinction between public (10.6 percent) and commercial (78.5 percent) channels is extraordinary. Obviously, the low share of American series on the public channels is directly connected to the high share of national series. The British channels programme relatively few American series. This not only benefits their own fiction, but also Australian fiction. About a quarter of all series shown on British channels is of Australian origin. Great Britain is the only European country where direct imports from Australia are important to such a degree (see Mohr and O'Donnell, 1996: 40), although we also registered a considerable percentage of Australian soaps on the Walloon public broadcasting station.

The import of non-national European series amounts to only 7.5 percent but up to 14.4 percent in prime-time. There are major differences per country: ranging from the total absence on the British channels to a third of all series on the Walloon public channels. In Wallonia this percentage is for the most part due to France again. French, German and British series have a similar but small share of European distribution (2 percent each) (see Table 4.6). They serve different markets: French series are shown in Wallonia and Italy. British series are shown in Flanders, the Netherlands and France and to a lesser degree in Germany. They also do relatively well in prime time. German series are successful in Wallonia, France and Italy (public channels) and to a lesser degree in Flanders and the Netherlands. France broadcasts 10.5 percent British and 11.5 percent German series, but neither Britain nor Germany broadcast French series. Great Britain limits itself with respect to series to national, Australian and American series, which means English-spoken series.

There are fewer co-productions for series than for films. Only 0.8 percent of the series are the result of a cooperation between European countries. Also, in this respect, the public channels (especially Dutch and German) score significantly better than the commercial ones.

The high percentage of series from other countries (17 percent) on the Italian commercial channels has to be attributed to the Latin American telenovelas. They are a purely Southern European (and recently also Eastern European) phenomenon. In Italy, the telenovelas are almost exclusively broadcast on Rete 4, one of the three Mediaset (formerly Fininvest) channels. Rete 4 specializes in soaps and telenovelas for a mainly female audience (Buonanno, 1998a: 53).

The analysis shows the cultural fragmentation of the European audiovisual market while at the same time the American audiovisual industry has succeeded in breaking through all these cultural barriers. The American success formulas are sufficiently well known by now. The themes of American television are derived from emotional, daily life and concentrate on personal conflicts. Love, jealousy, hatred, ambition and the lust for money are the major themes. The cause of all good and evil lies with the individual, not with society. Each serial is characterized by an intelligible content, identifiable situations and a touch of suspense. At the same time, American television fiction offers escapist dream material, which Vasterman (1981) and Berger (1992) compared with fairy tales, based on simple dichotomies of good and evil, and with a built-in hope for a better life, more happiness and prosperity. There is no room for experiments; 'safety first' is the motto of the American networks, which stands for imitation and following up of existing success formulas (De Bens, 1994: 92). Gitlin (1983) summarizes it as 'nothing succeeds like success'.

As for films, the evolution since 1991 has more or less stabilized (see Table 4.6). Between 1988 and 1991 there were still big shifts: a decrease in the share of national series and an increase in the share of American series. Between 1991 and 1997 the shifts are much less marked and are certainly less univocal if one takes into account the limited sample period. It looks as though the slight increase of national series is at the expense of non-national European series, but certainly not at the expense of American series.

European audiovisual policy

The results of our programme analysis from 1997, like the results of similar research – the Eurofiction reports for 1996 and 1997 (Buonanno, 1998a, 1998b) and the figures from the European Audiovisual Observatory (1999) – confirm that the same trends apply to the 1990s as to the 1980s:

- The importance of fiction on the European television channels;
- The dominant position of American fiction;
- The limited distribution of European fiction.

This is not self-evident in view of all the policy measures taken since the end of the 1980s to stimulate European audiovisual production and distribution in resistance to the dominant American industry. [...]

Total programming time vs fiction programming time

In the reports of the European Commission the share of European programmes is worked out with regard to the *total* broadcasting time, with exclusion of only a few programme categories such as news reports and sports and logically advertising and teletext.[7] Documentaries, but also talk shows, quizzes and shows are included. These programmes allow the channels to produce cheap, one-off domestic productions (the so-called 'quota quickies') and to attain the European quota. Often these programmes are no more than copies of American programmes, the formats of which are filled in accordance with the national culture (e.g. *Wheel of Fortune, Venture*).

In our study we have shown that the European production and programming of *fiction* on the various European channels present a more pessimistic picture. For the European Commission fiction is only one of the categories on which the quotas are calculated. However, it is the largest single programme category (about a third of transmission time), one of the most popular and consequently crucial in the development of the European audiovisual industry. Of all fiction examined, 63.4 percent is of American origin. Figures over a longer period show that the share of American fiction, instead of decreasing or stabilizing, has even risen slightly (see Tables 4.4 and 4.6; see also the figures for 1994–7 in the European Audiovisual Observatory, 1999: 186).

National vs non-national European fiction

Furthermore, the weak spot of the European audiovisual sector is the distribution of films and television programmes across the national borders. Whereas the American productions find a ready reception worldwide, European productions remain in the first place 'national productions'. The European Commission has calculated that 80 percent of the films made in the EU never leave the country of origin. The same goes for television programmes (De Bens et al., 1992: 95). Our research has shown that the inflow of American films and series in the 1990s has not been stopped at all, whereas the 'internal European' circulation of fiction remains stagnant. Prime-time is showing a bipolarization of national fiction on the one hand and US fiction on the other. European co-productions do not contribute to an increase of the European share but replace the single-country productions.

With regard to the internal European distribution of fiction, language and cultural proximity still play an important role. This is especially true for the large language groups (such as English, French, German) and to a lesser degree for the smaller language groups (such as Dutch, Italian). As a consequence, the fiction content on channels in small language communities is more diversified than the fiction content on channels in large language communities. Great Britain is a good example. Series on British channels are either British or American or Australian. Co-productions are almost exclusively concluded with English-speaking (and thus non-European) countries (such as the USA, Australia, New Zealand). Germany and France search for co-productions within Europe, but they also show a clear preference for cooperation with countries from the same language group. Germany co-produces with Austria and German-speaking Switzerland and France with French-speaking Belgium (Wallonia) and French-speaking Switzerland (Buonanno, 1998a: 18). Co-productions deteriorate into an extension of the national productions: deeply rooted in the cultural tradition of the dominant country which also provides the main market (Buonanno, 1998a: xvi).

Films vs series

In our survey, the category of 'fiction' was further subdivided into 'films' and 'series'. This brought to light some striking differences between both genres. The US dominance is, for both films (57.4 percent) and series (64.2 percent), an indisputable fact. It is striking, though, that the share of the American film increases in prime-time (up to 67.2 percent) whereas the share of American series decreases strongly (to 39.4 percent). The Hollywood movie dominates not only the European cinemas but also the European television screen and this during peak-time. American series on the other hand are used first and foremost to 'fill in' the broadcasting schedules on the commercial channels in the morning and afternoon and during the night.

The share of national series is everywhere much higher than the share of national films and their concentration in prime-time is striking. In the 1990s, the production of home-made series gained momentum in most European countries (such as Germany, the Netherlands, Flanders – countries with formerly an almost non-existent soap tradition). The increase of the domestic series coincides with an increase of series in general. Eurofiction speaks of the 'serialization of domestic products': 'more serials and soap operas were being produced [in 1997], having formats that extended over an undefined, and even infinite number of episodes' (Buonanno, 1998b: 302). According to Mohr and O'Donnell (1996: 62), the rapid evolution in the 1990s to more domestic series is the result of the increasing competition between the increased number of channels:

> The real 'soap wars' in Europe – both in relation to domestic *and* imported serials – are no longer between Europe and America, but between different stations competing within the same domestic market.

Series, and especially domestic series, attract viewers and commit them to daily channel loyalty. It is mainly economic motives that are at the basis of this evolution and not the concern about the national culture or European quota for national productions. However, a number of authors (e.g. Picard, 1999) predict that as a result of the future fragmentation of the television market and consequently of the advertising market, television channels will have at their disposal less and less revenue and fewer and fewer means to invest in their own productions. [...]

Public vs commercial channels

[…]

Our research shows that 67 percent of the films and 76 percent of the series on the German commercial channels are of American origin. This is well over 78 percent of the broadcasting time, devoted to fiction. Also with respect to the total broadcasting time (all programme categories together), the share of US programmes is still 52 percent. Is this the good example to which the Commission refers?

By no means do we dispute that the 'new' character of a channel, as the Commission puts it, is not beneficial to the share of European programmes. In the first months, or rather the first years of its existence, a new channel attempts to consolidate the home audience rapidly by a high level of imports and strip scheduling. Over time and once the station is established within its home market, it may begin to move towards domestic and European production (Commission of the European Communities, 1998: 53; De Bens et al., 1992: 77–8). But we do dispute the fact that the distinction between public and commercial channels is not at all relevant. Even the results of the Commission prove the opposite: the list of channels *not* achieving a majority of European works in 1995–6 does not include one public channel (Commission of the European Communities, 1998: 71–4).

Our own findings clearly confirm the distinction between public and commercial channels. Loyal to their assignment to provide a wide and balanced range of entertainment and informational programmes, public channels clearly devote more broadcasting time to programme genres such as information, education, sports and culture while commercial channels concentrate foremost on fiction. With regard to fiction, public channels offer a wider range of national and European fiction while commercial channels programme predominantly American fiction. Dupagne and Waterman (1998) examined the relation between the share of commercial channels in a country and the share of US import and found a clearly positive correlation: the more commercial channels in a country, the larger the share of US import. This leads them to conclude:

> … that political decisions to permit commercial television stations to operate in Western Europe may be a more important factor in determining the tendency to import US programs than economic or linguistic considerations. (Dupagne and Waterman, 1998: 216)

Conclusion

Television is mainly and increasingly a medium for entertainment, especially fiction. Fiction content is dominated by American films and home-made series, spread over an interminable number of episodes and modelled after American and Australian examples. Our investigation shows that this tendency is especially perceivable among the sharply increased number of commercial channels. It is true that public channels are dragged into the competition battle, but they continue to hold on to more programme diversity both in genres and in countries of origin. The European system of quotas has not been able to stem the 'Dallasification' of television content. Therefore, the conclusion of the investigation from 1991 is still relevant at the end of the 1990s (De Bens et al., 1992: 98): 'National governments face an important task: TV media policy needs a more cultural approach.' The broadcasting station and the audiovisual sector in general are too important to be left only to the market.

Notes

1. In 1988 (18–31 January), the Euromedia Research Group also carried out a similar enquiry among 20 European television stations.
2. The 36 broadcasting stations are: for Flanders, the Flemish-speaking part of Belgium: the public stations BRTN-TV1 and TV2 and the commercial stations VTM, Ka2 and VT4; for Wallonia, the French-speaking part of Belgium: the public stations RTBF1 and Tele21 and the commercial stations RTL-Tvi and Club RTL; for the Netherlands: the public stations NED1, NED2 and NED3 and the commercial stations Veronica, RTL4, RTL5 and SBS6; for Germany: the public stations ARD and ZDF and the commercial stations RTLtelevision, SAT1, PR07, VOX and RTL2; for France: the public stations FR2 and FR3 and the commercial station TF1; for Great Britain: the public stations BBC1 and BBC2 and the commercial stations Channel 4 and ITV; for Italy: the public stations RAI1, RAI2 and RAI3 and the commercial stations Italia 1, Rete 4 and Canale 5.
3. The comparability with the investigation from 1991 is obviously strengthened by the use of the same code book. We distinguished two main categories which in turn were subdivided into 10 subcategories. On the one hand, there is the 'popular' programme category which consists of (1) films, (2) series and serials, (3) entertainment/infotainment, (4) popular music and (5) sports. On the other hand, there is the 'serious' programme category which consists of (6) information, (7) culture, (8) education, (9) children's programmes and (10) others. In this article we go into only two programme categories, namely (1) films and (2) series, which together form the broader category of 'fiction'. The definition of prime-time used was 7 p.m. to 11 p.m.
4. Several authors point out the imitation of American genres on both public and commercial European channels: daily games and talk shows, reality shows, daily soaps and comedy (De Bens, 1994: 92–3; Hallenberger, 1998: 37). Hallenberger even speaks of the 'Americanization' of viewing patterns: 'channel hopping', switching channels during publicity breaks. Obviously, it is not only American formats that are imitated. Both the Dutch soap *Goede tijden, slechte tijden* (Good Times, Bad Times) and the German clone *Gute Zeiten, Schlechte Zeiten* are modelled on the Australian soap *The Restless Years*. *Wittekerke* (Flanders) too was modelled on an Australian series.
5. The category 'information' was defined rather narrowly: news bulletins and news reels. The category 'education', on the other hand, was broadly defined and includes school television, scientific programmes, documentaries, but also consumer programmes, economic programmes and others.
6. This conclusion is of course only valid for the commercial channels in the survey i.e. ITV and Channel 4. In addition, Great Britain has a comprehensive range of commercial cable and satellite channels with, on the whole, a very commercial, often thematic offering.
7. The directive also makes mention of a category 'games' but this is interpreted very narrowly.

Bibliography

Ang, Ien (1982) *Het geval Dallas. Populaire kultuur, ideologie en plezier.* Amsterdam: SU.
Berger, Arthur A. (1992) *Popular Culture Genres. Theories and Texts.* London: Sage.

Biltereyst, Daniël (1995) *Hollywood in het Avondland: over de afhankelijkheid en de impact van Amerikaanse televisie in Europa*. Brussel: VUB Press.

Biltereyst, Daniël (1996) 'Europees audiovisueel beleid en de beperkte interne stroom van tv-programma's. Een internationale diachronische flow-studie rond fictie', *Communicatie* 25(2): 3–26.

Blumler, Jay and W. Hoffman-Riem (1992) 'New Roles for Public Service Television', pp. 202–17 in J. Blumler (ed.), *Television and the Public Interest. Vulnerable Values in West European Broadcasting*. London: Sage.

Boyd-Barrett, Oliver (1977) 'Media Imperialism: Towards an International Framework for the Analysis of Media Systems', pp. 116–41 in J. Curran, M.Gurevitch and J. Woollacott (eds), *Mass Communication and Society*. London: Edward Arnold.

Buonanno, Milly (ed.) (1998a) *Imaginary Dreamscapes. Television Fiction in Europe. First Report of the Eurofiction Project. 1997*. Luton: ULP/John Libbey Media.

Buonanno, Milly (ed.) (1998b) *Eurofiction 1998. Secondo Rapporto sulla fiction telvisiva in Europa*. Rome: RAI-ERI.

Commission of the European Communities (1997) *Audiovisual Policy of the European Union 1998*. Brussels and Luxembourg: Office for Official Publications of the European Communities.

Contamine, Claude, Monique van Dusseldorp and Sophie Deleville-McGuire (eds) (1996) *7th European Television and Film Forum. Building the European Audiovisual Market – Creative Potential, Economic Trends, Societal Needs. Proceedings of the 7th European TV and Film Forum*. Düsseldorf: European Institute for the Media.

CSA (Conseil Supérieur de l'audiovisuel) (1995) 'La Fiction européenne sur les chaines françaises, britanniques et allemandes', *La Lettre CSA* (74): 5–9.

De Bens, Els (1997) 'Television Programming: More Diversity, More Convergence?', pp. 27–37 in K. Brants (ed.), *The Media in Question. Popular Cultures and Public Interest*. London: Sage.

De Bens, Els, Mary Kelly and Marit Bakke (1992) 'Television Content: Dallasification of Culture?', pp. 73–100 in K. Siune and W. Truetzschler (eds), *Dynamics of Media Politics*. London: Sage.

Dupagne, Michel and David Waterman (1998) 'Determinants of US Television Fiction Imports in Western Europe', *Journal of Broadcasting and Electronic Media* 42(2): 208–20.

European Audiovisual Observatory (1999) *Statistical Yearbook 1999. Film, Television, Video and New Media in Europe*. Strasbourg: European Audiovisual Observatory.

Featherstone, Mike (1991) *Consumer Culture and Postmodernism*. London: Sage.

Fiske, John (1987) *Television Culture*. London: Methuen.

Fiske, John (1991) 'Postmodernism and Television', pp. 55–67 in J. Curran and M. Gurevitch (eds), *Mass Media and Society*. London: Edward Arnold.

Ghijs, Inge (1997) 'Sterren en strepen op de buis. Vanwaar de Vlaamse appetijt voor Amerikaans tv-voer?', *De Standaard Magazine* 7 November: 4–6.

Gitlin, Todd (1983) *Inside Prime Time*. New York: Pantheon.

Hallenberger, Gerd (1998) 'Derrick's Children in the TV Supermarket. German Television Fiction in 1996', pp. 35–50 in M. Buonanno (ed.), *Imaginary Dreamscapes. Television Fiction in Europe. First Report of the Eurofiction Project. 1997*. Luton: ULP/John Libbey Media.

Hamelink, Cees (1978) *De mythe van de vrije informatie*. Baarn: In den Toren.

High Level Group on Audiovisual Policy (1998) *The Digital Age: European Audiovisual Policy. Report from the High Level Group on Audiovisual Policy*. Brussels and Luxembourg: Office for Official Publications of the European Communities.

Katz, Elihu and Tamar Liebes (1990) *The Export of Meaning. Cross-Cultural Readings of Dallas*. New York: Oxford University Press.

Krüger, Udo Michaël (1997) 'Programmanalyse 1996: ARD, ZDF, RTL, SAT1 und PRO SIEBEN im Vergleich. Unterschiede der Programmprofile bleiben bestehen', *Media Perspektiven* 7: 354–66.

Machet, Emmanuelle (1999) 'Ten Years of the "Television without Frontiers" Directive. How Successful Has the Directive Been and Will It Continue as a Separate Policy Area?', *Intermedia* 27(3): 40–2.

Mattelart, Armand and Ariel Dorfman (1975) *How to Read Donald Duck: Imperialist Ideology in the Disney Comic*. New York: International General.

Mohr, Paul J. and Hugh O'Donnell (1996) 'The Rise and Rise of Soap Operas in Europe', *The SCA Journal* 2: 34–70.

Morley, David (1980) *The Nationwide Audience. Structure and Decoding*. London: British Film Institute.

Morley, David (1992) 'Electronic Communities and Domestic Rituals', pp. 65–83 in M. Skovmand and K.C. Schrøder (eds), *Media Cultures. Reappraising Transnational Media*. London: Routledge.

Nordenstreng, Kaarle and Tapio Varis (1974) *Television Traffic, a One Way Street? A Survey and Analysis of the International Flow of Television Programmes Material, Unesco Reports and Papers on Mass Communication* 70. Paris: UNESCO.

Nordenstreng, Kaarle and Tapio Varis (1986) *La Circulation internationale des émissions de télévision, Unesco etudes et documents d'information* 100. Paris: UNESCO.

Picard, Robert (1999) 'Audience Fragmentation and Structural Limits on Media Innovation and Diversity', paper for the Second Expert Meeting on Mediaand Open Societies' Amsterdam School of Communication Research.

Pragnell, Anthony (1985) *Television in Europe*, Media Monograph No. 5. Manchester: European Institute for the Media.

Schiller, Herbert (1976) *Communication and Cultural Domination*. White Plains, NY: International Arts and Science Press.

Sepstrup, Preben (1989) 'Implication of Current Developments in West European Broadcasting', *Media, Culture and Society* 11(2): 29–54.

Sepstrup, Preben (1990) *Transnationalisation of Television in Western Europe*. London: John Libbey.

Silj, Alessandro (1988) *East of Dallas. The European Challenge to American TV*. London: British Film Institute.

Tunstall, Jeremy (1977) *The Media Are American*. New York: Columbia University Press.

Varis, Tapio (1984) 'The International Flow of Television Programs', *Journal of Communication* 34(1): 143–52.

Vasterman, Peter (1981) 'Televisie-Amusement. Een Spel zonder Grenzen', pp. 50–105 in J. Bardoel and J. Bierhoff (eds), *Media in Nederland. Deel I. Omroep, Film, Nieuwe Media, Invloed*. Amsterdam: Van Gennep.

Van Den Burghe, Philip (1998) 'La Culture à la télévision sur la voie de l'Europe', *La Libre belgique*, 23 April.

Section Two

Audience

---

5 Five Traditions in Search of the Audience

Klaus Bruhn Jensen and Karl Erik Rosengren

Introduction

In the beginning, the word was directly communicated, even to mass audiences. Building on their own experience, practitioners/theoreticians of oratory, rhetoric and poetics gradually accumulated a vast fund of systematic knowledge about characteristics of verbal messages (oral and written, fictional and non-fictional) supposedly affecting listeners in a powerful way. This fund of knowledge was codified in classic writings by, for instance, Aristotle, Cicero, Quintilian. Taught in schools and academies, it lived on through the Middle Ages, being revitalized and revised in the Renaissance and afterwards (Arnold and Frandsen, 1984).

In spite of the fact that modern mass communication is mediated rather than direct, parts of the truly classic fund of knowledge originally emanating from the rhetorics of antiquity have flowed into modern audience research. Tracing this influence in detail is not our task, however. Our task is broader and yet more specific to the field of communication research as it currently exists: to present and discuss the major research traditions focusing their interest on the nexus between the mass media and their audiences.

The approaches in the area have been many and diverse, drawing on a number of disciplines in the humanities and the social sciences. Even in cases where obvious similarities may be found between different traditions, their representatives have not always seemed to be aware of each other's existence. Recently, however, in this area as in some other areas of the emerging discipline of communication research, signs of increasing contacts between different research traditions

Source: *EJC* (1990), vol. 5: 207–238.

have become visible (Blumler et al., 1985; Dervin et al., 1989; Jensen, 1987a; Rosengren, 1985; Schrøder, 1987).

This article is an attempt to explicate, in terms of a number of basic characteristics of the various approaches, the confluences which have recently taken place in research on the reception, uses and effects of mass media content, while at the same time identifying the controversies arising from different theoretical and political orientations. Coming from different traditions, the authors wish to suggest that the process of dialogue and *détente* may lead to a dynamic state of coexistence, rather than final unification.

For analytical purposes, we note five main traditions of research in this area: (1) Effects research, (2) Uses and gratifications research, (3) Literary criticism, (4) Cultural studies, (5) Reception analysis. First short background histories, thumbnail sketches of the five broad traditions will be provided, rooted as they are in distinctive conceptions of the nature and purpose of science and scholarship. After this historically oriented background, we analyse in the next, more systematically oriented section of the article each of the five traditions, in turn, in terms of (a) their conceptualization of three constituents of mass communication processes: the message, the audience and the micro and macro aspects of the social system in which the whole process is embedded; and (b) their methodologies and modes of analysis. We finally proceed to a discussion of some pragmatic aspects of previous research and our own analyses: the politics of audience research in general, the social relevance and applications of audience studies and implications for further research.

History

Effects Research

The history of mass communication is the history of a series of new media being introduced: books, journals, newspapers, film, radio, television. At present, new and not so new developments of television are restructuring the international media scene: various combinations of computerized cable, satellite and video technologies. For each new medium, there has been widespread fear that its effects might be deleterious, especially to supposedly weak minds, such as those of children, women and uneducated people. 'Moral panics' of this type accompanied the introduction of film, comics, TV and video. Directly and indirectly, such panics gave rise to much research on the effects of the use of this or that medium (Cohen, 1980; Roe, 1985; cf. DeFleur and Ball-Rokeach, 1989). Indeed, mass-communication research owes at least part of its very existence to sometimes exaggerated and misapprehended notions of the effects of mass communication (McQuail, 1987).

Over the years, mass-communication research itself has started from, and arrived at, quite diverse notions about the strength of the effects of mass-media use. According to conventional wisdom, these notions have developed cyclically, from the idea of strong effects to that of weak effects, and back again. If that is so, it must be added, however, that at the same time the notions about the character of these effects have changed quite substantially – by and large, from short-term, direct and specific effects to long-term, indirect and diffuse effects (Mahle, 1986; Rosengren, 1988). At the same time, the notion of the individual presumably affected by the mass media has varied, from that of a passive recipient of powerful messages to that of a much more active and selective user of media content (Klapper, 1960; Levy and Windahl, 1985).

In addition to such variations over time, there has also been variation between different types of research in the area – experimental research probably being more inclined than survey research to seek and find direct, strong and immediate effects on passive recipients. Experimental effects research has recently experienced something of a revival, drawing on a combination of the strong demands inherent in the experimental design and developed versions of classic psychological, social psychological and sociological theories and models (Bradac, 1989; Bryant and Zillmann, 1986; Schenk, 1987). Moreover, the rise of sub-specialties in effects research, addressing issues ranging from the agenda-setting function of the media (McCombs and Shaw, 1972; McCombs and Weaver, 1985) to the impact of media on knowledge gaps between groups and categories in society (Tichenor et al., 1970; Gaziano, 1983), has served to differentiate the general area of effects studies considerably (cf. Rosengren, 1988).

Effects research, then, has recently been differentiated and revitalized. A partly parallel development has occurred in the other broad, social science-oriented audience research tradition, the 'uses and gratifications' (U&G) tradition.

Uses and Gratifications Research

'What do the media do to the individual?' – 'What does the individual do with the media?' According to the widespread adage, the two questions give us in a nutshell the difference between two broad research traditions which for a long time dominated research on the media/individual nexus. The former question, of course, refers to effects research; the latter, to U&G research. While originally there was much truth in the adage, recent developments have complicated as well as differentiated the picture of two distinct traditions of research.

Effects research as we know it today has some of its roots in American film research of the 1920s (Lowery and DeFleur, 1988). The beginnings of U&G research can be located about two decades later, in the early 1940s. As part of the ambitious mass-communication research programme initiated by Paul F. Lazarsfeld, Herta Herzog undertook the task of finding out what gratifications radio listeners might derive from daytime serials, quiz programmes, etc. (Herzog, 1942, 1944). Since then, U&G research may be said to have developed in four phases, moving from prima-facie descriptions, to typological efforts building on systematic operationalizations of central variables, to efforts at explanation, to systematic theory building (Palmgreen et al., 1985). In its attempts to build and test formal theories, U&G research has drawn on recent developments in social psychology, primarily the so-called expectancy-value approach

(Palmgreen and Rayburn, 1985; Babrow, 1989). This step is reminiscent of similar developments in effects research hinted at above.

As a matter of fact, the recent developments in effects and U&G research may well mark a final confluence between these two traditions. Such a confluence has been on its way for quite some time, and it has often been called for by a number of scholars, sometimes under the heading of 'uses and effects research' (cf. Belson, 1972; Klapper, 1960; Rosengren and Windahl, 1972; Trenaman, 1967; Windahl, 1981). This dynamic body of research is matched by the heterogeneous forms of enquiry which grew out of the humanistic tradition in the area.

Literary Criticism

For some 2500 years or more, the development of arts and sciences in the west has been closely related to the emergence of literate forms of communication (Havelock, 1963; Ong, 1982). A great deal of importance has traditionally been attached to the exegesis of texts carrying cognitive and/or aesthetic experience. Rules of interpretation have been a shaping force of social life and cultural practices generally, also in cultures with a relative separation of religious, cultural and other societal sectors. In the Christian tradition, of course, the interpretation of the Bible and other canonical texts has resulted in controversies which could make or break individuals as well as whole societies. (Actually, the potentially fatal implications of such a controversy in eighteenth-century Sweden helped to transform traditional textual interpretation into a very early case of quantitative content analysis; cf. Rosengren, 1981: 9)

With the development of the modern social order came the redefinition of literature as a form of communication addressing readers primarily as private individuals in a sphere of leisure (Watt, 1957). While this entailed a complex process of redefining also the purpose of literary criticism (Williams, 1977; Eagleton, 1983), one result was an emphasis on attempts at demonstrating that, and explaining how, literature, as mastered by specific historical authors, may give rise to aesthetic experiences supposed to transcend historical time and place. These efforts further implied a normative approach to the education of readers, at least to the extent that readers must learn appropriate responses to the literary tradition, thus, in a sense, learning the effects of literary communication. […]

Cultural Studies

The borderland of textual and social research has been given a distinctive, if often eclectic, articulation within cultural studies. Combining structuralist assumptions about the nature of society under industrial capitalism with culturalist assumptions about the relative autonomy of cultural forms and their contribution to social change (Hall, 1980), much work in this tradition proposes to study mass-communication processes as an integrated aspect of other everyday 'practices'. Practices may be defined briefly as meaningful social activities (Williams, 1977). The concept serves to underline a holistic perspective on social life, while recognizing the scope for intervention by individuals and the role of meaning for orienting social action. For cultural studies, then, the centre of mass-communication research is located outside the media, which are embedded, along with audiences, in broad social and cultural practices.

The roots of present-day cultural studies are many, including a number of nineteenth-century classics (Durkheim, Marx, Weber), as well as modern European and American pioneers such as Adorno and Horkheimer (1977), Hoggart (1957), Williams (1977), Carey (1989) and Gans (1974). It is normally assumed that a breakthrough took place when, building on these classics and pioneers, a Birmingham–Paris axis was established and, later on, re-exported to the American market. In other words, British cultural studies derived much of their impetus and appeal from the assimilation of French social and psychoanalytic theory to the critical study of contemporary social issues (Hall et al., 1980). In doing so, this tradition helped to redefine culture not as canonical works, but as processes of meaning production. It further served to revaluate popular culture as a worthy discourse and a relevant social resource, casting, for example, television as a modern bard (Fiske and Hartley, 1978). It should be added, perhaps, that although for some time British cultural studies dominated the scene, similar ideas were developed more or less independently in other European countries.

The tradition of cultural studies raises both theoretical and political issues concerning the audience. With Morley (1980) representing something of a breakthrough, a great deal of recent work has explored the extent to which audiences – drawing on frames of explanation outside the dominant social order – resist constructions of reality presented by mass media (Ang, 1985; Morley, 1986; Radway, 1984; Fiske, 1987). Theoretically, the relative power of different cultural practices in the social production of meaning is at stake. Politically, the question is whether this form of semiotic resistance is evidence of a long-term tendency towards social change, which might imply new political strategies.

Reception Analysis

Cultural studies blend into reception analysis in several respects, as exemplified by recent works such as Ang (1985), Morley (1986), or Radway (1984). Reception analysis, in this context, is taken as the more inclusive term, covering various forms of qualitative empirical audience research which, to different degrees, seek to integrate social–scientific and humanistic perspectives on reception (Jensen, 1986).

In broad theoretical terms, the tradition builds on a variety of theoretical frameworks ranging from symbolic interactionism to psychoanalysis. More specifically, it has one of its roots in the two traditions of reception aesthetics and reader-response theories mentioned above, another in the U&G research which some current reception analysts helped found (Katz and Liebes, 1984). In empirical terms, reception analysis has been concerned with cultural contexts both within and outside Europe and the United States (Liebes and Katz, 1986; Lindlof, 1987; Lull, 1988).

Reception analysis thus understood may be regarded as the most recent development in the area of audience studies. By and large it has taken as its points of departure what are seen as limitations in the modes of enquiry of both the humanities and the social sciences. On the one hand, it has questioned the validity of interpretive content analyses carried out in the humanities as a source of knowledge about the uses and effects of mass-media content. This criticism is generally held to be well-founded, sometimes even by those being hit by it, although, as traditionalists may remind us, qualitative empirical studies sometimes leave behind important theoretical and political issues regarding the epistemological status and aesthetic quality of different media texts (Gripsrud, 1989). On the other hand, reception analysis has questioned the predominant methodologies of empirical social–scientific research, a criticism which, while met with qualified enthusiasm, has at least contributed to debates across the field about the nature and purpose of media scholarship (Rosengren, 1989).

Thus, reception analysis develops what may be referred to as audience-cum-content analysis which is both qualitative and empirical in nature. While producing empirical data about the audience through in-depth interviewing and observation, studies normally apply qualitative methods in a comparative analysis of audience data as well as content data. The immediate aim, then, is to examine the very processes of reception, which, further, have a bearing on the use and impact of media content.

Systematics

Theories

Theories about mass-media audiences are being developed in all five traditions discussed in this article. In simplified terms, the sets of theories available in the area may be divided into the humanistic type and the social-science type, which are the legacy of 'arts' and 'science', respectively.

The social-science type theories have been developed mainly within the traditions of effects research and U&G research, often on the basis of more general psychological, social-psychological and sociological theories. They are usually transformed into graphical and statistical models of processes of influence whose elements and interrelations may be tested by formalized procedures. The humanistic type theories, in their turn, derive mainly from the traditions of literary criticism and cultural studies. They are systematic but as a rule not formalizable descriptions of how content structures – media discourses – come to carry specific meanings for recipients in a particular social context. In reception analysis, attempts are being made to combine the two types of theories.

Substantively, theories in the area may be thought of as specific conceptualizations of mass communication processes within the message/audience nexus.

Three constituents of such processes are of particular relevance for audience studies: message, audience and social system, or – in the terminology of the humanities – text/discourse, recipient and context.

Typically, the tradition of *effects research* tends to conceive of media messages as symbolic stimuli having recognizable and measurable physical characteristics. While originally the interest was often focused on isolated, undifferentiated stimuli – for example, an act of violence or a programme classified as 'violent' – the insight has gradually grown stronger that what must be studied are configurations of stimuli and stimuli differentiated according to context-oriented theory. An example is successful versus unsuccessful violence, committed by provoked or unprovoked agents, against powerful or weak victims. In short, wholes of differentiated stimuli have come to take the place of single, undifferentiated stimuli, the composition of the wholes and the type of differentiation being guided by formalized theories (Bradac, 1989; Bryant and Zillmann, 1986; Schenk, 1987).

On the audience side, a similar differentiation has taken place. Effects theories presently much in vogue – like for example, Gerbner's 'cultivation theory' (Signorielli and Morgan, 1989), or Noelle-Neumann's 'spiral of silence' (1983) – predict and find very different effects for audience members with different social and/or individual characteristics. Also the social context (macro, mezzo and micro) surrounding the communication process has been given increased attention. For instance, the spiral of silence has been shown to operate only under certain societal and communicative conditions (Noelle-Neumann, 1983, 1988). Similarly, cultivation effects have been shown to be different in different social surroundings and media systems (Melischeck et al., 1984; Signorielli and Morgan, 1989). To take a very specific example: effects of television viewing on children's and adolescents' social interaction with peers and family members have been shown to be radically different in the USA of the 1950s and in Sweden of the 1980s (Rosengren and Windahl, 1989). [...]

The majority of studies within *literary criticism* have focused on the structure of literary messages, or works. Traditionally, the literary work is seen as a rule-governed configuration of linguistic and rhetorical structures which in the aggregate make up genres as defined in aesthetics or hermeneutics (Frye, 1957; Eagleton, 1983). It is interesting to note that – for literary criticism as well as for effects research – meaning is taken to be immanent in content structures. While both specific texts and genres may give rise to different interpretations, literary analysis may be said to provide the appropriate response according to literary tradition or, alternatively, it may suggest a new, more insightful reading, sometimes from the viewpoint of an implied reader. Hence, the reader is most often a critical construct to be deduced from literary discourse or tradition. When empirical readers are studied, attention is frequently focused on individual readings or general sociological or psychological aspects of literary meaning rather than historically or demographically specific recipients. The social system in which literature is produced, then, is most often present as an abstract framework of the analysis, or sometimes as 'historical background' provided in an introductory section.

Work in *cultural studies*, similarly, focuses on the actual message or discourse of communication. Like literary criticism it also pays special attention to the genre in question, its implied reader positions and associated social uses. Unlike literary criticism, however, cultural studies are not centred on just high culture, but on popular cultural discourses as well. Thus, media messages are conceived of as generically structured discourses which are relevant for audiences in different cultural and social practices.

With the exception of some recent work (see, for instance, Morley, 1980; Radway, 1984), cultural studies have not examined empirical audiences, instead deducing them from media discourses as analytical constructs. Such analyses, however, are substantiated with extensive reference to the social and historical context. This context represents a social system of diverse practices which are said to mediate the flow and interpretation of communication, for example, through the existence of sub-cultures based on gender, class or ethnicity. This same social system also helps to generate interpretive strategies supposedly shared by individuals belonging to specific audience groups or publics which are referred to as interpretive communities (Fish, 1980; Lindlof, 1988; Jensen, 1990). In this way, cultural studies seek to combine a text-centred perspective with a social-systemic conception of reception.

Reception analysis has drawn the components of its theoretical framework from both the humanities and the social sciences. Like cultural studies, reception analysis speaks of media messages as culturally and generically coded discourses, while defining audiences as agents of meaning production. Like U&G research, reception analysis conceives of recipients as active individuals who can do a variety of things with media in terms of consumption, decoding and social uses. What characterizes reception analysis is, above all, an insistence that studies include a comparative empirical analysis of media discourses with audience discourses – content structures with the structure of audience responses regarding content. The results of this analysis are then interpreted with reference to the surrounding socio-cultural system, which, again, is conceptualized as a historical configuration of social practices, contexts of use, and interpretive communities. A common assumption of reception studies is that cultural practices as well as individual acts of interpretation are relatively autonomous, for example in relation to political and economic structures. Within this complex theoretical framework of *social semiotics,* the question to be addressed empirically by reception studies is how specific audiences differ in the social production of meaning.

Trying to sum up present theoretical developments in the five research traditions discussed, we note, first of all, how in all five traditions the audience members have come to stand out as increasingly active and selective in their use and interpretation of mass-media messages. In metaphorical terms, we could say that audiences, rather than 'reading out' messages from media, are seen to 'read in' quite diverse meanings into mass-mediated texts. In classical terms, *eisegesis* may be a more important aspect of audience activities than *exegesis*. At the same time the social context has also come to appear as ever more important in shaping both audience, mass-media genres and institutions, as well as the interaction between media and recipients.

Despite such conceptual differentiations within each tradition, however, the scope of each one of the two main types of theories – oriented towards the humanities and social science, respectively – stands out as somewhat limited when regarded in the light of the other. One basic reason for this state of affairs is that there are major differences not only in the *extent* to which our five traditions specify three constituents of communication processes fundamental to all audience research (message, audience and social context), but also in the *mode* in which this is being done.

Social science-oriented audience research has succeeded in differentiating, to varying degrees, the conception of the macro-social system, the media-institutional environment and the audience as social-psychological entities. It is on this foundation that social science successfully performs replicable studies of representative samples from well defined populations of audiences. Conversely, humanistically oriented audience studies have offered elaborate theories of meaning and representation to account for the sense which audiences attribute to media content and which may serve to explain cognitive and behavioural effects of media use. Recent reception studies have also successfully examined empirical recipients as social and psychological entities who think, feel and act in ways similar to those of characters represented in textual discourse.

This situation raises a number of issues regarding the compatibility of the traditions within the framework of a (hypothetically emerging) comprehensive theory of media reception and impact. An analysis of methodological similarities and differences in audience studies may help to clarify further these and related issues.

Methodologies and Modes of Analysis

Just as one may find two main types of theories in the area of audience research, one may distinguish between two forms of methodologies and modes of analysis. Social–scientific work puts great weight on establishing explicitly operationalized categories of analysis, and on keeping – in principle at least – the phases of theory and hypothesis formation, observation, analysis, interpretation and presentation of results separate from each other. Moreover, the assumption is that the researcher's role in the act of data collection and analysis can and should be minimized. The humanistic tradition, in contrast, assumes that in principle, no distinction can be made between the collection, analysis and interpretation of 'data'. The best a researcher can offer is said to be a reflexive accounting of the contexts, purposes and participant roles through which a piece of research is constituted (Lindlof and Anderson, 1988). Like other forms of science, however, humanistic scholarship generally is required to abide by the systematic procedures and explicit levels of enquiry which facilitate meaningful intersubjective agreement and/or disagreement.

These two mainstreams of general methodology are often referred to in terms of the distinction between quantitative and qualitative approaches. While much of the discussion that is premised on this distinction has obscured rather than clarified the similarities, dissimilarities and interconnections between the approaches, for want of a better terminology we use it occasionally.

Effects and U&G research – in parallel with their theoretical orientations – rely primarily on the social science type of methodologies. Literary criticism and cultural studies rely primarily on the humanist type, while in reception analysis both types may be found.

Within a general social science methodology, in both *effects research* and *U&G research* a number of specific methods and techniques have been used, including laboratory experiments, natural and field experiments, survey studies by means of questionnaires and standardized interviews, participant observations, in-depth interviews etc. The main difference between the two traditions is probably that effects research as a rule tends to prefer highly structured and standardized techniques, while U&G research seems to have been relatively more open towards less structured, 'naturalistic' techniques such as in-depth interviews and participant observation.

In general, and regardless of the specific methods applied, in both traditions today there is a tendency for researchers to try to apply a holistic perspective, locating media use and effects within as broad a psychological, social-psychological, and sociological framework as possible. Methodologically, this tendency gives rise to at least two types of efforts. [...]

It should be added, finally, that combinations of different research methodologies in a single study have existed for a long time in social science research, at least *in nascendi*. A majority of handbooks in social science methodology always recommended, sometimes actually as a *sine qua non*, that any large experiment and/or quantitative survey be preceded by small qualitative studies in which the researcher really could gain first-hand, intimate knowledge of the phenomena under examination. One important issue in this connection is how these standard procedures of social science may be drawn upon in current audience research, especially in the light of humanistic articulations of qualitative research. While qualitative methodologies remain relevant as indispensable generators of insights and hypotheses, representatives of the humanistic research traditions suggest that, in certain respects, qualitative studies may have independent explanatory value regarding the reception and uses of media.

A major difference between communication research of the social science type and the mainstream of literary studies is their conception of analysis and interpretation. Except for the social science-oriented literary research mentioned previously in the historical section, *literary criticism* does not normally make a methodological distinction between the analysis of 'data' and the subsequent interpretation of aggregated 'findings'. Instead, relying on a variety of text-critical methods developed within linguistics, literary theory and rhetoric, it aims at performing what may be regarded as analysis-cum-interpretation, in order to substantiate one, sometimes more, possible and reasonable readings.

The tool of research is the interpretive capacity of the scholar and the categories of analysis are grounded primarily in the literary works being examined. The meaning of each constitutive element is established with reference to the context of the work as a whole. Its wider significance may be assessed by considering the social context of historical and psychoanalytic factors, which offer cues to understanding particular authors, readerships or origins of literary themes. The role of the empirical reader, however, has rarely been operationalized or posed as an explicit methodological issue in literary studies, except in recent work which, by and large, has drawn its research designs from sociology, social psychology and psychology (cf. Schmidt, 1980–2; Svensson, 1985; Groeben and Vorderer, 1988).

While growing out of literary criticism, *cultural studies* perform their analysis-cum-interpretation through methods which refer explicitly to extra-textual frameworks of explanation. The discourses of literature and media are said to be inscribed in broader social and cultural practices. The categories of analysis, consequently, are grounded not only in literary theory but in theories of social structure and subjectivity as well – granting the fact that the primary tool of research still remains the interpreting scholar.

More specifically, a variety of cultural forms – from oral storytelling, to graffiti, to particular modes of everyday conversation – may be interpreted as the popular expression and maintenance of social and cultural identities which are based in interpretive communities. These communities, in their turn, are formed in processes of gendered, ethnic and sub-cultural socialization, which to no small extent feed on the mass media. While audience publics are thus seen as active participants in the social production of meaning, often challenging media constructions of reality, the focus of analysis has tended to be the over-arching discourses of culture, rather than their local, empirical producers and recipients.

Drawing on methods of analysis-cum-interpretation from the literary tradition and the conception of communication and cultural processes as socially situated discourses from cultural studies, *reception analysis* can be said to perform a comparative reading of media discourses and audience discourses in order to understand the processes of reception. Audience discourses are generated within small-scale empirical designs relying particularly on in-depth interviewing and participant observation. Comparing these discourses with the structure of media content, reception studies have indicated how particular genres and themes may be assimilated by specific audiences. With reference, moreover, to the social context of audience background variables as well as to other cultural and political institutions, reception analysis has explored how audiences may contribute to social meaning production and cultural patterns generally through their membership of socially specific interpretive communities. How mass-mediated meaning comes to orient social action and cognition, however, remains a question for more comprehensive audience studies.

One methodological difficulty of reception analysis in its current form is that, while it offers a theoretically informed, empirical examination of communication processes, its findings are not easily replicable. In fact they can only seldom be generalized beyond the small groups of individuals studied. The same difficulty besets cultural studies and literary criticism (except for most of the social science-oriented variants already mentioned). Generalizability, of course, is a widely accepted demand in audience research of the effects and U&G types, both of which aim at producing replicable studies of representative samples from well defined populations. This basic difference between effects and U&G research and literary criticism, cultural studies and reception analysis points to a general issue for audience research brought to the fore also in our theoretical considerations. If each tradition contributes a perspective which is thought to have relevance and explanatory value in itself, the question is how the field might arrive at terms of co-operation that would serve the interests of further research and, perhaps, those of the audience.

Trying to sum up the methodological similarities and dissimilarities between our five research traditions, one is struck by the parallel between, on the one hand, the functions of experimental research in effects and U&G studies, and on the other the empirical–qualitative approach of literary, cultural and reception studies.

In both cases, through intensive and careful observation of a small number of selected cases, new knowledge is produced about what happens under specified conditions. What 'happens' is audiences attributing particular meanings to a given media content; these meanings, in turn, may come to inform and affect the cognition and behaviour of particular audience members. These are forms of impact which can be established, for example, through experimental designs or participant observation in family settings. Quantitative survey research, however, using representative samples drawn from strictly defined populations, gains knowledge about what happens in these populations with a precise measure of probability. The survey methodology is, of course, designed with a view to recreate, so far as possible, a set of specified and uniform conditions under which the respondents can address, in a theoretically grounded and valid manner, the kind of audience response under examination. The verbal response by which an interviewee addresses an aspect of media and related attributes is thus the fundamental constituent of such methodologies. The correlation of such responses in terms of statistical procedures establishes the different forms of impact.

Eventually, survey research and experiments in the laboratory as well as empirical qualitative studies are interdependent. Not only do they represent complementary forms of evidence, reminiscent of the classical *in vitro* versus *in vivo* distinction. They also enter into a system of theoretical checks and balances in which the explanatory value of each mode of analysis – independently and in combination with other analytical modes – may be examined. This type of theory and methodology development is, indeed, one of the most important tasks for further research in the area of audience studies.

The main results of our overview of the theoretical and methodological characteristics of the five research traditions under discussion are schematically summarized in Table 5.1. [...]

Further Research

It is unrealistic to hope to completely reconcile the differential legacies of arts and sciences which inform the five traditions of audience research outlined in this article, and as stated this is not our ambition. Yet we do maintain that there are further possibilities of convergence at several levels of analysis, not least in terms of interdisciplinary *theory development*.

For such possibilities to be realized, it is first necessary, however, that the differential character of theory formation in the humanities and social sciences be clearly recognized. What humanistically oriented audience theory has to offer is

TABLE 5.1 MAIN CHARACTERISTICS OF FIVE AUDIENCE RESEARCH TRADITIONS

	Effects Research	Uses and Gratifications	Research Tradition Literary Criticism	Cultural Studies	Reception Analysis
Type of Theory	Semi-formalized	Semi-formalized	Verbal	Verbal	Verbal
Focus of Theory:					
Message	Less central	Less central	Central	Central	Central
Audience	Central	Central	Peripheral	Less central	Central
Social System	Less central	Central	Less central	Less central	Less central
Type of Methodology	Social science	Social science	Humanist	Humanist	Mainly Humanist
Approaches					
Experimental	Often	Seldom	Seldom	Almost never	Almost never
Survey	Often	As a rule	Seldom	Seldom	Seldom
In-depth Interview	Sometimes	Sometimes	Seldom	Often	As a rule
Message Analysis	Seldom	Seldom	As a rule	As a rule	As a rule
Techniques of Analysis					
Statistical	As a rule	As a rule	Seldom	Seldom	Seldom
Interpretive	Seldom	Sometimes	As a rule	As a rule	As a rule
Modes of Presentation					
Numerical, Tabular	As a rule	As a rule	Almost never	Seldom	Sometimes
Verbal, Analytical	As a rule	As a rule	Sometimes	Often	As a rule
Verbal, Narrative	Sometimes	Sometimes	As a rule	As a rule	As a rule

primarily verbal formulations of the rich heritage of finely nuanced insights gained during decades or even centuries of studies of texts and their hypothesized impact on audiences. In recent decades, this tradition has been formulated in theories of discourse, representation and general semiotics; methodologies of systematic textual analysis have been developed and applied to mass media (van Dijk, 1983; Jensen, 1987b).

However, the merits of audience theory developed within the social science tradition may lie as much in its formal characteristics as in its substantive results. The relatively strong demands for clarity, consistency and systematization traditionally upheld in most social and behavioural sciences have forged their theories into strong instruments for guiding the search for new knowledge, as well as for efficiently expressing and structuring knowledge already gained – in traditions of audience research oriented towards the social sciences and the humanities alike.

Substantively, our systematics suggest that a comprehensive theoretical framework for audience research requires at least three components: (1) a theory of the social structures in which media and audiences are embedded; (2) a theory of discourse or communication which accounts for the nature of media representation (print, aural, visual); and (3) a theory of socio-cultural and social–psychological dispositions with which individuals approach and interact with media content. Each of these three components, of course, needs further clarification and differentiation. A social structure theory, for instance, must encompass the macro (societal), the mezzo (institutional) and the micro (individual) level. At present there is no such theory at hand. *Mutatis mutandis*, the same applies to the other two components. Nevertheless, there are many useful fragments lying around, which, once they have been pieced together, might be used as efficient stepping-stones, if nothing else. […]

In terms of *methodology*, this implies that studies in the area should combine elements of content analysis with audience research in one design. Too often, research based in the humanities has neglected standard demographic classifications of the populations which it sets out to examine. Similarly, much social science research has tended to think of content in technical terms, as isolated bits of information rather than as culturally coded vehicles of meaning. Reconciling this split may be more important for the development of truly interdisciplinary methodologies than a routine examination of quantitative/qualitative and/or administrative/critical distinctions. As of today, only few broad, long-term studies of this type are to be found (cf. Hansson, 1959; Segers, 1978; Schmidt, 1980–82; Svensson, 1985).

The question about what general methodological standards can be applied in such empirical combinations of different methodologies presents a thorny problem. In the long run, however, this problem may be solved by the happy fact that in science and scholarship, Gresham's law does not apply. Good methodological currency drives out not so good methodological currency – not the other way round, as is the case in the marketplace.

The basic characteristic of both humanistic scholarship and social science is the demand for inter-subjective validity. In the social sciences, this demand has been explicated in some detail in the technical terms of reliability, validity and generalizability. Some such technical explications are presently being accepted in humanistic scholarship – at much the same pace as social science learns and re-learns humanistic techniques of textual analysis and interpretation, criticism of sources, etc. The development of systematic modes of analysis is thus being undertaken from several quarters of the field (Höijer, 1989, 1990; Jensen, 1989; Kirk and Miller, 1986). […]

In such co-operation, it is crucial that the standards of what constitutes scientific and scholarly acceptable analysis be made explicit. Humanistic researchers need to establish a terminology which will enable them to deal with issues of reliability, validity and generalizability (Höijer, 1989, 1990). Social science research, equally, needs to recognize that non-quantitative procedures of analysis, as developed within linguistics and semiotics in the course of this century, may well have an explanatory value in their own right (e.g. Van Dijk, 1988).

We believe that comparative studies across cultures would lend themselves very well to further developments in multi-method empirical research. As suggested by ethnographies both within anthropology and in recent media research (Lull, 1988), various forms of in-depth, naturalistic observation and interaction with audience respondents may be necessary in order to characterize and delimit the context of data gathering. At the same time, survey techniques may be used to examine particular issues which emerge in the course of the study, specifying in turn, the purposes of further observation or interviewing and providing an opportunity to assess comparatively two sets of findings regarding the same object of study. Contributing to an important and relatively underresearched area of international communication research, such studies would fit the recent strong trend towards an increased interest in comparative studies in communication. They would also be able to explore the extent to which current research methodologies, most of which embody a specific form of western rationality, apply to the reception and impact of media across cultures (cf. Liebes and Katz, 1986; Lull, 1988).

Third, audience research may return to community studies, as carried out by some early work in the field, in order to assess the explanatory value of different traditions (Lynd and Lynd, 1929; cf. Caplow and Bahr, 1983). Case studies of the cultural and communicative practices of specific communities represent an opportunity to examine in detail the kinds of micro and macro social contexts in which most media use takes place. Case studies also lend themselves specifically to the combination of several modes of empirical analysis. They thus offer excellent opportunities to complement the limitations naturally inherent in each and every single research tradition.

In the long term, of course, the combined approaches suggested above must in their turn be combined. In comparative studies based on the combination of several methodologies we may at last find the audience.

References

Adorno, T.W. and M. Horkheimer (1977) 'The Culture Industry', in J. Curran, M. Gurevitch and J. Woollacott (eds), *Mass Communication and Society*. London: Edward Arnold.
Ang, I. (1985) *Watching Dallas*. London: Methuen.

Arnold, C.C. and K.D. Frandsen (1984) 'Conceptions of Rhetoric and Communication', in C.C. Arnold and J.W. Bowers (eds), *Handbook of Rhetorical and Communication Theory.* Boston: Allyn and Bacon.

Babrow, A. (1989) 'An Expectancy-Value Analysis of the Student Soap Opera Audience', *Communication Research,* 16: 155–78.

Belson, W.A. (1972) *The Impact of Television.* London: Lockwood.

Blumler, J. and E. Katz (eds) (1974) *The Uses of Mass Communications: Current Perspectives on Gratifications Research.* Beverly Hills, CA: Sage.

Blumler, J.G., M. Gurevitch and E. Katz (1985) 'Reaching Out: A Future for Gratifications Research', in K.E. Rosengren, L.A. Wenner and P. Palmgreen (eds), *Media Gratifications Research: Current Perspectives.* Beverly Hills, CA: Sage.

Bradac, J.J. (ed.) (1989) *Message Effects in Communication Science.* Newbury Park, CA: Sage.

Bryant, J. and D. Zillmann (eds) (1986) *Perspectives on Media Effects.* Hillsdale, NJ: Erlbaum.

Caplow, T. and H.M. Bahr (1983) *Middletown Families.* Minneapolis: University of Minnesota Press.

Carey, J.W. (1989) *Communication as Culture: Essays on Media and Society.* London: Unwin and Hyman.

Cohen, S. (1980) *Folk Devils and Moral Panics.* Oxford: Robertson.

DeFleur, M.L. and S. Ball-Rokeach (1989) *Theories of Mass Communication* (5th edn). New York: Longman.

Dervin, B., V.L. Grossberg, B.J. O'Keefe and E. Wartella (eds) (1989) *Rethinking Communication* (1–2). Newbury Park, CA: Sage.

Eagleton, T. (1983) *Literary Theory: An Introduction.* Minneapolis: University of Minnesota Press.

Fish, S. (1980) *Is there a Text in This Class? The Authority of Interpretive Communities.* Cambridge, MA: Harvard University Press.

Fiske, J. (1987) *Television Culture.* London: Routledge.

Fiske, J. and J. Hartley (1978) *Reading Television.* London: Methuen.

Frye, N. (1957) *Anatomy of Criticism.* Princeton, NJ: Princeton University Press.

Gans, H. (1974) *Popular Culture and High Culture: An Analysis and Evaluation of Taste.* New York: Basic Books.

Gaziano, C. (1983) The Knowledge Gap: An Analytical Review of Media Effects', *Communication Research,* 10: 447–86.

Gripsrud, J. (1989) '"High Culture" Revisited', *Cultural Studies,* 3(2): 194–207.

Groeben, N. and P. Vorderer (1988) *Leserpsychologie: Lesemotivation – Lektürewirkung.* Münster: Aschendorff.

Hall, S. (1980) 'Cultural Studies: Two Paradigms', *Media, Culture & Society,* 2: 57–72.

Hall, S., Hobson, D. Lowe, A. and P. Willis (eds) (1980) *Culture, Media, Language.* London: Hutchinson.

Hansson, G. (1959) *Dikten Och Iäsaren.* Stochholm: Bonniers.

Havelock, E. (1963) *Preface to Plato.* Cambridge, MA: Harvard University Press.

Herzog, H. (1942) 'Professor Quiz: A Gratification Study', in P.F. Lazarsfeld and F.N. Stanton (eds), *Radio Research, 1941.* New York: Duell, Sloan and Pearce.

Herzog, H. (1944) 'What Do We Really Know about Daytime Serial Listeners', in P.F. Lazarsfeld and F.N. Stanton (eds), *Radio Research, 1942–3.* New York: Duell, Sloan and Pearce.

Hoggart, R. (1957) *The Uses of Literacy.* London: Pelican.

Höijer, B. (1989) 'Reliability, Validity and Generalizability: Three Questions for Qualitative Reception Research'. Paper presented to the IX Nordic Mass Communication Research Conference, Bergby, Sweden, 20–23 August.

Höijer, B. (1990) 'Studying Viewers' Reception of Television Programs: Theoretical and Methodological Considerations', *European Journal of Communication,* 5(1): 29–56.

Iser, W. (1970) *Die Apellstruktur der Texte.* Konstanz: Konstanz University Press.

Jensen, K.B. (1986) *Making Sense of the News.* Åarhus: Åarhus University Press.

Jensen, K.B. (1987a) 'Qualitative Audience Research: Toward an Integrative Approach to Reception', *Critical Studies in Mass Communication,* 4(1): 21–36.

Jensen, K.B. (1987b) 'News as Ideology: Economic Statistics and Political Ritual in Television Network News', *Journal of Communication,* 37(1): 8–27.

Jensen, K.B. (1989) 'Discourses of Interviewing: Validating Qualitative Research Findings through Textual Analysis', in S. Kvale (ed.), *Issues of Validity in Qualitative Research.* Lund: Studentlitteratur.

Jensen, K.B. (1990) 'When is Meaning? Communication Theory, Pragmatism, and Mass Media Reception', in J. Anderson (ed.), *Communication Yearbook*, 14. Newbury Park, CA: Sage.

Katz, E. and T. Liebes (1984) 'Once Upon a Time, in Dallas', *Intermedia*, 12(3): 28–32.

Klapper, J. (1960) *The Effects of Mass Communication*. New York: Free Press.

Kirk, J. and M. Miller (1986) *Reliability and Validity in Qualitative Research*. Newbury Park, CA: Sage.

Lazarsfeld, P.F. (1941/1972) 'Administrative and Critical Communications Research', in P.F. Lazarsfeld, *Qualitative Analysis: Historical and Critical Essays*. Boston: Allyn and Bacon.

Levy, M.R. and S. Windahl (1985) 'The Concept of Audience Activity', in K.E. Rosengren, L.A. Wenner and P. Palmgreen (eds), *Media Gratifications Research: Current Perspectives*. Beverly Hills, CA: Sage.

Liebes, T. and E. Katz (1986) 'Patterns of Involvement in Television Fiction: A Comparative Analysis', *European Journal of Communication*, 2: 151–72.

Lindlof, T. (ed.) (1987) *Natural Audiences*. Norwood, NJ: Ablex.

Lindlof, T. (1988) 'Media Audiences as Interpretive Communities', *Communication Yearbook*, 11: 81–107.

Lindlof, T. and J. Anderson (1988) 'Problems in Decolonizing the Human Subject in Qualitative Audience Research'. Paper presented to the Congress of the International Association for Mass Communication Research, Barcelona, Spain, 24–29 July, 1988.

Lowery, S. and M.L. DeFleur (1988) *Milestones in Mass Communication Research* (2nd edn). London: Longman.

Lull, J. (ed.) (1988) *World Families Watch Television*. Newbury Park, CA: Sage.

Lynd, R.S. and H.M. Lynd (1929) *Middletown: A Study in American Culture*. New York: Harcourt.

McCombs, M.E. and D.L. Shaw (1972) 'The Agenda-Setting Function of Mass Media', *Public Opinion Quarterly*, 36: 176–87.

McCombs, M.E. and D.H. Weaver (1985) 'Toward a Merger of Gratification and Agenda-Setting Research', in K.E. Rosengren, L.A. Wenner and P. Palmgreen (eds), *Media Gratifications Research: Current Perspectives*. Beverly Hills, CA: Sage.

McQuail, D. (1987) *Mass Communication Theory* (2nd edn). London: Sage.

Mahle, W. (ed.) (1986) *Langfristige Medienwirkungen*. Berlin: Spiess.

Melischeck, G., K.E. Rosengren and J. Stappers (eds) (1984) *Cultural Indicators: An International Symposium*. Vienna: Akademie der Wissenschaften.

Milawsky, J.R., H.H. Stipp, R.C. Kessler and W.S. Rubens (1982) *Television and Aggression: A Panel Study*. New York: Academic Press.

Morley, D. (1980) 'The "Nationwide" Audience: Structure and Decoding'. *British Film Institute Television Monographs*, 11. London: BFI.

Morley, D. (1986) *Family Television: Cultural Power and Domestic Leisure*. London: Comedia.

Noelle-Neumann, E. (1983) *The Spiral of Silence*. Chicago: University of Chicago Press.

Noelle-Neumann, E. (1988) 'The 'Event as Event' and the 'Event as News': The Significance of 'Consonance' for Media Effects Research', *European Journal of Communication*, 2: 391–414.

Ong, W. (1982) *Orality and Literacy*. London: Methuen.

Palmgreen, P. and J.D. Rayburn (1985) 'An Expectancy-Value Approach to Media Gratifications', in K.E. Rosengren, L.A. Wenner and P. Palmgreen (eds), *Media Gratifications Research: Current Perspectives*. Beverly Hills, CA: Sage.

Palmgreen, P., L.A. Wenner and K.E. Rosengren (1985) 'Uses and Gratifications Research: The Past Ten Years', in K.E. Rosengren, L.A. Wenner and P. Palmgreen (eds), *Media Gratifications Research: Current Perspectives*. Beverly Hills, CA: Sage.

Radway, J. (1984) *Reading the Romance*. Chapel Hill, NC: University of North Carolina Press.

Richards, I. A. (1929) *Practical Criticism*. New York: Harcourt, Brace and World.

Roe, K. (1985) 'The Swedish Moral Panic Over Video, 1980–1984', *Nordicom Review of Nordic Mass Communication Research* (June): 20–25.

Rosengren, K.E. (1974) 'Uses and Gratifications: A Paradigm Outlined', in J.G. Blumler and E. Katz (eds), *The Uses of Mass Communications: Current Perspectives on Gratifications Research*. Beverly Hills, CA: Sage.

Rosengren, K.E. (1981) 'Introduction', in K.E. Rosengren (ed.), *Advances in Content Analysis*. Beverly Hills, CA: Sage.

Rosengren, K.E. (1985) 'Communication Research: One Paradigm, or Four?', in E.M. Rogers and F. Balle (eds), *The Media Revolution in America and in Western Europe*. Norwood, NJ: Ablex.

Rosengren, K.E. (1988) 'The Study of Media Culture: Ideas, Actions and Artefacts', in *Lund Research Papers on the Sociology of Communication*, 10. Lund University: Department of Sociology.

Rosengren, K.E. (1989) 'Paradigms Lost and Regained', in B. Dervin, L. Grossberg, B.J. O'Keefe and E. Wartella (eds), *Rethinking Communication*, 1. Newbury Park, CA: Sage.

Rosengren, K.E. (1990) 'Media Use in Childhood and Adolescence: Invariant Change?' *Communication Yearbook*, 14.

Rosengren, K.E. and S. Windahl (1972) 'Mass Media Consumption as a Functional Alternative', in D. McQuail (ed.), *Sociology of Mass Communications*. Harmondsworth: Penguin.

Rosengren, K.E. and S. Windahl (1989) *Media Matter: TV Use in Childhood and Adolescence*. Norwood, NJ: Ablex.

Rosengren, K.E., L.A. Wenner, and P. Palmgreen (eds) (1985). *Media Gratifications Research: Current Perspectives*. Beverly Hills: Sage.

Schenk, M. (1987) *Medienwirkungsforschung*. Tübingen: Mohr.

Schmidt, S.J. (1980–2) *Grundriss der empirischen Literaturwissenschaft*, 1–2. Braunschweig/ Wiesbaden: Vieweg.

Schrøder, K.C. (1987) 'Convergence of Antagonistic Traditions?', *European Journal of Communication*, 2: 7–32.

Segers, R.T. (1978) *The Evaluation of Literary Texts*. Lisse: De Ridder.

Signorielli, N. and M. Morgan (eds) (1989) *Advances in Cultivation Research*. Newbury Park, CA: Sage.

Singer, J.L., D.G. Singers and W.S. Rapaczynski (1984) 'Family Patterns and Television Viewing as Predictors of Children's Beliefs and Aggression', *Journal of Communication*, 34(2): 73–89.

Svensson, C. (1985) *The Construction of Poetic Meaning*. Malmö: Liber.

Tichenor, P.J., G.A. Donohew and C.N. Olien (1970) 'Mass Media Flow and Differential Growth in Knowledge', *Public Opinion Quarterly*, 34: 159–70.

Tichenor, P.J., G.A. Donohew and C.N. Olien (1980) *Community Conflict and the Press*. Newbury Park, CA: Sage.

Trenaman, J.M. (1967) *Communication and Comprehension*. London: Longmans.

van Dijk, T.A. (1983) 'Discourse Analysis: Its Development and Application to the Structure of News', *Journal of Communication*, 33: 20–43.

van Dijk, T.A. (1988) 'Semantics of a Press Panic: The Tamil "Invasion"', *European Journal of Communication*, 3: 167–88.

Watt ,I. (1957) *The Rise of the Novel*. London: Penguin.

Weibull, L. (1985) 'Structural Factors in Gratifications Research', in K.E. Rosengren, L.A. Wenner and P. Palmgreen (eds), *Media Gratifications Research: Current Perspectives*. Beverly Hills, CA: Sage.

Williams, R. (1977) *Marxism and Literature*. London: Oxford University Press.

Windahl, S. (1981) 'Uses and Gratifications at the Cross-roads', in G.C. Wilhoit and H. De Bock (eds), *Mass Communication Review Yearbook* (2). Beverly Hills, CA: Sage.

Resisting American Hegemony: A Comparative Analysis of the Reception of Domestic and US Fiction

Daniel Biltereyst

Reception Analysis and the Impact of US Fiction

There is a growing awareness among communication scientists from different standpoints that studies of international television flows and the cultural imperialism thesis should be complemented by more analysis of the consumption (e.g. Collins, 1986; Fejes, 1981; Katz and Liebes, 1990; Nordenstreng and Varis, 1974: 11; Sepstrup, 1989; Tracey, 1985). As has been pointed out by Preben Sepstrup (1989: 395), most studies of these subjects have concentrated on the supply of television programmes, 'but not on the consumption of the import and the impact of this consumption'.

The same arguments may be used in the debate on the loss of 'cultural identity' – a concept that, with the advent of 'Europe 1992', as well as the ongoing transnationalization and commercialization of media structures, has become of central importance for contemporary European communication research (McQuail, 1990; Morley and Robins, 1990; Schlesinger, 1986, 1988). A crucial pivot in this flourishing cultural debate is the potential, growing influence of foreign (US) fiction programmes on the identity of European collectivities. The great quantity of US drama will, most scholars state, unquestionably imply a process of further 'Americanization' or homogenization of European cultural diversity.

As in the cultural imperialism debate, it is clear that these arguments start primarily from a causal relationship between supply and effects: conclusions about the possible effects are mainly based on the volume of imported foreign (US) television programmes. However, empirical data on the *consumption* of US fiction programming itself are practically unavailable. So we do not only need data on the *amount* of consumption (audience ratings, for example), but especially data on the *nature* or the qualitative aspects of it. The argument goes that if we could understand how audiences outside the USA really consume, experience and decode US fiction, we would have a more accurate view of its potential influence. [...]

Source: *EJC* (1991), vol. 6: 469–497.

Micro/Macro Problems

First it should be clear that reception analysis dissociates itself explicitly from the study of larger, long-term influences or 'effects' on a macro-level and focuses the analysis on the concrete individual consumption of specific programmes in specific contexts (micro-level). In contrast to most experimental studies on effects, reception analysis is not even really interested in isolating the specific influence of one factor (a stimulus), by eliminating or controlling all other contextual factors in an experimental design. In its ethnographic vein, reception analysis emphasizes the interactive processes between a 'text' and its 'readers' in their varying manifestations situated in a natural context (Curran, 1990: 150; LeCompte and Goetz, 1982: 33). [...]

Considering this formulation of the research problematic it is clear that the macro-problematic in relation to 'effects' will never be solved by reception analytical studies. Moreover, studying the long-term social consequences of a great quantity of American fiction programming faces insuperable difficulties from a research point of view. How can, for example, the cultural influence of these programmes be dissociated from influences of other socioeconomic developments? Yet, reception analysis can give extremely valuable information on the decoding of US fiction on a micro-level. According to Höijer (1990b: 30–1), 'any theory of long-term effects of mass media thus has to take short-term effects into account, although not equalizing the two levels'.

The Relationship between Decoded Meanings and Impact

A second problem deals with the question of how to relate decoded meanings to impact. Although several qualitative audience enquiries introduce their studies with a plea for the need to conduct research on audience responses in relation to the problematic of the influence of US fiction, they are obliged to talk with great caution about impact, influence or effects. Liebes and Katz (1986: 151–2) write that their study is 'not of effects but rather of the processes that might lead to effects'. In the same vein of well-considered restraint Herta Herzog (1986: 351; 1987: 95) presents her study of audience responses to *Dallas* as (only) a necessarily preliminary investigation to a possible study of impact.

As Katz and Liebes later wrote (1990: 58), it is appropriate and even necessary to reflect on how to interpret such reception analytical data with regard to effects. Here an ambivalent position can be observed.

On the one hand, it is obvious that researchers working within the reception perspective will always adopt a distant, cautious attitude towards a concept like impact. [...] On the other hand, there seems to exist a sort of consensus on some of the directions that a potential textual impact may take. This is quite clear in relation to the concept of *involvement*. For Liebes and Katz (1986: 151–2) this concept is important because it 'may hold the key to effect' and it designates '*dependence* on the message'. As involvement may say something about impact, one could argue that if involvement with the message is high, the dependence and impact are too. [...]

Essentialist, Decontextualized Positions

A third problem, which calls into question the relevance of existing reception analytical studies on the problematic, deals with central theoretical and analytical concepts, such as audience activity, (symbolic) resistance and textual polysemy and openness. Recently some of these concepts have been criticized virulently. The 'mythologized' status and the imperial resistant power of the audience in the process of meaning production have been under especially severe attack (Condit, 1989: Curran, 1990; Morris, 1988; Silverstone, 1990: 177–8). A certain exaggeration of the 'impermeability of audiences to media influence' (Curran, 1990: 151) has been described as a 'romanticizing and romanticist tendency in much work that emphasizes resistance' (Ang, 1990: 246). Following James Curran (1990) these tendencies even hold a real danger for the increasing incorporation of cultural relativism within the critical/cultural tradition. [...]

Summarizing this central position, Morley and Robins argue that American commercial television drama operates:

> ... at a very high level of abstraction, and the price of this approach to a universality of appeal is a higher level of polysemy or multi-accentuality. The research of Ang and Katz and Liebes reminds us just how open these types of programmes are to re-interpretation by audiences outside their country of origins'. (Morley and Robins, 1990: 29)

Of course, one can make several criticisms of this perspective. Among them is the point that these studies neglect economic, historical and production factors, in explaining why American drama is so successful (e.g., Gripsrud, 1990).

But even if one concentrates on the inherent qualities of US fiction, we can strongly question such statements on the text and spectator–text relationship. This article argues that the concentration on the reception of US fiction alone (exemplified in the number of studies on the soap opera *Dallas*) has stimulated an essentialist and a decontextualized position on the characteristics, the functioning, the decoding and thus the appeal and impact of US drama. By essentialist we mean that, in the past, differentiated nuances have rarely been drawn with respect to these issues. In order to study the impact of a text, one should not unquestioningly accept its potential characteristics or dissociate it from the manifestation of its decoding in specific contexts.

In order to understand the functioning, the polysemic potential and the decoding of mass-produced US fiction abroad, one must pay attention not simply to US fiction alone. A comparison of its decoding with the decoding of other types of television fiction, with which audiences have different kinds of relationships (e.g. non-commercial drama, fiction from another origin or tradition), can open new perspectives to an understanding of the cross-cultural appeal of US television programmes. [...]

Case Study Design: The Reception of US and Domestic Fiction

In this study we explore how people in a small European language community (in this case Flanders, the Dutch speaking part of Belgium) develop different strategies in decoding commercial US and domestic fiction. The choice of *domestic drama as the 'different text'* seems quite obvious because there clearly exists an opposite relationship between the (in this case Flemish) audience and the two types of drama, as one of them is strange and the other closely linked to the indigenous cultural background. In keeping with most television drama produced in European countries (Silj, 1988), Flemish domestic fiction is made for local consumption. As it often uses very specific regional accents, dialects and expressions, and also shows specific regional situations, Flemish TV drama is to a great extent comprehensible only from a specific cultural-historical background. In contrast with American commercial television programmes, mostly considered as 'open' and more or less 'culture-free' texts, Flemish drama can be seen as relatively 'closed' texts.

A second reason to choose domestic drama in this comparative analysis arises from its popularity. Research on the amount of television consumption (audience ratings) has shown that in many European and other countries US fiction loses when competing directly with comparable domestic productions (Silj, 1988; Tracey, 1985). While the dominance and popularity of US television drama have been widely studied on several levels, the significance of the higher popularity of home-produced drama still forms a complete wasteland from a research point of view. The success of US fiction seems to have overshadowed the fact that, as Ellen Seiter et al. (1989: 5) put it, 'other forms of television might also please us (and, possibly, please better)'.

Choice and Characteristics of the Programmes

Considering the question of the resemblance between the programmes, we selected one episode from the Flemish situation comedy *De Kollega's* (The Colleagues) and another one from the American sitcom *She's the Sheriff*.[1] Both sitcoms, that may be considered as representative for other programmes of this type in their culture, were tremendously similar in generic, narrative and other respects. So they can be considered as typical 'careercoms', where leading characters are for professional reasons obliged to work in one room.

Also on a narrative level both episodes showed strong similarities: in both series one of the younger women falls in love with a man, an actor not usually in the show. In both programmes this love affair has to contend with problems concerned with the environment of the professional situation. At the end these love affairs end badly for the women. In this sense both sitcoms relied on similar types of characterization (Eaton, 1978). One could say that the differences here were mainly situated on the paradigmatical level in a common narrative scheme (e.g., the American sitcom was situated in a police department, while in the Flemish one the action took place in a ministry).

On technical and production aspects both fiction programmes differed quite a lot, where the American sitcom was technically the 'better' product (for instance, the average shot length was considerably longer for the Flemish sitcom).

Respondents

In our case study both fiction programmes were shown to thirty-four respondents (seventeen women, seventeen men) in their homes with their families. This group could be subdivided into three major groups: younger adolescents (16 to 18 years old), younger adults (21 to 30 years old) and older adults (45 to 55 years old).

Data Collection

Methodologically this case study was designed as a multi-method piece of research, combining several techniques used in recent reception analyses. The data collection process consisted of three phases. Several days before the viewing sessions the respondents were asked to fill in a general questionnaire, that was designed to discover personal attitudes and opinions about situation comedy as a genre and about US television fiction and domestic drama on Flemish television (1: general questionnaire phase). The viewing sessions of both programmes were each time followed by individual open interviews, aimed to tap each respondent's experience of the programme (2: interview phase). After this session, another questionnaire booklet was given to each respondent. In this phase of the study the respondents were asked to attribute values for specific characteristics to six main characters in both sitcoms, using scaling techniques (Livingstone, 1987, 1988, 1989) (3: scaling phase).

Data Analysis

On an analytical level this combined use of multiple qualitative and quantitative data collection techniques was not only inspired by questions of reliability (Höijer, 1990a, 1990b; Jensen and Rosengren, 1990), but especially by the need to understand the reception of audiovisual programmes as a process. As has been rightly remarked by James Curran (1990: 150) many recent ethnographic studies on audiences have used notions of reception and, especially, decoding as plain, 'loose' concepts. Following Curran we could say that some practitioners of qualitative audience research seem to have forgotten that different methods of data collection also produce different types of information. Interviewing people, for example, produces totally different data than asking them to attribute values to specific characters, using scaling techniques.

In this sense, to have a better insight into reception as a process, the concept has for analytical reasons to be broken up into different substantial parts, which we call *moments* in the reception process. Although these 'moments' cannot be strictly delimited (in time nor meaning), they represent different aspects of the process of receiving and decoding a text. In this article we distinguish and introduce four major 'moments' (cf. Groeben, 1982). Placed in a (more or less) chronological manner, these are: (1) the horizon of expectations, or the totality of expectations with which the recipient encounters a (audiovisual) text; (2) the *recognition*, or the literal comprehension of specific configurations (characters, themes, actions, etc.) presented in the text; (3) the *interpretation*, or the inferential comprehension of those configurations; and (4) the *discussion*, or the applied comprehension of the programme within the recipient's own background.

In this case study we explicitly apply existing analytical methods in order to show how these methods can be incorporated into a more elaborated, changing and articulated reception process scheme. While this case study, based on multi-method approach and on the analytical scheme of diverse 'moments' in reception, provides a lot of information on the reception of both situation comedies by the same group of people, in this framework we only present the most central findings (see also Biltereyst, 1991).

Horizon of Expectations

A first structuring moment in the reception process is formed by the 'horizon of expectations' – a concept which refers to the aesthetic and cultural expectations with which the recipient encounters a programme (see Jauss, 1974). In this study, we attempted to reconstruct this horizon with regard to domestic and US fiction in general. Here we relied on the data from the general questionnaire phase which took place before the viewing sessions. Some passages from the interviews, however, also provided useful data on this 'horizon'.

Interpreting these data it was noticeable that viewers were quite critical in their attitudes to the quality of domestic television drama in general. While all respondents claimed to like American drama productions, especially their technical and entertaining qualities, only three (all older adults) of the thirty-four respondents claimed to like Flemish drama productions. All other respondents were quite neutral to it, stating that they had no or no specific preference for indigenous fiction drama. Analysing these data it became clear that people were especially critical of the technical and production qualities of domestic products (acting, editing, etc.).

This critical horizon also became apparent in the interviews after the viewing sessions. Although most respondents ($n = 33$) declared to have enjoyed and preferred *De Kollega's* far more than *She's the Sheriff*, they remained quite critical of domestic drama. A characteristic statement here was made by a 30-year-old female lawyer:

> Yes, I do prefer *De Kollega's*, but I admit that *She's the Sheriff* is better as an entertainment programme. OK, the story in *De Kollega's* is very attractive and everything is well-done, but *She's the Sheriff* is more like a slapstick.

Here the humour is very light and easy to enjoy. It strongly works on specific moments full of humour. That's why I prefer those American series. As pure entertainment. (interview 6A)

In this sense, the critical horizon of expectations seems to contradict the traditional 'popularity' of domestic drama and the concrete appreciation of both programmes. A possible explanation is that there is certainly no tradition or 'folklore' around the rarely produced domestic drama. US fiction, on the other hand, seems to be driven by its tradition of strong entertainment programming. This statement seems to be confirmed by the critical attitude towards the production and technical qualities of domestic drama, a domain where American commercial fiction products have traditionally high standards.

To understand this 'contradiction' one has also to distinguish people's declared needs and expectations from their concrete involvement in the reception process. They do not always coincide (as in this case), nor do they exclude each other. As is argued later, a higher involvement with domestic drama also embraces a certain critical, normative attitude towards technical and other aspects.

Recognition

A central question in this approach is how the different cultural distance between the audience and the two texts influences and structures the reception process. So it is important to know if there really was a better understanding or recognition of the diegetical world, i.e. the world depicted by the programme (see Genette, 1972). Here we identify recognition as the mere literal comprehension of specific separate elements (configurations such as characters) in the diegetical world. Still how can such loose concepts like 'recognition' or 'literal comprehension' be operationalized and objectively approached?

In this case study we translated the concept of mere literal comprehension into the concept of 'unanimity'. Is high recognition by a group of respondents not a question of similar comprehension? When all respondents attribute the same value to a particular property, this can be considered as perfect unanimity (low variability or dispersion) and indicative of high recognition.

Operationalizing recognition into the 'degree of unanimity within a group', we used data from the scaling phase, where respondents were asked to rate twenty-one characteristics of six characters in each sitcom, using a five-point scale. Focusing on characters provides interesting possibilities because characters may be considered as clean-cut units and as clearly recognizable bearers of values. This method of using quantitative social psychology techniques in relation to reception and textual analysis has already proved to be fruitful and challenging (Livingstone, 1987, 1988, 1989).

Did the recipients really recognize the characters in both sitcoms in different ways? Did they have a better control over the codes used in the indigenous programme for designating the characters? This might be expected, especially because *De Kollega's* was firmly rooted in a Flemish sociocultural context.

TABLE 6.1 MEAN AND DISPERSION RATE FOR EACH CHARACTERISTIC OF THE SIX
CHARACTERS FOR BOTH SITCOMS

Characteristics	American Sitcom		Domestic Sitcom	
	s	$\bar{x}$	s	$\bar{x}$
1. Looking for pleasure	1.019	3	0.905	3.13
2. Social sense	0.793	3.13	0.781	2.91
3. Modern	0.921	2.81	0.678	2.5
4. Organization talent	0.866	2.86	0.793	2.76
5. Piteous	0.964	2.28	0.953	2.51
6. Hard	0.842	2.63	0.83	2.61
7. Active	0.787	3.06	0.781	2.71
8. Comic, funny	1.044	2.95	0.871	3.06
9. Rational	0.905	2.81	0.866	2.8
10. Masculine	0.894	2.88	0.748	2.91
11. Feminine	0.848	2.33	0.793	2.06
12. Moral dignity	0.768	2.93	0.806	2.81
13. Family values	0.854	3.11	0.871	3.08
14. Warmth	0.888	3.25	0.728	3.05
15. Social ability	0.824	3	0.741	2.9
16. Mature	0.877	2.85	0.768	2.73
17. Dominant	0.894	2.78	0.8	2.75
18. Sexy	0.964	2.43	0.8	2.05
19. Intelligent	0.781	2.93	0.842	2.83
20. Rascal	1.034	2.5	1.086	2.65
21. Rough	0.964	2.31	0.877	2.3

Note: Dispersion rate in standard deviation (s); central tendency in mean ($\bar{x}$).

In Table 6.1 we present the mean dispersion rate (in standard deviation) for
each characteristic of the six characters in both sitcoms. As demonstrated by this
table, the study clearly confirmed our hypothesis that viewers more readily
recognized the characters in the domestic sitcom. The scores attributed to traits of
the characters were systematically more dispersed in the American fiction programme (less unanimity). Only in four cases (characteristics 12, 13, 19 and 20) was
the dispersion rate higher in relation to the domestic drama. The values, attached
by the thirty-four respondents to different characters of the domestic programme,
were systematically less varied (higher unanimity). This part of the study thus
showed that the recipients had a better recognition of and command of the codes
used for the creation of the diegetical world in the indigenous programme – a
finding that also seemed to be confirmed in the interview phase, but which is
quite difficult to prove objectively. Respondents claimed on several occasions that
the specific situations and characters in the US sitcom were strange to them.

Interpretation

What are the consequences of this better recognition for the further decoding
and involvement of both sitcoms? In the first instance we were interested in the

interpretation of the diegetical world, as depicted by both sitcoms. Interpretation is defined here as the inferential comprehension of both programmes – or the consideration of how the different elements are meaningfully related to each other. Here the same questionnaire booklet (scaling phase) can be used, providing important data on differences of interpretation.

General Specialization

The first finding of note in this part of the study is that the recipients *attributed* systematically *higher* scores to the characters in the American series (see Table 6.1, where the average mean scores for the twenty-one characteristics are reported). This was the case for most characteristics (sixteen of the twenty-one). So, the characters in the American fiction programme were considered to be a lot warmer in their social and moral relations, more modern looking, active, rational, sexy, intelligent and rough, but also harder and more dominant. One major exception, however, is that the highest scores for the characteristics within the 'comic dimension' (characteristics 1, 8 and 20) were systematically reserved for characters in the domestic sitcom.

This central finding of the *generally higher values for the US fiction programme versus the higher estimation of the comic functioning of the domestic sitcom* suggests that, for the recipient, commercial American television drama exploits better and deeper a broader set of properties (codes) within social, cultural and moral dimensions. Compared to this general achievement of the American drama, the domestic programme seems (for the recipients) to have concentrated on the dominant dimension in sitcoms, the comic one.

Complex Comic Effect

Still, it is not advisable to wrench different dimensions from each other; situation comedies do not function in just the comic dimension. Sitcoms, and the characters in them, function in very specific social, moral and cultural contexts (Eaton, 1978). The comic effects of some characters are strongly generated by specific interrelations between codes and dimensions. The most comic character in the domestic drama (the character with the highest scores for the comic characteristics) also scored extremely high on other characteristics (like 'rough', etc.). In this sense any analysis of the functioning of specific characters has to be closely connected to the recipients' reconstruction of the interplay of several dimensions on moral, cultural, social, comic and other levels.

Analysing the data in this way (see Bilvereyst, 1991) indicates clearly that the viewers have been decoding the domestic programme *on more complex, extreme levels,* using several dimensions. To give just one example, it was clear that the recipients made a quite logical connection between the intellectual status of a character and its comic effect in the domestic drama: people with extreme low or high scores for the characteristic of 'intelligence' (characteristic 19) were attributed with extreme scores on comic characteristics. Here the comic effect (characteristic 8) not only worked meaningfully in relation to this intelligence code ($r = -0.519$), but also in connection with social (characteristic 2; $r = 0.861$) and moral codes (characteristic 12; $r = 0.868$). This type of strong correlation was not evident during the decoding of the US fiction programme. The intelligence ($r = -0.079$), social ($r = 0.330$) and moral ($r = -0.157$) codes were not strongly correlated with the comic code. In the case of the domestic comedy these and other codes were important in creating the comic effect of the programme, while in the American sitcom this important effect was experienced in a quite linear, less complex manner.

Such major differences in the interpretation of both sitcoms cannot be derived on a convincing basis from a textual analysis: both programmes as texts seem to generate the comic effects by an interplay of extreme characteristics on several levels.

Discussion

When the recipients recognize the character and their actions (literal comprehension) and interpret the different dimensions in them (inferential comprehension), one can question how they discuss or 'apply' the programmes to their *own* lives: how they relate both programmes to their own experiences? Were they involved differently? What differences can be made here between both types of 'encounters'?

Here an open, unstructured in-depth interview was the appropriate method: during the interview phase the respondent could discuss the programme and his or her experience of it. The analysis of the transcripts of these interviews was inspired by the studies of Katz and Liebes on the decoding of *Dallas*. Central to this approach was the study of patterns of involvement. To treat such a complex concept as 'involvement' the different statements have to be systematically analysed, using different indicators, focused on 'how viewers discuss' fiction programmes (Liebes and Katz, 1986: 152).

Referential vs. Meta-Linguistic Frame

A first important category of the analysis of the interview material is the distinction between *referential* and *meta-linguistic* frames. In referential statements the recipients treat (see Katz and Liebes, 1986) the programme as applicable to real life, whereas in meta-linguistic ones they consider it as a fictional construction with specific aesthetic law and formulae. For Katz and Liebes referential decodings primarily imply a more emotionally involved attitude of the recipient. Meta-linguistic statements, on the contrary, are to be considered as more distant and critical. An example of this type can be found during an interview with a 45-year-old school teacher:

TABLE 6.2   REFERENTIAL VS. META-LINGUISTIC STATEMENTS: PROPORTIONAL (%) AND ABSOLUTE NUMBER

	American Sitcom	Domestic Sitcom
Referential Statements	51.9%	55%
	109	126
Meta-linguistic Statements	48%	45%
	101	104

When I watch *She's the Sheriff*, I think: 'It must be very cheap to produce this type of programme.' Everything happens in a studio, always with the same decor. You can see that everything in this production is made quickly. (interview 23A)

Using this analytical category it became clear that the recipients discussed both series in a mixed referential and meta-linguistic frame. Analysing all interview statements showed that the overall ratio was in both cases about 1:1. Still, as indicated in Table 6.2, there are some slight differences between decodings of the domestic and American dramas. Although the difference between the coding of *De Kollega's* (55 percent referential versus 45 percent meta-linguistic, a difference of 10 percent) and of *She's the Sheriff* (51.9 percent referential versus 48 percent meta-linguistic, a difference of 3.9 percent) looks small, it seems that the viewers are somewhat more involved and more likely to view the domestic programme as applicable to real-life events.

Personal, Normative Involvement

More important however for the analysis of these statements is their value orientations. In their *Dallas* study Liebes and Katz consider value-free and normative statements (1986: 163–4). Utterances can carry explicit personal judgements or evaluations, based on specific value-systems (i.e., normative). Interpretative statements, not characterized by such personal judgements, were called 'value-free'. Data on the value orientations of the statements indicate the need of the recipients to take a personal view on different aspects of the programme.

Analysing the statements this way made clear that the proportion of normative statements is far higher in response to the indigenous programme than to the American programme (see Table 6.3). Comments about formal and technical aspects of the domestic programme especially were nearly always (79.8%) normatively loaded. As indicated in an interview with a 23-year-old female student, it seems that talking in a meta-linguistic frame in relation to the domestic programme involves strong approval or disapproval:

TABLE 6.3   NORMATIVE VS. VALUE-FREE STATEMENTS: PROPORTIONAL (%) AND
ABSOLUTE NUMBER

		American Sitcom	Domestic Sitcom
Referential	Normative	40.3%	70.6%
Statements		44	89
	Value-free	59.6%	29.3%
		65	37
Meta-linguistic	Normative	46.5%	79.8%
Statements		47	83
	Value-free	53.4%	20.1%
		54	21

> I like several characters in *De Kollega's*, but some of them really bother me.
> And then there is that typical disease of many Flemish actors, who try to
> speak perfect Dutch, but will never succeed in speaking it naturally. Then I
> prefer the use of specific dialects as some characters do. And this can be
> very, very funny. (interview 28B)

Such explicit personal judgements were also abundantly present in the referential statements on the domestic programme (70.6 percent). This may not be
surprising: opinions about the indigenous programme were more connected with
personal experiences and sometimes even ideologically loaded. Such a view was
clearly expressed in the interview with a 58-year old technical designer:

> I had that experience too. In those days, bosses used to be men with little
> intellectual capacity. They had been working their own way up. Then, when
> they became the boss, they became arrogant, like real *arrivists*. Then they
> took measures that cannot be labelled as clever, skilful or socially justified …
> (interview 22B)

In the case of the American programme there was an overall ratio of (roughly)
1:1 in relation to the value orientation of the statements, somewhat in favour of
value-free statements (59.6 percent for referential statements and 53.4 percent for
meta-linguistic ones). Respondents spoke quite fluently about several aspects of
the US programme and their experiences of it, but they did not feel so strongly
the need to take an explicit personal view on most items. It seemed that the
recipients were strongly led by the narrative thread in the US programme,
retelling and interpreting the story in a mixed normative/value-free way. […]

Bringing the 'Moments' Together

The use of different reception-inspired methods proves to be fruitful when the
different moments of the reception process are related. It is in this interplay of
moments that the dynamic complexity of receiving a text is manifested.

As illustrated in Table 6.4, summarizing the main tendencies of the case study, this interplay takes quite divergent forms: people clearly developed different decoding practices in relation to comparable domestic and US commercial fiction programmes. People were, as expected and in spite of the critical horizon of expectations, considerably more involved with the home-made drama. This high involvement on many levels seems to be grounded in a better literal comprehension or recognition of the configurations in the indigenous drama. This better command of the codes in this programme provokes a generally more complex and extreme decoding, explicit normative positions, 'politicized' discussions and divergent views. Here the domestic programme functioned as a strongly value-loaded discourse (Barthes, 1972), provoking an open forum on different social, cultural and political issues. While the recipients, as an interpretive community, were characterized by a higher degree of unanimity in the mere 'literal' comprehension of the characters in the domestic drama, it seems that this unanimity ebbed away during the discussion. This type of reception process could be called a process of introspection: a higher form of recognition and interpretation of 'common' codes is confronted with a critical, politicized application of them on the basis of recipients' own lives and experiences.

A quite different evolution in the interplay of 'moments' can be found in the reception process of the US drama, where the involvement of the (same) recipients was of another order. Here we could speak of more fixed, linear decodings, a mixed personal involvement and consensus-forming process in relation to the presented configurations. While the reception process of the domestic drama was characterized by an evolution of 'high unanimity' to 'divergent positions' in the discussion, the reception of the US drama developed from 'low unanimity' to 'consensus'.

It is safe to say that the indigenous drama functioned as a forum for introspection to consider themes of identity and current political, cultural and social issues, while in the responses to the US programme such issues hardly ever arose (cf. Katz and Liebes, 1990: 59).

Conclusions: Impact, Decoding and Characteristics of US Fiction

What can be learned from our case study about the world-wide success and hegemonic functioning of American programming? Here several central concepts on the impact and appeal of US fiction have to be questioned and re-evaluated. Of course, the results of this study are only indicative on many levels and care is needed in venturing generalizations (due to the rather small sample size and limited choice of programmes). One could also argue that several findings in this case study are quite predictable in a comparative construction with domestic drama. Indeed, this study is only one way of treating the problem of the consumption of imported American programming; other studies in other cultural collectivities, using other types of programmes and other genres, should be conducted in order to gain a better view of the nature of such consumption and the

TABLE 6.4 DIFFERENT MOMENTS IN THE RECEPTION OF US AND DOMESTIC FICTION: SUMMARIZING TENDENCIES

Moments	Reception of the American Sitcom	Reception of the Domestic Sitcom
0. Horizon of expectations	Promising Routine, tradition Folklore	Critical (especially on formal aspects) Scarcity Absence of folklore
1. Recognition (literal comprehension)	Relatively low Lower degree of unanimity Variated positions	Relatively high Higher degree of unanimity Close positions, consensus
2. Interpretation (inferential comprehension)	General specialization Attractive at many levels (high values) Fixed, linear decoding	Specific specialization Strong comic effect Complex decoding
3. Discussion (applied comprehension)	Mixed position on value orientation Resigned mood of consensus, unanimity Led by the narrative strain	Personal, normative involvement 'Politicized' discussion, divergent views Forum for introspection

threats to cultural identity posed by an increased supply of US fiction. Although many current concerns are understandable and have to be taken into account, they must not stand in the way of a fuller contextualization of the prevalent essentialist statements about the impact, decoding, functioning and characteristics of US commercial fiction. What new elements have to be brought into the discussion?

The Active Process of Negotiation with US Fiction

If 'negotiation' refers to the process of exchange between the actual position of the viewer and the one proposed by the text (cf. Fiske, 1987), one can say that in this case the negotiative actions between the group of recipients and the American sitcom were not exceptionally developed. Although this programme was certainly not consumed passively, it did not invite open discussions or applications to real life. People paid more attention to the narrative strain of this programme.

High Involvement with US Fiction

The same arguments can be applied to the (much-praised) high involvement with US drama – a central issue in the functioning of popular commercial fiction. We found that Flemish Belgians' involvement with the US television drama was not all that high, penetrative or personal. This observation certainly does not imply that one has to adopt an extreme opposite position. As observed in the study, the reception of both sitcoms was shaped by a constant interaction between involvement and distance. However, compared with domestic drama, the involvement with US fiction was not that high and was less personal; its decoding looked quite linear and less complex.

The Polysemic Decoding of US Fiction

This case study also questions the open, polysemic character and decoding of US drama – mostly considered as crucial to its international success. This question is very important because, as indicated by Jensen (1990), it is in the different decoding practices that the relative power of media and audiences has to be explored.

In our study strong arguments can be found to question and contextualize the link that has been made between the (potential) polysemic character of US fiction and its concrete divergent decoding. It was much more the domestic drama that functioned as an open forum for discussion of viewers' own identity and problems. The case study clearly showed that the (so-called) 'closed' domestic Flemish drama provoked in this context extremely open discussions, multiple interpretations on several issues and complex, oppositional decodings, while the 'open, polysemic' US drama was predominantly decoded in a quite linear, closed, consensus-forming manner. This finding, which can be considered as the crystallizing point of interest in this study, indicates that the relationship between a polysemic textual character and multiple decoding is far from mechanical. It should also be kept in mind that the (ever-changing) sociocultural relationship between a community of readers and a text is crucial in structuring political power. The political power of texts is only one potential factor in this game (Jensen, 1990). [...]

One could question how far those remarks, especially the one on strong narrative guidance, are attacking the concept of the textual polysemy of US fiction. At least we can say that the polysemic character of US fiction has to be questioned as its main textual force. The success of US drama as a text has in this sense to be seen in its inviting combination of several attractive textual, narrative and technical features, working within a rich tradition.

Statements on the Impact of US Fiction Should be Redefined, Revised and Contextualized

What then can be said about the impact of both programmes on the audience – at least within the limits of the reception analysis perspective and by carefully using the indicators presented in this study? As indicated at the beginning of this article, the link between the decoded meanings and impact has to be considered in the complexity of all elements in play within a specific context. Our case study shows that it is no easy matter to interpret the decoding processes, possibly leading to effects, as some data incorporate multiple possible conclusions on impact.

If one considers 'involvement' as the pivot in the impact processes, then it is safe to say that the data in our case study tend to minimize the impact of US fiction, especially in comparison with domestic drama, or at least that one has to consider the relativity of it.

If 'dependence' is seen as different from involvement and crucial to impact, it is already a lot more difficult to conclude that the recipients were more dependent on the domestic drama. In fact we have to speak here of different types of dependence. On the one hand, the domestic drama gave rise to a forum for 'introspection': people were relating the characters, themes and situations in the programme to their own lives. The American programme, on the other hand was, as indicated, strongly guiding the recipient into its diegetical world. This narrative force, supported by its technical, production and other qualities, clearly tends to intensify the dependence of the recipient on the US fiction programme during the decoding process.

This position can also be taken in relation to the concept of 'negotiation process', which in the case of the US sitcom was not strongly developed from the recipient's point of view. As clarified further, its strong dependence on the American narrative did not generate strong negotiative activities, so that the part played by the viewer cannot be labelled as highly active.

In this sense and in contrast with many other reception-inspired studies on the problematic, we argue that a more integrated vision of the functioning and the different, divergent forms of impact of US fiction should be adopted. While involvement with American drama may (generally) not be so high as with domestic drama, US fiction employs powerful instruments to create a spectacular world with specific cultural value-systems, strengthening the possibility of impact on the viewer. So, different elements in this reception analytical case study seem to point to a revision of theories on the unproblematically limited impact of US fiction on a micro-level. Whether this, to quote Richard Collins (1986), is 'equally bad for audiences' is a totally different question.

Note

1. The series *De Kollega's* is a production of the Belgische Radio en Televisie (BRT, Brussels), the Dutch-speaking public broadcasting company. *She's the Sheriff* is a Lorimar Telepictures Company production, shown on Vlaamse Televisie Maatschappij (VTM), the Flemish commercial television station.

References

Ang, Ien (1985) *Watching Dallas: Soap Opera and the Melodramatic Imagination.* London: Methuen.

Ang, Ien (1990) 'Culture and Communication: Towards an Ethnographic Critique on Media Consumption in the Transnational Media System', *European Journal of Communication* 5(2–3): 239–60.

Barthes, Roland (1972) *Le degré zéro de la'écriture.* Paris: Seuil.

Biltereyst, Daniel (1991) 'Identificatie en Culturele identeit. Een analyse van de receptie en de populari teit van eigen en Amerikaans drama', in J. Servaes and L. Heinsman (eds), *Televisie na 1992.* Leuven: Acco.

Collins, Richard (1986) 'Wall-to-Wall Dallas: The US–UK Trade in Television', *Screen* 21(3–4): 66–77.

Condit, Celeste M. (1989) 'The Rhetorical Limits of Polysemy', *Critical Studies in Mass Communication* 6: 103–22.

Curran, James (1990) 'The New Revisionism in Mass Communication Research: A Reappraisal', *European Journal of Communication* 5(2–3): 135–64.

Eaton, Mick (1978) 'Television Situation Comedy', *Screen* 19(4): 16–89.

Fejes, Fred (1981) 'Media Imperialism: An Assessment', *Media, Culture & Society* 3(3): 281–9.

Fiske, John (1987) *Television Culture.* London: Methuen.

Genette, Gérard (1972) 'Discours du récit', pp. 65–273 in G. Genette (ed.), *Figures 111.* Paris: Seuil.

Gripsrud, Jostein (1990) 'Toward a Flexible Methodology in Studying Media Meaning: Dynasty in Norway', *Critical Studies in Mass Communication* 7(2):117–28.

Groeben, Norbert (1982) *Leserpsychologie: Textverständnis. – Textverständlichkeit.* Aschendorff: Münster Westfalen.

Herzog, Herta (1986) 'Dallas in Deutschland. Eine Pilotstudie,' *Rundfunk und Fernsehen* 34(3): 351–67.

Herzog, Herta (1987) 'Decoding *Dallas*: Comparing American and German viewers', pp. 95–103 in Arthur Asa Berger (ed.), *Television and Society.* New Brunswick: Transaction Books.

Höijer, Birgitta (1990a) 'Reliability, Validity and Generalizability. Three Questions for Qualitative Reception Research', *The Nordicom Review* 5: 15–20.

Höijer, Birgitta (1990b) 'Studying Viewers' Reception of Television Programmes: Theoretical and Methodological Considerations', *European Journal of Communication* 5(1): 29–56.

Jauss, Hans Robert (1974) *Literaturgeschichte als Provokation.* Frankfurt: Suhrkamp Verlag.

Jensen, Klaus Bruhn (1990) 'The Politics of Polysemy: Television News, Everyday Consciousness and Political Action', *Media, Culture and Society* 12(1): 57–77.

Jensen, Klaus Bruhn and Karl Erik Rosengren (1990) 'Five Traditions in Search of the Audience', *European Journal of Communication* 5(2–3): 207–38.

Katz, Elihu and Tamar Liebes (1985) 'Mutual Aid in the Decoding of *Dallas:* Preliminary Notes from a Cross-Cultural Study', pp. 187–98 in P. Drummond and R. Paterson (eds), *Television in Transition*. London: BFI.

Katz, Elihu and Tamar Liebes (1986) 'Decoding *Dallas:* Notes from a Cross-Cultural Study', pp. 97–109 in G. Gumpert and R. Catheart (eds), *Inter/Media: Interpersonal Communication in a Media World*. Oxford: Oxford University Press.

Katz, Elihu and Tamar Liebes (1990) 'Interacting with *Dallas:* Cross-Cultural Readings of American TV', *Canadian Journal of Communication* 15(1): 45–65.

LeCompte, Margaret D. and Judith P. Goetz (1982) 'Problems of Reliability and Validity in Ethnographic Research', *Review of Educational Research* 52(1):31–60.

Liebes, Tamar (1984) 'Ethnocriticism: Israelis of Moroccan Ethnicity Negotiate the Meaning of *Dallas*', *Studies in Visual Communication* 10(3): 46–72.

Liebes, Tamar (1988) 'Cultural Differences in the Retelling of Television Fiction', *Critical Studies in Mass Communication* 5: 277–92.

Liebes, Tamar and Elihu Katz (1986) 'Patterns of Involvement in Television Fiction: a Comparative Analysis', *European Journal of Communication* 1(2): 151–71.

Livingstone, Sonia M. (1987) 'The Implicit Representation of Characters in *Dallas*. A Multidimensional Scaling Approach', *Human Communication Research* 13(3): 399–420.

Livingstone, Sonia M. (1988) 'Viewers' Interpretations of Soap Opera: The Role of Gender, Power and Morality', pp. 83–107 in P. Drummond and R. Paterson (eds), *Television in Transition*. London: BFI.

Livingstone, Sonia M. (1989) 'Interpretive Viewers and Structured Programmes. The Implicit Representation of Soap Opera Characters', *Communication Research* 16(1): 25–57.

McQuail Denis and the Euromedia Research Group (1990) 'Caging the Beast: Constructing a Framework for the Analysis of Media Change in Western Europe', *European Journal of Communication* 5(2–3): 313–31.

Morley, D. and K. Robins (1990) 'Spaces of Identity: Communications Technologies and the Reconfiguration of Europe', *Screen* 30(4): 10–34.

Morris, Meaghan (1988) 'Banality in Cultural Studies', *Block* 14: 15–25.

Nordenstreng, K. and T. Varis (1974) *Television Traffic – a one-way street?* Unesco Reports and Papers on Mass Communication, No. 70.

Schlesinger, Philip (1986) 'Any Chance of Fabricating Eurofiction?', *Media, Culture & Society* 8: 125–31.

Schlesinger, Philip (1988) 'L'identité culturelle européene: au – delà du slogan', *Médiapouvoirs* 12: 54–63.

Seiter, Ellen, Hans Brochers, Gabrielle Kreutzner and Eva-Maria Warth (eds) (1989) *Remote Controle, Television, Audiences, and Cultural Power*. London: Routledge.

Sepstrup, Preben (1989) 'Research into International Television Flows: a Methodological Contribution', *European Journal of Communication* 4(4): 393–407.

Silj, Alessandro (1988) *East of Dallas. The European Challenge to American Television*. London: British Film Institute.

Silverstone, Roger (1990) 'Television and Everyday Life: Towards an Anthropology of the Television Audience', pp. 173–89 in M. Ferguson (ed.), *Public Communication: The New Imperatives*. London: Sage.

Tracey, Michael (1985) 'The Poisoned Chalice? International Television and the Idea of Dominance', *Daedalus:* 17–56.

Section Three

Policy and Politics

Accountability of Media to Society: Principles and Means

Denis McQuail

A crisis of accountability

The relationship between the media and society is currently problematic on two main grounds. First of all, the media are widely believed to have gained in their centrality and potential influence for good or ill in society. Second, they are undergoing rapid change, mainly as a result of new technology with the consequence that existing frameworks of regulation and social control are becoming obsolete. The principal dilemma faced is how to reconcile the increasing significance of media with the declining capacity to control them, on behalf of the general good. This applies especially to television, which is the dominant medium for public communication in most countries and which has traditionally been most subject to regulation. […]

The very notion of what counts as the general good of society is itself less clear-cut than it used to be in the days when national elites largely decided what it was and applied their criteria to media systems within national frontiers. The transnationalization of media – as much as their multiplication and transformation – is a potent source of uncertainty, since individuals can claim wider allegiances and flows of public communication are no longer determined by national governments alone.

The problematic circumstances described are widely experienced and have featured in criticism of media and concern about their effects, reminiscent of the early days of television, with persistent demands by public opinion that 'something should be done', despite the difficulties. In the United States, where

Source: *EJC* (1997), vol. 12, no. 4: 511–529.

the challenge to regulation has been less, because there was less regulation, we find, nevertheless, a flood of critical studies of the performance of press and broadcasting in relation to news, politics and cultural values (e.g. Picard, 1985; Entman, 1989; Kellner, 1989; Bogart, 1995; Fallows, 1996). In Western Europe, there is anxiety about the effects of transnational and commercial trends on traditional values which used to be upheld by broadcasting and other quality media (e.g. Blumler, 1992). Concern is even stronger and more justified in Eastern Europe and Russia, where systems of publicly controlled media have largely disintegrated and commercialism operates in the least favourable economic conditions for serving public purpose as well as profit (Androunas, 1993; Paletz et al., 1995; Price, 1995). It seems that in Japan too, television has received some of the blame for recent crises of society. [...]

We can summarize the situation outlined above as a potential crisis of media accountability to society, meaning essentially a breakdown in the systems by which media have been led or constrained in the past to put the interests of society on a par with their self-interest. This article is concerned with two main questions. First of all, how should we adapt existing media accountability institutions to changing conditions? Second, in doing so, how can we square the circle of reconciling media freedom with media accountability? In order to answer these questions it is necessary to examine the meaning of the accountability concept and to consider the various forms it takes. I will propose a framework of analysis for media accountability, evaluate the merits and demerits of the means available for dealing with the dilemma outlined above and suggest some lines of action which are both coherent and consistent with media freedom.

Assumptions

In doing so, I make certain basic assumptions, which I do not have time here to support by argument. One assumption is that there is such a thing as a public interest, despite the problems of practice and principle mentioned. Second, 'society' can still legitimately hold the media, as one of its key institutions, to account on public interest grounds. Essentially the public interest is expressed in the form of (often competing) claims, based on certain values and principles, which have to be settled in some political or judicial forum (McQuail, 1992). Third, accountability need not be fundamentally inconsistent with liberty, if only because the full notion of freedom cannot be detached from ideas of responsibility. Nor does accountability have to take the form of more regulation. All the same, accountability does in practice often entail limits on freedom to publish and any claims and sanctions which are backed by society have to be consistent with reigning principles of freedom.

Although I cannot argue in detail for these assumptions, there are pragmatic grounds for accepting them, since contemporary societies which do value and protect liberty of expression also maintain quite extensive controls over media, which at least set limits to what can be published without risk of sanction.

Contemporary issues of accountability

Some of the issues on which the media are held accountable are perennial and universal, while others are variable and particular to certain places and times. In the first category, belongs the requirement to respect the *rights of individuals*, when these are touched by publication, especially in respect to reputation and material interests (e.g. copyright). While law normally protects such rights, there is a disputed frontier zone where the public interest in publication may transcend individual and private rights. Matters to do with *public order and the security of the state* have also been perennial topics for claims against the media by authorities, especially in relation to defence, terrorism or civil disturbance. Again, there is a disputed territory where governments may use public interest claims to maintain secrecy and deny legitimate claims for information and freedom to publish.

In a second category of more variably arising issues, we can find a number of *public sphere expectations*. These particularly relate to media contributions to the working of political and other social institutions. This is achieved through: publishing full, fair and reliable information; assisting in the expression of diverse and relevant opinions, including criticism of government; giving access to significant voices in society; facilitating the participation of citizens in social life; abstaining from harmful propaganda. All these are necessary conditions for an effective democracy. There are also increasing calls for the media to take account of the greater interdependence of nations and to observe international norms for good conduct.

In the sphere of *cultural values* there is more diversity, less clarity and more disputation. The media are widely expected to respect if not support the dominant values and moral standards of a society and, though less strongly, to give expression to the culture, arts and language of the national society. The media seem more often to be criticized for their failures than praised for success in this area. We often find firm measures of control on matters where great public offence is caused, or where the welfare of children and rights of certain minorities are involved. In general, we need to keep in mind that issues of accountability are not confined to potential harm, but also include positive expectations.

Concerning responsibility and accountability

The terms 'responsibility' and 'accountability' are often used interchangeably, but it is useful to distinguish them. Here, responsibility refers essentially to obligations which are attributed, in one way or another, to the media, and relating to the issues just outlined. Accountability refers to the processes by which media are called to account for meeting their obligations. Hodges (1986: 14) puts it simply:

> The issue of *responsibility* is the following: to what social needs should we expect journalists to respond? The issue of *accountability* is as follows: how

might society call on journalists to account for their performance of the responsibility given them. Responsibility has to do with defining proper conduct; accountability with compelling it.

The case is, however, more complicated since there are different kinds of obligation and alternative ways of attributing them to the media. The notion of responsibility, for instance, includes at least the following: the occupational tasks going with a particular media role, such as film director or editor, thus essentially professional matters; the restrictions laid on media by law and regulation; the positive tasks assigned to some media by law or other binding agreement (as with public broadcasting); voluntary promises to serve society in some way; actual liability for the effects of publication, including harm caused.

Essentially we are dealing with, various potential *claims* made against the media on diverse grounds and the processes of accountability (the rendering of accounts) has to vary accordingly.

One important dimension of responsibility is the degree of compulsion involved in any obligation. Responsibilities range on a scale from the completely voluntary to the completely compulsory, like the prohibition of deliberate incitement to violence. The variation can be captured in terms of four main types of media responsibility, distinguishing between those that are *assigned, contracted, self-imposed* or *denied* (see Hodges, 1986).

Assigned responsibilities include many matters covered by law and regulation, against which the media may have no legitimate grounds for appeal. In free societies, these are kept to a minimum and mainly serve to balance media freedom with the rights of other members of society and the public interest. Contracted obligations arise because of some implied covenant between press and society, maintained by convention and mutual agreement. They also relate to promises of quality of service implied in the commercial transaction between a media business and a paying customer. Self-imposed obligations mainly refer to voluntary professional commitments to observe certain ethical standards and to serve public purposes. The category of 'obligations denied' is needed to cover numerous instances where claims are laid against the media but are not accepted, with varying degrees of legitimacy. To deny responsibility may be an essential expression of freedom as easily as an evasion of duty.

A full consideration of media accountability has to take account of all four categories. Each has its own place and each presents different problems. Moreover, it is arguable that, along with other changes mentioned at the outset, there are some basic shifts in the distribution of these types of media responsibility. I have no measure of such shifts, but it seems likely that the relative share of both assigned and self-imposed responsibilities is falling, while the share of obligations contracted or denied is rising as a result of the extension of media activities, driven by market considerations and protected by market freedoms. Obligations to society are more likely to be denied where they involve the provision of unprofitable services.

In general, the probable trend of modern society and of mass media is towards a loosening of collective social bonds and a weakening of mutual obligations of a moral kind, including public duties. In the case of media, the growing scale and complexity of the process of production and distribution tends to increase the distance in every sense between the originators of communication and the receivers, making it difficult for a sense of personal or moral responsibility for publication to develop or a response to be made.

As we have seen, accountability follows on from responsibility and I leave the *content* of media responsibilities behind (the specific issues which arise and the values involved) and concentrate on the *means* by which they might be 'enforced'. A more precise definition of accountability (Brummer, 1991: 14) has been worded as follows: 'being accountable [refers to] the capacity, willingness, need or requirement to render an account of one's actions or inactions'. Moreover, it has four facets: being accountable *to* someone, *for* something (a task or consequence), *on the basis of some criterion* and with a varying degree of *strictness*. I return later to the question of *to whom* the media may have to render account and deal with the question of degree of obligation.

There are always alternative ways of seeking to enforce obligations, whatever their strength. In general, these ways can range from a more or less coercive mode, in which the emphasis is on potential material *liability* for the consequences of publication, to a non-confrontational mode in which accountability is equated with *answerability* (Blatz, 1972; Christians, 1989).

The liability mode is characterized by an adversarial relationship, while answerability refers to a readiness for debate, negotiation and interaction designed to achieve some reconciliation and resolution of differences. The emphasis in the first instance is likely to be on issues of harm caused by the media, in the second on issues of mass media quality.

There is a range of possibilities in between these alternative models, between the extreme cases of punitive enforcement and reliance on purely verbal and interactional forms of accounting. Each may have its place, but the second has a wider potential range of application and seems more consistent with publication freedom. Reliance on voluntary cooperation with non-coercive forms of accountability for publication is less likely to have a 'chilling' effect on media, fearful of economic penalties, and is more conducive to a reasoned liberation defence of publication which goes against majority norms or private right and interests.

Other arguments for preferring this 'softer' mode of accountability include: the frequent difficulty of proving liability for consequences of publication (think of the low success rate of mass media effects research); the problem of enforcing judgements concerning harm caused; the relative lack of clear criteria of good or bad media performance; the considerable doubt as to whether 'speech acts' can properly be treated in the same category as other acts (Bracken, 1994); the difficulty of balancing costs of private harm against potential public benefits from publication.

Nevertheless, while the preferred mode of accountability seems clear enough, it may not be consistent with current media trends. Modern mass media are less inclined to make voluntary commitments to society, less able to have any meaningful relationship with their audiences and those whom they affect, less ready to enter into dialogue. In practice, they may only respond to formal controls backed up by the threat of coercion which touches their material

FREE MEDIA
have
RESPONSIBILITIES
in the form of
OBLIGATIONS
which are either:

ASSIGNED   CONTRACTED   SELF-IMPOSED or DENIED

for which they are held
ACCOUNTABLE
(legally, socially or morally)
either in the sense of:

LIABILITY   ANSWERABILITY
for harm caused   or   for quality of performance

FIGURE 7.1   THE RELATIONSHIP BETWEEN MEDIA FREEDOM, RESPONSIBILITY
AND ACCOUNTABILITY

interests. These comments serve to reinforce the view that we face a major
dilemma in reconciling the interests of society with current trends of media
development. Not only is it more difficult to control the media directly, but the
forms of accountability, which are more desirable on libertarian grounds, and
more suited to an information society, are also becoming less easy to realize.

Figure 7.1 presents a summary of these points concerning responsibility and
accountability.

Lines of accountability

As we have noted, to be accountable is to answer to some particular claimant
outside the media, implying some kind of a relationship. In reality the situation
is very complex with an important distinction to be made between lines of
accountability *within* a media organization and those *between* it and outside
claimants. Internal accountability is not the main issue here, although it is
extremely important and has implications for relations with society. The
fulfilment of obligations to society often depends on the willingness of owners
to apply internal controls and the capacity of managers to put them into effect.

It is not only a matter of effective control but also of legitimacy, since some
certain media roles can claim a degree of autonomy on grounds of professionalism,
personal conscience, artistic licence or simply free speech. The tension between
accountability and freedom is also manifested within the walls of the media,
even if it is often concealed from outside view. This means that we cannot rely
on strong management to deal with the alleged sins of the media. In an age of
media moguls, this would be a recipe for totalitarianism.

There are also times when a media organization may fail to meet some external obligation on the grounds of a freedom claimed by an employee, for instance in the matter of disclosure of sources. Although ultimately the media organization as a corporate entity can usually be held responsible, the question of exactly *who* in an organization can be called to account is not always clear, and the issue is more than one of minor detail.

I return to the question of *to whom* accountability is due. If we consider only external relationships, we can identify a range of potential claimants. In general terms, these include: those to whom a legal or contractual duty exists; those to whom a promise has been made; those affected by some publication; those with power to act in response to publication. More concretely, the main claimants who call the media to account, aside from the owners (including shareholders) can be classified in terms of proximity, vocality and prima facie legitimacy.

The strongest and most direct accountability claims are likely to come from: sources (e.g. providers of news stories); clients (e.g. advertisers); audiences (as paying customers or as citizens and members of the public); those affected by the media (directly reported on or experiencing effects of some publication); and regulators (a general category for those with responsibility for control, whether from government or by self-regulation). Less directly involved, but important are: different pressure and interest groups; politicians; commentators, critics and those who claim to express public opinion.

Not only are the lines of accountability which arise in what are (in principle) mutual relationships between the media and these potential claimants very numerous and diverse, they also differ in the 'currency' which is employed. The 'accounts' deployed in media accountability are cast in several forms. Sometimes the currency is cash money, but in other cases it is a matter of esteem, loyalty, trust, allegiance or affection. The services supplied by the media are not usually material and they receive not only cash in return. A full consideration of accountability has to recognize the special character of the institution. A major implication of these remarks is that sanctions against the media can take non-material as well as material forms. At the same time, recent trends in media have tended to give more weight to money as the main 'currency'. Modern media are probably less concerned about loss of their own public reputation, their social influence or professional standing than about their financial balance sheet.

The accountability process

It is clear from this summary sketch that multiple and overlapping criteria, meanings, rules and procedures are involved in the business of holding media socially accountable. The situation varies from one medium to another and from one type of responsibility to another. In essence the accounting process which accompanies and follows publication is a matter of continually matching promises and obligations on the one hand with expectations and claims on the other.

The time-scale of accountability also varies greatly. Every issue of a daily newspaper and each television news bulletin is routinely tested immediately by a variety of potential claimants, not least by the audience. In the longer term, we find media systems being assessed by research, reviewed by commissions or subject to debate in parliaments, especially at or after critical moments in society. Accordingly, it is obvious that the particular means or mechanisms by which accountability is exercised include very many disparate entities and follow several alternative logics.

Any of the following may be involved: the working of the media market; political debate; the justice system; commissions of inquiry; independent research; comment and criticism by the media themselves; the pressure of public opinion; media self-regulatory agencies; media professional associations; special lobbies and interest groups; political parties; associations representing the audience.

In order to consider the questions raised at the outset it is useful to consider a small number of basic 'accountability frames', each one representing an alternative, though not mutually exclusive, approach to accountability, with its own typical logic, forms and procedures. A 'frame' in this sense involves several elements. First of all there must be a relationship between a media 'agent' on the one hand and a 'claimant' on the other, often with a third party as adjudicator. The relationship is actively concerned with some disputed issue and thus with certain normative principles. Finally there are some accepted rules, procedures and forms of account. Such frames can be distinguished along several dimensions, especially the following: the particular issues and normative principles which they deal with; the forms and discourse in which accounts are rendered; the procedures for accounting; the degree of constraint or compulsion involved.

The three most generally prevalent accountability frames in the sense intended are: a *legal-regulatory* frame; a *financial/market* frame; and a *public service/ fiduciary (or public trust)* frame. The history of media institutions can provide other examples, the most prominent being the frame of *government control*, which is still to be found, or that of media based on *religious or political party* allegiance, which is also not completely extinguished. The three selected frames can be characterized in more detail as follows.

The *legal-regulatory* frame typically sets the basic principles and ground rules for the operation of media institutions and establishes the rights and duties of individuals in relation to the media. In modern liberal and law-based societies, the law guarantees rights of free publication and also sets limits to freedom for purposes of protecting the rights of others and taking care of the general good of society. The main accountability issues handled within this frame include: intellectual property rights; freedom of expression; ownership and monopoly questions; claims of harm to individuals, groups, organizations, the state and society; and the needs of the judicial and political system. The relevant logic and discourse is legal-rational and administrative in character. The procedures involved are clearly laid down and formal in character, involving a process of adjudication. The forms of account are normally written texts which specify promises, obligations, arguments, justification, judgements, and so on. There is nearly always a high degree of constraint and settlements of disputes are usually involuntary.

The *financial/market* frame refers primarily to the normal disciplines of the market applied to publication issues. Laws of supply and demand secure an approximate balance between the needs and interests of communicators and those of consumers and between the interests of the media industry and those of the wider society. In principle the market system works in an open and self-correcting way. Free market principles support freedom to publish and to receive communication. They also work against unpopular forms of publication. The main issues handled within this framework are those to do with property rights (and duties), freedom again (including access and diversity), with the quality of communication goods and services (as seen by the consumer) and with techno-logical development. The underlying logic emphasizes freedom, efficiency, choice, profitability and majority preference.

The market system appears to work without direct reference to normative principles. However, for present purposes, we can note that media markets usually involve mechanisms which are sensitive to some norms. For instance, audience and market research reports on public preferences, likes and dislikes and social attitudes. Media publicity and public relations help media to keep in touch with the public mood and lead to publication decisions which are not just a direct reflection of immediate consumer demand. The economic interests of the media require some sensitivity to the views and interests of government and other powerful social institutions. Finally, the media market system has to work within some limits set by law and regulation on behalf of the public interest and is not fully autonomous.

The third frame, described as one of *public responsibility or trust*, is more complex and less clearly manifested, but real enough and still serviceable as a means of accountability. It is identified more by goals than by procedures (although it also includes public service broadcasting). The relevant goals reflect a primary concern with society, the public good and with the ideal purposes of public communication as information, opinion and culture. Its basis lies in the idea that organized rights to publication involve some form of 'public interest', whether written or unwritten. There is a historic commitment on the part of many media organization as well as of individual communicators and their professional associations to behave in a 'socially responsible' way. The frame includes, besides the activities of public service broadcasting, private media in their more voluntary pursuit of social and communication goals. Again, we find an overlap between the range of application of the market frame and this one.

The issues which fall within the scope of the 'social responsibility' frame are diverse, but essentially concern: informational and cultural 'quality' measured by non-market criteria; potential benefit or harm to the wider community, especially in matters of morals and public order; social cohesion; and support for the national culture and the working of democracy. The typical discourse is normative and judgemental, often assuming a consensus of social values.

The media themselves often organize self-regulatory procedures to deal with individual or more collective complaints. Professional organizations within the media supplement industry procedures. Codes of professional norms and ethics usually specify minimum standards of conduct which should not be breached for personal or commercial gain. Public opinion is constantly expressed by politicians, by many special interests and by routine research. Public commissions and enquiries into issues of media and society add their voice from time to time. There is continual debate in many different fora about the doings of the media and the media themselves can play a key part by self-criticism and publication of reports and critical views.

These three thumbnail sketches are intended to encapsulate the main alternative means which are available to society, as it were, to maintain a balance between freedom to publish, the needs of media industries and the wider interests of society, and its constituent individuals and groups. It is hard not to be struck by two points. First, that the means available are rich and varied; second, that they are immensely complex, fragile, interrelated and culturally dependent. Accountability processes cannot simply be invented overnight, nor can they be easily manipulated or changed according to some project of media reform, however well intentioned. In effect, we are limited by the means we have at our disposal and may have to make the best of these means. These reflections underline the particular difficulty faced when the media themselves change fundamentally, as they are doing at the moment. It is easier to appreciate how difficult it is to respond effectively and in time to such changes.

The relative merits and demerits of the main accountability frames

The frames as described are not equally suited to all purposes and each has its own characteristic strengths and weaknesses. It is useful to reflect on what these are, even if we do not have a free choice between them. The *legal-regulatory* model has the apparent advantage of being able to implement the public will in a clear and binding way. In a free society its application is likely to be kept to a minimum and it serves to secure as well as limit freedom. In principle it is above sectional interests and is fair and open in its working. There are also obvious drawbacks, not least the fact that implementing legal controls does diminish freedom in some way and often benefits the powerful, who can better afford to use legal instruments. The legal model tends to be coercive, depending on concepts of harm and liability which are arguably not so appropriate for judging communication actions. Legal control is not easy to exercise under present conditions and is often only effective in the last resort. It is also often ineffective and unpredictable in its outcomes. Laws are not easy to change when conditions change, since they serve certain vested interests and acquire a permanent character. The general trend of deregulation reflects the drawbacks of legal means of control as much as it does the influence of liberal ideology.

The market model as a means of accountability has equally ardent and persuasive proponents as critics. It is certainly very flexible, adaptable and effective in its own terms. It is continually self-adjusting and sensitive to the interests of many different parties. It provides a consistent and predictable basis for making judgements on disputed issues. In some respects the media market is egalitarian and it is generally non-coercive. It is not insensitive to questions of values, since good ethics can also be good for business.

The limitations of the market are also well known, quite aside from the fact that markets are imperfect and lead predictably to certain 'failures', especially to conditions of monopoly. In the present context, perhaps the most serious charge against the market is that its very workings seem intrinsically flawed. The perceived low 'quality' of communication content is often directly blamed on market forces – the extraction of profit and extreme competition for a mass market, the subordination of the interest of audiences to those of advertisers. Profitable and popular content is not necessarily 'good' content and serving the needs of consumers is not the same as serving citizens' needs.

Markets lead to concentrations of media power, a reduced professional autonomy for employees, an imbalanced relationship between suppliers and consumers and an attenuation of the direct relationship between communicator and audience. This relationship becomes distant, calculative and manipulative. The more successful media become, the more powerful they are and the less inclined to listen to complaints from society or their own audiences, especially where these imply lower profits. The market cannot really police itself effectively, since the media are mostly directly accountable to the same interests they are supposed to keep an eye on, according to 'watchdog' concepts of media functions.

The third frame described appears to be the most suitable for expressing and implementing the public interest and holding free media to account in a free society. It meets criteria of voluntariness, normative richness, wide range and participative value. On the debit side, however, the frame is very fragmentary, variable in its coverage of issues and circumstances and often weak in the means of implementation. As already noted, large multinational corporations are not usually very public spirited in distant markets.

It works on a voluntary basis where media organizations choose to comply (or where they have to), but only selectively. Media promises are often not kept and professional associations are not always strong enough to enforce codes of norms and ethics. Claims to social responsibility can often be self-serving and more for self-protection against effective regulation than genuinely intended. Service to the 'public good' may often involve support for dominant values and powerful interest groups. In the end, the effectiveness of the public trust model depends very much on the traditions of the particular media system and on there being an active participatory democracy already in place.

Conclusions to be drawn

Against this background and with the materials presented one can draw a number of general conclusions about what should be done to protect and advance the public interest in broadcasting under changed conditions. […] My aim is not to propose new means of control, but rather to suggest broad principles of policy and practice for achieving social accountability. Accountability arrangements have to meet three general aims which are not easy to reconcile. A most general requirement is that accountability itself should actually protect and promote media freedom. A second aim is to prevent or limit harm which the media might cause. Third, accountability should promote positive benefits from media to society. No single one of the frames discussed is ideal or necessarily superior to the others, and it is also clear that none of the three discussed is adequate on its own. What is needed is to encourage the aspects of each framework which (1) are most likely to maximize the achievement of these three aims and (2) most capable of reconciling the divergent tendencies of the three frameworks.

According to my analysis, the aim of freedom is best served by making certain choices which I can only summarize. First, intervention should be kept to a minimum and self-regulation is generally preferable to external regulation. Additionally, just as freedom is served by a diversity of media, so is it likely that diverse, overlapping and even conflicting forms of accountability are more desirable, on grounds of freedom, than unified and consistent forms. This is an argument *against* convergence of regulation whether or not the media converge, which seems less likely as time goes on. The more alternatives there are for framing and testing issues of accountability the more courts of appeal there are and the less 'chilling' are the effects of control. The very inconsistency of accountability can promote freedom, even if it offends against administrative and even market logic. Multiple models of freedom and regulation are also more likely to reflect the genuine diversity which exists in society concerning conceptions of what is in the public good. There is no single prescription for freedom or for virtue.

The preferable forms for accountancy will be those which are spontaneous and interactive and which involve the greatest mutuality between the parties concerned, providing the best conditions for media *answerability*. Freedom is not well served by coercive forms of control or by making the media more *liable* for consequences which are considered harmful. But dialogue and negotiation between the parties to communication is impossible where relations between media agents and those affected by the reactions are completely detached and calculative.

It should consequently be the objective of policy to promote routine relations of dialogue between media and society (audiences, public, groups, government) which reduce the need for arbitrary and restrictive measures at moments of crisis. This means that any interventions relating to media structure should aim to encourage smaller-scale and more local (and also national) media and discourage global conglomeration. It also means that encouragement should be given where possible to strengthening the voice of the audience and of 'intermediate' public exposure and settlement of disputes with media rather than private procedures.

In line with the aim of promoting positive contributions to society, forms of accountability which reward 'good' media behaviour are also to be preferred to those which punish offences. In this respect, the questions of 'internal' media freedom deserve particular attention, where liberty of the press is valued, even if law is not the best way to increase the autonomy of journalists and other media professionals. Improving the status of professional associations of media workers and encouraging education and self-regulation are more appropriate avenues to follow and can help to provide a counterweight to the extremes of commercial motivation and to multinational conglomerates.

Even if it is quite clear that the market on its own is as much a danger as a benefit to the public interest, there are advantages to including the market within the range of accountability procedures, rather than treating it only as something to be restrained, especially when the market is by far the dominant driving force of media change and expansion. The market clearly protects and promotes some important freedoms and it can also discourage some undesired media freedoms and promote some positive ones by way of mechanisms of consumer response and public relations. There are also ways of encouraging business ethics which can reinforce professional ethics.

The position of public broadcasting is a special case (and still of critical significance) in this general discussion. It is arguably the best single device for reconciling the three divergent aims set out above, assuming that democratic control can take care of essential freedoms. It has no equal in its capacity to secure positive communication benefits, at the behest of society. However, it is also not universally available, it is declining in its extent relative to less regulated market forms and is not likely to provide a solution for new areas of media expansion. It is also increasingly hard to maintain the distinction between broadcasting and other media which legitimates its special position. However, the implication of my analysis, especially the desirability of diversity of structure and means of control, is that public broadcasting should be preserved wherever possible for as long as possible. It can also be gradually reconfigured into the framework of a public trust model with a wider remit, with other media borrowing from its strengths.

Current technological changes do seem to undermine or bypass the regulatory systems instituted for broadcasting and broadcasting itself becomes harder to distinguish from the new interactive media. However, according to the line of argument advanced, the latter do not require any fundamentally new systems of control. In some ways they are intrinsically suited to the kinds of accountability which have been favoured in this account. Their interactivity makes dialogue with audiences more possible and they are diverse and fragmented. We can also expect the market increasingly to influence the organization and uses of new interactive media, with some losses for freedom as well as gains for accountability through setting limits to undesired effects. Whatever the degree of control, new interactive media, even if powered by the market, can be expected to contribute to the public good by way of information and the formation or strengthening of social ties.

Concluding remarks

In general, the 'crisis of accountability' has probably been exaggerated and also misrepresented. It has always been too easy to blame the media for the ills of society and even for the ills of the media themselves. It is hard to escape from the fact that the media generally do follow the tastes and interests of their audiences and also the needs of their sources and clients, including the politicians and governments who are supposed to look after the public interest. The performance of media reflects the imperfections of society as much as their own failings. The public, in its capacity as audience, also has its responsibility and we cannot be sure that, even with more opportunities, the public would welcome 'better' media or embrace the more desirable forms of accountability which requires some continuing effort on their part. It is also illusory to suppose that better media would necessarily lead to a better society.

We also need to keep in mind that free media have the right to be 'irresponsible' and that some perceived 'misuses' of autonomy will be a necessary price for potential benefits of invention, creativity, opposition, deviation and change. More important is the question of whether the freedom to be irresponsible on the one hand and the power to call media to account, on the other, are equitably distributed. On the face of it, the present state of media in the world and current tendencies suggest that the answer is 'no' on both counts. But that is a larger question, which I have to leave for others to deal with.

Note

This article is the text of keynote to Symposium on Broadcasting Ethics organized by The British Council and NHK, Tokyo, 18 March 1997.

References

Androunas, E. (1993) *Soviet Media in Transition*. Westport, CN: Praeger.

Blatz, C.V. (1972) 'Accountability and Answerability', *Journal for the Theory of Social Behaviour* 2: 1–120.

Blumler, J.G. (ed.) (1992) *Television in the Public Interest*. London: Sage.

Bogart, L. (1995) *Commercial Culture*. New York: Oxford University Press.

Bracken, H.M. (1994) *Freedom of Speech: Words are not Deeds*. New York: Praeger.

Brummer, J. (1991) *Corporate Responsibility: An Interdisciplinary Analysis*. Westport, CN: Greenwood Press.

Christians, C. (1989) 'Self-regulation: A Critical Role for a Code of Ethics', pp. 35–54 in E.E. Dennis, D.M. Gillmor and T.L. Glasser (eds), *Media Freedom and Accountability*. New York: Greenwood Press.

Entman, R.M. (1989) *Democracy without Citizens*. New York: Oxford University Press.

Fallows, J. (1996) *Breaking the News: The Profit Factor in News Selection*. Westport, CT: Greenwood Press.

Hodges, L.W. (1986) 'Defining Press Responsibility: A Functional Approach', pp. 13–31 in D. Elliot (ed.), *Responsible Journalism*, Beverly Hills, CA: Sage.

Kellner, D. (1989) *Television and the Crisis of Democracy*. Boulder, CO: Westview Press.

McQuail, D. (1992) *Media Performance: Mass Communication in the Public Interest*. London: Sage.

Paletz, D., K. Jacubowitz and P. Novosel (1995) *Glasnost and After*. Creskill, NJ: Hampton Press.

Picard, R.G. (1985) *The Press and the Decline of Democracy*. Westport, CN: Greenwood Press.

Price, M.E. (1995) *Television, the Public Sphere and National Identity*. New York: Oxford University Press.

8   Who's Afraid of Infotainment?

Kees Brants

When, on the eve of the 1994 elections in the Netherlands, parliamentary candidate and future Minister of the Interior Hans Dijkstal put his saxophone to his mouth, closed his eyes and played the first tunes of a bluesy ballad, the local pundits of political communication who watched the entertainment show on television first laughed their heads off. Here was a free market Liberal who had been watching too many American election campaigns, notably Bill Clinton's in 1992. But to be honest, he did not do too badly. It wasn't Elvis Presley's 'Heartbreak Hotel' and the Dutch host was a far cry from Arsenio Hall, but Hans Dijkstal knew how to play and certainly thrilled the studio audience that had not come for heavy-handed political talk. And he reached a good size audience at home as well, many with little political interest, and all potential voters.

After the laughter had died down, the same commentators were quick to exclaim that commercialization had now come to the Low Countries. The dykes had apparently been unable to stop the flood of 'Americanization', they lamented as latter-day Hans Brinkers. They did not explain what the label exactly meant, but it was obviously no good and a violent contrast with the serious attitude with which they thought politics should be approached. And later they dwelt upon the good old days, when public broadcasting still had a monopoly and when everyone seemed to agree that commercial television was something that the Americans should keep for themselves – in short, the days when political communication was still meant to inform about issues and points of view and not to entertain with personalities and images.

The pundits must have suffered a memory loss in linking the coming of commercial television in the Netherlands (1989) with infotainment elements that supposedly characterize American-style television. Already in the 1970s a prime minister and a prime minister to-be had used a talk show in their campaigns. A predecessor of Hans Dijkstal was interviewed in a sauna, dressed in a towel barely hiding his substantial size. Commentators with a better memory recalled many an occasion where politicians – obviously expecting to find the floating voter – had not shunned the entertainment programmes of the public broadcasters. They might not always have been at ease (one prime minister radiated exuberantly in 1981 when being interviewed and half ridiculed by a Dutch comedian), but they felt it was part of the game.

These examples of what would now be called 'infotainment' only prove, of course, that the phenomenon is not new in the Netherlands; andI am sure every country in Europe has its own historic examples. The question is whether

Source: *EJC* (1998), vol. 13, no. 3: 315–35.

infotainment has become a more structural phenomenon in Europe, whether it has changed systematically the content of television's portrayal of politics and whether, as many claim, this has resulted in and, at the same time, is proof of a crisis in politicial communication's role in democracy.

The scary world of commercial television and beyond

Many authors in the United States (e.g. Brokaw et al., 1997; Hallin, 1996; McManus, 1994; see also the 1996 Annals of the American Academy of Political and Social Sciences) and in Europe (e.g. De Bens, 1998; Franklin, 1994; Kavanagh, 1997; Siune, 1998; see also Pfetsch, 1996, and others in Germany, Belgium and Scandinavia who research the so-called 'convergence hypothesis') have linked the commercial basis of television in the USA and the recent changes in the broadcasting system in Europe with developments in the level of political knowledge and participation in and, more generally, with the quality of the democratic system. It is sometimes called 'infotainment' or 'tabloidization', when addressing the same issue in newspapers. Usually the picture is as bleak as the topic is hot.

American Jay G. Blumler (who, until his recent retirement, worked at the University of Leeds in the UK and the University of Maryland in the USA) is probably the most outspoken and certainly the most repetitive in his critical assessment of the causal link, its origins and effects. In following him (often in collaboration with his colleague Michael Gurevitch) in what he has dubbed alternatively a 'crisis of public' or 'civic communication', and a 'crisis of communication for citizenship', Blumler stands for many political scientists and communication scholars who worry about what he calls the 'commercial deluge' inundating Europe, and its consequences for democracy.

As with many of his colleagues, Blumler's starting point is democratic theory, or the idea of collective decision-making through deliberative communication and debate among the members of the public. In the ideal democracy, of course, individuals participate equally in the decision-making process. But most modern democratic states have, for all practical and political purposes, been constituted with forms of representative democracy, wherein the people delegate political authority to others representing them. The devices intended to link citizens to their representatives were elections, political organizations and public opinion generated and conveyed through the mass media. A prerequisite for a well-functioning democracy in this theory is an actively and rationally participating citizenry that has access to a free market-place of ideas and is fed by relevant information and that knows something about the actual issues on the political agenda. Democracy thus requires that the media (and for Europe particularly, public service broadcasting) perform and provide a number of functions and services for the political system. Notably:

> Surveillance of the sociopolitical environment, reporting developments likely to impinge, positively or negatively, on the welfare of citizens. Meaningful

agenda setting, identifying the key issues of the day, including the forces that have formed and may resolve them.

Platforms for an intelligible and illuminating advocacy by politicians and spokepersons of other cause and interest groups.

Dialogue across a diverse range of views, as well as between power holders (actual and prospective) and mass publics.

Mechanisms for holding officials to account for how they have exercised power.

Incentives for citizens to learn, choose and become involved, rather than merely to follow and kibitz over the political process.

A principled resistance to the effects of forces outside the media to subvert their independence, integrity and ability to serve the audience.

A sense of respect for the audience members, as potentially concerned and able to make sense of his or her political environment. (Blumler and Gurevitch, 1995: 97)

That is quite a handful. But if media and especially public service television is to bear some sense of 'responsibility for the health of the political process and for the quality of the public discussion generated within it', their role is 'pivotal' (Blumler, 1992b: 1). Until the coming of the commercial deluge, the broadcasting organizations in Europe had done a fine job, thanks to – 'being creatures ultimately of the state' – their politicized structure. [...]

In short, Blumler (and he is not alone) is afraid of commercial television, because its political communication is a mixture of information and entertainment – politics as popular culture instead of the serious business of popular discourse. And because competition forces public broadcasters to adapt to the wishes of the (politically less interested) consumers, they will contribute to the growth of the turned-off voter. It is a scary causal link which taps the life-blood of democracy.

Blumler presents a convincing case for the dangers of infotainment, based on decennia of reflection on the dynamics of change in European (notably British) and American political communication. His study is embedded in a conviction that system-based features of political communication give characteristic shape to a society's public sphere and his description of the changes he has noted over the years is well stocked with examples from different countries. Empirical support for content changes, however, is limited. And it is in this pudding that the proof lies, of course – proof that can only come from longitudinal, cross-national and cross-system comparison.

There is little of this, but in the course of this article I look at two obvious domains of political communication to put Blumler's claim to the test: television news and campaign communication. The first rests on secondary literature about the (changing?) place of politics in television news in different European countries, the second on first-hand research on the infotainment orientation of politicians and television journalists in the 1994 elections in the Netherlands. Whatever the outcome, I contend at the end that much about the infotainment scare is based on questionable premises.

Entertaining news in the multi-channel reality

Following the infotainment hypothesis one might expect several changes in the television news of those European countries that have had a strong public service tradition: a certain degree of depoliticization, in the sense of less attention for or marginalization of political news; a different, more populist picture of politics through focusing on human interest, personalization and sensationalism in the presentation of politicians and the political process – and these developments at first more significantly so with commercial than with public channels, but (after some time) the latter following suit.

Although extensive comparative and longitudinal European content analysis of television news is very limited (Heinderyckx [1993] is a notable exception but his comparison of 16 channels in eight countries focuses mainly on public stations) and operationalizations of political news content in these research projects differ markedly, separate country studies give a generally ambiguous and sometimes contradictory picture of the 'infotaining' of news and of a programmatic convergence between public and commercial channels.

Contrary to what one might expect, news programmes on the public channels did not move to the periphery of or outside prime-time in order to compete with popular drama on commercial television. On the contrary, most commercial channels have followed the public schedule and seem to compete with public broadcasters more on their 'home ground' than with different content and formats. Hotelling's Law of Excessive Sameness of Products, which claims to show mathematically that in competitive markets it is rational for producers of goods to make their products as similar as possible, might be one explanation for this phenomenon (see Van Cuilenburg, 1997). Legitimizing the commercial channel as a serious television station, and thus attracting the same, for advertisers particularly interesting, audiences, has been another driving force. Being an established commercial station might explain why in 1993 and early 1998 programme managers of Britain's ITV suggested rescheduling the long established *News At Ten* to 11 p.m. Growing competition, they claimed, forced them to stretch the length of attractive prime-time entertainment programming. Recent discussions on the BBC 'dumbing down' its coverage of Westminster politics, though exemplary of anxiety over the more market-driven and competitive approach of the public broadcaster, is based more on examples than on longitudinal analysis of changes in its political output.

In most countries commercial television has not marginalized political news. In eight West European countries, almost six out of an average of 13.3 items per newscast in the early 1990s were about politics, with French TV5 (public) broadcasting above the average and Belgian VTM and French TF1 (both commercial) and French A2 and Italian RAIUNO (both public) broadcasting below the average (Heinderyckx, 1993). In Sweden, where commercial television has not yet got a real stronghold, Hvitfelt (1994) noticed that, overall, air time devoted to politics declined sharply between 1990 and 1993.

Pfetsch (1996) and Bruns and Marcinkowski (1996) found, however, that both public and commercial channels in Germany have increased their political information in the news since the mid-1980s. Private channels have even doubled political references in news stories, putting it almost at a par with public news. In looking at the total programme supply in Germany of two public and three private channels over a four-week period in 1995, Kruger (1996), however, found a substantial difference: the former had on average 27 percent political information in its programming (out of a ratio of 42 percent information), the latter just over 5 percent (with PRO 70 percent; out of an average of 13 percent information). Apparently, if they do it, commercial channels restrict their political information mainly to newscasts.

In Denmark Powers et al. (1994) did not find much distinction between the news of the public DR-TV and the commercial TV-2; they even claim that commercial competition has led to more varied news from more sources, but their research was not longitudinal. Van Poecke and Van der Biesen (1991), on the other hand, found a marked difference in political news content between the Flemish public BRT and the commercial VTM (23 and 16 percent respectively). For the Netherlands, Van Engelen (1997) found an increase in national political items of the public NOS news between 1990 and 1993 from 23 to 32 percent, while the commercial RTL news remained at around 17 percent over that same period. Van Praag and Van der Eijk (1998), in looking at Dutch campaign news at three consecutive elections (1986, 1989 and 1994), noticed a marked decrease of politically informative news with the public channel and, alternatively, an increase of campaign rituals and horse race between 1986 and 1994. The decrease of political information set in, however, long before competition started in 1989, when the first commercial station was introduced in the Netherlands.

According to the infotainment hypothesis we can expect a growing importance of sensationalism and human interest, following the example of the tabloid press that we find in several European countries. Again, the picture is ambiguous, though tabloid television news – the car, star and royalty chasing format that we know from local television in the US – is still practically absent in Europe, including most private channels. Where for the European countries as a whole we might see a slight tendency towards a popularization of news, there is little evidence that politicians and politics are dramatically more personalized and sensationalized than before.

In Belgium (Canninga, 1994), Sweden (Hvitfelt, 1994) and Denmark (Powers et al., 1994) there is evidence towards more sensationalism in news reporting as a whole (in choice of items: more crime news, and/or in news angle and visuals) as well as more 'soft' news. For Germany Kruger found in 1995 that the three commercial channels had on average 37 percent of what he calls 'boulevard' news – crime, drugs, catastrophies, sexual abnormalities – against 7 percent for the two public channels. Bruns and Marcinkowski (1996) note, however, that between 1986 and 1994 human interest and violence items in the commercial news dropped to the same level as the public channels. Using Nimmo and Combs's (1985) distinction between on the one hand elitist/factual news and on the other populist/sensationalist, Van Engelen (1997) claims that between 1990 and 1996 almost all items of the commercial and the public news he looked at fitted the first category. However, in tackling declining advertising income, the managing director of Dutch RTL in 1998 not only cut the news budget, but also suggested the news be made more 'juicy'.

We do see several examples of adaptation by the public news to the styles and modes of presentation that one generally ascribes to the commercial channels. Double presentations and 'happy talk', especially in daytime news, are not uncommon with the public stations anymore. Moreover, the anchor person begins to show star features and behave accordingly. From the archetypal 'pillar of wisdom and independence', he or she sometimes enters the world of popular culture, like the two main BBC news presenters who also host respectively a reality television show and a quiz. Apart from the 'talking heads' of anchors, moving pictures dominate all 17 channels in the eight countries Heinderyckx (1993: 435) looked at, which made him conclude that the editors are apparently afraid of boring the viewers. Hvitfelt (1994) notes for Sweden more of what he calls 'dramaturgically crafted' techniques of story telling in the news. Together with Bruns and Marcinkowski (1996) for Germany and Van Engelen (1997) for the Netherlands, Hvitfelt also sees an increase of interviews with 'the person in the street', as proof that identification for the viewing public is taken more into consideration. Though contrary to Germany and the Netherlands, the Swedish public channel focuses more on the 'wielders of power' and 'spokespersons'. In comparing Dutch and Belgian public and commercial stations, Canninga (1994) concluded that the latter usually show shorter items, a tendency noticed elsewhere too (Hvitfelt for Sweden). But according to Van Engelen the tendency in the Netherlands is the opposite, as is the case in Germany: the items have become longer and of a more narrative nature.

Although she found conflicting evidence for the hypothesis that German public channels would follow commercial stations in their entertainment focus, Pfetsch (1996) claims that in Germany 'serious' politics on television is reduced to the traditional news format, while new genres have appeared that blur the boundaries between political information and entertainment. With the fragmentation of audiences, politicians feel more or less obliged to use all channels of political communication available. In a separate study of news during the 1994 elections in the Netherlands, a colleague and I looked specifically at how politicians adapted to the new, multi-channel situation and whether they did indeed aim for more popular types of programmes.

Up and down the infotainment scale

In a six-week, round-the-clock content analysis of three public and two commercial channels, prior to the 1994 elections in the Netherlands, we looked at where the politicians of the different parties appeared on television (see Brants and Neijens (1998) where this is reported more extensively). In total, approximately 12,000 cases on Netherlands 1, 2 and 3 (public) and RTL 4 and 5 (private) were coded, as well as the name and the political party of the politician. To get some idea of the degree to which politicians geared their television appearances to the range of programmes available to the public, the amount of attention to politicians was broken down according to seven programme genres: news, (heavy) information (like discussion programmes and documentaries),

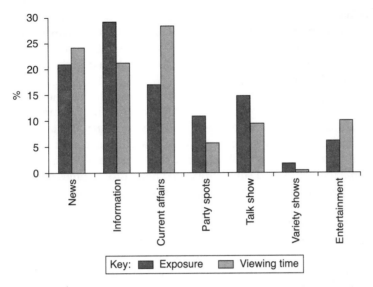

FIGURE 8.1 EXPOSURE AND VIEWING TIME POLITICIANS ACCORDING TO GENRE

current affairs, party political broadcasts, talk shows (both vox-pop and light interview programmes) and entertainment (game shows, music programmes).

The classification assumes an ideal type, 'traditional' continuum ranging from informative to entertainment programmes, in which we followed the standard division used by the Dutch broadcasting corporations for analysing audience data. The use of this so-called People Meter (providing data based on a representative sample of the Dutch population) in combination with the different programme types thus enabled us to calculate how many and which people were watching the politicians and for how long. Or in other words: did the politicians actually reach the audience/electorate they wanted?

Contrary to the expectation that – with an electorate scattered over channels and genres – politicians would follow the audience, the traditional informative programmes still accounted for more than three-quarters of the air time with politicians (see Figure 8.1). Talk and variety shows and entertainment programmes only had a limited share (22 percent) of politicians' performances. With the exception of party political broadcasts, which generally seem to talk in relative emptiness, and entertainment, the audience was also more interested in the informative programmes. As it turned out, the informative programmes were also for the politically less interested the main window for seeing politicians at election time.

There was a marked difference between parties and between party leaders and other candidates. The new leader of the Christian Democratic Party (CDA) had opted for an American-style, image-oriented and human interest campaign and, as his campaign manager claimed in interviews, his media focus was on infotainment genres. He was, however, underrepresented in the kind of programmes on that side of the informative–entertainment continuum. Internal party differences over his campaign style, and the fact that he was named in a fraud scandal, meant he had a lot of explaining to do and made him a prime target for news and current affairs. The infotainment genres seemed to have lost interest in the personal characteristics he so emphasized in the period prior to the six-week election campaign.

Opinion polls long before election day had shown that the Labour Party (PvdA) leader, present prime minister Wim Kok, had his own image problem: both he and his party were seen as unreliable, uncaring and lacking in social feeling, characteristics rather disastrous in a social democratic candidate. The campaign team succeeded in changing Kok's 'technocrat' image; their strategy of avoiding the critical and conflict-oriented news programmes and the fact that almost 40 percent of his television appearances were in talk shows must have helped.

The two smaller parties – free market Liberal Party (VVD) and the socially progressive Liberal Party (D66) – had more or less mirror problems. The leader of the former party was considered a poor, far too high-brow communicator and the party therefore opted for a campaign team in which prominence was given to a popular former sportswoman. As it turned out, 15 percent of the total VVD television appearances were in entertainment programmes, more than in news and current affairs. When someone watched a VVD politician on television, 29 percent of the cases were during an entertainment programme. The D66 leader on the other hand, was – being a great communicator and popular with large segments of the public – in great demand with infotainment genres. As the polls promised success, D66 could only lose in the campaign and they consequently decided to play it more low key. Their politicians hardly appeared in entertainment programmes, but they focused on informative programmes and, for their leader, on talk shows.

The 'infotainment' of politics has, of course, potentially two sides. Next to politicians aiming at more entertainment-focused programmes, genres themselves can have changed. The ideal typical information–entertainment scale described in the previous paragraphs is based on the role ascribed to mass media in democratic theory, as discussed earlier in the article, whereby informative programmes are considered to have content conducive to rational participation in the political-electoral process; entertainment programmes are for distraction and pleasure (thus assuming that politics is serious business and no fun). Between the two ideal typical extremes of the continuum, however, a whole range of subgenres has emerged, in which aspects of human interest, degree of information, sensationalism, drama and entertainment have been mixed (Just et al., 1996).

In covering the whole range of television genres in their political signification process at election time, we combined topical content characteristics with style and format elements and applied these to the information–entertainment continuum. On the one side of the scale are the programmes with hard and serious news, on the other the emphasis lies on taste, pleasure and lifestyle. On the 'serious side' we could, with regard to topic, expect more factual content aspects such as stories about party manifestos, policy, issues and party political disagreements, while with regard to journalistic style politicians would be addressed with respect to their expertise or political involvement, as policy-maker or expert, serious, from a certain professional distance, meant to inform and with a tone of objectivity. The format would be business-like, no showy additions like active audiences and accompanying music.

On the 'entertaining side' of the continuum we could expect topics with a more human interest content in which politicians appear as individuals with specific characteristics. Here, image and drama are more important than the message, the latter being simple, preferably light hearted and with an emotional under- or even overtone. The style would be more informal, personal and open, in general: meant to entertain, instead of emphasizing independence and critique. The format is entertaining, which could be both slightly sensational as well as lightly dramatic. Audiences would participate actively and show appreciation or dislike.

Infotainment is situated between the two poles and mixes political informative elements in entertainment programmes or entertainment characteristics in traditionally informative programmes.

Analysing the topic, style and format of a number of programmes of both public and private channels in the pre-election six-week period allowed us to say something about the relative infotainment of political communication on Dutch television during an election. We randomly chose 16 programmes of the seven genres we previously distinguished in which one or more politicians appeared. Due to classification differences with the People Meter this resulted in a rather uneven distribution over the different genres, but still enabled us to compare both genres and public and private channels. For each programme, the presence of informative and/or entertainment characteristics was coded and attributed to topic, style and format, resulting in scores ranging from 'i' (fully informative), via 'i/e' and 'e/i' to 'e' (fully entertaining).

Almost all programmes we analysed had entertainment aspects (see Table 8.1), in topic, style and format. Little attention was paid to policy positions of the various parties and little or no attention to party political fundamentals, ideology and electoral programmes. The campaign was mostly connected with conflicts between parties and the consequences for possible coalition formation within the context of the so-called horse race and hoopla. Although there are notable exceptions with regard to style, the programmes generally followed the traditional continuum. More so than in style, we see in the format a strong presence of entertainment elements and more so with private than with public programmes.

On the whole, as to the information–entertainment scale, the picture is hybrid though: a talk show may be more informative about the qualities of a candidate than a news or current affairs programme is about issues and policies, and private channel's programmes are not necessarily more geared to entertainment in their portrayal of politics than the programmes of the public broadcasters.

Coming to terms with popularizing politics

So, who's afraid of the infotainment of politics? Certainly not only Jay G. Blumler, who is treated here maybe a bit unfairly because his analysis of the

TABLE 8.1   THE DEGREE OF INFOTAINMENT OF SEVEN TELEVISION GENRES

Genre and channel	Informative – entertainment		
	Topic	Style	Format
Talk show 1 (public)	i	i	i/e
Information 1 (private)	i	i	e/i
News 1 (public)	i	i/e	i
Current affairs 1 (public)	i/e	i	i
News 2 (public)	i/e	i	i
News 3 (private)	i/e	i	i/e
Information 2 (public)	i/e	i	i/e
Current affairs 2 (public)	i/e	i/e	e/i
News 4 (private)	e/i	i/e	i/e
Talk show 2 (private)	i/e	e/i	e/i
Entertainment 1 (public)	i/e	e/i	e
Talk show 3 (public)	e/i	e/i	e
Party spot (CDA)	e/i	e	i/e
Party spot (PvdA)	e/i	e	e/i
Variety show (private)	e	e	e
Entertainment 2 (private)	e	e	e

Note: i = informative; e = entertainment; i/e = mostly informative; e/i = mostly entertainment.

crisis of civic communication covers more ground than infotainment alone. While he and other academics, journalists and politicians in different European countries seem to hold it very much against the bad influence that is coming from across the Atlantic, scholars in the United States are also increasingly worried about the entertainment focus of many a candidate and about 'talk show democracy' (Brokaw et al., 1997).

To weigh the pros and cons one has to be sure what the dangers are. The infotaining or popularization of politics on television is, I believe, problematic under three conditions: if that is the dominant form in which politics is portrayed; if it is done to hide something else; or, if it leads to a distorted image of politics. Neither of these conditions seem to be unconditionally the case.

Dominance of infotainment

A longitudinal, cross-Europe content analysis could give an answer to this, but so far research is scattered. In the overview of studies on television news in a number of West European countries, there is many an example of entertainment elements in the content and style of political reporting. But on the whole, the picture is at best ambiguous and certainly does not point to infotainment taking over and to an unequivocally bad influence of commercial television. With most private stations and the public broadcasters, the news remains at the heart of their programming, and politics still forms a substantial part of most news programmes. The coming of commercial television may have resulted in somewhat more human interest and sensationalism, but hardly so in political reporting. Television programme makers cannot very well be blamed for using their medium and visualizing the news, as long as relevant topics are not omitted because of lack of pictures. Also the fact that, in trying to gain empathy with the viewer, the 'person in the street' has gained prominence in interviews is hardly proof of an entertainment focus, certainly when officials and power wielders still dominate the news.

The study of infotainment in different television genres in the Dutch election campaign of 1994 also presented an ambiguous picture. More than three-quarters of politicians' television appearances were on the traditional platforms of political communication: news and current affairs programmes and party political broadcasts.[1] On the other hand, looking at the content, style and format of different programmes of genres ranging from information to entertainment, it turned out also that the informational programmes to a more or less degree contained elements of entertainment. On the whole, however, there seems to remain enough television to choose relevant information from and to gain knowledge in order to participate in the democratic process.

More problematic, or from another perspective reassuring, is, however, that a number of recent research projects have dampened the belief in the cognitive ability of television. In an extensive overview of American surveys, Robinson and Davis (1990) conclude that, compared to reading daily newspapers, watching television news is a poor aid to getting informed. Television is seen and treated as a pleasure machine and that attitude alone already poses difficulties for understanding. In comparing Dutch commercial and public television news, Kleinnijenhuis et al. (1991) sketched a more complex picture whereby acquiring knowledge is dependent on previous knowledge, motivation and information on offer. They concluded that television news is less suitable for acquiring complex knowledge necessary to make a rational choice. Moreover, as John Zaller (1997) claims, because election outcomes have more impact on individuals than individuals can have on election outcomes, the rational voter will be more interested in information about how the election is likely to come out than in information that will help her or him to cast a wise vote. Whether one likes it or not and whether or not one disagrees with the rational choice approach, these findings put political communication in a different light.

Infotainment as hideout

If a campaign strategy is aimed at infotainment in order to avoid the professional scrutiny of political journalists, we might have a problem. And it is worse if it is meant to mislead, or at least to hide something from the public, not to tell the whole story and thus to project an image which, if unveiled, might have made people decide otherwise. One of the pivotal functions of journalists in a participatory democracy – holding officials to account for how they have excercised power – cannot be fulfilled. An example of this can be found in Clinton's successful bypass strategy in 1992, which was expressly meant to avoid the critical Washington-watchers and focused very much on the non-traditional media format of talk shows and (supposedly uncritical) local media (Rosenstiel, 1993: 83–92).

There are probably examples of such political communication behaviour in European countries too, but, as far as I know, no systematic research on this topic exists. Present prime minister Wim Kok applied a bypass strategy in the Netherlands in 1994 when he sometimes refused to comment on national televison news on issues brought forward by his opponents, while gladly attending many a talk show or visiting local television stations. But even when 38 percent of his television appearances were on talk shows, the majority were still in the informative programmes. Moreover, the realization that most viewers are to be found watching politicians in the latter programmes and that television news is considered to be the most trustworthy medium, makes these genres, in a way, an unavoidable part of the media strategy of political parties.

There is also a paradoxical risk in this strategy, which Blumler (1990) labelled the 'modern publicity process' and which Zaller (1997) has developed into what he calls the 'Rule of Product Substitution': the more effectively reporters are challenged for control of a news jurisdiction, the more strenuously they will seek to develop new and distinctive types of information that they can substitute for what politicians are providing and that affirm overall journalistic control of mass communication. The reaction to politicians trying to gain control over the media's agenda has, in the US at least, resulted in journalists predominantly evaluating political leaders in a negative way. They use opponents as a means to undermine each politician's claim (Patterson, 1994).

Though only based on one example, the irritated journalistic reaction to Wim Kok's bypass strategy and attempts to confront him with his opponents might point to a comparative development in the Netherlands (Brants and Van Praag, 1995: 249ff.). Cappella and Jamieson (1996) and Patterson (1994) have argued and empirically substantiated that this type of negative and conflict-oriented reporting has led to public cynicism and declining confidence in the US political system. If this holds true for European countries as well, it puts both infotainment as a bypass strategy and the resulting type of political journalism in a different light.

Infotainment as seduction

More than anything else probably (but usually implicitly), the critique of infotainment is based on the assumption that if many people are attracted by personalities and avoid the hard stuff of politics, it is bad for them. They are seduced by imagery hiding the reality of necessary choices in political matters, they miss out on the information relevant for political participation, and they thus might make the wrong or at least an irrational decision at places like the ballot box, or do not vote at all. These assumptions are based, of course, on a highly questionable hypodermic needle theory of the workings of mass media; they define the private and the personal away to the affective domain of the assumed irrational; and they turn the *opportunity* for access to information and participation in politics, which lies at the heart of democratic theory, into an *obligation*, and that begs for unwarranted disappointment.

The fear of losing the citizen and trading him or her for the consumer is based on a distinction which seems to miss the point in thetelevision age. In political communication, the affect of the supposed consumer should be taken as seriously as the cognitive of the acclaimed citizen. The kind of vox-pop talk show where politicians are confronted with live audiences is probably the only public space where 'ordinary people' as 'experience-based experts' can put the issues they deem relevant on both the media and the political agenda. Blumler (1997), on the other hand, claims that it also tends

> ... to stage politics as spectacle and theatre and can suffer from glitziness and shallowness. The upgrading of popular views often entails the downgrading of expertise, and all too often populist programmes degenerate into bear pits. The role of the studio audience becomes little more than that of providing a range of conflicting views with minimal exchange, a process of argument-hopping with some ideas cut off abruptly in mid-stream, a plethora of points without structure. In short, communication-for-citizenship requires 'deliberative' not 'simplistic' populism.

In this description of some forms of popular journalism, Blumler assumes at the other side a kind of political journalism: with experts, intelligent and comprehensible discourse based on exhange of arguments and people listening to each other, and discussions that are placed in relevant contexts and that come to conclusions, a kind of journalism that barely exists and, if so, only attracts an audience usually limited to already-knows. The mixture of entertainment and consciousness raising that is to be found in some talk shows could, on the other hand, re-establish the popular in politics.

In societies where ideologies disappear and differences between political parties become less and less important and visible, for the public much understanding of politics has the structure of narratives centred around individual characters (Crigler and Jensen, 1991: 189). Under such circumstances, personal characteristics of politicians are not unimportant and irrational elements in choices and evaluations of politics. Personalization may also be an important strategy for understanding political information and placing social issues in a personal perspective. Democracy, as Dahlgren (1998: 91) has pointed out, is not 'just about official politics, but also has to do with the norms and horizons of everyday life and culture'. Civil society should not only include the discursive and decision-making domain of politics but also the vast terrain of domestic life.

Note

1. The first results of a similar analysis of the 1998 elections point in the same direction: almost 80 percent of politicians' television appearances were in the informative genres.

References

Blumler, J.G. (1990) 'Elections, the Media and the Modern Publicity Process', pp. 101–14 in M. Ferguson (ed.), *Public Communication: The New Imperatives*. London: Sage.

Blumler, J.G. (ed.) (1992a) *Television and the Public Interest*. London: Sage.

Blumler, J.G. (1992b) 'The Civic Communication Task of Public Service Broadcasting: Lessons from Election Observation at the BBC', paper presented to the conference on 'What Future for Public Service Broadcasting?' London.

Blumler, J.G. (1997) 'Origins of the Crisis of Communication for Citizenship', *Political Communication* 14(4): 395–404.

Blumler, J.G. and M. Gurevitch (1995) *The Crisis of Public Communication*. London: Routledge.

Brants, K. and Ph. Van Praag Jr (1995) *Verkoop van de Politiek. De verkiezingscampagne van 1994*. Amsterdam: Het Spinhuis.

Brants, K. and P. Neijens (1998) 'The Infotainment of Politics', *Political Communication* 15(2): 149–65.

Brokaw, T., J. Fallows, C. Hall Jamieson, M. Matalin and T. Russert with M. Kalb (1997) 'Talk Show Democracy '96', *Press/Politics* 2(1): 4–13.

Bruns, T. and F. Marcinkowski (1996) 'Konvergenz Revisited. Neue Befunde zu einer alteren Diskussion', *Rundfunk und Fernsehen* 44(4): 461–79.

Canninga, L. (1994) 'Een vergelijkende analyse van de nieuwscultuur in de buitenlandse berichtgeving op BRTN, VTM, NOS en RTL', *Media & Maatschappij* 4(1): 91–114.

Cappella, J. and C. Hall Jamieson (1996) 'News Frames, Political Cynicism and Media Cynicism', *The Annals of the American Academy of Political Science* (Special edition 'Media and Politics'): 71–84.

Crigler, A. and K. Bruhn Jensen (1991) 'Discourses on Politics: Talking about Public Issues in the United States and Denmark', pp. 176–95 in P. Dahlgren and C. Sparks (eds), *Communication and Citizenship. Journalism and the Public Sphere in the New Media Age*. London: Routledge.

Dahlgren, P. (1998) 'Enhancing the Civic Ideal in Journalism', pp. 89–101 in K. Brants, J. Hermes and L. van Zoonen (eds), *The Media in Question. Popular Cultures and Public Interests*. London: Sage.

De Bens, E. (1998) 'Television Programming: More Diversity, More Convergence?', pp. 27–38 in K. Brants, J. Hermes and L. van Zoonen (eds), *The Media in Question. Popular Cultures and Public Interests*. London: Sage.

Franklin, Bob (1994) *Packaging Politics. Political Communication in Britain's Media Democracy*. London: Edward Arnold.

Hallin, Daniel (1996) 'Commercialism and Professionalism in the American News Media', pp. 243–64 in James Curran and Michael Gurevitch (eds), *Mass Media and Society*. London: Edward Arnold.

Heinderyckx, F. (1993) 'Television News Programmes in Western Europe: A Comparative Study', *European Journal of Communication* 8(3): 425–50.

Hvitfelt, H. (1994) 'The Commercialization of the Evening News: Changes in Narrative Techniques in Swedish TV News', *The Nordicom Review* 2: 33–41.

Just, M.R., A.N. Crigler, D.E. Alger, T.E. Cook, M. Kern and D.M. West (1996) *Crosstalk. Citizens, Candidates and the Media in a Presidential Campaign*. Chicago, IL: The University of Chicago Press.

Kavanagh, D. (1997) 'Media and Elections: An Unhappy Marriage?', keynote address and paper presented at the conference 'Images of Politics', Amsterdam.

Kleinnijenhuis, J., A. Peeters, A. Hietbrink and N. Spaans (1991) 'Het nieuwsaanbod van NOS en RTL4 en wat de kijkers ervan leren', *Massacommunicatie* 19(3): 197–226.

Kruger, U.M. (1996) 'Boulevardisierung der Information im Privatfernsehen', *Media Perspektiven* 7(96): 362–75.

McManus, J. (1994) *Market-driven Journalism: Let the Citizen Beware?* Thousand Oaks, CA: Sage.

Nimmo, D. and J. Combs (1985) *Nightly Horrors. Crisis Coverage by Television Network News*. Knoxville: University of Tennessee Press.

Patterson, T.E. (1994) *Out of Order*. New York: Vintage.

Pfetsch, B. (1996) 'Convergence through Privatization? Changing Media Environments and Televised Politics in Germany', *European Journal of Communication* 11(4): 427–51.

Powers, A., H. Kristjandottir and H. Sutton (1994) 'Competition in Danish Television News', *Journal of Media Economics* 7(4): 21–30.

Robinson, J.P. and D.K. Davis (1990) 'Television News and the Informed Public', *Journal of Communication* 40(1): 106–19.

Rosenstiel, R. (1993) *Strange Bedfellows. How Television and the Presidential Candidates Changed American Politics*. New York: Hyperion.

Siune, K. (1998) 'Is Broadcasting Policy Becoming Redundant?', pp. 18–27 in K. Brants, J. Hermes and L. van Zoonen (eds), *The Media in Question. Popular Cultures and Public Interests*. London: Sage.

Van Cuilenburg, Jan (1997) 'Access and Diversity in Communications and Information', paper presented at the opening conference of ASCoR, Amsterdam, 18–19 September.

Van Engelen, Marcel (1997) 'Televisienieuws onder druk', unpublished MA thesis, University of Amsterdam.

Van Poecke, L. and W. Van der Biesen (1991) 'Programma- en nieuwsaanbod op BRT en VTM', pp. 24–48 in *Strategieen van openbare omroepen versus commerciele omroepen*, Referaten 13e Vlaams congres voor Communicatiewetenschap, Rijksuniversiteit, Gent.

Van Praag, Ph. and C. Van der Eijk (1998) 'The Coverage of a Historic Campaign', *Political Communication* 15(2): 165–85.

Zaller, J. (1997) 'The Political Economy of Election News', paper presented at the APSA conference, Washington.

Political Communication Systems All Change: a Response to Kees Brants

Jay G. Blumler

Almost everything to do with political communication seems to be in flux these days: social formations and lifestyles; strategies of persuasion; politician–journalist relations; and media technology, organization and finance. Critical in the last sphere has been the shift from a situation where limited-channel, nationwide television was the dominant medium of political communication, to a more abundant and fragmented system, providing not only more outlets for political messages but also more opportunities for audiences to ignore (or only cursorily scan) those messages in favour of more sheerly enjoyable fare. Some observers even suspect that the turbulent currents of change are ushering in a quite new political communication order in place of the older one (Blumler and Kavanagh, 1998; Wyatt, 1998).

In 'Who's Afraid of Infotainment?' (*European Journal of Communication*, 13(3), 1998: 315–35), Kees Brants casts a penetrating and challenging eye on one consequence of these developments – the marked blurring of conventional distinctions between media genres that set out to inform and those that entertain. His approach is creative but raises certain issues that need further discussion.

Wherefrom infotainment?

The upsurge of new-found 'infotainment' springs from systemic impulses: the exigencies of increased competition in multi-channel conditions; the exigencies of tighter media finance, requiring news and current affairs producers to show that they can earn their keep; and the tendency for many citizens to approach politics more like consumers (instrumental, oriented to immediate gratifications and potentially fickle) than believers. Even in Britain, the birthplace of missionary public service broadcasting, television today offers more slice-of-real-life 'docusoaps' than analytically pedagogic documentaries; single-subject current affairs programmes are being replaced by faster paced magazine programmes; the main news bulletins have been cosmetically revamped; news readers have become celebrities, paid and promoted as such; and the daytime

Source: *EJC* (1999), vol. 15, no. 2: 241–249.

schedules are full of *Oprah*-like talk shows, including the infamous Jerry Springer show.

Enter Kees Brants

How should scholars relate to this disconcerting trend? Will it drag down the public service standards of European political communication? Is it ultimately corrosive or restorative for engaged citizenship? Kees Brants makes three welcome contributions to these questions.

First, he shows that it would be premature for civic-minded Europeans to succumb to a full-blown panic over infotainment. After reviewing published content analyses of the public and private television news services of several European countries, Brants concludes that, in an admittedly mixed picture, traditional standards are still largely being upheld. Public channels have not moved the news to the margins or out of prime-time to compete with popular drama on commercial television. On the contrary, commercial channels differ little from the public schedules and seem to be competing more on terms set by public broadcasters than with different content and formats.

Second, Brants offers a promising research tool, termed an 'infotainment scale', for further investigation in this area. This codes programmes for the presence of defined informational and/or entertainment characteristics in respect of their topics, styles and formats, ranging in each case from 'i' (fully informative), via 'i/e' and 'e/i' to 'e' (fully entertaining). When Brants applies this scale to 16 programmes from seven different television genres that covered the 1994 election campaign in the Netherlands, a hybrid but not dismaying picture emerges. Although the programmes mixed the elements in varying ways and degrees, Brants concludes that the evidence 'does not point to infotainment taking over' (p. 329).

Third, Brants proposes a discriminating way to evaluate the emergence of infotainment, depending essentially on whether it seems to be getting out of hand. A trend to infotainment would be problematic, he suggests, if: (1) it became the dominant form in which politics was portrayed; (2) it was used by politicians to avoid the professional scrutiny of political journalists; or (3) it distracted audiences from 'the hard stuff of politics'. And Brants considers that as of now these criteria are far from being violated in European political television.

But more needs to be said about four matters dealt with in Brants' article.

Wherefrom the crisis of public communication?

First, why have some of us discerned in certain current trends the seeds of a crisis of public communication (Blumler and Gurevitch, 1995; Blumler, 1997)? Here Brants misses the point. The nub of our concern is not the march of infotainment, as he seems to suppose. I certainly have no quarrel with the argument that there may be more than one way or one television genre to inform citizens about politics, ranging from mainstream news and current affairs through call-in programmes, talk shows, other hybrid infotainment formats, as well as soap operas and dramas in realistic settings that highlight current issues. Inasmuch as (1) television is the primary medium of political communication, (2) television offers a cornucopia of diverse genres and programme types and (3) uses and gratifications research has often spotted 'surveillance' and 'reality-seeking' motives for viewing such programmes, the notion that only programmes formally labelled as 'informational' should be regarded as legitimate outlets for civic communication is unsustainable. Of course, whether all such programmes actually do stimulate and inform their audience members, or whether some are perniciously seductive (deflecting people from the 'hard stuff' as Brants puts it), are still largely unexplored empirical questions.

A need to be open-minded about infotainment also arises from the strong currents of populism that are suffusing the worlds of politics and the media these days. They emanate from the expansion of media outlets, which 'has created new opportunities and pitfalls for the public to enter the political world' (Delli Carpini and Williams, 1998). But they also stem from the decline of ideology, leaving a sort of legitimacy gap that populism helps to fill; from the growth of political marketing as an adjunct to campaign strategy; and from the diminished standing of political, media and other elites in popular eyes. In such conditions, paternalistic discourse is no longer an option. Communicators who wish to inform and empower their auditors must therefore adapt more closely than in the past to what ordinary people find interesting, engaging, relevant and accessible. It is also important, however, whether such communicators actually *do* wish to inform and empower or just want to grab eyeballs and sop up ratings. And that is why it is worth holding on to our distinction, scorned by Brants, between 'simplistic' and 'deliberative' approaches to populist political communication (Blumler and Gurevitch, 1995: 221).

Brants' belittling of our concern about the crisis of public communication is also unhelpful. One can endorse the need for a balanced take on 'infotainment' without arguing that the crisis of public communication is not real and serious. Does voter turnout of 36 percent in the recent US mid-term elections or a historically low turnout since the Second World War at the last British General Election not signify a serious problem about voters' perceptions of and attitudes towards politics? Is it implausible to associate the growth of electoral indifference and cynicism with the advance of a communication process, in which (to exaggerate a bit!) the 'permanent campaign' wears everybody out, negative campaigning tarnishes everybody and campaigns that are heavily mediated by journalists continually spotlight the manoeuvring of politicians for publicity advantage?

So what forces are ultimately responsible for this state of affairs? Our diagnosis of it was based on a longitudinal examination of changes that have taken place in communicators' approaches to television and in the sociopolitical environment over the past quarter century. It is not a snapshot of the situation in the last couple of years, and we never ascribed the crisis of public communication to the coming of commercial television, as Brants alleges. Instead we traced its sources to what we called the 'dynamics of inter-communicator relationships'

(Blumler, 1997: 397). They included such interconnected developments as: (1) the thorough-going professionalization of political advocacy (initially by parties and candidates but subsequently spreading to interest group and social cause campaigns of all kinds); (2) the fight back by journalists against politicians' attempts to narrow their news choices (e.g. fixation on 'the game' rather than policy substance; inordinately heavy coverage of politicians' gaffes, however trivial); (3) frequent coverage of spin-doctoring as an inherent part of the political story; (4) the collapse of norms about the ethical rules of the publicity game; (5) widespread projection of an image of the 'turned-off' citizen; and (6) signs that politician–journalist relations have entered a new phase, one we termed 'a chronic state of partial war' (Blumler and Gurevitch, 1995: 215).

Two huge problems follow inexorably from this whirlpool of developments. One is the suppression of substance. If it is the case, as John Zaller (1998) has convincingly argued, that voters mainly hold governments to account for their delivery of such fundamentals as prosperity, peace and moderation, then much of what passes for political communication among the fevered frenzies of the modern publicity process will simply appear irrelevant to their civic interests. That is surely a recipe for yet more scepticism, disregard and disrespect.

The enormous power of the media in the new dispensation is the other main problem of concern. A whiff of this is conveyed by the reason for giving up his Cabinet post that was given by Peter Mandelson in his December 1998 letter of resignation after remarkably hyped media coverage of the relatively trifling 'offence' of having concealed his acceptance of a large loan from another government minister some years earlier:

> I do not believe that I have done anything wrong or improper. ... But we came to power promising to uphold the highest possible standards in public life. We have not just to do so, *but we must be seen to do so.* (emphasis in original)

But who determines whether one is *seen* to behave properly nowadays? This is predominantly *media* controlled – and at a time when the news media are becoming increasingly competitive, aggressive and uninhibited in chasing scandalous stories.

About none of this should we be so complacent as Kees Brants seems to be.

Now for the good news

Brants' reassuring impression that in Europe broadcast news and current affairs have not been overwhelmed by depoliticization, personalization and sensationalism in the wake of commercially driven multi-channel competition also merits further consideration. The contrast with experience in the USA, where some of the consequences of increased competition have been pretty drastic, is intriguing. For example, the US networks almost closed up civic shop altogether during the 1996 presidential campaign – reducing their coverage of both the primary and general election races by about 40 percent compared with 1992. And it was not just the amount of attention to politics that was affected. Also favoured, according to David L. Swanson (1997: 1269), was 'a style of coverage driven by entertainment values and a desire not to be left behind by the tabloids in attracting the mass audience'.

So what explains the greater resilience of European civic communication in the face of increased competition? Two explanatory factors come to mind.

First, differences of political culture may have been involved. Traditionally at least, what Semetko et al. (1991: 5) have termed 'the valuation of politics as such' was lower in the US than in most European societies. And although some of the sources of this difference may be receding, e.g. Europe's stronger and more ideologically inspired party systems, European publics may still be more receptive to news agendas led by serious politics than is the US electoral audience. But cultures do change – which gives yet another reason to deplore the potentially undermining cynicism that is spawned by the modern publicity process.

Second, differences of broadcasting structure and history may have also played a part. From the onset of radio much of Europe was exposed to the crucial system-straddling, standards-setting and expectations-forming role of public service broadcasting, which the USA never experienced. Thus, the impact of multi-channel competition in a fully privately owned and commercially run media system may be different from its impact in a media system that was shaped from an early stage by the establishment of large public service organizations. But whether the ravages of competition can be withstood over the longer term remains to be seen. Amid so much ongoing media change and social change, the continuing ability of public service television to hold the line against communication trivialization cannot be taken for granted. To do so, its news providers will have to muster a formidable combination of qualities: principled commitment, courage, imagination and an ability to adapt to the needs of new-style audiences while retaining faith in their receptivity to a serious agenda.

Researching infotainment

Brants' article has also reminded me of how tired I have become of attitudinally charged disputes between 'critical traditionalists' on the one side, who apply blanket terms of abuse like 'dumbing down' to many recent trends in political journalism, and 'popular culturalists' on the other side, who seem disposed to applaud almost any cultural form so long as it is popular, typically lauding the populist thrust in broadcast programming for inviting people 'to rethink and possibly revalue' their stands on moral, social and political issues (Hermes, 1997: 160). Although Brants aligns himself with neither of these extremes, a tinge of popular culturalism does shine through such statements as, 'The mixture of entertainment and consciousness raising that is to be found in some talk shows could … re-establish the popular in politics', and 'Personalization may also be an important strategy for understanding political information and placing social issues in a personal perspective' (p. 332).

But my complaint is that both sides in this dispute tend to rely too heavily on what Stromer-Galley and Schiappa (1998: 27) have termed 'audience conjectures' – that is, 'claims about specific effects on audiences or claims describing the determinate meaning of a text for audiences', without offering confirming data. As Stromer-Galley and Schiappa argue, those who make such claims should 'support' them 'with audience research'. Applying this stricture to the subject in hand, it seems to me that the academic study of infotainment and related phenomena has been lopsidedly skewed towards trend analyses of media content. Of course it is vital that such trends be monitored. But we will not be able to fathom their civic significance until attempts are made systematically to undertake research into the range of audience responses to the range of newer formats. In fact Brants' 'infotainment scale' could play an important part in such a project of comparatively designed reception research, enabling us to gauge whether there are important differences (and if so, of what kinds and for whom) in viewers' politically relevant responses to programmes graded differently on the scale.

New world, new citizenship?

Finally, some revisionist ideas about the meaning of 'citizenship', incomple-tely thought through, appear in the conclusion to Brants' article. He is not alone in this. Quite a few commentators have latterly been striving to 'rethink citizenship' without claiming to have found problem-free answers (Buckingham, 1997). Many influences have fed this effort: the assumption that the so-called Enlightenment project is dead; a fuller appreciation that no real-life public sphere is anything like an academic seminar and that very few real-life citizens approach political issues like model students; a recognition that the informational needs and processing styles of many younger people are radically different from those of their elders (Buckingham, 1997); and the increased visibility of more raw ways of addressing social issues common in talk shows and other populist forums.

Brants' response to this development appears in the following two statements:

In political communication, the affect of the supposed consumer should be taken as seriously as the cognitive of the acclaimed citizen. (p. 332)

Civil society should not only include the discursive and decision-making domain of politics but also the vast terrain of domestic life. (p. 333)

What troubles me about these remarks is the impression conveyed that almost any approach to citizenship could be acceptable. If we want to think things through, fine; but if we just want to get worked up about them, that's equally fine. And if we are interested in more structural issues of economic management, social distribution and power structures, great; but if we are hooked on divergent sexual behaviours, conflicts and deviations, that's equally all right.

I personally doubt whether such a tolerant balancing act is sufficient for any concept of citizenship that includes the ideal of 'empowerment'. Of course 'affect' has a proper part to play in determining the ends that people wish to achieve in politics, but those ends will only be socially defensible and viably attainable if they are also shaped by a cognitive awareness of surrounding interests and circumstances. Similarly, although the conditions and tensions of everyday life in people's domestic, workplace and neighbourhood milieux raise many issues that are suited to public discussion, it would be highly unfortunate if the sphere of official politics was left to the activities of highly motivated and better informed elites. As William A. Gamson (1998) has recently declared in a brilliantly all-encompassing phrase, we should look for ways of 'integrating the language of the lifeworld into the policy discourse'.

Note

The terms of this response benefited greatly from consultation with Michael Gurevitch.

References

Blumler, Jay G. (1997) 'Origins of the Crisis of Communication for Citizenship', *Political Communication* 14(4): 395–404.

Blumler, Jay G. and Michael Gurevitch (1995) *The Crisis of Public Communication*. London and New York: Routledge.

Blumler, Jay G. and Dennis Kavanagh (1998) 'A Third Age of Political Communication: Where Is It Heading?', paper presented at the Round-table on Seeking Responsible Futures for Political Communication, London, July.

Buckingham, David (1997) 'News Media, Political Socialization and Popular Citizenship: Towards a New Agenda', *Critical Studies in Mass Communication* 14(3): 344–66.

Delli Carpini, Michael X. and Bruce A. Williams (1998) 'The Politics of "Popular" Media', paper presented at the Workshop on Mediated Politics, Annenberg School for Communication, Philadelphia, October.

Gamson, William A. (1998) 'Promoting Political Engagement', paper presented at the Workshop on Mediated Politics, Annenberg School for Communication, Philadelphia, October.

Hermes, Joke (1997) 'Cultural Citizenship and Popular Fiction', pp. 157–67 in Kees Brants, Joke Hermes and Liesbet van Zoonen (eds), *The Media in Question: Popular Cultures and Public Interests*. London, Thousand Oaks, CA and New Delhi: Sage.

Semetko, Holli A., Jay G. Blumler, Michael Gurevitch and David H. Weaver (1991) *The Formation of Campaign Agendas: A Comparative Analysis of Party and Media Roles in Recent American and British Elections*. Hillsdale, NJ: Lawrence Erlbaum.

Stromer-Galley, Jennifer and Edward Schiappa (1998) 'The Argumentative Burdens of Audience Conjectures: Audience Research in Popular Culture Criticism', *Communication Theory* 8(1): 27–62.

Swanson, David L. (1997) 'The Political-media Complex at 50: Putting the 1996 Presidential Campaign in Context', *American Behavioral Scientist* 40(8): 1264–82.

Wyatt, Robert O. (1998) 'After 50 Years, Political Communication Scholars Still Argue with Lazarsfeld', *Journal of Communication* 48(2): 146–56.

Zaller, John (1998) 'The Politics of Substance', paper presented at the Workshop on Mediated Politics, Annenberg School for Communication, Philadelphia, October.

'Four Mothers': The Womb in the Public Sphere

Dafna Lemish and
Inbal Barzel

'Four Mothers' is a protest movement calling for Israel's withdrawal from the occupied territories of southern Lebanon. Israel invaded south Lebanon on 6 June 1982 in an attempt to solve security problems on its northern border. While planned as a limited operation, it escalated to a full-scale war and has culminated in a problematic occupation. The unresolved situation has claimed many lives: over 1200 Israeli soldiers have been killed in the region, and numerous (numbers unavailable) soldiers and guerrilla fighters and citizens have lost their lives on the other side of the border.

The Four Mothers movement was established after a tragic crash involving two military helicopters on 5 February 1997, resulting in the wasteful death of 73 soldiers on their way to assignments in southern Lebanon.

Originally, four women, all mothers of combat soldiers, residents of the vulnerable Israeli north, initiated the protest, to be joined by scores of others, men included. A year later, the movement reported on 600 activists around the country, and 15,000 supporting signatures on a protest petition (Ringel-Hoffman, *Ma'ariv*, 27 March 1998). Moreover, the term 'Four Mothers' possesses a symbolic meaning in Jewish tradition, since it represents the four biblical mothers (Sara, Lea, Rebecca and Rachel), thus serving as the emblem of 'motherhood' of the nation as a whole.

On 7 February 1997, a mother named Zabarie wrote in a letter to a weekly paper (*Ha'ir*):

> Woman, mother! Why do you give them your son, so they would sacrifice him? Your flower is 18, and he is the most important thing for you in the world – more so than yourself. You won't eat because of him. You won't sleep because of him. And now, you let him go straight to hell, instead of telling him: 'My child, they die there! Don't go there!' ... Lebanon is a monstrous altar. Tell him the truth, don't let him go so easily. Don't give them your child. He wants to live.

Motherly love and the instinctive desire to protect one's child are perceived in our society as an essential characteristic of femininity. The mythical strength assigned to motherly love seems to legitimize almost any form of action, including

Source: *EJC* (2000), vol. 15, no. 2: 147–169.

rebellion and even crime. The power conferred by motherhood and the
ization of its calling, camouflages women's impotence as citizens. This
larly true in a society like Israel which glorifies motherhood as a 'public
erve the national goals. As bearers of children, women are entrusted
iological and social reproduction of the national collective (Berkovitch,
unique mission of the woman, the mission of motherhood – there is
no greater mission than that in life', declared the pronounced first prime
minister of Israel, David Ben Gurion, in 1949, in a debate about releasing married
women from compulsory military service.

These essentialist maternal qualities have been used by some theoreticians and
politicians, including many feminist thinkers and activists, to explain and justify
women's involvement in anti-war protest movements (Lorentzen and Turpin,
1998). The assumption inherent in these arguments is that the essence of
'woman' includes natural inflexible qualities resulting from her role (or potential
role) as a mother: a mother produces life and destroying it is against her nature.
A mother is used to providing care, to nourishing and nurturing, and therefore
will seek cooperation, and object to violence and the exploitation of power.
Universalistic notions suggest that through centuries of socialization, women
have become more equipped to resolving conflicts through peaceful means
rather than through competition and violence, which are more in line with
masculine norms of behaviour (Galblaum, 1997/8; Harris and King, 1989).
However, for maternal practice to become 'a natural resource for peace politics'
(Ruddick, 1989: 157), it needs to be transferred from the private lives of women,
to the public sphere of politics, as Azmon (1997) so rightfully states. Indeed, this
'motherist' posture has many manifestations and was the leading argument of
many of the women's peace movements of the century worldwide (York, 1998).

Although many argue over the notion of the essential peaceful nature of
women (Elshtain, 1987), their involvement in peace work in many countries
is well documented (Lorentzen and Turpin, 1998). Specifically, research on protest movements in Israel against war and occupation suggests that women's
involvement in them is significantly higher than their proportion in the popu-
lation at large, and that women also tend to establish their own movements
(Chazan, 1992). Over the past decade in Israel, such movements have included
'Mothers Against Silence' (protesting against the war in Lebanon), as well as
'Women in Black', 'Shani – Women Against the Occupation', 'Women for
Political Prisoners', 'Tandi – Democratic Women's Movement in Israel', 'Bat
Shalom' and others (all protesting against the occupation of the Palestinian
Territories). [...]

In an attempt to understand why women's movements and women's issues as
a whole have been either ignored or displayed in news coverage, Rakow and
Kranich (1991: 9) suggest that news is essentially a masculine narrative 'in which
women function not as speaking objects but as signs'. Their absence from the
public sphere and lack of status as authority figures legitimizes their common
presentation as ordinary people bearing the meaning of 'woman'. Their presentation in the news illustrates the consequences of public events rather than their
being political actors in those events. When women threaten the social order,
their actions are attributed to the nature of 'woman' and its essential personality

fault, their disruptive character and their inability to get along with each other. The recent growth of intimacy in news coverage, including intensified increased attention to human interest stories and personalization of political behaviours allows a growing visibility of women as news presenters, yet it does not guarantee the recognition of private sphere feminine values and perspectives as appropriate for a public sphere context (van Zoonen, 1991).

Given this framing of women's marginality in the public sphere and their relegation to the private one, the case of the Four Mothers movement is of particular interest. Here is a movement openly declaring itself as 'mothers' (rather than 'citizens'), although it has embraced interested fathers and encouraged others to join in, claiming their space in the national discourse on one of the burning issues on the public agenda – security of the northern border. How did the media portray this movement? How did coverage of its members and their messages present the 'voice' offered by motherhood in the rational debate over the future of Israel's presence in south Lebanon? What room is the female world allowed in the masculine discourse of power and dominance? These are the questions at the heart of this analysis on the portrayal of the Four Mothers movement in the Israeli press.

The study

A retrospective search of news items making overt and detailed references to Four Mothers resulted in a pool of 57 items, between February 1997 (time of the triggering accident) and April 1998 (two months following the one-year memorial and a period of public soul-searching). The news coverage included 17 news items, 16 in-depth articles and 24 personal commentaries and letters to the editors, in the three major daily papers (two popular and one quality press, 44 items in all) and from various local papers (13 in all). While the sample is clearly limited in scope and not all-inclusive (and therefore inappropriate for a systematic quantitative content analysis), it serves amply to delineate the dominant themes in the representation of Four Mothers in the public sphere.

Each item was analysed for the following: (1) the type of coverage (hard news; article; personal commentary), placement in the newspaper and salience (hard news/soft news sections; headline size; visuals; spread); (2) the main themes discussed in relation to Four Mothers (information; political opinions; issues of femininity and motherhood); (3) the nature of the discourse surrounding the phenomenon (emotional/rational; descriptive/supportive/critical; personal/ structural); and (4) the main themes hinted at in the headline and sub-headline and their relationship with the item as a whole (item expanding on the headline; headline irrelevant to the item; item contradictory to the headline).

In addition, in-depth interviews were conducted by one of the authors with the key leader of the group as well as with three additional central activists, concerning their perceptions of the movement's position in the general discussion over Israeli military presence in southern Lebanon and their unique position as women participants in this debate. Interviews were transcribed and analysed.

Analysis of newspaper coverage

The critical analysis of the newspaper coverage highlights several recurring themes suggesting a discourse of struggle with the infiltration of women into the public sphere through the framing of the Four Mothers movement's activities within the private sphere. The following suggests the discourse strategies through which this framing was achieved.

Naming and its essence

The first and most prominent theme is related to the naming of the movement 'Four Mothers', a label used by both the journalists and the members themselves. The first article to adopt this name appeared in a local paper, following the informal gathering of the four soldiers' mothers who initiated the protest against the drafting of young men to an unchallenged war. Since the article appeared just before the Passover holiday, when according to Jewish tradition the story of the exodus of the Jewish slaves from Egypt is celebrated and the four biblical Jewish mothers are mentioned, the journalist's choice of the symbolic title of 'Four Mothers' was timely. Ben-Dor, the initiator of the movement, recalls:

> We decided to adopt the name, but we didn't conceive that motherhood and femininity would serve our opponents as an opportunity to divert attention from the issue and dwell on us and on our name. We tried time and again to say that fathers and many good citizens are partners in our protest, but the exposure was mainly to us as a phenomenon. (interview, 21 July 1998)

Most of the newspaper items include a reference to this name in their titles: 'Mothers', 'What do mothers say in the days and in the nights', 'Mothers' voice', 'Four mothers and one war', 'A mother's plan', 'Ten mothers joined four mothers', 'Four mothers and a deputy minister', 'We all have mothers', 'The minister and the mothers', 'Girlfriends of soldiers join mothers', 'Mothers' war-games', 'Mothers and withdrawal plans'.

The titles' framing of this civil resistance to the war, as rooted in the dependency role of motherhood, strongly reflects the dominant theme in the articles themselves. Motherhood serves as the means of legitimizing these women, thereby validating their right to express their views and for the media practitioners to give them a voice.

As one article opens:

> When their sons were drafted to the Israeli Defense Forces [IDF], it was clear to the mothers that this is what needs to be done. Four mothers ... wiped their tears and knew that from this time on a new way of life begins for them: elite units, a life of worries from one leave to the next, relief when destiny skips over them, and a terrible pain when it did not skip over their friends. (Shneid, *Ma'ariv*, n.d.)

'We are mothers of soldiers in combat units who are serving or are going to serve in Lebanon', one mother is quoted to have said. 'The turnabout was the helicopter disaster. We decided we had to do something. We felt that we wanted to do something to help our children' (local northern paper, May 1997). 'I bore you, no slogan could convince me to sacrifice you', stated a known female media professional, in a personal commentary (Moskuna-Lerman, *Ma'ariv*, 19 January 1998).

Motherhood was often anchored as an irrational, highly emotional voice. Interviews with activists highlighted a discourse of feelings of love and caring. In one double-spread article, a few quotes are given prominence: 'Every day there is word of another friend who died. What do you do with the feeling that you are raising a child whose every need you took care of and who now is facing an existential problem?'; 'We pray for the safety of the soldiers, we hug them and love them. The nastiest saying is "You are weakening the soldiers". How can one say something like that to a mother?'; 'In one poster we wrote: "What do we get out of Lebanon? Only children in coffins"' (Shneid, *Ma'ariv*, n.d.). Many of the articles devoted space to lengthy descriptions of mothers' emotions, fears, prayers and sense of helplessness.

Interviews with activists highlighted their mixed feelings over the choice of this frame.

> It's a double edged sword ... all along they characterized us as mothers. ... It's true, I am guilty of being a mother, but come on, come listen to what I have to say. Leave that aside! All the time they latched onto the female thing rather than to the problem at hand. It allowed them to cling to the motherhood issues and not go in depth into the problem. It afforded them a way to escape the problem. On the other hand, it was a-political, a mothers' cry ... it worked ... it touched people somehow ... in their own relationships with their mothers, on the private level. (Ben-Dor, interview, 21 July 1998)

It also became clear from the interviews that the journalists actively chose to stick to the motherly frame. When referred to the official spokesman of the movement, they refused to interview him: 'They didn't want us to send a man – only a mother, who has a son in Lebanon. That's what the "ratings" dictated' (Ben-Dor, interview, 21 July 1998).

Motherhood was such an overriding meta-perspective attached to the movement and its message, that it even overrode the possibility of the common stereotypical treatment of women in the Israeli media in their sexual role. Nowhere in the reports was there a reference to the activists' appearance, beauty or dress code, so typical of women's portrayals, including those of women politicians. The surprising absence of the sexual overtone suggests that the 'motherhood' anchor of the 'Madonna–Whore' dichotomy was the overriding frame in the coverage, leaving no breach for alternative interpretations.

Motherhood as a source of delegitimization

Motherhood serves as a double-edged sword, since it is also the major source of delegitimizing the arguments put forward by the movement. Mothers were presented as egocentric, emotional, inconsiderate members of society, worrying 'only' about the welfare of their own flesh and blood, and not about the common good of society. Such treatment was mainly expressed in private letters to the editors, commentaries and quotes from others in articles, but never explicitly stated by journalists themselves. 'As a father to three sons in this tiresome country, I want to say truthfully what I think about such articles of women who "send" their son to the army. When a person does not learn to control his [sic] fears, he [sic] clings to slogans', writes a citizen in response to a commentary in support of the Four Mothers (Fromkin, Ma'ariv, 19 January 1998). 'The attempt to camouflage a personal egocentric worry (although understood and justified), in ideological-moral arguments is too transparent and cannot deceive us', writes another male citizen (Zaharoni, Ma'ariv, 23 September 1997).

The opinion that mothers lack the skills, experience and knowledge to make judgements related to security matters was often stated. 'Mothers do not understand a thing about security', states a quote in a subtitle (Glikman, Yediot Acharonot, 3 February 1998). 'If we were men it would have been easier', confesses one of the activists, 'the male establishment has a hard time accepting us and reacts in sentences such as "what do you understand in logistics and strategy"' (Shneid, Ma'ariv, n.d.).

Interestingly enough, even the members of the movement themselves are sometimes quoted to concur with this line of argument: 'We do not pretend to be able to give advice regarding security, but we are sure that there are other options to guarding the northern border' (Glikman, Yediot Acharonot, 3 June 1997).

This theme is highlighted by juxtaposing the irrational, non-experienced voice of mothers with that of the rational, experienced 'men'. In covering a major demonstration, the reporter describes: 'Besides mothers of soldiers, there were also fathers, senior reserve officers, and released soldiers, who were going to try to explain that there is an alternative to the IDF's stay in Lebanon' (Glikman, Yediot Acharonot, 3 June 1997). Interestingly enough, women who are not mothers are not even counted among participants in this gathering, the assumption being that only mothers of soldiers are involved, and not women as concerned citizens.

Similarly, the joining of men into the movement sheds a new light on the message put forward: 'Only fathers talked in an assembly of Four Mothers', states a headline, followed later in the article by a protest quote from one of the movement's representatives. '"I insist that there will also be time for women to talk ... the fact that I wasn't a pilot or a fighter in the military – that doesn't mean I don't have something to say."' Following a detailed description of the various opinions expressed by men in this gathering, the article continues:

> Only toward the end of the conference, when the last of the men had had his say, did a few women approach the microphone and express their opinions. In the next conference, that's what the organizers promised, mothers and

women too will be invited to join the parade of speakers. (Am-Ad, *Ha'Kibbutz*, 27 November 1997)

While this report criticizes the silencing of the women, the journalists themselves add to it through lengthy descriptions of the content of the men's speeches, and only stating that the spokeswoman for the movement 'spoke', with no reference to the content of her speech. Similarly, a different article suggests that the women initiated a debate, but the detailed explanations for withdrawal from Lebanon were reported based on the words of a male politician present at the meeting and not from the women's debate (Gavish, northern local paper, May 1997).

Not only were women described in terms of the voice of inexperience and irrelevant emotion, but attention was devoted to some of those who blamed them for betraying the national ethos by demoralizing the military and causing actual damage. A right-wing female Knesset member is quoted as saying:

The legitimacy of this case seems to me completely out of place. I don't think these women should have a monopoly or copyright over the opinions of dozen of thousands of soldiers, and speak in their name. Even if they had asked their own children, it is reasonable to assume that they would have a different opinion. I think it is very illegitimate these days to sow demoralization among soldiers when they are doing their job faithfully. (Shneid, *Ma'ariv*, n.d.)

Similarly, another right-wing political leader argued: 'All these calls for withdrawal from Lebanon cause unimagined damage. They hurt our deterrence abilities and they have no grounding in reality. It causes the terrorists to think that they can defeat us by putting pressure on us' (Rapapport, *Yediot Acharonot*, 7 April 1998). 'They are dancing over [the spilled] blood', 'They are the Hizbollah's agents', accused others (Ringel-Hoofman, *Ma'ariv*, 27 March 1998).

The Four Mothers' political challenge is thus perceived as a betrayal of the national ethos of strength and determination against all enemies, and treachery to national goals. As is often the case with protest movement (van Zoonen, 1996), the public discourse feeds back into the movement's self-perception and serves to cultivate their own identity. One of the activists shared her internal conflict on the issue of causing damage:

I, for one, when joining the movement at the beginning, I did it in secrecy, so the children wouldn't know, because I didn't know what their reaction would be. At a certain point I was also afraid that maybe our activity here could affect events somehow, that maybe the Hizbollah ... I thought maybe the Hizbollah want us out of there, and I thought that if they see that there is pressure here, they would attack even more forcefully so we would get out of there. So I said to myself that I am really endangering the soldiers. On the other hand, later I started understanding ... you need to believe that what you are doing is right. (Horovitz, interview, 10 November 1998)

Introductory patterns

One discursive mechanism through which Four Mothers members have been delegitimized in newspaper reports is through their presentation in dependency roles as mothers, devoid of professional titles and credentials, as has been recorded in previous research (Ariel, 1988; Lemish and Tidhar, 1991; Tidhar and Lemish, 1993). Most journalists reported on the activists by specifying their names, their place of residence (close to the Lebanese border) and the fact that they are mothers of combat soldiers. Rarely is there a reference to their profession or to their education. The reduction to their roles as mothers is in sharp contrast to the treatment of men joining the movement. [...]

An additional aspect of this pattern is the personal nature of the typical journalist interview, approaching the activists on a first name basis, stripping them of their titles and framing the discourse as a personal, informal exchange perceived appropriate in female discourse. This is in sharp contrast to the form of approach reported in interviews with men in relation to the movement and its activities.

Compartmentalization

Analysis of the various news items suggests that there is a strategy of compartmentalization in reports on Four Mothers in local newspapers, as well as within magazine sections of the major newspapers. It is characterized with a more 'human interest' and soft gossip type journalism than the reporting of hard news of central importance to society. This discursive strategy, common in the coverage of women politicians in Israel (Herzog, 1999) as well as elsewhere (Kahn and Goldenberg, 1991; Norris, 1997; Sapiro, 1993), serves to frame the movement within the private sphere, and to marginalize its calling.

This tendency is highlighted by the fact that the movement finds its way to the front pages mostly on those occasions when Four Mothers react to injury or to the death of soldiers, or when a prominent male leader (or the 'wife of' one) joins their protest. This was clearly expressed in interviews with members of the movement, as one activist attested:

> What happens now with the media is that the minute a soldier gets killed in Lebanon, they call us immediately and want an interview. But we don't want to be associated with a movement that wakes up only at times of bereavement ... because we are active all the time, but that is when the media seek us out. ... People who are against us conceptually say: 'They are mothers, and that's the way mothers feel and that's why they act like this'. That's why we often feel that we need the assistance of a military man, because it is very important to have someone that is perceived to understand what he is talking about. That's the kind of perception we have in this country. (Horovitz, interview, 10 November 1998)

Once more, women activists are denied a political voice in their own right, but gain it when they are joined by a legitimate mainstream one.

Displaying the womb – conflicting interpretations

The media coverage of Four Mothers, as in the case of other social movements, can be perceived as an instrument for realizing the movement's goals (van Zoonen, 1996). It assists in mobilizing a consensus for the ideas put forward by the activists, provides symbolic links to other political and social participants, strengthens the commitment and dedication of the members themselves and serves the process of collective identifying. At the same time, however, as has been documented in the case of other social activists, media–movement inter-actions are characterized by a process of limiting and restricting the group's collective identity in favour of the ideas that adhere to consensual political paradigms (van Zoonen, 1996). In this particular case, it is the framing of Four Mothers as a movement whose legitimacy derives from the private sphere. […]

How can such achievements be understood in light of what seems from the analysis presented herein to be consistent biases restricting the legitimacy of the movement? Possible answers include reference to the general weariness of the Israeli public of the war in Lebanon and the price it exacts, as well as the readiness of the political establishment to seek alternative solutions to the situation. The willingness thereby of several prominent male political leaders to jump on the bandwagon capitalizing the momentum, has certainly strengthened the movement significantly. This perspective assumes that Four Mothers has capitalized on existing changes in the political system and public opinion. However, a complementary interpretation suggests that Four Mothers served as a catalyst stimulating the public to put pressure on sympathetic politicians to express their silenced, non-popular ideas and therefore to break the mainstream 'spiral of silence' (Noelle–Neumann, 1974). We argue that the newspapers treated the phenomenon of Four Mothers within an easily acceptable frame of motherhood (private sphere), rather than the alternative threatening one of citizenship (public sphere). This form of news management allowed the incorporation of Four Mothers and the radical discourse of maternal resistance into mainstream consensual media discourse. This very process of seemingly depoliticizing women actually facilitated the voicing of a female political alternative. […]

Two clear perspectives can be drawn from the resonance that the Four Mothers movement has had in the public discourse.

In search of the 'civic' voice

The first suggests that the time is finally ripe to accept women's voice as a civic, rational voice, equal in its legitimacy and persuasive power to that of a man. This is clearly expressed in the commentary of an academic woman who moved to a political career:

> Being a mother and a wife is a wonderful thing, but this position has nothing to do with the public rights women have: those are derived from their status as citizens and it has nothing to do with their marital status. It is time in the State of Israel that women's opinions will be listened to on any issue, including that of foreign affairs and security, in their own right and not through the mercy of others. The time has come for women to allow themselves to express their opinions without the need for the sponsorship of the men in their lives. (Tamir, *Yediot Acharonot*, 15 January 1998)

According to this perspective, equality for women would mean accepting their arguments as genderless citizens. Playing on their femininity and unique perspective as mothers thus defeats the grand goal of claiming equal status. This frustration is expressed by one of the founding activists:

> What difference does it make if I am a mother? If what I am saying is true, why does it matter who said it? If I am a mother, does it mean that only the lower part of my body is functioning and the upper part not? Why does it connote shrieking and yelling? Being a mother is one of my functions that I am proud of, but it doesn't degenerate my brain! I am presenting the problem as a citizen. And I expect an answer. And what about the men? Are they completely disassociated from emotions? Only the rational works for them? Only the rational leads them to war? (Ben-Dor, interview, 21 July 1998)

This line of argument challenges the potential long-term contribution of Four Mothers to women's presence in the public sphere, as another feminist author suggests:

> The female voice in the public debate is not necessarily beneficial to both the political issue and the women's issue. ... Peace movements in Israel take upon themselves, in many ways, the traditional division of roles between the sexes: the boys fight, the girls pacify; the men speak in the name of global considerations, the women speak in the name of the private; the men produce violence, the women withdraw from conflict. ... To engage in politics in the name of the 'female voice' means to fixate ourselves in 'women's roles' ... is it women's right to express themselves in regard to security matters derived from their womb? ... does a woman who does not have children need to be silent when we talk of war and peace? 'Worried mothers', 'terrified mothers', 'hysterical mothers', are typical expressions through which politics can continue to ignore any woman who stands in the political debate in the name of motherhood. Well, the woman is hysterical. Let us stroke her head and resume talking about important matters. She continues to scream outside? Never mind, let her yell a bit if it makes her feel better. We all have mothers, we can understand. Significant political

influence is not going to grow from this, and it is very doubtful if it empowers the women as a public. (Hareven, *Ma'ariv*, 4 March 1998)

A similar perspective is suggested by Gillath's (1991) analysis of an earlier movement against the occupation of south Lebanon, 'Parents Against Silence' (dubbed by the media, 'Mothers Against Silence'), which was active from about 1983 until about 1985. This group too, according to Gillath, was perceived as one of worried mothers and not as a general anti-war movement. The activists themselves, after retiring from their specific mission, had not become involved with feminist or political organizations and did not attempt to realize their potential power beyond the limited timely goal. Political movements in the name of 'motherhood' had not, thus far, had a lasting impact on political life in Israel.

The legitimacy of the 'mother's' voice

The same argument is turned upside down by other writers, presenting a rival interpretation of the role Four Mothers has been playing. It suggests that being women is indeed the source of a different kind of strength, and a different kind of logic.

The revolt, if we may call it so, is not against the military service of the children ... but against the unwillingness of the establishment, mostly male, to listen seriously and with respect to the female calling, that is certainly coming out of a different place. Somebody said it is coming from the womb. That is a very good and respectable place to come from ... there is room for logic that comes from the womb, and not only for logic that comes from combat experience ... women think differently from men, especially in issues of war and peace ... there is a need to bring the female perspective to the process of decision making. For us, women, to be able to fight over the female perspective, we have to liberate ourselves from the stigma with which we have been living for many years, that this perspective is inferior. (Paz-Melamed, *Ma'ariv*, n.d.)

One of the activists even suggests that this perspective is superior:

I have an advantage over the man, because he says 'I have to go to the army', that machismo, going to combat units, and those fathers who educate their sons to follow in their footsteps to combat ... to be loyal to your homeland, to your roots ... my feminist thinking is totally different ... I am the first one who needs to worry about this, and yell about it, and cry about it ... I gave life, you see, life ... because they are taking my son away from me and they are telling him go serve in the army, and serve in combat units, and maybe even forsake his life. I am the first one who has to say what she has to say. (Shpigel, interview, August 1998)

In their protest activities, women blur the distinction between the spheres. Although they act in the male-dominated military area, they bring to it values and issues which have been traditionally perceived as marginal to the discussion of foreign politics and security (Sasson-Levy, 1995). Indeed, many women who have infiltrated political life in Israel find it of value to present themselves as mothers. Motherhood provides them with the legitimacy of voicing their opinions, since they have already 'paid their traditional dues' to society. What they would otherwise not dare to voice, they are allowed to express 'as mothers'. This tactic has become an official strategy even in formal political life. Lemish and Tidhar (1999) have found, for example, that during the televised election campaign for national elections in 1996, 'women as mothers' was the dominant message across all parties. Women appeared with babies in their arms and children by their sides and as mothers who talked about their children as well as mothers who talked about children in general. In this capacity women spoke about peace, the future, education, equality, personal safety, poverty, religion, retirement, minorities, military service and more. It seemed that their roles as mothers officially provided legitimacy to their presence on the screen and to the message they were delivering. [...]

Conclusion: subversive playing to expectations

The fierce debate over the two perspectives among feminist journalists, professional commentators and the public at large clearly echoes the trap proposed by essentialism. This school of thought in feminist thinking assumes inherent personality differences between men and women: women are a priori nurturers and life-givers and therefore presumed to be more inclined towards anti-violent and pacifist views. As in the intellectual debate over essentialism, and its potential role in the oppression of women, the public debate too is torn over the essentialist qualities of the 'display of the womb' in the political discussion about the withdrawal from Lebanon. While the first perspective would measure the success of the movement by the gradual shift from the emotional 'mother's voice' to the 'civic' one, the second perspective is in search of the legitimization of the 'mother's voice' in its own right.

Both perspectives, however, would agree that Four Mothers gained legitimacy 'despite' its framing as the traditional 'mother's voice'. It is with this perception that we would like to take issue and suggest a rival interpretation: it is possible that Four Mothers' achievements were the result of working within the 'rules of the game' rather than going against them. In their non-threatening, legitimized and accepted roles as concerned mothers, life-bearers and caregivers, the public was willing to lend an ear to their message and was able to sympathize with their call. Since women are assigned the 'emotional work' in society, they, rather than men, are expected and have the right to publicly express vulnerable emotions such as fear and sadness (Mazali, 1997). Through these expressions they are also reflecting men's emotions, which are prohibited in the normative world of militaristic masculinity so typical of Israeli society. Mourning, lamenting and crying are almost always the behaviours of women, and as such, they are perceived as marginal to rational decisions and to practical lines of action. Women expressing their fear over the fate of their soldier-sons illustrate how crucial the military service is, how significant and important, a matter of life and death. A mother's anxiety and pain serve as a mirror to society's values. Public expressions of such anguish as is manifested in women's protests can therefore be seen as an extension of women's traditional role as 'mourners' rather than a revolutionary act of empowerment (Tidhar and Lemish, 1993; Lemish and Tidhar, 1999). As such, they are perceived as non-disruptive and acceptable and are allowed into the public discourse. [...]

The case study of Four Mothers thus raises the more general issue of the rhetoric of the female voice in the public sphere. The civic voice of women is allowed and expressed, among other things, through the discourse of motherhood. This is one possible process of gaining authority for the otherwise silenced female experience and worldview.

References

Ariel, M. (1988) 'Female and Male Stereotypes in Israeli Literature and Media: Evidence from Introductory Patterns', *Language and Communication* 8(1): 43–68.

Azmon, Y. (1997) 'War, Mothers, and a Girl with Braids: Involvement of Mothers' Peace Movements in the National Discourse in Israel', *Israeli Society Science Research* 12(1): 109–28.

Berkovitch, N. (1997) 'Motherhood as a National Mission: The Construction of Womanhood in the Legal Discourse in Israel', *Women's Studies International Forum* 20: 605–19.

Chang, C. and J. Hitchon (1997) 'Mass Media Impact on Voter Response to Women Candidates: Theoretical Development', *Communication Theory* 7(1): 29–52.

Chazan, N. (1992) 'Israeli Women and Peace Activism', pp. 152–61 in B. Swirski and Marilyn Safir (eds), *Calling the Equality Bluff*. New York: Pergamon Press.

Elshtain, J.B. (1987) *Women and War*. New York: Basic Books.

Galblaum, A. (1997/8) 'Women in Times of War and Peace', *Zmanim* 61: 14–25 (in Hebrew).

Gillath, N. (1991) 'Women Against War: "Parents Against Silence"', pp. 142–6 in B. Swirski and M. Safir (eds), *Calling the Equality Bluff*. New York: Pergamon Press.

Halevi, S. (1999) 'The Premier Body: Sarah Netanyahu and the Discourse of Womanhood in Israel', *National Women Studies Association (NWSA) Journal* 11(2): 72–87.

Harris, A. and Y. King (eds) (1989) *Rocking the Ship of State: Toward a Feminist Peace Politics*. Boulder, CO: Westview Press.

Herzog, H. (1998) 'More than a Looking Glass: Women in Israeli Local Politics and the Media', *Press/Politics* 3(1): 26–47.

Herzog, H. (1999) *Gendering Politics: Women in Israel*. Chicago, IL: Michigan University Press.

Kahn, K.F. and A. Gordon (1997) 'How Women Campaign for the U.S. Senate: Substance and Strategy', pp. 59–76 in P. Norris (ed.), *Women, Media and Politics*. Oxford: Oxford University Press.

Kahn, K.F. and E.N. Goldenberg (1991) 'Women Candidates in the News: An Examination of Gender Differences in U.S. Senate Campaign Coverage', *Public Opinion Quarterly* 55: 180–99.

Lemish, D. and C.E. Tidhar (1991) 'The Silenced Majority: Women in Israel's 1988 Television Election Campaign', *Women and Language* 14(1): 13–21.

Lemish, D. and C.E. Tidhar (1999) 'Still Marginal: Women in Israel's 1996 Television Election Campaign', *Sex Roles* 41(5/6): 389–412.

Lemish, D. and C.E. Tidhar (1999) '"Where Have All the Young Girls Gone?" The Disappearance of Female Broadcasters in War Times', *Women and Language* 22(2): 27–32.

Lorentzen, L.A. and J. Turpin (eds) (1998) *The Women and War Reader*. New York: New York University Press.

Mazali, R. (1997) 'I Refuse', *Noga* 32: 17–20 (in Hebrew).

Norris, P. (ed.) (1997) *Women, Media and Politics*. Oxford: Oxford University Press.

Rakow, L. and K. Kranich (1991) 'Woman as Sign in Television News', *Journal of Communication* 41(1): 8–23.

Ruddick, S. (1989) *Maternal Thinking: Towards a Politics of Peace*. London: The Women's Press.

Sapiro, V. (1993) 'The Political Uses of Symbolic Women: An Essay in Honor of Murray Edelman', *Political Communication* 10: 141–54.

Sasson-Levy, O. (1995) 'Radical Rhetoric, Conformist Practices: Theory and Praxis in an Israeli Protest Movement', *Shaine Working Papers* 1. Jerusalem: The Hebrew University, the Shaine Center for Research in Sciences (in Hebrew).

Sharoni, S. (1996) 'Gender and the Israeli–Palestinian Accord: Feminist Approaches to International Politics', pp. 107–26 in D. Kendiyoti (ed.), *Gendering the Middle East*. London: I.B. Tauris.

Tidhar, C.E. (1988) 'Women in Israel's Broadcasting Media and on Israeli Television', pp. 112–28 in Y. Kawakami (ed.), *Women and Communication in the Age of Science and Technology*. Tokyo: Atom Press.

Tidhar, C.E. and D. Lemish (1993) 'Women in the Intifada: The View of Television News Coverage', pp. 142–59 in A.A. Cohen and G. Wolfsfeld (eds), *Framing the Intifada: Media and People*. Norwood, NJ: Ablex.

York, J. (1998) 'The Truth about Women and Peace', pp. 19–25 in L.A. Lorentzen and J. Turpin (eds), *The Women and War Reader*. New York: New York University Press.

van Zoonen, L. (1991) 'A Tyranny of Intimacy? Women, Femininity and Television News', pp. 217–35 in P. Dahlgren and C. Sparks (eds), *Communication and Citizenship: Journalism and the Public Sphere*. London: Routledge.

van Zoonen, L. (1996) 'A Dance of Death: New Social Movements and Mass Media', pp. 201–22 in D. Paletz (ed.), *Political Communication in Action: States, Institutions, Movements, Audiences*. Cresskill, NJ: Hampton Press.

A Critical Review and Assessment of Herma[Chomsky's 'Propaganda Model'

Jeffery Klaehn

Introduction

The 'propaganda model' of media operations (henceforth PM) laid out and applied by Edward S. Herman and Noam Chomsky (1988) in *Manufacturing Consent: The Political Economy of the Mass Media* avows to the view that the mass media are instruments of power that 'mobilize support for the special interests that dominate the state and private activity' (Herman and Chomsky, 1988: xi). The model argues that media function as central mechanisms of propaganda in the capitalist democracies and suggests that class interests have 'multilevel effects on mass-media interests and choices' (Herman and Chomsky, 1988: 2). Media, according to this framework, do not have to be controlled nor does their behaviour have to be patterned, as it is assumed that they are integral actors in class warfare, fully integrated into the institutional framework, and act in unison with other ideological sectors, i.e. the academy, to establish, enforce, reinforce and police corporate hegemony.[1]

At least two commentators have referred to the PM as 'an almost conspiratorial view of the media' (Holsti and Rosenau, n.d.: 174). Herman and Chomsky (1988: xii) respond to this, stressing that the PM actually constitutes a *'free market analysis'* of media, 'with the results largely an outcome of the working of market forces'.

> With equal logic, one could argue that an analyst of General Motors who concludes that its managers try to maximize profits (instead of selflessly labouring to satisfy the needs of the public) is adopting a conspiracy theory. (Chomsky, 1982: 94)

The term 'conspiracy theory' implies secret controls that operate outside normal institutional channels. Herman and Chomsky's PM explains media behaviour in terms of institutional imperatives (see Rai, 1995: 42).[2]

Source: *EJC* (2002), vol. 17, no. 2: 148–182.

One can infer that there are three reasons why Herman and Chomsky violently reject the 'conspiracy' label. First, the term itself, 'conspiracy theory', is *precisely that*, a *label*, one that has been used as a means of dismissing the PM without granting a minimal presentation of the model or a consideration of evidence.[3] Second, Herman and Chomsky acknowledge that deliberate intent is in fact sometimes an intervening factor which can have intended and/or unintended outcomes, depending upon the specific case (see Herman, 1996a). The PM's own emphasis, however, is on patterns of media behaviour, in relation to institutional imperatives. The model itself assumes that patterns of media behaviour should be explained in structural terms, and not assume conspiracy. Third, Herman and Chomsky can be seen to presume that there are at least five major 'filtering' mechanisms which structure news content.[4] The authors also presume that deliberate intent ('conspiracy') and unconscious hegemony ('professional ideology') are for the most part unknowable and unmeasurable. Herman (2000) stresses that 'intent is an unmeasurable red herring'. Moreover, Chomsky writes that,

> The term 'conspiracy theory' is particularly revealing. I've always explicitly and forcefully opposed 'conspiracy theories,' and even am well known for that. … My work (and Ed Herman's, and others') is about as much of a 'conspiracy theory' as a study of GM that suggests that its management seeks to maximize profit and market share. But to the intellectual classes, to suggest that institutional factors enter into policy is like waving a red flag in front of a bull – for very good reasons.[5]

The PM can be seen to imply intent, and while it is not concerned with intervening processes, there is a vast scholarly literature specifically devoted to theorizing about the values, motivations and outlooks of individual editors, reporters and media commentators.[6] Herman and Chomsky postulate that the filter constraints have powerful unilinear effects, such that media 'interests' and 'choices' serve class interests on a consistent basis.

Herman and Chomsky (1988: 304) concede that the PM cannot account 'for every detail of such a complex matter as the working of the national mass media'. The authors acknowledge that several secondary effects are left unanalysed and cede that the PM is not concerned to analyse practical, organizational or mundane aspects of newsroom work.[7] At the same time, however, critics charge that the PM's overall view of media behaviour is in general deterministic and can be seen to be plagued by sociological reductionism.[8] The phrase 'manufacturing consent' encapsulates a functionalist logic. Herman (2000) has replied to both criticisms, declaring that, 'Any model involves deterministic elements' and, to those who have condemned the PM for presuming functional necessity, noting that while the PM explains patterns of media behaviour in terms of 'mechanisms and policies whereby the powerful protect their interests naturally and without overt conspiracy'.[9] Elsewhere, Chomsky writes that,

> The propaganda model does not assert that the media parrot the line of the current state managers in the manner of a totalitarian regime; rather, that the

media reflect the consensus of powerful elites of the state-corporate nexus generally, including those who object to some aspect of government policy, typically on tactical grounds. The model argues, from its foundations, that the media will protect the interests of the powerful, not that it will protect state managers from their criticisms; the persistent failure to see this point may reflect more general illusions about our democratic system. (Chomsky, 1989: 149)

The PM *is* to be distinguished from the 'gate-keeper model' of media operations. The PM does not assume that news workers and editors are typically coerced or instructed to omit certain voices and accentuate others. Rather, the model outlines circumstances under which media will be relatively 'open' or 'closed' (see Herman, 2000).[10] Whereas the PM is an 'institutional critique' of media performance (see Herman and Chomsky, 1988: 34), the gate-keeper model is principally concerned with micro-analysis and focuses on how decisions of particular editors and journalists influence news production and news selection processes (see White, 1964; Carter, 1958).

The kind of micro-analyses is not the task of the Propaganda Model. The model provides an overview of the system at work, making sense out of a confusing picture by extracting the main principles of the system. (Rai, 1995: 46)

Ericson et al. (1989: 378) point out that the instrumentalist underpinnings of the gate-keeper model are empirically unspecifiable due to 'variation in who controls the process, depending on the [particular] context, the types of sources involved, the type of news organizations involved, and what is at issue'. Thus, the gate-keeper model of media operations is generally regarded as overly simplistic (Cohen and Young, 1973: 19).[11] The PM acknowledges that journalists and editors do play central roles in disseminating information and mobilizing media audiences in support of the special interest groups that dominate the state and private economy. But the PM assumes that the processes of control are often unconscious. Its basic argument in this context is that meanings are essentially '*filtered*' by the constraints that are built into the system. Herman and Chomsky (1988: 2) argue that meanings are formed and produced at an unconscious level, such that conscious decisions are typically understood to be natural, objective, commonsense.[12] [...]

In presuming that media personnel act in ways that effectively serve the interests of dominant elites, however, 'the PM can be seen to infer structural processes by appealing to psychological processes in individuals.'[13] At the same time, it can be seen to presume various 'self-interested' or ideological motives from structural patterns in news coverage.[14] The PM argues that how events are analysed, represented and evaluated by the elite media effectively demonstrates the extent to which editors and reporters can be seen to have 'adapted' to constraints of ownership, organization, market and political power. It contends further that elite media interlock with other institutional sectors in ownership, management and social circles, effectively circumscribing their ability to remain analytically detached from other dominant institutional sectors.[15] [...]

The most glaring criticism of the PM that may be voiced in this context is that the model can be seen to take for granted yet still presume intervening processes. While it does not theorize audience effects, it presumes that news content is framed so as to (re)produce 'privileged' interpretations of the news which are ideologically serviceable to corporate and state monied interests. If one assumes that 'ideologically serviceable' means that the interpretations can and typically do propagandize and/or mislead audiences, then on logical grounds one can infer that the PM does in fact presume and expect that media do have consequential influence and effects.[16] The critic might charge that the model itself takes for granted that media content serves political ends in alleged myriad ways. 'It clearly implies that media effects are sometimes quite deliberately intended and presumes that media coverage does have consequential effects. At the same time, the model focuses exclusively on media content, rather than expanding its scope to studying media effects directly. Nor does it "test" actual beliefs and motivations of media personnel or seek to investigate the possible range of effects on government officials, lower-tier media or audiences.[17] A critic might charge further that 'Its preferred explanation relies not just on antecedent conditions of media (interests and outlooks coincident with other members of the dominant class) but of additional "intervening" processes which come between objective similarities of interest and outlook.'[18] This is not to dismiss its preferred explanation. 'Many who are familiar with Noam Chomsky's voluminous polemical writings on US foreign policy, for instance, agree that he provides circumstantial and other evidence thatdoes constitute 'proof' of hegemony and media complicity.' Concurrently, however, the critic might charge that 'the PM does infer self-interested or ideological motives (complicity, repressive tolerance) from structural patterns in news coverage and infers, and can be seen to explain away, structural processes by appealing to psychological processes in individuals.'[19] [...]

Herman and Chomsky concede that the PM does not explain 'everything' and in every context.[20] While it is true that the PM does not 'test' effects directly, 'it is important to note that this was not Herman and Chomsky's intention in the first place.[21] In fact, as highlighted earlier, 'they deliberately state that their PM is one that deals with patterns of media behaviour and performance, and not effects. It is equally true that some media models focus almost entirely on "audience effects" and largely ignore the structural dimensions which Herman and Chomsky emphasize.'[22] Active audience studies, for instance, emphasize micro-level analysis.

While conceding that there are 'important elements of truth and insights in active audience analysis', Ed Herman (1996b: 15) characterizes active audience studies as 'narrowly focussed and politically conservative, by choice and default'. Herman (1996b: 15) stresses that the focus on micro-issues of language, text interpretation, and gender and ethnic identity is 'politically safe and holds forth the possibility of endless deconstruction of small points in a growing framework of technical jargon'. [...]

Another criticism of Herman and Chomsky's PM is that it presumes that the ideas of a unified ruling class and ruling-class interests may be taken for granted as straightforward and relatively unproblematic.[23] The PM does assume class cohesion, and argues that mass media interlock with other institutional sectors. Moreover, it concedes that the powerful have individual objectives and acknowledges that these are manifest in disagreements over tactics. The PM assumes that elite institutional sectors share common interests and subscribes to the view that a unified ruling class and institutional nexus exist, with common political, economic and social interests.[24] The model presumes that media behaviour will reflect these interests. Media performance is understood as an outcome of market forces. [...]

The authors state that media serve to foster and enforce an intellectual and moral culture geared towards protecting wealth and privilege 'from the threat of public understanding and participation' (Chomsky, 1989: 14). Herman (2000) comments that, 'Because the propaganda model challenges basic premises and suggests that the media serve antidemocratic ends, it is commonly excluded from mainstream debates on media bias' (see also Herman, 1996a, 1999).

Herman and Chomsky's (1988) view of media as an ideological apparatus for dominant elites mirrors the thesis put forth by William Domhoff (1979) in his book, *The Powers That Be: Processes of Ruling Class Domination in America* (published nine years before *Manufacturing Consent*). Domhoff contends that there are four basic processes through which the ruling capitalist class 'rules': (1) the special interest process; (2) the policy formation process; (3) candidate selection; and (4) the ideological process. [...]

Herman and Chomsky argue that mass media behaviour is patterned and shaped by interlocks in ownership, common institutional imperatives and shared goals, market forces and internalized assumptions. The PM does not, however, argue that media are monolithic, or determined to the extent that they are entirely closed to dissent or debate.[25] It does not ignore dissent.[26]

> Whatever the advantages of the powerful ... the struggle goes on, space exists and dissent light breaks through in unexpected ways. The mass media are no monolith. (Herman, cited in Schlesinger, 1992: 308)

Elsewhere, in the final pages of *Manufacturing Consent*, Herman and Chomsky (1988: 306) make this same point, acknowledging that the 'system is not all powerful'.

> Government and elite domination of the media have not succeeded in overcoming the Vietnam syndrome and public hostility to direct US involvement in the destabilization and overthrow of foreign governments. (Herman and Chomsky, 1988: 306)

In conclusion, Herman and Chomsky's PM has been criticized for its basic assumptions regarding political economy, for its view of the major mass media as purveyors of ideologically serviceable propaganda, and for overall generalizability. Having introduced the article by overviewing several of the criticisms that have been levelled against the propaganda model, the article now provides a critical assessment and detailed review of the model itself.

A critical assessment and review of Herman and Chomsky's propaganda model

Herman and Chomsky's PM, initially referred to as a 'general theory of the Free Press', contends that America's elite agenda-setting media play an important role in establishing cultural hegemony, primarily by establishing a general framework for news discourse that is typically adhered to by lower-tier media.

For Herman and Chomsky, there is a clear demarcation between elite media – *The New York Times* and *The Washington Post* – and the 'quality press' – a term they use to refer to more 'populist' newspapers, such as *The Boston Globe*, *The Los Angeles Times* and *The Philadelphia Inquirer*, among others (Chomsky, 1987: 135).

Chomsky remarks that the extent to which ideological constraints typically relax varies according to the geographic proximity of particular media organizations to the centres of economic and political power.

> What happens in areas that are marginal with respect to the exercise of power doesn't matter so much. What happens in the centres of power matters a great deal. Therefore the controls are tighter to the extent that you get closer to the centre. (Chomsky, 1988: 629)

Within the geographic nexus of corporate–state power, however, Chomsky emphasizes that ideological control is typically extremely tight.

The PM contends that the agenda-setting media function as mechanisms of propaganda in several ways. The elite media determine what topics, issues and events are to be considered 'newsworthy' by the lower-tier media and establish the general premises of official discourse. Furthermore, elite media establish limitations on the range of debate and general boundaries for subsequent interpretation (Herman and Chomsky, 1988: 1–2).

> They determine, they select, they shape, they control, they restrict – in order to serve the interests of dominant, elite groups in the society. (Chomsky, cited in Wintonick and Achbar, 1994: 55)

Herman and Chomsky do not claim that media function only to circulate propaganda.[27] The PM, however, is concerned to describe 'the forces that cause the mass media to play a propaganda role' (Herman and Chomsky, 1988: xi–xii).

First and foremost, the PM constitutes an institutional critique of media performance. Herman and Chomsky argue that media serve the political and economic interests of dominant elites and charge that 'the workings of the media ... serve to mobilize support for the special interests that dominate the state and private activity' (Herman and Chomsky, 1988: xi). [...]

The PM argues that regularities of misrepresentation in news accounts flow directly from concentration of private power in society. It holds that elite media interlock with other institutional sectors in ownership, management and social circles, effectively circumventing their ability to remain analytically detached from the power structure of society, of which they themselves are an integral part. The net result of this, the authors contend, is self-censorship without any significant coercion. Media performance is understood as an outcome of market forces. [...] Herman and Chomsky tell us that the institutional nexus is extremely tight, such that media share close interlocks with the state and corporate sectors.

The PM argues that media serve 'political ends' by mobilizing bias, patterning news choices, marginalizing dissent, by allowing 'the government and dominant private interests to get their messages across to the public'[28] (Herman and Chomsky, 1988: 2).

According to this framework, media serve to foster and reinforce an intellectual and moral culture geared towards protecting wealth and privilege 'from the threat of public understanding and participation' (Chomsky, 1989: 14).

> The general picture is of a media machine acting as a self-regulating system where propaganda is produced voluntarily and in a decentralized way by media personnel who censor themselves on the basis of internalized sense of political correctness. (Rai, 1995: 46)

Market forces in action: the five 'filter elements' (constraints) explained

Herman and Chomsky (1988: 1–35) argue that the 'raw material of news' passes through a series of five interrelated filter constraints, 'leaving only the cleansed residue fit to print'. These filter elements continuously 'interact with and reinforce one another' and have multilevel effects on media performance (Herman and Chomsky, 1988: 2). The five filter elements are:

> ... (1) the size, concentrated ownership, owner wealth, and profit orientation of the dominant mass-media firms; (2) advertising as the primary income source of the mass media; (3) the reliance of the media on information provided by government, business, and 'experts' funded and approved by these primary sources and agents of power; (4) 'flak' as a means of disciplining the media; and (5) 'anti-communism' as a national religion and control mechanism. (Herman and Chomsky, 1988: 2)

The first filter constraint emphasizes that media are closely interlocked and share common interests with other dominant institutional sectors (corporations, the state, banks) (Herman and Chomsky, 1988: 3–14). As Herman and Chomsky point out: 'the dominant media firms are quite large businesses; they are controlled by very wealthy people or by managers who are subject to sharp constraints by owners and other market-profit-oriented forces' (Herman and Chomsky, 1988: 14).

The second filter highlights the influence of advertising values on the news production process. To remain financially viable, most media must sell markets (readers) to buyers (advertisers). This dependency can directly influence media performance.[29] Chomsky (1989: 8) remarks that media content naturalizes, reflecting 'the perspectives and interests of the sellers, the buyers, and the product' (see also Herman, 1999).

Herman (2000) contends that the relevance of the first and second filters have enhanced since *Manufacturing Consent* was first published:

> The dramatic changes in the economy, the communications industries, and politics over the past dozen years have tended on balance to enhance the applicability of the propaganda model. The first two filters – ownership and advertising – have become even more important.

The third filter notes that dominant elites routinely facilitate the news-gathering process: providing press releases, advance copies of speeches, periodicals, photo opportunities and ready-for-news analysis (Herman and Chomsky, 1988: 19). Thus, government and corporate sources are attractive to the media for purely economic reasons. Such sources are favoured and are routinely endorsed and legitimized by the media because they are recognizable and viewed as prima facie credible. Information provided to the media by corporate and state sources does not require fact checking or costly background research and is typically portrayed as accurate.

In sum, Herman and Chomsky highlight not only the symbiotic nature of the relationship between journalists and their sources, but the reciprocity of interests involved in the relationship. The third filter constraint stresses that the opinions and analyses that are expounded by corporate and state sources are adapted to dominant class interests and market forces (Herman and Chomsky, 1988: 23; see also Martin and Knight, 1997: 253–4). Cited by the corporate media as experts and/or 'authorized knowers', their opinions are often accepted without scrutiny. Dissenting views are frequently excluded from public forums. In this way, core assumptions that cannot stand up to factual analysis can find widespread support.

Herman and Chomsky stress that the nature of the symbiotic relationship between media and sources directly influences media performance. [...] Importantly, the authors contend that preferred meanings are structured into news discourse as a result of the dominance of official sources who are identified as 'experts'. In this way, news discourse 'may be skewed in the direction desired by the government and "the market"' (Herman and Chomsky, 1988: 23). Concurrently, the '*preferred*' meanings that are structured into news discourse are typically 'those that are functional for elites' (Herman and Chomsky, 1988: 23).[30]

Flak, the fourth filter, means that dominant social institutions (most notably the state) possess the power and requisite organizational resources to pressure media to play a propagandistic role in society. Herman and Chomsky (1988: 26) explain that:

> Flak refers to negative responses to a media statement or program. ... It may be organized centrally or locally, or it may consist of the entirely independent actions of individuals.

In sum, the authors maintain that there are powerful interests that routinely encourage right-wing bias in media (Herman and Chomsky, 1988: 27–8).

According to the PM, these filter constraints are the most dominant elements in the news production process, and they continuously interact with one another and operate on an individual and institutional basis (Herman and Chomsky, 1988: 2; Rai, 1995: 40). According to Herman and Chomsky, the filter constraints excise the news that powerful interests deem *not* fit to print. [...]

Herman and Chomsky state that these five filter constraints capture the essential ingredients of the PM. The authors argue that there is 'a systematic and highly political dichotomization in news coverage based on serviceability to important domestic power interests' (Herman and Chomsky, 1988: 35). Herman and Chomsky contend that this dichotomy is routinely observable in 'choices of story and in the volume and quality of coverage' (Herman and Chomsky, 1988: 35). They maintain that choices for publicity and suppression are bound to the five filter constraints just outlined. The authors argue that media shape public opinion by controlling how ideas are presented, and also by limiting the range of credible alternatives. [...]

Media: threatening democracy, inducing avoidance, self-indulgently hypocritical?

The PM argues that the elite agenda-setting media legitimize dominant ideological principles and social institutions by systematically defending the principal 'economic, social and political agendas' of dominant elites and social institutions (Herman and Chomsky, 1988: 298). In Chomsky's view, it is not surprising that they fulfil this function:

> If you look at the institutional structure of media and the pressures that act on them and so forth and so on, you would tend on relatively uncontroversial assumptions to expect that the media would serve this function.[31]

As noted, Herman and Chomsky's view of media as an ideological apparatus for elites mirrors the thesis put forth by William Domhoff (1979) in *The Powers That Be: Processes of Ruling Class Domination in America*. [...]

Like Herman and Chomsky, Domhoff stresses that the ideological network is both 'extremely diverse and diffuse' (Domhoff, 1979: 173), and such that media interact with other institutional sectors in circulating knowledge and shaping public opinion on a range of foreign policy and key domestic issues, such as the functioning of the economy (Domhoff, 1979: 179–83).[32]

It bears noting that Herman and Chomsky appropriated the phrase 'manufacturing consent' from the influential American journalist Walter Lippmann, who advocated consent engineering early in the 20th century. For Lippmann, the 'manufacture of consent' was both necessary and favourable, predominantly because, in Lippmann's view, 'the common interests' – meaning, presumably, issues of concern to all citizens in democratic societies – 'very largely elude public opinion entirely'. Lippmann postulated that 'the common good' ought to be 'managed' by a small 'specialized class' (Lippmann, cited in

Wintonick and Achbar, 1994: 40). Lippmann recommended that the role of the electorate – the 'bewildered herd', as he called them – be restricted to that of 'interested spectators of action' (Lippmann, cited in Rai, 1995: 23). Lippmann predicted that the 'self-conscious art of persuasion' would eventually come to preface every 'political calculation' and 'modify every political premise'. Lippmann stressed that consent engineering is not historically inconsistent with the overall 'practice of democracy'. […]

In 1947, in an article titled 'The Engineering of Consent', published in *The Annals of the American Academy of Political and Social Science,* Edward Bernays put forth a similar argument in support of 'the manufacture of consent'. Like Walter Lippman, Bernays declares that the interests of 'democracy' are particularly well served by 'the application of scientific principles and tried practices' to the 'the engineering of consent'. Bernays asserts that consent engineering is at the heart of democracy and characterizes it as 'among our most valuable contributions to the efficient functioning of society'. […]

Chomsky notes that the conception of democracy which underlies such doctrines is relatively consistent with the fundamental principles and ideals of America's founding fathers.

In his various political works Chomsky (1988: 679) frequently cites a statement made by John Jay – 'Those who own the country ought to govern it' – to illustrate this. John Jay was the first chief justice of the Supreme Court and president of the Constitutional Convention.

In translation, Chomsky remarks that 'we're subject to democracy of the marketplace'.

> It's a game for elites, it's not for the ignorant masses, who have to be marginalized, diverted, and controlled – of course for their own good. (Chomsky, cited in Wintonick and Achbar, 1994: 40)

According to Chomsky, the effectiveness of thought control in democratic societies owes much to the fact that ideological indoctrination is combined with a general impression that society is relatively open and free (Chomsky, 1982: 91f.). […] The PM argues that because 'thought control' is virtually transparent in democratic societies, the propaganda system is actually more effective and efficient than it is in totalitarian states.

This view of dominant social institutions as autocratic, oppressive, deterministic and coercive can be understood as the bedrock upon which the foundations of the PM are constructed. Herman and Chomsky, in arguing that the mass media mobilize support for corporate and state monied interests, contend that media play a key role in engineering or manufacturing consent. Thus, it is important to highlight their argument that media performance is 'guided' by dominant elites. Media content is directly relevant to the manufacture of consent. Herman and Chomsky (1988: 35) state that there is a 'systematic and highly political dichotomization in news coverage' that is 'based on serviceability to important domestic power interests'. They maintain that the propaganda function of the mass media is observable in choices of story selection, in the quantity and quality of coverage, and in modes of handling some stories as opposed to others. The authors explain that 'the modes of handling favoured and inconvenient materials (placement, tone, context, fullness of treatment) differ in ways that serve political ends' (Herman and Chomsky, 1988: 35). Thus, it is assumed that media content serves 'political ends', by 'mobilizing interest and outrage' and by generating interest and sympathetic emotion in some stories while directing attention away from others (Herman and Chomsky, 1988: 35). [...]

Nexus: interrelations of state and corporate capitalism and the corporate media

In sum, the PM constitutes an institutional critique of mass media. It highlights the multilevel ways in which money and power influence media performance, argues that media interests and choices routinely amount to propaganda campaigns, and suggests that media performance reflects the fact that dominant media firms share interlocking and common interests with other institutional sectors.

The PM assumes that dominant elites are the major initiator of action in society. They dominate economic decision-making processes, as well as the political processes.[33] As noted, the PM hypothesizes that elites share common interests and goals that are largely integrated.[34] Herman and Chomsky acknowledge that elites can disagree but stress that such disagreements are largely confined to tactics on how they can achieve common goals. Disagreement over tactics will be reflected in mass media discourse.

> The mass media are not a solid monolith on all issues. Where the powerful are in disagreement, there will be a certain diversity of tactical judgments on how to attain shared aims, reflected in media debate. But views that challenge fundamental premises or suggest that the observed modes of exercise of state power are based on systemic factors will be excluded from the mass media even when elite controversy over tactics rages fiercely. (Herman and Chomsky, 1988: xiii)

The PM acknowledges that a careful and thorough reading of the mass media will bear this out. However, 'the filter constraints are so powerful, and built into the system in such a fundamental way, that alternative bases of news choices are hardly imaginable' (Herman and Chomsky, 1988: 2). Furthermore, the PM holds that the illusion of genuine debate serves to reinforce the overall effectiveness of the propaganda system in society (Herman and Chomsky, 1988: 298). Chomsky remarks that:

> The more vigorous the debate, the better the system of propaganda is served, since the tacit, unspoken assumptions are more forcefully implanted. (Chomsky, 1982: 81)

While emphasizing its extensive reach and resiliency, Chomsky describes the propaganda system as 'inherently unstable', commenting that, 'Any system that's based on lying and deceit is inherently unstable' (Chomsky, 1987: 49). Even so, the authors contend that the filter constraints have powerful unilinear effects, such that media interests and choices serve class interests on a consistent basis.[35] [...]

Concluding remarks

Herman and Chomsky's institutional critique of media behaviour is forceful and convincing, as is their analysis of the ideological formation of public opinion and of the 'Orwellian' abuse of language in western democracies.

'Brainwashing under freedom' is Chomsky's catchphrase for the hypocrisy of western liberal opinion and its relationship to power.

The thesis put forth in *Manufacturing Consent,* that consent in a 'free society' is manufactured through manipulation of public opinion, perhaps even more now than when their book was originally published, bespeaks journalistic self-censorship in an era in which corporate ownership of media has never been as concentrated, right-wing pressure on public radio and television is increasing, the public relations industries are expanding exponentially, and advertising values dominate the news production process.[36] If ever there was a time for the PM to be included in scholarly debates on media performance, it is now.

This paper is dedicated to the memory of Suzanne Kondratanko (3 March 1974–11 September 2001).

Notes

I wish to thank Dr Valerie Scatamburlo-D'Annibale, Department of Communication Studies, University of Windsor, for her insightful feedback.

1. This view echoes Miliband, who wrote that:

    There is nothing particularly surprising about the character and role of the major mass media in advanced capitalist society. Given the economic and political context in which they function, they cannot fail to be, predominantly, agencies for the dissemination of ideas and values which affirm rather than challenge existing patterns of power and privilege, and thus to be weapons in the arsenal of class domination. (Miliband, cited in Clement, 1975: 278)

2. In *Chomsky's Politics,* Milan Rai (1995: 42) remarks: 'If the explanation is based on the nature of institutions, not the machinations of individuals, it cannot, by definition, be given the name "conspiracy theory".'
3. Herman (2000) takes this up in 'The Propaganda Model: A Retrospective'.
4. It bears mentioning in this context that Herman was the principal author of the first chapter of *Manufacturing Consent,* in which the filter mechanisms are laid out. A new edition of the book, with a new introduction, was published in January 2002.
5. Personal correspondence, 8 December 1998.
6. For analysis of the influence of owners and media professional ideals on news discourse see Gans (1979) and Tuchman (1978).

7. Chomsky (1982: 14) does, however, acknowledge seductions of privilege.

8. Personal correspondence, Dr Peter Archibald, Sociology, McMaster University, Hamilton, Ontario, Canada, November 2001.

9. Edward Herman (2000) adds that, 'This would seem to be one of the model's merits; it shows a dynamic and self-protecting system in operation.'

10. Specifically, when elites are divided over tactics, 'space' is created, allowing room for debate (see Herman, 2000). Hackett (1991: 281) also points out that dissent is likely to find expression in the major mass media only when certain conditions are met. These conditions, however, can be seen to favour the explanatory logic of the PM.

11. Despite the gate-keeper model's theoretic inadequacies, Hackett (1991: 98) states that it is an appropriate description of the work that newspaper editors actually do 'with regard to news about national and international affairs: They select and disseminate, rather than generate, such news'.

12. Stuart Hall explains that preferred codes are 'rendered invisible by the process of ideological masking and taking-for-granted. ... They seem to be, even to those who employ and manipulate them for the purposes of encoding, simply "the sum of what we already know"' (Hall, cited in Winter, 1991: 44).

13. Personal correspondence, Dr Peter Archibald, September 2001.

14. Personal correspondence, Dr Peter Archibald, November 2001.

15. Other scholars contend that media are far more pluralistic. Doyle et al. (1997: 243) state that 'media are more open, pluralistic, and diverse than the more pessimistic dominant ideology suggests'.

16. Personal correspondence, Dr Peter Archibald, November 2001.

17. Personal correspondence, Dr Peter Archibald, November 2001.

18. Personal correspondence, Dr Peter Archibald, November 2001.

19. Personal correspondence, Dr Peter Archibald, November 2001.

20. No one theory is all-encompassing, but this does not detract from the fact that the PM can still be effective in certain cases.

21. Personal correspondence, Dr Valerie Scatamburlo-D'Annibale, November 2001.

22. Personal correspondence, Dr Valerie Scatamburlo-D'Annibale, November 2001.

23. Chomsky (1997a: 61) prefers not to use the term 'ruling class', thinking it insufficient for serious class analysis. Instead, he prefers the term 'elites' or 'dominant elites', but concedes that because 'political discourse is so debased', it is only possible to 'talk vaguely about the establishment', or about 'people in the dominant sectors'.

24. The debate here effectively mirrors the Marxist response to the liberal-bourgeois thesis within Canadian sociology.

25. At the same time, however, Herman and Chomsky (1988: 301) do state that media behaviour is determined, to the extent that most mass media are themselves interlocked with the ruling bloc.

26. In *Media Control: The Spectacular Achievements of Propaganda*, Chomsky stresses that dissent culture continues to thrive, despite the structural forces present in the mainstream media. This is echoed, strongly, by Herman (1996a, 2000) who states that critics often fail to recognize that the PM is 'about how the media work, not how effective they are'.

27. In the Preface to *Manufacturing Consent* Herman and Chomsky (1988: xi) note that: 'We do not claim this is all the mass media do, but we believe the propaganda function to be a very important aspect of their overall service.'

28. Herman and Chomsky (1988: xii) describe the PM as a 'guided market system' within which the *guidance* is 'provided by the government, the leaders of the corporate community, the top media owners and executives, and the assorted individuals and groups who are assigned or allowed to take constructive initiatives'.

29. Cohen and Young (1973: 16); Clement (1975: 280–1); Martin and Knight (1997: 253); Bagdikian (1983: 160–73); Lee and Solomon (1990: 65–72); Nelson (1989).

30. Herman (2000) writes that 'Studies of news sources reveal that a significant proportion of news originates in public relations releases. There are, by one count, 20,000 more public relations agents working to doctor the news today than there are journalists writing it.'

31. Source: transcript, 'Noam Chomsky Meets the Washington Press', National Press Club, DC, 11 April 1989, p. 2.

32. Domhoff (1979: 57) asserts that the sum total of special interest is class rule, i.e. 'what is *not* done and *not* debated defines ruling-class domination even if the class as a whole does not act consciously to realize its will and to subordinate other classes'.
33. See Chomsky (1988: 189) for a qualification.
34. For Chomsky there is a clear demarcation between the state and the government. Chomsky asserts that the state comprises, institutions that set the conditions for public policy and is relatively stable. The state constitutes, the actual nexus of decision-making power ... including investment and political decisions, setting the framework within which the public policy can be discussed and is determined (Chomsky, 1985: 230). In contrast, Chomsky views government as more visible, consisting of 'whatever groups happen to control the political system, one component of the state system, at a particular moment' (Chomsky, 1985: 230).
35. As noted above, Chomsky clearly distinguishes the state from the government. The PM would explain hegemonic crises or shifts in political alignment, i.e. the massive defeat of the post-Mulroney Tories, in this context. Government is a visible and inherently transitory organ of the state. In contrast, the state, which Chomsky identifies as the actual nexus of decision-making power in the society, is remarkably stable in comparison.
36. See Herman (1996a, 2000) for a detailed discussion of the enhanced relevancy of the PM.

Bibliography

Carter, R. (1958) 'Newspaper Gatekeepers and their Sources of News', *Public Opinion Quarterly* 22: 133–44.

Chomsky, Noam (1973) *For Reasons of State*. London: Collins.

Chomsky, Noam (1979) *Language and Responsibility*. Hassocks: Harvester Press.

Chomsky, Noam (1982) *Towards a New Cold War: Essays on the Current Crisis and How We Got There*. London: Sinclair Browne.

Chomsky, Noam (1985) *Turning the Tide: US Intervention in Central America and the Struggle for Peace*. London: Pluto.

Chomsky, Noam (1987) *The Chomsky Reader*, ed. James Peck. New York: Pantheon.

Chomsky, Noam (1989) *Necessary Illusions: Thought Control in Democratic Societies*. Toronto: CBC Enterprises.

Chomsky, Noam (1992a) *Deterring Democracy*. New York: Hill and Wang.

Chomsky, Noam (1997a) *Class Warfare*, Interviews with David Barsamian. Vancouver: New Star.

Chomsky, Noam (1998) *The Common Good*, Interviews with David Barsamian. Berkeley, CA: Odonian.

Clement, W. (1975) *Canadian Corporate Elite: Analysis of Economic Power*. Toronto: McClelland and Stewart.

Cohen, Bernard C. (1963) *The Press and Foreign Policy*. Princeton, NJ: Princeton University Press.

Cohen, Stanley and Jack Young (eds) (1973) *The Manufacture of News: Social Problems, Deviance and Mass Media*. London: Constable.

Domhoff, William G. (1979) *The Powers That Be: Processes of Ruling Class Domination in America*. New York: Vintage Books.

Doyle, Aaron, Brian Elliot and David Tindall (1997) 'Framing the Forests: Corporations, the BC Forest Alliance, and the Media', pp. 240–68 in William K. Carroll (ed.), *Organizing Dissent: Contemporary Social Movements in Theory and Practice*, 2nd edn. Toronto: Garamond Press.

Ericson, Richard V., Patricia Baranek and Janet Chan (1989) *Negotiating Control: A Study of News Sources*. Toronto: University of Toronto Press.

Gans, H. (1979) *Deciding What's News*. New York: Pantheon.

Garnham, Nicholas (1990) *Capitalism and Communication: Global Culture and the Economies of Information*. London: Sage.

George, A. (ed.) (1991) *Western State Terrorism*. New York: Routledge.

Hackett, R. (1991) *News and Dissent: The Press and the Politics of Peace in Canada*. Norwood, NJ: Ablex.

Herman, Edward S. (1996a) 'The Propaganda Model Revisited', *Monthly Review* July.

Herman, Edward S. (1996b) 'Postmodernism Triumphs', *Z Magazine* January: 15–17.

Herman, Edward S. (1999) *The Myth of the Liberal Media: An Edward Herman Reader*. New York: Peter Lang.

Herman, Edward S. (2000) 'The Propaganda Model: A Retrospective', *Journalism Studies* 1(1): 101–12.

Herman, Edward S. and Noam Chomsky (1988) *Manufacturing Consent: The Political Economy of the Mass Media*. New York: Pantheon.

Holsti, Ole R. and James N. Rosenau (n.d.) *American Leadership in World Affairs*. Boston, MA: Allen and Unwin.

Lee, M. and N. Solomon (1990) *Unreliable Sources: A Guide to Detecting Bias in the News Media*. New York: Carol.

Martin, Michele with Graham Knight (1997) *Communication and Mass Media: Culture, Domination and Opposition*. Toronto: Prentice-Hall.

Nelson, J. (1989) *Sultans of Sleeze: Public Relations and the Mass Media*. Toronto: Between the Lines.

Rai, Milan (1995) *Chomsky's Politics*. New York: Verso.

Tuchman, Gaye (1978) *Making News: A Study in the Construction of Reality*. New York: Free Press.

White, David M. (1964) 'The Gatekeeper: A Case Study in the Selection of News', in L.A. Dexter and D.M. White (eds), *People, Society and Mass Communications*. New York: Free Press.

Winter, J. (1991) *Common Cents*. Montreal: Black Rose.

Wintonick, Peter and Mark Achbar (1994) *Manufacturing Consent: Noam Chomsky and the Media*. Montreal: Black Rose.

Section Four

Journalism

<hr>

12 The Sacred Side of Professional Journalism

Thorbjörn Broddason

The idea of sacredness as a key element in the maintenance of social cohesion has been one of the best-established fixtures of sociological thought since its introduction by Emile Durkheim (1976/1915). In this paper the idea is discussed that some occupations, journalism being one of them, are invested with sacredness while others are not. It will be argued that the sacredness of occupations derives from a combination of sources, the most important being the mysteriousness of exclusive, but vital knowledge and the nobleness of self-sacrifice. My argument suggests also that if we add the dimension of sacredness to current definitions of professionalism we shall have improved our understanding of this latter concept and increased its usefulness in sociological discourse. I shall, in other words, attempt to demonstrate that a profession is a sacred occupation in the Durkheimian sense.

The prolific sociological literature of recent decades on professionalism abounds with definitions of the concept, most of which include exclusive knowledge and self-sacrifice as core items but do not explicitly take into account the mysterious or sacred aspect. Thus, Armstrong (1990: 691) lists esoteric knowledge and a service ideal as 'essential' professional attributes while Wilensky (1964: 140) notes that the 'service ideal is the pivot around which the moral claim to professional status revolves'. According to Goode (1970: 28): '... the two generating qualities are (1) a basic body of abstract knowledge and (2) the ideal of service.' Freidson (1986: 123), while acknowledging the service aspect, lays heaviest emphasis on 'gaining a living by virtue of possessing credentials based on higher education'. Abbott (1988: 318) concludes that '... a firm definition of profession is both unnecessary and dangerous ...' and notes laconically that the 'tasks of professions are human problems amenable to expert service' (Abbott, 1988: 35). Although admirably simple, this statement is too indiscriminate as it

Source: *EJC* (1994), vol. 9: 227–248.

stands. The following is a representative example of a more comprehensive definition of professionalism: Collective control over entry to the group; a code of altruistic service, supported by scrupulous self-policing; a special set of skills based on the absorption of a definable body of knowledge and a set of 'client-type' relationships with the public (Smith, 1980: 153). [...]

The idea I wish to pursue – that there is a sacred aspect to all true professions – is not explicit in those analyses I have come across, but some authors appear to acknowledge it at least indirectly (Bakewell and Garnham, 1970: 305; Gans, 1980: 293; Parsons, 1968: 537). A main objective here is to clarify the position of journalism, an occupation with strongly contested claims to professional status. This will be done with reference to two other occupations with long-established professional credentials – the clergy and medicine.

The Sacredness of Professions

The mysteriousness of esoteric but supposedly essential knowledge is clearly manifested in the offices of religious functionaries in historic societies and among so-called primitive peoples: they possess knowledge which is denied others and, as this knowledge is thought essential for the well being of individuals and the community at large, these leaders wield significant power over their fellow human beings.[1] We also find among the clergy evidence of another main source of reverence, that is, the nobility of self-sacrifice: the priestly vocation is very much defined in terms of sacrificial service to others. [...] I have taken the priesthood as the point of departure for my argument concerning sacred occupations, not necessarily because the clergy should be considered to be the best contemporary example of such groups, but rather because through it the essence of the sacred occupations can easily be recognized. [...]

Has professional power, then, been secularized? Is it more 'worldly' than it used to be? That is not my conclusion; I argue that the sacred aspect of the power and service of professionalism is present in modern industrialized societies, but that it has largely been transferred from the clergy to other occupational groups, one of which – mass communication – I now consider more closely. This view is inspired by Thomas Luckmann's argument that 'religion is present in non-specific form in all societies and all "normal" (socialized) individuals' (1967: 78) and that 'what are usually taken as symptoms of the decline of traditional Christianity may be symptoms of a more revolutionary change: the replacement of the institutional specialization of religion by a new social form of religion' (Luckmann, 1967: 90–1). [...]

The Sacredness of Journalism

There is nothing original in pointing out the religious aspects of mass communication. Bakewell and Garnham (1970) named their book on British Television, *The New Priesthood*, and Altheide and Snow (1979: 199) write: 'Since the eighteenth-century enlightenment period in Europe, media gradually have replaced religion as the dominant institutions in western society'. Gans (1980: 293) acknowledges the analogy with religion but warns against taking it without 'a large grain of salt'. Dayan and Katz (1992: 7) speak of 'the reverence and ceremony' associated with media events and 'the almost priestly role played by journalists' on particular occasions. There is also a long-standing debate about professionalism in the mass media (Beam, 1988; Dennis, 1989; Goldstein, 1985; Olen, 1988; Schudson, 1988; Smith, 1980). However, the tie between sacredness and professionalism in mass communication has received little attention. For the sake of simplicity, I now focus exclusively on the mass media in their capacity as sources of news, political and otherwise. I should also concede at this point that my argument is primarily aimed at 'quality' newspapers and other media with public service pretensions.

Information about events that occur beyond the sphere of personal experience is clearly valuable to ordinary persons in industrial democracies. In sharp contrast, individuals and societies in former, pre-industrial, predemocratic, times could manage without information about events that occurred beyond their immediate existence. In other words, what they could not experience by means of their own senses or gather through local gossip was of little more than curiosity value. This was so for two reasons: first, simple societies are self-sufficient to a high degree and do not depend on other societies for their subsistence; and second, those events in far-away places which might affect them were so completely outside their control that it mattered very little whether they received advance news or not.

All this changed in the wake of the Age of Discovery and the Industrial Revolution. In modern times self-sufficiency is virtually unattainable for any one society. Any spot on earth may be immediately affected by an economic, political or military decision taken by a state on the other side of the globe. Hence, the relevance of events to a particular nation is no longer inversely related to their distance from that nation.[2] Add to this the basic assumption of democracy that every member of society should carry his or her share of the responsibility for political decisions and we are bound to conclude that news belongs to 'human problems amenable to expert service' (Abbott, 1988: 35). Without news we could neither exercise our political rights nor fulfil our political obligations (Thurén, 1989). In this sense the modern journalist resembles the priest of former times who held the key to our salvation. Thus, I think it is well established that newsgatherers and newscasters 'serve the vital needs of man'. But are we getting 'expert service' from the news media? The answer is affirmative in terms of special skills (technical or practical), but a 'definable body of knowledge' possessed by newspeople probably does not exist.[3] Indeed, journalism is considered by some to be typical of occupations that 'seem to be less suitable to professionalization than others ... because the knowledge they require is not easily expressed and transmitted in theoretical form' (Kocka, 1990: 69). Although a growing proportion of newspeople are graduates of schools of journalism or similar institutions, a 1984 report (echoing, as it might seem, the lamentations of 19th-century critics of medicine) concluded that 'the general state of journalism and mass communication education is dismal' (quoted by Goldstein, 1985: 162). Mass communicators do not exercise 'collective control over entry to the group' nor are they ever likely to gain such control, as it would be irreconcilable with the doctrine of the freedom of the press. While it would be difficult to maintain the proposition that every mass communicator abides by 'a code of altruistic service, supported by scrupulous self-policing', it is nevertheless true that there exists among newspeople an awareness of a unique responsibility towards the general public. The strength of this awareness is a key factor in deciding the issue of professionalism and sacredness. As regards '"client-type" relationships with the public' these definitely do exist, but they are shaped by their corporate character in the sense outlined by Abbott (1983: 856; see also Goode, 1970: 47).[4]

There is no dearth of authoritative statements denying professional status to journalists. Thus Goldstein (1985: 162) states flatly that 'journalism is not a profession' and, according to Olen (1988), '... journalism is not a profession ... more important, it should not be one ... Freedom of the press ... is not a right that belongs to the *institution* of journalism'. This argument seems to miss the point as there is no reason to contrast the responsibilities of journalists with the question of freedom of the press. Kepplinger and Köcher (1990: 307) contend that '... journalists cannot really be counted among the professional class. In contrast to members of the professions, journalists can behave in an extremely selective manner toward themselves and toward third parties'. This is highly debatable. First, it might be argued that 'members of the professions' are allowed some selectivity as regards their occupational behaviour and second, it could be argued that journalists who take their work seriously are expected to deal with certain issues in certain ways and will ignore them at their peril. Merrill (1988) considers characteristics of a 'profession' to be 'restrictive factors' and comes to the conclusion that such professionalizing factors[5] as he dealt with 'are prone to discipline the press, to keep it in line, to regiment it and ultimately place it under increasing control'. Merrill is right, but only because he is highly selective in his choice of 'professionalizing factors'. Smith (1980: 153) maintains that the 'key criteria of professionalization are missing' with regard to journalism in the West. Windahl and Signitzer (1992: 128) claim without reservation: 'Research has shown ... that journalists may attain only semi-professional status because, among other reasons, their knowledge base does not command the same respect as does that of occupational groups such as civil engineers'.[6]

On the other hand, according to McQuail (1992: 186): 'A ... factor at work in the historical development of modern news was the rise of a journalistic *profession*, which has entailed a claim to autonomy, a promise of some ethics of performance and of certain standards of service'. Lichter et al. (1986: 27) also recognize that change is in the air: 'In keeping with their newfound status, leading journalists are increasingly likely to see themselves as professionals who translate the news rather than craftsmen who merely transmit it'. Finally, considering how programme staff of the BBC use the word 'professional' to imply the invocation of some moral order which endows them with a legitimacy and authority, distinguishable from loyalty to the organization or compliance with outside demands, Tom Burns (1977: 126) finds that 'professionalism of the broadcaster can be regarded as having supplanted the idea of public service as it was defined and established under Reith, and as it was developed during the thirties and forties'. As the idea of public service has definitely not been abandoned, however, a proper reading of this observation seems to be that professionalism and a redefined idea of public service are not only compatible, but mutually supportive. According to Rosengren et al. (1991: 70) there is indeed 'some reason to believe that public service broadcasting is conducive to professional quality in programming'.[7]

Although newspeople fall short on some of the previously listed professional requirements, they satisfy other important ones, especially the one referring to the service of vital needs. In accordance with this, the public has begun treating mass communicators with veneration and trust which closely resembles that bestowed on ministers and doctors and their paraphernalia. This veneration, in all three cases, as it rises or recedes, can be understood with reference to the concept of sacredness as it is defined by Durkheim. Such an understanding emphasizes the integrative role of the mass media.[8] If we want to carry the analogy with traditional religion further it must be recognized that we do not construct temples, comparable to cathedrals and hospitals, for the public worship of the mass media; we do, however, dedicate one corner – or even a whole room – in every one of hundreds of millions of homes to the TV set and we gather in front of it daily, in a ritualistic manner, in order to reaffirm and update our picture of the world. The particular time which is devoted to news on television may even be referred to as 'a sacred hour', distinct from other parts of the daily programme which, not being as relevant to our continued existence, may be treated less reverently. When the news slot is desecrated by the news reporters themselves, as occasionally happens, for example, with so-called news recreations, there is no lack of indignant responses and even outrage.[9] This is comparable to public reactions to sinning priests and malpractising doctors.

Newspeople, much like priests and doctors, must put up with long and irregular working hours and their work never leaves them (Broddason et al., 1987). That their work can be extremely hazardous is manifested in the fate of journalists who have paid with their lives for their efforts to expose corrupt or tyrannical conditions.[10] Thus, there seems little doubt that many journalists provide 'altrustic service' and even reveal a nobleness of self-sacrifice. However, it is acknowledged that under authoritarian or tyrannical conditions there is no shortage of journalists who run the errands of the rulers. Clearly, they do not meet the standards of professionalism, no more in fact than doctors, judges or clergy who abuse their calling by turning their knowledge and power to the service of despots.

If our salvation in the here-after is one of the chief concerns of the clergy, and our health and longevity in the temporal sense is the preoccupation of the doctors, and the success of these professions in their respective fields explains their elevated status, what then lies at the bottom of the trust and veneration afforded journalists? I have already mentioned their role as identifiers and mediators of vital information for the democratic process.[11] Taking this point to its logical conclusion, it could be argued that respect for mass communicators rests on the belief that they are key agents in averting the imminent environmental disaster brought upon us by the very scientific progress that was supposed to solve all our problems.

It could be said that newspeople cannot be motivated by altruism as they frequently manifest contrary tendencies, such as spite, vengefulness and deceit. My answer to this is that these are malpractices which are uniformly condemned while there is an ongoing vigorous debate about the ethical boundaries media people must observe in the pursuit of their calling.[12] It could also be argued that the press is not held in high esteem by the general public and indeed some social surveys seem to confirm this (Harris, 1984; Lambeth, 1986: vii), while others do not. For instance Kepplinger and Köcher report that 'the German public today puts greater trust in journalists, when assessing nuclear energy, than in experts ...' (1990: 305) and that 'in the United States ... the population ascribes a higher degree of effectiveness and integrity to the different mass media than to the different political institutions' (1990: 286). Summarizing the findings of a number of researchers examining changing values in western industrial nations, Kepplinger and Köcher conclude: 'Because of the general significance of the mass media, journalists are important, if not the most important, transmitters of changed values' (1990: 289). Perhaps the integrating and sacred functions of the mass media are best demonstrated by the status of American network television anchors who seem to have established a standing even above politicians (Robinson and Kohut, 1988). This could account for the pronounced irreverence with which established broadcasters frequently treat members of the political elite.[13] The profound shaking of the House of Windsor by the UK mass media is particularly noteworthy in this context.

[...] [T]he introduction of computers will drastically alter the working conditions [...] of journalists and other mass communicators. Jaspin (1989) demonstrates how the skilful handling of computerized information can dramatically add power to the watchdog role of investigative journalism. In the short or medium term, it seems to me that the computerization of journalism might well speed up the professionalization of the occupation,[14] depending on how well journalists meet the challenges of the new technology. In the long term, however, as newsgathering expert systems become available to the general public, the gate-keeping function of newspeople will diminish and, as a group, they will probably experience deprofessionalization, or even worse:

> If journalism does not give persuasive and compelling reasons, it may become obsolete in the coming 'every person an editor' era when we can dial up information without the benefit of trained reporters who select and interpret to help make sense of things. (Dennis, 1989: 119)

Or, in Durkheim's words: '... there is no institution where deterioration does not set in at some point in its history' (1958: 23).

Conclusion

The central argument in this paper has been that only those occupations that are perceived to serve the vital needs of the human race, as well as possessing esoteric knowledge, qualify for the designation of 'profession' and, further, that there is always a sacred aspect to a true profession. The question of sacredness. which has been somewhat neglected in the literature on professionalism, is found to be intimately related to the idea of self-sacrifice. This goes a long way in explaining the elevated status of the clergy and doctors and also throws light on the erosion that the former and, to some extent, the latter occupation is going through in terms of public esteem.

The division of labour has hit professional workers with full force and is traditionally regarded as furthering professionalization. I find fault with this argument as it seems to me that exactly the opposite happens, that is, as the 'dirty work' is given over to subordinates, the professional loses his/her grasp of the whole task. Thus, the delegation of professional tasks to people with restricted qualifications might actually be contributing to deprofessionalization.

When the case of journalism is examined, it falls short on some traditional criteria, but it is evident that both its perceived function as a vital service and its sacred aspect – which I find essential for a comprehensive definition of professionalism – are present in at least some sectors of journalism. It is more questionable whether journalists possess a definable body of esoteric knowledge, but this again depends on how narrowly we define 'knowledge'.

The sacred aspect of professional journalism has been presented in this paper as being intimately linked to democracy. At the same time it was noted that the nobility of self-sacrifice may find its expression under tyrannical conditions. Thus the democratic value of professional journalism is perhaps best exemplified under nondemocratic conditions.

Notes

In the process of writing this article I benefited from comments from colleagues at the University of Lund, Michigan State University and the University of Iceland. I also had access to library and other facilities at these universities, all of which are gratefully acknowledged. I also wish to acknowledge the valuable comments which I received from an anonymous reviewer and the editor of the *European Journal of Communication*. An earlier version of the article appeared in *Pressens Årbog* (Broddason, 1990).

1. Indeed, as suggested by Foucault (1980), knowledge and power become integrated to the point of being indistinguishable; the power of knowledge and the knowledge of the powerful reinforce each other.
2. For a while the concept of cultural distance was much in vogue; see, for example, Galtung and Ruge's (1970) classic article. It is becoming obsolete as it is increasingly evident that distance so defined offers industrialized nations no protection from the consequences of Third World events, actions or decisions.
3. An extensive survey among American newspaper journalists revealed a heterogeneity of attitudes and working conditions in the newsrooms and a mixture of professional and non-professional responses: '... the majority views news as what they – reporters and editors – think it is ... But the notion of what makes news appeared too personal to achieve even a newsroom consensus' (Burgoon et al., 1982: 2).
4. 'Rules governing the practitioner/client relationship may be formal, written rules or merely normative routines and controls of everyday professional life. A similar distinction holds for rules governing relations between colleagues. It does not hold for corporate obligations, which are generally unwritten cultural assumptions, even though they may appear in formal ethics codes.

In a theoretical sense, then, the professions have two levels of obligation, corporate and individual' (Abbott, 1983: 856).

5. Merrill concentrated on the following six factors: (1) in-country licensing; (2) international licensing; (3) identification cards or accreditation; (4) university education; (5) in-country codes of ethics; and (6) international codes of ethics.

6. It is interesting that Windahl and Signitzer should single out civil engineers as a definite example of professionals, as this occupational group has often been seen as problematic in this respect. Thus, according to Collins: 'There is no doubt at all that engineers have valid scientific knowledge (and indeed have had it. ... for at least 2000 years). But engineers have had the greatest difficulty in getting themselves organized as a self-governing occupational group, and they have rarely had high prestige ...' (1990b: 18).

7. Rosengren et al. also draw attention to the relevance of normative theories of the media in this respect: 'Professional quality of programming is most central in the Free Press Theory, the Social Responsibility Theory, and the Democratic Participant Theory, while under the Authoritarian, the Soviet and the Development Media Theories, professional quality of programming is leading a much more precarious existence' (Rosengren et al., 1991: 68).

8. 'The symbolic representations of integration are what Durkheim called "religion"' (Berger and Luckmann, 1967: 198). McQuail (1987: 88–94) provides a useful discussion of the relationship between mass media and social integration.

9. See, for instance, the *New York Times*, 30 October and 2 November 1989.

10. The Committee to Protect Journalists (1986a) has compiled a list which includes the names of 293 journalists who were killed or disappeared between 1976 and 1986. The list is not meant to be conclusive as many cases go unreported. Furthermore, it does not include journalists killed in crossfire or random attacks or those murdered for strictly personal reasons. Rather, it classifies those who appear to have been targeted for what they investigated, wrote, broadcast or photographed, or because they were identified as journalists and were perceived as threats. The Committee (1986b) also compiled a list of 328 attacks on the press in 1985. While the list reflects all the cases the Committee investigated, the Committee says it should not be regarded as complete as many cases go unreported. The early 1990s have seen ample evidence of the hazards that journalists in many conflict-ridden areas of the world have to face. Even in a country supposedly at peace such as Turkey, journalists were being killed at the rate of one a month in 1992.

11. Others have acknowledged the criterion of vital importance with regard to journalists. But this acknowledgement is liable to be put in a derogatory context: 'Aside from the stories they are paid to tell, professional journalists also invent myths about themselves. One such myth stresses the socially edifying features of their occupation. According to that story, journalists gather and disseminate the vital information democracy needs to function' (Pauly, 1988: 246).

12. Kepplinger and Köcher (1990: 305) point out that the *Washington Post* and the *New York Times* have started to document errors in reporting and to discuss questionable editorial decisions.

13. Lichter et al. (1986: 27) provide an illuminating anecdote of a television network employee who said to a prominent politician being interviewed by Dan Rather, anchorman of CBS News: 'Senator, Mr Rather will only have time for one more question'.

14. Windahl and Rosengren (1978) make a useful distinction between individual professionalization and the professionalization of an occupation.

References

Abbott, Andrew (1983) 'Professional Ethics', *American Journal of Sociology* 88(5): 855–85.

Abbott, Andrew (1988) *The System of Professions. An Essay on the Division of Expert Labor.* Chicago: University of Chicago Press.

Altheide, D.L. and R.P. Snow (1979) *Media Logic.* London: Sage Publications.

Armstrong, David (1990) 'Medicine As a Profession: Times of Change', *British Medical Journal* 301(3 October): 691–3.

Bakewell, Joan and Nicholas Garnham (1970) *The New Priesthood. British Television Today.* London: Allen Lane, The Penguin Press.

Beam, Randal A. (1988) 'Professionalism as an Organizational Concept', paper presented at the Annual Meeting of the Association for Education in Journalism and Mass Communication, Portland, Oregon (July).

Berger, Peter L. and Thomas Luckmann (1967) *The Social Construction of Reality.* New York: Doubleday (Anchor Press).

Bjarnason, Thoroddur and Thorolfur Thorlindsson (1993) 'In Defense of a Folk Model: The "Skipper Effect" in the Icelandic Cod Fishery', *American Anthropologist* 95(2): 371–94.

Broddason, Thorbjörn (1990) 'Präster, läkare, masskommunikatörer. Profession-alismens sakrala dimension', *Pressens Årbog:* 87–94.

Broddason, Thorbjörn, Akiba E. Cohen, Walter Gantz and Bradley S. Greenberg (1987) 'News Diffusion After the Palme Assassination Among Journalists in Iceland, Israel and the US', *European Journal of Communication* 2(2): 211–26.

Broddason, Thorbjörn and Elías Hédinsson (1986) 'A World Without Media', *Nordicom Review* 1986(1–2): 1–5.

Burgoon, Judee K., Michael Burgoon and Charles K. Atkin (1982) 'What's News? Who Decides? And How?', a preliminary report on the world of the working journalist, conducted for the American Society of Newspaper Editors (May).

Burns, Tom (1977) *The BBC, Public Institution and Private World.* London: Macmillan.

Collins, Randall (1990a) 'Market Closure and the Conflict Theory of Professions', in Michael Burrage and Rolf Torstendahl (eds), *Professions in Theory and History*, pp. 24–43. London: Sage.

Collins, Randall (1990b) 'Changing Conceptions in the Sociology of the Professions', in Rolf Torstendahl and Michael Burrage (eds), *The Formation of Professions*, pp. 11–23. London: Sage.

Committee to Protect Journalists (1986a) 'Journalists Killed and Disappeared Since 1976', mimeo.

Committee to Protect Journalists (1986b) 'Attacks on the Press 1985', mimeo.

Darling-Hammond, Linda (1988) 'Policy and Professionalism', in Ann Lieberman (ed.), *Building a Professional Culture in Schools*, pp. 55–77. New York: Teachers College Press.

Davis Michael (1990) 'The Ethics Boom: What and Why?', *The Centennial Review* 34(2): 163–86.

Dayan, Daniel and Elihu Katz (1992) *Media Events. The Live Broadcasting of History.* Cambridge: Harvard University Press.

Dennis, Everette E. (1989) *Reshaping the Media. Mass Communication in an Information Age.* London: Sage.

Durkheim, Emile (1976/1915) *The Elementary Forms of Religious Life.* London: George Allen & Unwin Ltd.

Durkheim, Emile (1958) *Professional Ethics and Civic Morals.* Glencoe: The Free Press.

Foucault, Michel (1980) *Power/Knowledge.* London: Penguin.

Freidson, Eliot (1986) *Professional Powers. A Study of the Institutionalization of Formal Knowledge.* Chicago: The University of Chicago Press.

Galtung, Johan and Mari Holmboe Ruge (1970) 'The Structure of Foreign News', in Jeremy Tunstall (ed.), *Media Sociology*, pp. 259–98. London: Constable.

Gans, Herbert J. (1980) *Deciding What's News.* London: Constable.

Goldstein, Tom (1985) *The News at Any Cost.* New York: Simon and Schuster.

Goode, William J. (1970) 'The Theoretical Limits of Professionalization', in Arthur W. Foshay (ed.), *The Professional as Educator.* New York: Teachers College Press.

Harris, Louis (1984) 'Does the Public Really Hate the Press?', *Columbia Journalism Review* (March–April): 18.

Jaspin, Elliot (1989) 'Out With the Paper Chase, In With the Data Base', lecture at Gannett Center for Media Studies, Columbia University, New York, mimeo.

Kepplinger, Hans Mathias and Renate Köcher (1990) 'Professionalism in the Media World?', *European Journal of Communication* 5(2–3): 285–311.

Kocka, Jürgen (1990) '*Bürgertum* and Professions in the Nineteenth Century: Two Alternative Approaches', in Michael Burrage and Rolf Torstendahl (eds), *Professions in Theory and History*, pp. 62–74. London: Sage.

Lambeth, Edmund B. (1986) *Committed Journalism. An Ethic for the Profession.* Bloomington: Indiana University Press.

Lichter, Robert, Stanley Rothman and Linda S. Lichter (1986) *The Media Elite.* Bethesda, MD: Adler and Adler.

Linderman Alf (1989) 'Människans möte med tv-religionen', paper presented at the IXth Nordic Conference for Mass Communication Research (20–23 August), Borgholm, Sweden.

Luckmann, Thomas (1967) *The Invisible Religion.* London: Macmillan.

McQuail, Denis (1987) *Mass Communication Theory. An Introduction.* London: Sage.

McQuail, Denis (1992) *Media Performance.* London: Sage.

Merrill, John C. (1988) 'Inclination of Nations to Control Press and Attitudes on Professionalization', *Journalism Quarterly*, 65(4): 839–44.

Murphy, Raymond (1990) 'Proletarianization or Bureaucratization: The Fall of the Professional?', in Rolf Torstendahl and Michael Burrage (eds), *The Formation of Professions*, pp. 71–96. London: Sage.

The New York Times (1989), 30 October and 2 November.

Numbers, Ronald E. (1988) 'The Fall and Rise of the American Medical Profession', in Nathan O. Hatch (ed.), *The Professions in American History.* Notre Dame, IN: University of Notre Dame Press.

Olen, Jeffrey (1988) *Ethics in Journalism.* Englewood Cliffs, NJ: Prentice Hall.

Parsons, Talcott (1968) 'Professions', in David L. Sills (ed.), *International Encyclopedia of the Social Sciences*, Vol. 12, pp. 536–46. London and Glencoe: Macmillan and The Free Press.

Pauly, John J. (1988) 'Rupert Murdoch and the Demonology of Professional Journalism', in James W. Carey (ed.), *Media, Myths and Narratives*, pp. 246–61. London: Sage.

Pétursson, Pétur (1983) *Church and Social Change. A Study of the Secularization Process in Iceland 1830–1930.* Vänersborg: Plus Ultra.

Robinson, Michael, and Andrew Kohut (1988) 'Believability and the Press', *Public Opinion Quarterly* 52(2): 174–89.

Rosengren, Karl Erik, Mats Carlsson and Yael Tågerud (1991) 'Quality in Programming: Views from the North', *Studies of Broadcasting* 27: 21–80.

Schudson, Michael (1988) 'The Profession of Journalism in the United States', in Nathan O. Hatch (ed.), *The Professions in American History.* Notre Dame, IN: University of Notre Dame Press.

Smith, Anthony (1980) *The Geopolitics of Information. How Western Culture Dominates the World.* New York: Oxford University Press.

Thurén, Thorsten (1989) 'Journalistik som yrke – en omöjilig rou?', paper presented at the IXth Nordic conference on Mass Communication Research (20–23 August) Borgholm, Sweden.

Wilensky, Harold L. (1964) 'The Professionalization of Everyone?', *American Journal of Sociology* 70(2): 137–58.

Windahl, Sven and Karl Erik Rosengren (1978) 'Newsmen's Professionalization', *Journalism Quarterly* 55(3): 466–73.

Windahl, Sven and Benno Signitzer (1992) *Using Communication Theory.* London: Sage.

13 Telling Stories: Sociology, Journalism and the Informed Citizen[1]

Peter Golding

Journalism and sociology have had an uncomfortable relationship. At times the academic study of the media has seemed a protracted *'j' accuse'*, endlessly contrasting the compacted and flawed account of social reality provided in the media with some other, more adequate narrative. Inevitably this has produced its tensions. What journalists perceive as accusations of deceit and incompetence, researchers prefer to cloak in the language of social process, organizational imperative, or ideology. While journalists concentrate on the immediate and intentional aspects of communication, their academic critics are focused on the longer term and 'unwitting' byproducts of structures of dominance, culture and hegemony. It is, too frequently, a dialogue of the deaf.

Yet, while journalism has seemed to suffer at the hands of academia, sociology has certainly never had a kind press. *The Times* (17 October 1989) warned that 'The teaching of sociology in schools is sapping Britain's industrial strength by encouraging pupils to develop an anti-business bias'. A year before that the *Daily Telegraph* had discovered that 'More than 250,000 people a year are being trained as critical saboteurs of Britain through their study of contemporary sociology'. I am delighted to say it is a lot more now.

The fictional image encouraged by such lampoons as Malcolm Bradbury's (1975) novel *The History Man*, or the television adaptation of Anne Oakley's *The Men's Room* (1988), in which the sociology don becomes an opinionated, bed-hopping libertine, have not helped.

My aim in this paper is to assess the relative contributions of sociology and journalism to the task of providing for an informed citizenry. For, if the accumulated findings of several decades of media research are correct, that task cannot be fulfilled by an increasingly inadequate media system. Where then will critical commentary on social and political affairs be generated, if not from an independent and dynamic academy?

Source: *EJC* (1994), vol. 9: 461–484.

Democracy and the Mass Media:
The Sublime and the Ridiculous

This paper is entitled 'telling stories', and my first story takes us to the House of Commons in the late 18th century. The heroic and often told battle to obtain the right to report parliamentary proceedings had been won in 1771. But still the struggle continued (Aspinall, 1956; Kinnear, 1905). Imagine if you will the cramped, dark seats in the Gallery. One man sits intense and still amidst the hub-bub, staring into the Chamber, listening to the speeches. Hours later he is still there, unmoving and concentrated. This is William Woodfall, editor, printer, and indeed sole reporter of the *Morning Chronicle*. For his prodigious feats William has gone down in history as 'Memory Woodfall', because his legendary talent was the ability to commit to memory complete debates, often after sitting through the night listening to the House at work. Note-taking at this time was still prohibited. Many readers will have seen his heirs, no doubt, sitting glassy-eyed in the front rows of lectures. In the cold early morning Memory would return to his office and write verbatim accounts of the proceedings in the House (Smith, 1978). Undoubtedly, like Samuel Johnson a few years later, his ability to embellish the speeches with a lucidity and oratory beyond the skills of the orig-inal speakers did much to keep criticism and prosecution at bay. But he was engaged in developing that central art of what we later came to call the mass media, namely, political communication.

It has become a central assumption of modern times that Woodfall's heirs play a key role in making modern society work. The mass media, it is assumed, are the vital arteries through which the information which is our democratic life-blood flows between rulers and ruled. Those who govern keep a watchful eye on the public mood by scanning the front pages and headlines, while for the citizen at large, the media provide a rich and diverse diet of political information. We read and watch, then consider judiciously among the many alternatives put to us before arriving at conclusions and voting wisely. If journalism is 'history's first draft', then we all take part in the ritual of editing its final polished manu-script. The media provide a supermarket of ideas, around whose counters we freely wander before approaching the electoral check-out, our choices made from amongst a comprehensive selection of political packages.

This view is inscribed on the hearts of those who work in and manage the mass media. Here is Charles Curran, a distinguished former Director-General of the BBC:

> It is the broadcaster's role, as I see it, to win public interest in public issues. The organisation of political consent is more difficult in a complex society than it has ever been before. If broadcasting can arouse public interest it can increase public understanding. ... Broadcasters have a responsibil-ity, therefore, to provide a rationally based and balanced service of news which will enable adult people to make basic judgements about public policy in their capacity as voting citizens of a democracy (Curran, 1979: 114).

There one hears the patrician tones of the BBC mandarin. But the sentiment is clear. A different voice is that of Chris Moncrief, the recently retired Press Association lobby correspondent, who argues that:

> For myself I have never yet been able to locate a conscience even if I had wanted to struggle with it. We are in the business to write stories to sell newspapers. I think we are part of the entertainment industry at the down-market end. We do it for the money. And if that serves the public at the end of the day – well, that's a bonus (cited in Goodman, 1989: 4).

Whose story do we believe? The twin role of the media in our lives is manifest and, for the sociologist, it inevitably commands attention. On the one hand, the media are vast industries on which we spend an increasing and considerable proportion of our disposable income. On the other they are a major source of the imagery, values and ideas with which we make sense of the world around us.

On average, adults in Britain now spend 26 hours a week watching television, and a further 10 hours a week listening to radio. Over half the population read the three most successful daily newspapers every day. There is no other activity, except for the exceptionally athletic or the disgustingly lucky, which takes up more of people's time.

To what extent, though, do the media keep us informed, parading before us the great issues of the day, analysed, debated, and provided in full? How much do we learn of the complex relationship between the intelligence services and the state in a story about 'MI5 Wife in Secret Love Split' (*Sun*, 18 December 1991)? For informed insight into Britain's role in the world and the variety of international affairs, exploring the subtle nuances of cross-national relations, we can turn to the complexities unveiled in 'Up Yours Jacques' (*Daily Star*, 24 November 1992). Equally significant for our understanding of the changing structure of family life in contemporary society would be such front-page features as 'Sex Op Sister Stole My Man' (*Daily Star*, 7 December 1992). New patterns of diet and environmental concern are another matter of great public interest, no doubt highlighted in such front-page spreads as the story about Beatle Paul McCartney's wife: 'Gobsmacca: Linda's Outrage as She Finds Steak in Her Veggie Pies' (*Daily Star*, 10 October 1992), while reports and information about urban environment and road planning can be found in such articles as 'Man Who Made Love to Pavements' (*Sun*, 19 February 1993). The morning after the most stunning byelection and local government election results for a generation, the front page of Britain's second most popular national daily revealed the keynote news that: 'Bananarama Star in £300 a Day Mental Clinic' (*Daily Mirror*, 7 May 1993).

The increasing conflation of the daily popular press with the entertainment industry is, of course, nothing new, though it has reached new peaks of intensity in recent years. In 1992 content analysis by the Communication Research Centre at Loughborough University of the most popular national daily in Britain, read by over one in five of the adult population every day, showed 7 percent of front page stories dealt with political issues of some kind (either national or international) while 37 percent featured royalty or show business stories. But then we are not alone: on the day Nelson Mandela returned to Soweto and Europe agreed to the unification of Germany, most US papers devoted their front pages to the divorce of Donald and Mrs Trump.

We accept that events are as they appear in newspapers, and increasingly on television. That most televisual of dramas, the Gulf War, remains a recent high-point of the subjection of information to the irresistible logic of news management and the demands of TV. The introduction of tanks to the ground forces in the war took place, said a government spokesman at the time, because 'we need a force that is militarily worthwhile, self-sufficient, and looks good on television'. This is what you might call the breakfast-TV approach to campaign strategy. [...]

Telling Stories: News Media and Social Policy

In the mid-1970s I became interested in the way the media were responding to the growing concern about poverty in affluent Britain. The so-called 'rediscovery of poverty' 10 years earlier had come as a shock. What had been believed to be mere pockets of remediable poverty amidst the generally rising living standards of the post-war welfare state turned out to be, on closer inspection, intractable and large proportions of the population – about seven million people, half of them children – living on or below the poverty line. This needed explaining. The welfare state was becoming more and more expensive; yet here was clear evidence of a problem that refused to respond to the cure. Providing clear and acceptable explanations is part of the media's role, and together with Sue Middleton I began to examine how this circle was being squared (Golding and Middleton, 1982).

Lengthy investigation of both press coverage and popular attitudes revealed a number of themes, deeply rooted in the ancestry of British political culture and practice, surfacing in the simplicities and mythologies of media portrayals. Some old stories were being revisited. Gradually through this period the story we are told shifts from the problems of poverty to the crimes of the poor, in a rewriting of one of the core problems of the post-war welfare state.

Several themes among these stories became prominent and recurrent at this time. First was the notion of a necessary crack-down on the excesses of social security claimants. A number of headlines began to appear such as 'Big New War on the Dole Cheats' (*News of the World*) or 'War on the Welfare Scroungers' (*Daily Mail*, 25 July 1976). In the *Daily Mirror*, 22 September 1976, readers were advised that there was a 'War on Cheats' being waged, recalling its own story a few weeks previously beginning 'Britain's army of dole-queue swindlers were on the run last night as a government minister warned he was gunning for them'. Such language is terse, pithy and effective, redolent of the punchy adversarial jour-nalism of the sports pages. The difference is that it defines the line of opposition as that between society and a deviant minority, the social security claimant. Very often a racist tinge is not far from the surface (*Daily Star*, 24 April 1991: 'House That for Cheek: Asian Family of 9 Jet Straight into Council Flat').

Secondly, news coverage extracted from the national psyche the emotive dis-tinction between the deserving and undeserving poor. Social security policy has always felt the need to sort the feckless and workshy, the immoral and seedy, from the helpless and worthy. Classification is, equally, a popular sport in populist journalism. Welfare, in the rhetorical mix which inevitably flows from this combination, becomes a burden which we, the decent tax-paying, hard-working majority, have to bear to support the inadequate and unscrupulous.

It soon became a recurrent refrain that benefits were being lavished on millions who did not need them, and who lived a life of luxury on the proceeds. If something is too easily available and harmful to those who get it, the damage to the national fibre is obvious, and the medical analogy this invites was soon to appear. As a *Daily Mail* (26 September 1977) feature headed 'The Welfare Junkies' put it: 'there is a dangerously addictive influence at work in the welfare system'. Of course the implication is clear: there is a subplot in this story – the naturally healthy state of the social organism is one without the plague of wide-scale benefits; the welfare 'cure' is the root of the disease.

With the growing recession of the 1980s the wilder excesses of scroungerphobia began to retreat. But the ideology that had permitted and endorsed a major shift in the administration of social security from the promotion of benefits to people who needed them but don't claim, to the policing of the few whose claims were dubious, was never allowed to subside. The language and vocabulary of the 1970s have been a constant in more recent press reporting of this central area of social policy. Still we read of the continuing battle to rid us of this burden of wasters, spongers and loafers, in such stories as 'War on the Something for Nothing Brigade – Big Welfare Crackdown' (*Sun*, 21 September 1987); 'Hippy Dole Blitz' (*Daily Express*, 8 August 1992); 'Scroungers Will Be Nicked: It's War on the Loadsamoney Lot' (*Daily Star*, 12 May 1988); 'Stuff the Spongers' (*Daily Star*, 8 October 1992).

This tirade was brought to a fine dénouement in the *Sun's* splendidly public-spirited new panel game 'Shop a Scrounger' (29 April 1993), in which readers were given a phone line to provide the names of neighbours they suspected of claiming undue social security.

Following that research I undertook a series of studies into the ways in which the various components of the welfare state, and the policy apparatus generally, were explained and conveyed to the electorate at large. Health, for example: 'it's all sex and heart transplants in' it', as a tabloid friend explained to me, thus saving major expenditure of time and money on endless content analysis to arrive at the same conclusion. The pillorying of social workers (Golding, 1991), truncated accounts of crime (in which massive over reporting of crimes against the person has led to concern over public misapprehensions of criminality and the legal system), and of fields like education, all began to build up a pattern. [...]

But the cumulative lessons of all this research, and that conducted by others, point to a conclusion that, if predictable, is nonetheless alarming. What it highlights reflects concerns that are increasingly disturbing the more thoughtful of journalism's practitioners. Wherever we look, in coverage of race, industrial relations, welfare, foreign relations, or electoral politics, the media have failed democracy. We live in a political society in blinkers.

A Wired Wonderwork: New Technology and the Social Order

But surely, this is an information society? We are deluged with information at every turn. Aren't new technologies locking us all into a new wonderworld in

TABLE 13.1 OWNERSHIP OF COMMUNICATION RESOURCES AMONG HOUSEHOLDS AT SELECTED INCOME LEVELS (UK, 1992)

	% of households with:				
Weekly Household Income (£)	TV	Cable TV	Telephone	Video	Home computer
80–100	98.4	6.5	74.5	40.7	6.5
160–200	98.6	6.8	87.1	62.9	12.5
280–320	98.6	9.8	92.0	80.3	16.3
640–800	99.5	17.1	99.5	91.8	36.9
All households	98.3	9.3	88.4	69.3	19.1

Source: Central Statistical Office (1993).

which wired households can draw on a cornucopia of technical advances? To press a button is to know. It's a tempting vision. But there is a price to be paid to enter this playground. As information becomes increasingly a commodity, to be bought and sold, then having the admission price becomes ever more crucial for citizens in a society claiming to be informed.

The information society is a myth. We live in a media society, in which information is available at a price, or not at all. We assume that all have the means to partake of this new rich information diet, but even a cursory glance at the evidence shows how far this is from the truth.

The figures in Table 13.1 show the ownership of different communications goods among high-, low- and medium-income groups. As you might expect, TV is more or less universally available, though this disguises the difference between the well-heeled media academic with his slimline fastext Nicam stereo sound master set, and portables in every room in the house, and the dodgy four-channel secondhand small screen in the parlour of his less affluent neighbour.

But if we look at other goods, a gap begins to appear. For example, video ownership, though relatively widespread in Britain (much stimulated by the royal wedding in the early 1980s), is much more common among higher income groups. Ownership of a video recorder doubled from 30 percent to 60 percent of the population between 1985 and 1990, but it remains well below half among poorer households, who have the least opportunity for alternative entertainment outside the home. Home computers, though increasingly available, are very inequitably distributed through the population. Even telephones, widely assumed to be universally available, are in fact not found in nearly one in eight households, overwhelmingly those in lower income groups. Indeed, if those figures are broken down further, we find that phone ownership is even lower among single pensioner households and lone parents – just those groups we might assume are most in need of such facilities. Among single parent households containing two or more children, the figure for telephone ownership drops to 64 percent.

It is sometimes argued that this gap will diminish over time, just as it did for new 'white goods' in the 1950s. But this is unlikely to be so for two reasons. First, it is intrinsic to the nature of these goods that their ownership imparts cumulative advantage to those able to sustain them. This is because these goods require more than a single expenditure. They must be fed. Computers require updating, software, add-ons such as printers or modems. Video recorders require blank or prerecorded tapes. Increasingly with the spread of cable and satellite reception, purchase of leisure goods is recurrent rather than single and capital only. Secondly, the 1950s and 1960s, during which the previous generation of domestic electrical goods became commonplace, were periods of boom and declining inequality. Such economic dynamics are not likely to be replicated in the period in which the new communication goods are being established (Golding, 1990).

What we have in the misinformed society is, in a cliché which nonetheless carries an unavoidable truth, the growing gap between information-poor and information-rich. Where information is only available at a price, we need to examine carefully from whom and how that information arrives. Research I have carried out with colleagues in recent years has broadened to address this issue. This work has focused on the profound changes in, firstly, the structure of the communications media, and, secondly, the society within which they operate. The gulf between those with a full citizenship season ticket into the information society, and those left outside with their noses pressed against the windows, results from changes in each.

Media Monoliths and the Centripetal Society

We need, at this point, to address two issues: first, shifts in the media; second, the social changes which are their backdrop.

For over 20 years, in collaboration with Graham Murdock, I have investigated what we have come to label the political economy of the mass media (Golding and Murdock, 1991). Mapping the boardroom machinations of the Robert Maxwells and Rupert Murdochs of this world has its own fascinations. But we have to recognize the implications of an information market in which three-quarters of the national daily circulation of newspapers, and over four-fifths of the Sunday circulation, is controlled by three corporate groups. This is hardly guaranteed to widen the scope and range of views and voices in the public arena.

Not surprisingly, the last Royal Commission on the Press came to a conclusion which has been manifestly obvious to any observer of British newspapers, when it noted that:

> There is no doubt that over most of this century the labour movement has had less newspaper support than its right wing opponents and that its major beliefs and activities have been unfavourably reported by the majority of the press (cited in Golding and Murdock, 1991: 26).

While it is possible to argue that partisanship has declined as newspapers remorselessly struggle to survive in an adverse financial climate, it is difficult to sustain any argument that the press as a whole provides a full range of possible means of expression and opinion.

As for the press, so for other media. The diversification and internationalization of companies like Murdoch's News International, Sony of Japan, Bertelsmann in Germany, and so on, create a network of control over what one ad man once called the 'syndication of experience'.

The major alternative to this corporate monolith has traditionally been the public service broadcasters. The model of the BBC, claiming to provide education, entertainment and information as a public service at high professional standards in the public interest, has informed the statutory basis and occupational ideologies of most national broadcasting systems, both across Europe and further afield. Indeed commercial systems, like the ITV network in this country, have themselves readily assumed the mantle of public service broadcasting as enthusiastically, and sometimes more so, than quasi-public bodies such as the BBC.

The emergence of new technologies providing for a major diversification of delivery systems, via cable and satellite especially, together with the rapidly rising cost of maintaining national public broadcasting systems without substantial advertising support, have conspired to threaten the very fabric of the public service broadcasting systems in many European countries. Where buttressed by governments already ideologically inclined to commercialization and privatization, as in the UK, the move away from the public service model has been rapid. [...]

It is clear then, that, at the very least, the public space represented by a national broadcasting system dedicated to providing extensive, prominent and diverse cultural resources for an informed citizenry is uncertain to survive current scrutiny.

But if the media are moving into a new market-driven era in which information is available, but at a price, what of the social processes which lay behind this shift? Sociologists have watched and described, with varying language and conclusions, two twin processes over the last couple of decades – greater inequality and growing centralization.

The widening gap between those with the disposable income enabling them to enjoy the new playthings of 'the information society', and those left uncomfortably juggling the consuming realities of survival in hard times, is the most fundamental social change in recent years. Between 1979 and 1989 the poorest tenth of the population saw a drop in their real living standards of 6 percent compared to a rise of 46 percent for the top tenth. The poorest third of society are becoming increasingly detached from the precarious rise in living standards enjoyed by those above them. By the end of the 1980s over 11 million people (1 in 5 of the population) were living on or below the poverty line, a rise of roughly 50 percent in a decade (Oppenheim, 1993: 29).

This mundane arithmetic of domestic economy places huge barriers between large sections of the community and the turnstiles through which the information paradise is gained. For those with the spending power to enjoy the communications bounty, the future beckons enticingly. For others, such goods and services remain luxuries displaced by the pressing needs of food, clothing and shelter.

But the second social change we have explored is what, in a number of writings, I have called the 'centripetal society' – a society in which all things spin increasingly towards the centre. After all, that simple couplet of 'free market and strong state' has been our conceptual lodestone for some little while. [...]

The most significant feature of the centripetal society in this context is the growth of the public relations state. All states seek to promote the best view of their policies and practices. But in recent years the UK media have been under unprecedented pressure to reflect and disseminate government views. [...] At the same time, governments have been engaged in a build-up of their own publicity and press relations activities on an unprecedented scale. [...]

But public relations has both negative and positive elements. The growing unease felt in many areas of public life about the use of government information as a tool of secrecy came to a head in the publication just over two years ago by that madcap radical body, the Royal Statistical Society, of a report (1990) into official statistics, suggesting their preparation and form had become too much an instrument of state public relations. The Society declared itself no longer confident that 'the organisational framework in which [government statisticians] work offers the best protection against undue pressure ... we are clear that the indirect result of the post Rayner reforms have been harmful to quality'. There has been, it said, 'a serious erosion of public confidence' in UK official statistics. The Rayner report had declared that government statistics were for the benefit of government, not for the public. In its wake the government statistical service moved into the dark clutches of the Treasury. [...]

That the elementary accounting of public life can no longer be made available for public and independent scrutiny is one of the most serious blows to critical social science in the post-war period.

The barriers this places to innovative and profoundly important work investigating the dynamics of benefits and incomes are inexcusable. Instead we have the panglossian evasions of *Social Trends*, an official survey of good news statistics sufficient to gladden the heart of television newsreader Martyn Lewis (who has campaigned for more 'good news' to be included in bulletins), but recently disowned as misleading and incomplete even by its distinguished first editor.

We live, then, in a society increasingly ignorant of itself. A society not self-informed is not an information society.

Witness to History: Sociology as Trustee

But what then of sociology, for this is my final story. I write primarily of sociology, but what I say holds, I hope, for the social sciences as a whole. For the need for independent and critical inquiry into social conditions has never been more urgent, nor more threatened, than today. Sociology stands as witness and storyteller or it fails completely. We must insist on that task in a society which is otherwise denied the means for self-reflection – indeed, the means for people to be citizens.

It has often seemed to me that we sometimes labour, as sociologists, under a false modesty – when gathered in throngs, sociologists seem a seething mass of humility. How wonderful it would be, we sometimes feel, to be able to come to the podium at some prestigious conference and announce a startling medical breakthrough, a staggering advance in technological ingenuity. Too often our brief seems merely to act as the bearers of bad tidings, while others crow the good news and get the plaudits. It is not surprising that media social researchers frequently succumb sheepishly to the charge that they fail to be fans in their quest to be critics.

The corrective can be simple. I have often hankered after the example of Auguste Comte, the 19th-century French writer who gave sociology its name. Comte would demand that his manservant wake him each morning by shaking him briskly by the shoulders and admonishing him: 'Wake master, you have great things to do.' Sadly, my own household has not remotely matched this performance.

But the tradition is an honourable one. It may have been the stench of urban poverty and the fear of destructive social disorder that drove the development of the blue books, the social surveys and urban anthropology of Victorian England. Still, the legacy it created, that of engaged documentary, survived in the work of Booth and later of Rowntree, and in the 20th century in the film making of John Grierson, the heroic journalism of *Picture Post*, and the ambitious if flawed social narratives of Mass Observation. Their aims were simple: to tell the truth and make things better. We lose that simple objective at our peril.

Dangers to our enterprise remain, however, and the dangers are both external and internal. In Britain we face a culture as sublimely anti-intellectual as any in Europe. As our Prime Minister observed recently: 'We should understand a little less and condemn a little more.' He has managed both with commendable skill, but it is a credo to bring the hairs on one's nape to attention.

The industrialization of higher education confronts so much of our ambition. Over three-quarters of a century ago two books appeared which should stand on the shelf of every higher education civil servant in the country. In *The Higher Education in America* the great sociologist Thorstein Veblen shrewdly and ironically surveys the intrusion of business culture into academic life. He writes:

> The underlying business-like presumption accordingly appears to be that learning is a merchantable commodity, to be produced on a piece-rate plan, bought and sold by standard units, counted and reduced to staple equivalence by impersonal mechanised tests. ... So far as this salesmanlike efficiency goes freely into effect it leads to a substitution of salesmanlike efficiency ... in the place of scientific capacity and addiction to study. This process ... [produces] the stale routine of futility (Veblen, 1965/1918: 221–2).

This fear was even more dramatically highlighted in Upton Sinclair's magnificent polemic *The Goose Step* (Sinclair, 1923) which, just a few years after Veblen's essay, railed against the 'New Department Stores', which he observed the American universities to have become. [...]

This is the onward march of those whom George Orwell labelled the 'striped trousered ones' – threatening what he called 'a bureaucratic tyranny' (Orwell, 1961: 323). The shadow of the 'striped trousered' looms large over sociology. Their language, of total quality management, audit, throughput and efficiency, is not our language. Their stories are not our stories, and the telling of our tales must resist the diverting and tempting rhetoric of the market-place. This is the language and philosophy of those who know the price of everything and the value of nothing.

But if there are dangers without, we cannot ignore the threats from within. The first and not least of these is the retreat from public issues. The postwar bifurcation of sociology and social policy and administration in British Higher Education institutions was one of the most destructive, politically emasculating and intellectually diminishing episodes in British social science.

Sociology suffers from the temptations of introspection, a theoreticism that is not theory but a turning of our collective backs on the link between biography and history that is sociology's core concern. The 'culture of contentment' identified by J.K. Galbraith, which settles readily on the comfortable and successful in a divided society, can so easily blunt the critical edge of sociology. Once again Orwell's warning of the irresponsibility of noncommitment – hiding, as he put it, 'inside the whale' – should stand before us. If we lose sight of the mundane cruelties of social structure the essential integrity of critical social research is abandoned.

It now becomes urgent to rediscover the firmly-rooted concerns with such old-fashioned nostrums as power and inequality if we are to recover the story-telling potency of sociology. The questions we ask can so easily migrate into the internal world of the private and away from the pressing task of constructing, with reasoned argument and credible evidence, the critique of public life.

Secondly, we face the temptations of grand design. Anxious to stand large on the horizon of history we see new eras at every turn. The coming of postindustrialism, postmaterialism and most recently of postmodernism in our academic discourses reflects this desperate premonition of cataclysm. We live in a time dwarfed by a sense of transition, creating a 'first past the post' mentality. As the millennium approaches we succumb readily to such rhetoric as that of the Club of Rome: 'We are in the early stages of forming a new world society ... dense with information technology, confused about morals and ethics, and in social and educational chaos' (1972).

Thank goodness for the reassurance of British Foreign Secretary Douglas Hurd that 'history has not ended'. We are foolish to disagree. From fears of the new ice age in the 1970s to global warming in the 1980s, and suggestions of the end of history more recently, we have seen the dangers of being drawn into this game. Rapid and dramatic shifts in the political order in eastern Europe and the third world, environmental uncertainty, the globalization of production and the emergence of a new international division of labour, all undoubtedly feed this intimation of change. But we should be wary of hasty labelling.

With the help of my former research assistant Beckie Walker I have precisely located the start of postmodernism in the middle of 1986. The term originates in discussion of Latin American poetry in the 1930s (Osborne, 1992). But in the UK before 1986 there were just 25 books or articles which referred to postmodernism or postmodernity in their title. In the next three years there were nearly 300. Obviously something happened in 1986. Far be it from me to suggest we would learn more about the onset of postmodernism by assessing the marketing ploys and methods of academic publishers, but I offer the finding freely. The temptations of era-labelling taunt us all, and must be resisted.

Thirdly stands the threat of clientism – the definition of our enquiries from without by those who fund and legislate for research. The transmutation of the national statutory body which funds academic social science research in Britain from the 'Social Science Research Council' into the 'Economic and Social Research Council' some years ago was but the first warning shot in this battle. The growth of research funding through government-inspired programmes rather than to diverse and original researchers, driven by curiosity and invention rather than application and competence, is one of the most insidious detractors from sociology's role as critical story-teller in recent years. [...]

At best sociology becomes part of our common sense. The very linguistic air we breathe is suffused with sociological understanding. Class, charisma, life-style and a myriad other terms have drifted into everyday understanding. There *is* such a thing as society.

In Manhattan there is a boutique named Gemeinschaft after one of the key terms in the German sociologist Max Weber's classic work in social theory. One waits with bated breath for the opening of the Weltanschauung coffee bar in central London. But sustaining that intervention into everyday thought must remain our core task, using reasoned argument and incontrovertible evidence to argue and challenge the orthodoxies and precepts that rule our lives.

How much more true this is of social research into communications. Abandonment of that search for the links between systems of communication and the dynamics of power and inequality which roots media research in the heartland of social inquiry can only ultimately impoverish and marginalize our labours.

Coda: Story-Telling and Telling Stories

The story I have been trying to tell is in some ways a tragedy. It has been said that 'democracy is the precious right of the British not to have to think about politics'. But the clouds have silver linings. How heartening it was to hear a dis-tinguished back-bench Member of Parliament, Sir John Stokes, tell a Committee of Members recently, 'People never talk about politics in the pubs. But now they are starting to. I regard that as a sinister sign'.

He may be right. But that culture of dissent, debate and informed citizenship can only survive if a critical academy stands firm in defence of independent social research and scholarship. In Salman Rushdie's *Satanic Verses* we are told that the poet' s task is 'to name the unnameable, to point at frauds, to take sides, start arguments, shape the world and stop it going to sleep' (Rushdie, 1992: 97). I can think of no better task for the sociologist.[2]

In a society riven by growing inequalities, in which large sections of the population are increasingly being left behind by the denizens of comfortable Britain, in which reports of racial harassment have soared in the last two years and the sour stench of racism once again corrodes our culture, in which millions live those 'public issues which become private troubles' – in this society we have stories to tell. All around us are other tellers of stories and keepers of secrets – powerful, venal, mendacious and effective. Our task is also to tell stories, and in doing so we must make the stories we tell *telling* stories.

Notes

1. This paper is adapted from and based on the author's inaugural lecture at the University of Loughborough, 19 May 1993.
2. This view of sociology as a story-telling witness is similarly developed by Marris who, in my view, convincingly argues that 'sociologists are tellers of exemplary stories, whose moral represents a general truth' (Marris, 1990: 82). As he concludes, 'storytelling, in the full sense, is not merely recounting events but endowing them with meaning by commentary and dramatic structure' (Marris, 1990: 86).

References

Aspinall, A. (1956) 'The Reporting and Publishing of the House of Commons' Debates', in R. Pares and A. Taylor (eds), *Essays Presented to Sir Lewis Namier*. London: Macmillan.

Billig, M., D. Deacon, P. Golding, and S. Middleton (1993) 'In the Hands of the Spin Doctors: Television, Politics, and the 1992 General Election', in N. Miller and R. Alien (eds), *It's Live – But is it Real?* London: John Libbey.

Bradbury, Malcolm (1975) *The History Man*. London: Secker and Warburg.

Central Statistical Office (1993) *Family Spending*. London: HMSO.

Club of Rome (1972) *The Limits to Growth*. London: Earth Island Publications.

Curran, C. (1979) *A Seamless Robe: Broadcasting Philosophy and Practice*. London: Collins.

Fitzwalter, B. (1992) 'The Cheap and Cheerful Channel', *The Guardian*, 7 September: 23.

Golding, P. (1990) 'Political Communication and Citizenship: the Media and Democracy in an Inegalitarian Social Order', in M. Ferguson (ed.), *Public Communications: The New Imperatives*. London: Sage.

Golding, P. (1991) 'Do-Gooders on Display: Social Work, Public Attitudes, and the Mass Media', in B. Franklin and N. Parton (eds), *Social Work, The Media and Public Relations*, pp. 88–104. London: Routledge.

Golding, P. and S. Middleton (1982) *Images of Welfare: Press and Public Attitudes to Poverty*. Oxford: Martin Robertson.

Golding, P. and G. Murdock (1991) 'Culture, Communications, and Political Economy', in J. Curran and M. Gurevitch (eds), *Mass Media and Society*. London: Edward Arnold.

Goodman, G. (1989) 'Editorial', *British Journalism Review* 1(1).

Kinnear, A. (1905) 'Parliamentary Reporting', *Contemporary Review* LXXXVII: 369–75.

Marris, P. (1990) 'Witnesses, Storytellers, or Engineers? Roles of Sociologists in Social Policy', in H.J. Gans (ed.), *Sociology in America*. Newbury Park, CA: Sage.

Oakley, Anne (1988) *The Men's Room*. London: Virago.

Oppenheim, C. (1993) *Poverty: The Facts*. London: Child Poverty Action Group.

Orwell, G. (1961) *Collected Essays*. London: Seeker and Warburg.

Osborne, P. (1992) 'Modernity is a Qualitative not a Chronological Category', *New Left Review* 192: 65–84.

Royal Statistical Society (1990) *Official Statistics: Counting with Confidence*, p. 4. London: RSS.

Rushdie, S. (1992) *The Satanic Verses*. Dover, DE: The Consortium.

Sinclair, U. (1923) *The Goose Step*. Chicago: the Author.

Smith, A. (1978) 'The Long Road to Objectivity and Back: The Kinds of Truth We Get in Journalism', in G. Boyce, J. Curran and P. Wingate (eds), *Newspaper History: From the 17th Century to the Present Day*. London: Constable.

Veblen, T. (1965/1918) *The Higher Learning in America*. New York: Augustus M. Kelley.

14 Beyond Journalism: A Profession between Information Society and Civil Society

Jo Bardoel

Is journalism becoming redundant? Is the profession, slowly but surely, losing its prominent place in communication between the citizen and government? Over the past years, it has repeatedly been said that the function of journalism is gradually being eroded. Underlying such concerns are the changes that have taken place in the journalistic dissemination of news as a result of new media technology.

Several years ago, this concern was directed towards the steady advance of broadcasting stations like Cable News Network (CNN) and the satellites that allow them to bring direct, uncut reports of world events, from the Gulf War to peace keeping in the former Yugoslavia. [...]

More recently, the advent of new, interactive communication services such as the Internet, 'free nets' and 'digital cities' has given rise to expectations that in the future journalistic intervention in political communication will no longer be necessary. Mitchell Kapor, founder of the American digital citizens' movement Electronic Frontier Foundation, gives the example of vice-president Al Gore's appearance on *CompuServe*:

> It was the first live interactive news conference by the vice-president. The *New York Times* observed: This actually might be like when Franklin Roosevelt went on television at the New York World Fair in 1939. Symbolically it could be marking the beginning of an era, in which public officials are available to discuss and interact in real time. (Wiering and Schröder, 1994)

These developments pose questions as to the significance of the new information technology for the traditional task of journalism. What will the information society mean for the position of journalists in political communication? Will they become redundant, as some have suggested? Will the advance of the direct registration of news smother the journalism that seeks to explain its background? Or might it be the other way round? Will individuals lose their way on the information highway and feel a greater need for journalistic direction? In this context we are of course

Source: *EJC* (1996), vol. 11, no. 3: 283–302.

less interested in the changes in the day-to-day working routines of journalists that might occur (see Bardoel, 1993) than in the broader mission that is attributed to the profession in relation to political democracy and social integration in any society. Although the latter function of comment and critique is all too often identified with the written press, the same holds true, in principle, for the 'workers of the word' in audiovisual and electronic media.

We start by charting the opposing points of view and then go on to develop a vision of the future of journalism. First, the arguments that state that the profession of journalism will become redundant.

Will journalism become redundant?

The gradual but inexorable *shift* in the current media landscape from *print to audiovisual means* (Sociaal en Cultureel Planbureau, 1994) is not doing the profession any good, so the first assumption goes. Because of the written word and the greater level of abstraction and selectivity, the journalistic surplus-value of the old print media is, it is argued, almost by definition greater than that of the audiovisual media. Television prefers easy-to-follow problems and short 'sound bites' (Rosenblum, 1993). Shocking images make a greater impression than deep debate on the underlying problems. These substantive objections against television journalism will carry even more weight as people come to rely more on television for information on 'serious' subjects. Politicians make use of television's strong position in order to address the electorate directly, circumventing the (critical) press. Over the past few years there have been some telling examples: Ross Perot, Bill Clinton and Silvio Berlusconi. Perot's sudden success fuelled a debate in the United States on what Sandel (1992) has called 'electronic bonapartism'. In Europe, a comparable discussion on 'tele(vision-demo)cracy' took place after the meteorite-like rise of Silvio Berlusconi and his electoral association Forza Italia.

As well as shifts within the existing media – from print to audiovisual – there is also the impact of new technology. First, we notice the *explosion of information* as more new information is produced and the accessibility of existing sources of information, such as databases, increases. Within this growing flow of information, the part played by journalistic products will decrease proportionately, the assumption being that the 'communication pressure' it creates reduces both journalism's scope and the citizen's accessibility.

A primary element of this increasing communication pressure is the *amount of information*, the increase in the volume of information. By now it is well known that the supply of information is expanding explosively, while the amount of time available to the receiver remains more or less constant (Van Cuilenburg et al., 1992: 51–68). In order not to lose track, or to miss as little as possible, consumers have taken refuge in increasingly impatient communication behaviour of which 'zapping' has become the symbol.

But there is more. The *speed* at which news and information circulate in society is also assumed to be steadily increasing (Sociaal en Cultureel Planbureau, 1994: 427). News circulates ever faster and the public adjusts its pattern of expectations accordingly. For the journalist, faster reporting means less time for selection and processing. Across the board, the time difference between event and report is decreasing, those involved are allowed less time to give their reactions (Van der Donk and Tops, 1992: 54) and increasingly, moreover, it is the public's opinion that is sought through instant opinion polls, 'The politicians reach the people via television; the people reach the politicians via polls' (see Abramson et al., 1988: 90). The life of public issues is shortened as the publicity process speeds up. This whirling communication carousel of immediate action and reaction within the publicity process decreases rather than increases the scope for journalistic signification.

Finally, increased opportunities for telematic communication also lead to a greater concentration, a greater *density* (Münch, 1993: 262–3; Weischenberg et al., 1994: 27) of available information. In principle, each message can now reach everyone and, in principle, be received by everyone. Journalists are finding it increasingly difficult to attract the public's attention within this densely packed public space. There is a parallel increase in employment opportunities for professional attracters of attention such as government information officials and public relations (PR) officers, the natural antipodes of journalists. Recent research in the Netherlands shows that the first group already outnumbers the latter by 2:1 (Van Ruler and de Lange, 1995: 24).

When we wish to summarize the preceding trends into a formula, the 'communication pressure' in society consists of a multiplication of volume, speed of circulation and density of public communication:

Communication pressure = Volume × Speed of circulation × Density.

The most distinguishing feature of the new communication services based on telematics, *interactivity* (Bardoel, 1993: 57), undermines the position of journalism yet again. The emphasis shifts from 'allocution' to 'consultation' (Bordewijk and Van Kaam, 1982; McQuail, 1987: 41), from undirected dissemination to a directed search for information. Increasingly, it is the receiver to whom the task of selection falls. Although it is fair to say that only a limited public, as yet, will actually make use of such (inter)active opportunities, as a matter of principle their significance is considerable, for they infringe on the exclusive access to many different sources that journalists have enjoyed up till now.

Interactive services may also provide an incentive for increased communication between citizens, for *horizontal communication* in society. It has been predicted that this development will be at the expense of the existing vertical communication between the state and the citizen, in which journalism has traditionally played such an important part. The advance of what Abramson et al. (1988: 113) refer to as 'unmediated media' may exert extra pressure on the position and the filtering effect of the established media. Moreover, the combination of computers and networks provides additional opportunities for communication in fields of social life hitherto practically untouched by the media. We are already seeing the emergence of many new circles of communication, bound together by common interest, through services such as the Internet. The 'media gap'

(Neuman, 1991: 9–10) between interpersonal communication and mass communication is gradually being closed. In other words, 'civil society' is also being 'mediatised' (Bardoel, 1993: 57). There is, however, little or no journalistic intervention involved in these new, direct forms of media communication.

The existing *vertical communication* between citizens and the state is also expected to become easier and to bypass such traditional intermediaries as political parties and journalists. Many observers have remarked that the modern technological opportunities for direct interaction with citizens and direct democracy are even a panacea for the limitations of representative democracy. [...]

The position of journalism is not only under debate as a direct result of the trends in technology, such as the advance of (satellite) television, the surplus of information and the advent of interactive media. These are also reflected in wider developments in society that are equally threatening to the journalist's position.

This technology reinforces the tendency both to decentralization through horizontal communication and to centralization in the form of a globalized communication flow. As new and old media are linked in a global network, the individual journalist is reduced to just a cog in an ever widening 'communication machine'. Of course, the globalization of the communication structure began long ago with the advance of internationally operating press agencies. But the pace of development is increasing with the advent of worldwide news stations such as CNN, databases and expert systems. Separate media and individual journalists are increasingly helpless in the face of this global flow of information. Münch (1993: 276) compares the modern journalist with a disc jockey playing their choice of music for a dancing public. The material is produced elsewhere; the disc jockey's job is simply to select and present.

A further threat is presented by the *erosion of the nation-state*, until now an important breeding ground and source of support for the journalistic profession. This traditional centre of political power and sovereignty is losing powers in two directions, to more central and to more decentralized centres of power: on the one hand to Europe, on the other to regional and local entities. During the greater part of the 20th century, states Sandel (1992), the nation-state was regarded as the centre of democratic self-government and as the expression of a collective social identity. In the Western world, however, the nation-state seems no longer able to fulfil those two historical functions – because it is too big to allow the expression of certain feelings of local identity and too small to maintain its hold on global economic processes. Dahlgren (1991: 12) concludes: 'Today, the nation-state as a political entity is in deep crisis, beset not only with fiscal dilemmas but also with problems of legitimation. This crisis of course goes in tandem with the transnationalization of capital and the dispersion of production with the international economy.'

Globalization and the diminishing significance of the nation-state have both tangible and psychological implications. The development of individual lifestyles on the one hand and global connections on the other, leads to a socio-cultural 'Umwertung aller Werte', in which politics are given a different, more modest role to play. These changes have been defined in such terms as *postmodern culture* and cultural value-relativism. McQuail (1992: 4) summarizes, referring to Harvey (1989):

> Its political implication is that the 'Enlightenment project' of rational social progress has drawn to an end, especially in respect of applying bureaucratic means to achieve socially planned collective objectives. As a social-cultural philosophy 'post-modernism' stands opposed to the traditional notion of a fixed and hierarchical culture. It favours forms of culture which are transient, superficial, appealing to sense rather than reason. Postmodern culture is volatile, illogical, kaleidoscopic, inventive, hedonistic. It certainly favours the newer, audiovisual over the older, print media.

It puts an end to several old certainties, without offering a new, normative basis to replace them. This applies to both (ideas on) politics and culture in general and more specifically to journalism. In today's culture, for example, politics occupy a less prominent place, the significance of norms and values is more relative, and the borders between once divided domains (such as information and entertainment, high and low culture) are being blurred.

At the same time, there are fewer objections to *commercial exploitation* – once widely held in the field of the media – and less fear of monopolization, so that there is also less justification providing public amenities to the media. Solutions based on liberal ideas and market conformity apparently provide the foundations for an emerging 'new consensus' on new media policies, both in the United States and in Europe (McQuail, 1993: 196). This (post)modern (media) culture may also have implications for the special social status and protection upon which the profession of journalism has always been able to count.

Will journalism remain?

Now that technology has rendered journalistic intervention less necessary, the future of the profession will depend more than ever on other *social factors* and considerations. The development of a global system of communication and growing 'communication autonomy' of the citizen outlined above, offer new opportunities, but also create new dilemmas and problems. Against this backdrop, these developments and their significance remain, to a certain extent, questionable – both empirically and normatively.

First, it should be noted that the advance of CNN – which indeed prompted many a sombre thought – seems to have passed its zenith. The original agitation around CNN is reminiscent of the unease that accompanies each new technological development upon which new and more direct forms of reporting are based. We may expect the new direct and global television reporting to carve itself a niche alongside – and not primarily instead of – existing forms of journalism. More international news stations will join CNN in providing the daily menu of television. At a national and local level too, comparable news stations will emerge, as has long been the case in the United States.

In general, the shifts in media use outlined above, *from print to audiovisual* – including their assumed disadvantages to journalism – are less impressive than they appear at first sight. Research from the Dutch Social and Cultural Planning Agency (Sociaal en Cultureel Planbureau, 1994) shows that 'loss of reading' occurs mostly in relation to 'popular newspapers, regional papers and the tabloid press', in short 'newspapers and magazines that, in their presentation and simplicity, address the same broad public as broadcasting stations' (Knulst, 1994: 334–5). The generalizing and depreciating approach of television in the recent debate on the 'loss of reading culture' completely ignores the professionalization that television journalism has gone through in the last decades.

Moreover, the first articulated fears that the public would literally be flooded out by the rising tide of information are disappearing. It is becoming clear that receivers develop their own strategies for dealing with the flow. At the same time, technology – itself partly responsible for the flood in the first place – also provides solutions. Artificial memories such as the answering machine, video recorder, fax and personal computer (PC) afford an escape from the pressure of permanent accessibility and direct communication and allow messages to be received later – or not at all. According to Van Cuilenburg (1994: 146–54), in the midst of this surfeit, the modern citizen has an increasing need to be 'absently present', to reserve the right of non-communication. The increase of directed consultation and interaction services at the expense of undirected 'allocutive' communication also provides a defence against an embarrassment of unsolicited communication. The increase in segmentation and 'targeting' may prove a social anomaly. The well-known 'information gap', the inequality between citizens in terms of access to information and participation in the political process, is increasing, and reinforces existing social and political inequality. The fact that certain groups of the population (well-educated, young, male) seem better able to deal with new forms of communication, merely serves to reinforce that inequality further.

Again, the suggestion that the new technology provides a solution for a different gap – the participation gap in democracy, shall we say – is at least questionable. As we have seen, techno-optimists argue that electronic networks offer hitherto unknown opportunities for such matters as dialogue, participation and direct democracy. The technological opportunities for self-representation allow citizens to participate directly in political debate and decision-making and are said to negate the reason for the existence of *intermediary agencies* such as political parties and the mass media. While the first experimental experiences have shown that electronic meetings may contribute to sociopolitical debate, they cannot replace representative democracy (Van Dijk, 1991: 80–90). Electronic communication differs too much from face-to-face communication, like in gatherings. Via electronic networks citizens are approached separately, without there being a common identity or a shared signification system. The handling of the agenda proves to be a problem in electronic meetings. This direct democracy lacks the mechanisms of common consideration and compromising that are inherent in representative democracy.

The nature of direct, electronic communication is often elusive: it is well suited to consumerism marketing (in politics too), but does not provide an alternative to existing forms of opinion formation and decision-making. According to

Van Dijk (1994: 9), it is primarily populist political movements such as that of Ross Perot and short-lived campaign organizations (à la Clinton) that make use of media and information technology.

The assumption that the individual citizen will make the most of all of the political and personal opportunities that unlimited information affords, is also receiving more and more criticism. The most important consequence of the new media situation may well lie, as is increasingly acknowledged, in the field of social integration and political participation (Weischenberg et al., 1994). In an electronic and individualized society, such notions as 'community' and 'debate' will inevitably be less self-evident. Abramson et al. (1988) point to the function that the national media have had as an important source of common civic culture, in which the goals are a common political vocabulary, a common political agenda and the formation of public opinion. Indeed, one of the paradoxes of the new technology is that, in principle, it greatly increases the opportunities for getting together, but in practice decreases the chances of that happening accordingly. At best, once stable communities evaporate into 'shared moments' (Tracey, 1993: 14–16).

The transformation from traditional, physical community to a modern, abstract public sphere (Öffentlichkeit) renders the organization of social debate increasingly difficult. The concept of 'debate' itself suggests still a unity of time, place and action that is, in the modern media reality, 'stretched out' to a process of – in relation to time and place – scattered contributions to the discussion. Nevertheless, terms such as 'conversation' (Hallin, 1992: 10) or 'debate' remain the dominant metaphors in relation to the public sphere, a position that the 'market' metaphor holds in the economic sector.

Despite the reduced chance of getting together, modern society shows an increasing need for common orientation and debate. Absolute norms and values, derived from conviction or religion, are less and less functional. More and more, we live according to relative guidelines, permanently redetermined and adapted in mutual debate. Knapen (1994: 362) has concluded correctly: 'Whoever is unable or unwilling to draw socio-political guidance from the Bible, from Allah or the Pope, will have to get it from mutual discourse.'

New journalistic practices

Within this framework, individualization of communication can be seen as a threat to social dialogue. Habermas (1992: 438) emphasizes the importance of a *discursive public sphere* that is more than a mere statistical majority. The social basis for an active political Öffentlichkeit in this sense is 'civil society' (Dekker, 1994). This concept has become increasingly popular in social science over the past years. It stands for the organizations, societies and movements that, at an intermediate level, determine political democracy and social cohesion in a given society. It presupposes an open and pluralistic field of voluntary organizations and informal groups, as an alternative to relationships between people that are governed by market forces or a hierarchical, state-dominated model of opinion formation and power blocs (Edwards, 1994: 317). In a notion of 'civil society', a certain involvement is expected of the citizen, and in that sense there is a link with recent debate in the Netherlands on *citizenship and civic consciousness*. More generally, there are arguments in favour of broadening the concept of 'citizenship', from its classical, rational-political content to a more (post)modern, sociocultural interpretation. This is in line with the above-mentioned eroding primacy of politics in society and with the real, not compartmentalized, outlook of people on life and society. […]

Concepts such as 'public sphere' and 'civil society' allow us to reach a more well-considered conclusion on the effect of the new media on public communication and the position of journalism within these developments. Taking the concept of civil society as a starting point, the new technology is easily recognized as a facilitating device for social contact and relationships at a meso-level, positioning between traditional mass media and person-to-person communication. We have already seen that this technology, based on computers and networks, is likely to affect society at a meso-level most, a domain that as yet is barely 'mediatised' (Bardoel, 1993: 57), overcoming the limitations of distance/space and time and offering more opportunity for horizontal communication between citizens. If it is true that, to paraphrase Peters (1993: 566), that mass media are splendid in representation but horrid for participation, the opposite may hold for the new information and communication technology. According to Tops et al. (1995: 104–5), the use of this new technology opens up opportunities for forms of direct democracy and for a more 'responsive' representational democracy. Although we should be very cautious not to fall into the trap of technological determinism we must acknowledge that certainly there are new opportunities. The extensive interest in the Internet could be possibly interpreted as the first sign of this development.

However, it is a very different matter to assume that new opportunities for communication will make the old intermediary frameworks (like mass media and political parties) superfluous. Inevitably, they will be somewhat crowded, but not crowded out, for in general we may assume that *new relationships* will *add to* rather than replace old ones. Both old and new media will assist in recognizing and defining the problems that politics must address. Compared to the new communication technology and information services, the mass media and political parties mainly operate at a different stage of social issue formation. It is possible to represent the mechanism of public cq. political debate graphically. Unlike Habermas, who seems to think of social communication in terms of concentric circles (he refers to it as centre and periphery), our figure (Figure 14.1) – following McQuail's (1987: 6) figure of 'communication processes in society' – contains a *communication pyramid*.

The shape of a pyramid has been chosen to illustrate the bottom–up process of problem selection and definition by citizens and the top–down process of producing decisions, measures and solutions by the political establishment. Going up in the pyramid means more support and fewer issues (issue filtration). It shows the position of the mass media (and therefore also of journalists) and of political parties as 'higher up' in the pyramid than the new interactive communication technology. If new technological developments further down in

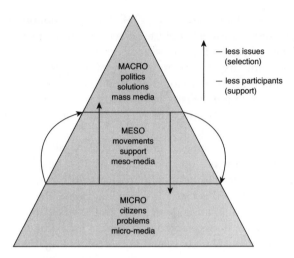

FIGURE 14.1   COMMUNICATION PYRAMID–PUBLIC/POLITICAL DEBATE
Source: Bardoel (1995)

the pyramid – so the assumption goes – lead to greater opportunities for mediated communication on the meso-level, the selection and filtering of relevant issues higher up in the pyramid may be expected to gain in significance. Journalism will therefore, in my view, continue to play a crucial part in recruiting and processing relevant issues from the growing plurality of public spheres towards the political centre (Habermas) or towards the top (in my model). Therefore the function of journalism as a director of social debate will be more essential than ever in a society in which the pressure of communication is steadily increasing. Journalism will not, as in the era of mass media, control the public debate, but can take the lead in directing and defining the public agenda. As journalists are no longer the indispensable intermediaries between the outside world and the public, they must prove their position in this respect. It is important that journalists take this aspect of their intermediary task more seriously than they seem to do at present. […]

Orientating and instrumental journalism

The position of journalism as a 'unified' profession that encompasses many very different activities at very different levels, seems no longer tenable. The advent of new media formats, based on multimedia applications and the increasing (inter)activity of the user, make this presumption less realistic then it already was. Ideal-typically, I see two sorts of journalism developing (Bardoel, 1993: 117–20). First, there is *orientating journalism* whose job it is to provide a general orientation (background, commentary, explanation) to a general public. Second, there is *instrumental journalism*, geared to providing information (functional, specialistic) to interested customers. (I gladly leave to the reader the question of whether all of these activities should be called journalism.)

	ORIENTATING	INSTRUMENTAL
Goal:	orientation	action
Function:	stage, forum	file, memory
Emphasis:	attention	information
User:	public/citizens	individual/role player
Info-mode:	one way/'allocution'	interactive/'consultation'
Product:	'fax paper'	'PC paper'
Profession:	'old' journalism	'new' journalism

FIGURE 14.2   IDEAL-TYPES OF JOURNALISM

Source: compare Bardoel (1993: 119).

The main differences between these journalistic ideal-types are indicated in Figure 14.2. It will be clear that the new information services require mostly 'new' journalists (or information brokers), while the classical media seek 'old' journalists. As we have said, these are ideal-types; all sorts of mixtures are possible.

We can see, therefore, that as the media sector segments, the integrating, centripetal task gains in importance as well. There will be employment for journalists in both fields in the future. The difference is that the first task will expand while the second will shrink, and thus journalistic intervention will be threatened, both in quantitative and qualitative terms.

What will happen to *classical journalism*? In a society held together less by geographical and physical relationships than by medial and symbolic links, the good journalist functions as a conductor of social debate and a broker of social consensus. Peters' (1993: 550) thesis that – referring to Bentham and Mill – the press functions as the 'social superego' and the 'moral regulator' for the coordination of society contains more truth then ever before. In the new surfeit of information, the traditional task of journalism will evolve from sending messages to offering orientation to the citizen and the emphasis will shift from 'content' to 'context'. We have already suggested that the emphasis in journalistic intervention will shift from 'getting' information to 'bringing' information (Bardoel, 1989: 49). Within the profession itself, however, the emphasis is still very much on collecting information (the traditional 'TinTin romanticism' in journalism) and less on directing the social flow of information and public debate. More than ever, the task of journalism will lie in filtering relevant issues from an increasing supply of information in a crowded public domain and its fragmented segments. Journalism evolves from the provision of facts to the provision of meaning. In the new ocean of information, 'navigation' is desperately needed. Information in itself is less important than information shared with others. Communication rather than information becomes the key word, and journalists have a long tradition in bringing minds together. In fulfilling this function the – higher educated – public expects the journalist to put aside all traces of old-fashioned paternalism.

At the same time, it should be noted that journalism does not seem adequately equipped to deal with this new task. Blumler (1992: 104) has said: 'A threading suture of these analyses is that a weakened political sphere confers on journalism functions and responsibilities that it is at best half-equipped to assume: agenda definition, interest aggregation, civic correlation, and sense-making.' The recent increase in news 'hypes' in the Netherlands and elsewhere – as a result of the speeding up, competition and concentration in the dissemination of news – shows that journalistic ethics and practice vis-á-vis its role in public communication are lagging behind. The new challenges require responsibilities beyond traditional journalism.

On the other hand, the new media offer scope for 'instrumental journalism', as I have called the work in the new information services. As yet there are no clear professional profiles or training requirements in this field. The new information broker appears to be an unspecialized Jack-or-Jane-of-all-trades. The emphasis will be, for the time being, on exploring and developing new techniques in the direction of meaningful and profitable exploitation by information services (product development). A knowledge of the technology, of layout (computer graphics) and of the compact, brief and sequential presentation of information via menus and trees, is essential. Of course, basic journalistic skills remain important. Moreover, information and database management – skills thus far mostly found among documentation professionals – will gain in importance, while knowledge of and orientation towards target groups are basic conditions. Indeed, the individual user pays the piper and calls the tune, thanks to direct feedback via interactive techniques and paying per unit used. Journalism and marketing will have more to do with each other than many an old press dog would wish.

A number of these changes will have repercussions for journalism in general. Digital techniques join previously separate flows of information in networks and increase the options for users. The importance of *journalistic distinction*, the recognizable surplus value of journalism vis-á-vis the products of documentation professionals (such as documentalists) and publicity professionals (such as PR agents) is increasing, not in the last instance because journalistic information has its price.

Moreover, the journalist's work will be increasingly less bound to specific media. 'Single source, multiple media' is a term often heard in this connection. This means that journalists will find themselves more frequently on publishing desks, together with layout and marketing staff, and that they will work individually and from a distance as modern teleworkers. This threatens the *collective culture* of the editorial desk, always an important factor in and guarantee for the transfer of professional skills and values. The threat will increase as the different provisions that have always served to protect editorial space against commercial and political interests, come under pressure. Public broadcasting is in deep water here, both as a matter of principle (legitimation) and of practice (finance). The scope of responsible journalism – in practice especially the press – in the market sector, is increasingly dependent on a decreasing number of owners. There is a risk that the 'enlightened' media owner of yesteryear, with their understanding of journalism's specific position, will be replaced by owners with an eye to 'return on investment' only. The risk increases as new players flow in from 'outside' as a result of the convergence of media and telecommunication, but by definition lacking all affinity with media culture. In that light, it may be necessary to create new guarantees or to develop new media ethics (Dennis, 1994; Harwood Group, 1995). It goes without saying that training and education should play an important role here.

At the end of the 20th century, journalism must once again seek its place in a changing society. A society that is secular, open, more dependent on media, transnational and whose members are relatively well educated. This implies that the profession can be bypassed more easily, but it makes journalism more valuable at the same time. The concerns outlined in the introduction are legitimate. There *is* ever more direct, unmediated television reporting – both worldwide and local. There *are* ever more interactive communication media. The social dissemination of information *is* increasingly individual and it *is* increasingly difficult to organize getting together and debate. 'Journalism' – if it ever existed as such – is falling apart. On the one hand, there is a need for information brokers, on the other, for directors and conductors of the public debate.

The function of classical journalism will probably shift to the latter position, also because the profession is one of the last strongholds of generalism in an increasingly specialized and fragmented society (Bardoel, 1988: 157). Greater individual freedom for citizens produces, more than ever, the need for common orientation. This might be the most important mission for journalists in the future – a mission that calls for responsibilities and skills beyond the present journalistic practice.

References

Abramson, J.B., F.C. Arterton and G.R. Orren (1988) *The Electronic Commonwealth. The Impact of New Technologies upon Democratic Politics*. New York: Basic Books.

Bardoel, J. (1988) 'Nieuwe informatietechnologie en journalistiek domein', pp. 149–67 in L. Heinsman and J. Servaes (eds), *Hoe nieuw zijn de nieuwe media? Een mediabeleid met een perspectief*. Leuven and Amersfoort: ACCO.

Bardoel, J.L.H. (1989) 'Journalistiek en nieuwe informatietechnologie', pp. 41–55 in J. Bardoel (ed.), *De krant van morgen. De elektronische toekomst van de schrijvende pers*. Amsterdam: Stichting 'Het Persinstituut'.

Bardoel, Jo (1993) *Zonder pen of papier. Journalistiek op de drempel van een nieuwe eeuw*. Amsterdam: Otto Cramwinckel Uitgever.

Bardoel, Jo (1995) 'Journalistieke tussen komst overbodig? Professie tussen informatienaatschappij en civile samenleving', *Massacommunicatie* 23(3): 136–59. (This article is an older and longer version in Dutch of this article.)

Blumler, J.G. (1992) 'News Media in Flux: An Analytical Afterword', *Journal of Communication* 42(3): 100–8.

Bordewijk, J.L. and B. van Kaam (1982) *Allocutie. Enkele gedachten over communicatievrijheid in een bekabeld land*. Baarn: Bosch en Keuning.

Calhoun, C. (1992) *Habermas and the Public Sphere*. Cambridge, MA: MIT Press.

Dahlgren, P. (1991) 'Introduction', pp. 1–25 in P. Dahlgren and C. Sparks (eds), *Communication and Citizenship. Journalism and the Public Sphere in the New Media*. New York: Routledge.

Dekker, P. (1994) *Civil Society. Verkenningen van een perspectief op vrijwilligerswerk*. (Vol. 1), pp. 42–9. Rijswijk and Den Haag: Sociaal en Cultureel Planbureau/VUGA.

Dennis, E.E. (1994) 'An Ethic for a New Age', *Media Studies Journal* (Freedom Forum Media Studies Center) 8(1): 143–53.

Edwards, A.R. (1994) 'Informatisering, democratie en staatsburgerrol', pp. 309–21 in A. Zuurmond, J. Huigen, P.H.A. Frissen, I.Th.M. Snellen and P.W. Tops (eds), *Informatisering in het openbaar bestuur. Technologie en sturing bestuurskundig beschouwd.* 's-Gravenhage: VUGA Uitgeverij.

Habermas, J. (1992) *Faktizität und Geltung. Beiträge zur Diskurstheorie des Rechts und des demokratischen Rechtsstaats.* Frankfurt am Main: Suhrkamp.

Hallin, D.C. (1992) 'We Keep America on Top of the World. Television Journalism and the Public Sphere', *Journal of Communication* 3(4): 14–26.

Harvey, D. (1989) *The Condition of Postmodernity. An Enquiry into the Origins of Cultural Change.* Oxford and Cambridge: Blackwell.

Harwood Group (1995) *Timeless Values. Staying True to Journalistic Principles in the Age of the New Media.* Reston: American Society of Newspaper Editors.

Knapen, B. (1994) 'Hoe au courant is de krant?', *De Gids* May: 356–65.

Knulst, W. (1994) 'Omroep en publiek', pp. 300–38 in H. Wijfjes (ed.), *Omroep in Nederland. Vijfenzeventig jaar medium en maaatschappij, 1919–1994.* Zwolle: Waanders.

McQuail, D. (1987) *Mass Communication Theory; An Introduction.* London: Sage.

McQuail, D. (1992) 'Public Interest Theories of Mass Communications in an Information Society', *The Bulletin of Institute of Journalism and Communication Studies* (The University of Tokyo) 45: 2–17.

McQuail, D. (1993) 'Informing the Information Society; The Task for Communication Science', pp. 185–99 in P. Gaunt (ed.), *Beyond Agendas. New Directions in Communication Research.* Westport and London.

Münch, R. (1993) 'Journalismus in der Kommunikationsgesellschaft', *Publizistik* 38(3): 261–80.

Neuman, W.R. (1991) *The Future of the Mass Audience.* Cambridge: Cambridge University Press.

Peters, J.D. (1993) 'Distrust of Representation: Habermas on the Public Sphere', *Media, Culture and Society* 15(4): 541–71.

Rosenblum, M. (1993) *Who Stole the News?* New York: Wiley.

Sandel, M. (1992) *De Volkskrant* 19 October. (The article was first published in *New Perspectives Quarterly.*)

Sociaal en Cultureel Planbureau (1994) *Sociaal en Cultureel Rapport 1994.* Den Haag: VUGA.

Tops, P.W., C.A.T. Schalken and S. Zouridis (1995) 'ICT en veranderende relatiepatronen tussen burgers en bestuur', in I. Baten and J. Ubacht (eds), *Een kwestie van toegang. Bijdragen aan het debat over het publieke domein van de informatievoorziening.* Amsterdam: Otto Cramwinckel Uitgever (with Rathenau Instituut, Den Haag).

Tracey, M. (1993) 'A Ceremony of Innocence. An Interpretation of the Condition of Public Service TV', pp. 39–65 in W. Stevenson (ed.), *All our Futures. The Changing Role and Purpose of the BBC.* The BBC Charter Review Series. London: BFI.

Van Cuilenburg, J.J. (1994) 'Een toekomst vol informatie en communicatie', pp. 146–54 in A.C. Zijderveld (ed.), *Kleine geschiedenis van de toekomst: 100 thesen over de westerse samenleving op weg naar de eenentwintigste eeuw.* Kampen: Kok Agora.

Van Cuilenburg, J.J., O. Scholten and G.W. Noomen (1992) *Communicatiewetenschap.* Minderburg: Dick Coutinho.

Van der, Donk, W.B.H.J. and P.W. Tops (1992) 'Informatisering en demokratie: Orwell of Athene?' pp. 33–75 in P.H.A. Frissen et al. (eds), *Orwell of Athene? Democratie en informatiesamenleving.* Den Haag: SDU/NOTA.

Van Dijk, J.A.G.M. (1991) *De netwerkmaatschappij. Sociale aspecten van nieuwe media.* Houten: Bohn Stafleu Van Loghum.

Van Dijk, J.A.G.M. (1994) 'De programma's dreigen het van de kiezers te verliezen', *NRC-Handelsblad* 15 April: 9.

Van Kaam, B. (1991) *Het taaie leven van de dode letter.* Amsterdam: Otto Cramwinckel Uitgever.

Van Ruler, B. and R. de Lange (1995) 'Kwantiteit is geen probleem, nu de kwaliteit nog. Onderzoek onder 700 bedrijven schetst helder beeld communicatiebranche', *Communicatie* 1(1): 24–5.

Weischenberg, S., K.D. Attmeppen and M. Löffelholz (1994) *Die Zukunft des Journalismus.* Opladen: Westdeutscher Verlag.

Wiering, F. and R. Schröder (1994) 'Beeldstorm', transcript of a television documentary 'Van McLuhan tot Virtual Reality', broadcast by Nederland 3, 4 September 1994. Hilversum: VPRO.

15

Journalistic Codes of Ethics in Europe

Tiina Laitila

Introduction

This article is based on my MA thesis 'European Media Ethics. In Search of a Common Basis' which deals with the possibility of a common code of ethics for European journalism.[1] The notorious Resolution and Recommendation on ethics of journalism moved by the Parliamentary Assembly of the Council of Europe in 1993 have served as my provocateurs, the European journalists' ethical codes as my starting point.

The Resolution and Recommendation suggested an establishment of a media ombudsman functioning on a European level, in addition to a set of ethical principles for European journalism. These suggestions were based on an idea that the media in Europe share similar problems and practices to a degree that they could be regulated by common rules and mechanisms. But do the journalists, editors and owners of the media – the real actors in the field – share similar norms and ideals in their work? This is the framework for my elaboration in this article.

The elaboration is made with the help of the national codes of ethics, which are seen to represent journalists' values and norms. The comparison of the codes shows whether the European journalists share similar rules and ideals, and whether it would thus be possible to create common ethical guidelines for European journalists. Here possibility is regarded as a theoretical, not as a practical question. The starting point is the codes of ethics of the European journalists, and the ideals of good journalism they offer.

While my research addresses the ethics of journalism in contemporary Europe, it can also be regarded as a part of the tradition to accumulate documentation about professional codes of ethics – a tradition already initiated at the University of Tampere in the mid-1970s (Leppänen, 1977; Alanen, 1979; Juusela, 1991). The next stage will be an electronic database including the texts of these codes.

Codes and their founders

Thirty-one journalistic codes of ethics representing 29 European countries were included in the comparison (see Table 15.1). Two-thirds of them are adopted by

Source: *EJC* (1995), vol. 10, no. 4: 527–44.

TABLE 15.1   THE ADOPTING BODIES OF THE EUROPEAN CODES

Code by journalists of	Journalists only	Journalists and publishers	Press council	State and journalists	Press council[a]
1. Austria			X		X
2. Belgium		X			X
3. Bulgaria	X				
4. Catalonia[b]	X				
5. Croatia	X				
6. Czech Republic	X				
7. Denmark				X	X
8. Finland	X				X
9. France	X				
10. Germany			X		X
11. Greece		X			X
12. Hungary	X				
13. Iceland	X				X
14. Ireland	X				
15. Italy	X				X
16. Latvia	X				
17. Luxembourg			X		X
18. Malta	X				X
19. Netherlands	X				X
20. Norway		X			X
21. Poland		X			
22. Portugal	X				X
23. Russia	X				
24. Slovak Republic	X				
25. Slovenia	X				X
26. Spain	X				
27. Sweden		X			X
28. Switzerland	X				X
29. Turkey			X		X
30. UK I	X				
31. UK II			X		X
Total	20	5	5	1	18

[a]Here the existence or non-existence of a press council in the countries examined is presented according to Sonninen and Laitila (1995). In addition to the ones listed here, there are councils also in Estonia and Romania.
[b]The Catalan code is the only regional code of ethics included in the study.

the unions or associations of journalists (20 codes). The second and third largest groups include the codes adopted by press councils (five codes) and the codes adopted by the journalists' and publishers' associations jointly (five codes). Finally, one code, that of Denmark, is adopted by the state and the journalists together.

Denmark's National Code of Conduct is unique among the codes examined, being introduced as a part of the Danish media law, the Media Liability Act, in

1992. In the Act, the journalism ethics are given their own chapter where it is stated that media contents and conduct must correspond to 'sound press ethics'. A press council was also created together with the new law in order to supervise ethics (Nissen Kruuse, 1993: 24). Strictly the Danish code should not have been part of the comparison, since it is a legal code. However, I included it in the study because it was adopted in cooperation with the Danish Union of Journalists. Before its adoption the journalists had no code whatsoever, only the publishers' association had a set of principles, which dated from 1981 (Juusela, 1991: 14).

When compared to another self-regulatory system, that of press councils, it seems that the codes of ethics are more often the instruments of the journalists themselves than are the councils. Among the 20 press councils functioning in Europe at the moment, six (those of Iceland, the Netherlands, Romania, Slovenia, Switzerland and Turkey) are founded solely by journalists' associations, and almost as many are established by the state (the Belgian, Danish, Greek and Portuguese councils). The rest of the councils are founded by different cooperation boards consisting of journalists, editors, publishers and/or the state (Sonninen and Laitila, 1995: 10–11).

Recent revisions

Most (21) of the codes have been adopted or revised in the 1990s. Six codes (those of Austria, Belgium, Iceland, the Czech Republic, the Netherlands and Turkey) date back to the 1980s, the Swiss and Greek codes to the 1970s, and one, that of the French journalists, to the 1930s.

Many of the codes originally date back further than the last 25 years. Four out of the 31 codes were adopted before the Second World War. The French code dates back to 1918, the Swedish one to 1923, the Finnish to 1924 and the Norwegian to 1936 (Bruun, 1979: 18–19).

The second spate of codes were introduced during the post-war period, from the late 1940s to 1960. Six codes were adopted during this time. The British National Union of Journalists established its first code in the late 1940s. The ethical code of Belgium was adopted in 1951, the International Federation of Journalists' (IFJ) code followed by the Dutch and the Czech journalists was set up in 1954, the Italian in 1957 and the Turkish in 1960 (Bruun, 1979: 20–2).

The 1970s and early 1980s saw a third boom, when seven more codes were adopted. The Austrian code was created in 1971, the Swiss in 1972, the German in 1973, the Greek and the Spanish in 1978, the Portuguese in 1979 and the Danish code in 1981.

The Bulgarian, Croatian, Hungarian, Latvian, Slovak, Slovenian, Polish and Russian codes have all been adopted in the 1990s. The Central and Eastern European journalists already had codes of ethics, but after the democratization of their countries they have all established new sets of principles that differ to a great extent from the old ones. This is why the codes applying to those countries are considered to be originally adopted in the 1990s. [...]

Functions as a basis for the comparison

I believe these codes of ethics have two main functions. On the one hand, their function is to specify accountability with regard to different outside interests; mainly the state, the public, the sources and the advertisers. Behind this is partly the need to 'look good' in the eyes of the regulators; to convince them that no further surveillance is needed. The need to show accountability is also a direct consequence of the duties of journalists in democratic societies; their role as informers of the public and watchdogs over the ruling powers.

On the other hand, a function of ethical codes and other self-regulatory mechanisms is also to protect the integrity and identity of the profession itself, both from external (state, interest groups, etc.) and internal (plagiarization, yellow press, and so forth) pressures.

The two-fold nature of self-regulation is emphasized by Ari Heinonen (1995). According to him, some kind of normative system (such as codes of ethics) which self-regulation implies, can be constructed only in relation to some articulated role expectations, as in relation to those of public interest demands. But since self-regulation to a great degree also reflects the values and norms of the journalistic profession, its substance can be regarded as 'the profession's interpretation of the public interest demands, amended by the aspects connected to the professional integrity' (Heinonen, 1995: 45, 63). For Heinonen self-regulation and its mechanisms represent a certain kind of compromise between the claims of society and the needs of the profession. [...]

From the two general functions of the codes six more specific ones can be derived. Four are named after – in my opinion – the most important groups regulating journalists. Through their codes of ethics the journalists show accountability (1) to the public, (2) to the sources and referents, (3) to their employers and (4) to the state. The latter two functions, on the other hand, concern the journalists' professional identity by protecting (5) the professional integrity of journalists and (6) the status and unity of the journalistic profession. The fifth function refers to external interference on the part of, for instance, the advertisers, whereas the sixth function refers to the clauses consolidating the good reputation of and solidarity among the journalists; thus protecting the profession from inside pressures.

I highlighted these particular six functions partly by selectively following the lines of accountability within the media and between the media and the outside world, drawn up by Denis McQuail (1994) (see Figures 15.1 and 15.2). The thoughts of several other scholars (e.g. Bruun, 1979; Jones, 1980; Harris, 1992) and the texts of the codes themselves have also led me to concentrate on this 'group of six'.

The six chosen functions constituted the basic classification for comparing the topics covered by national codes. The six functions were further divided into 13 categories as follows:

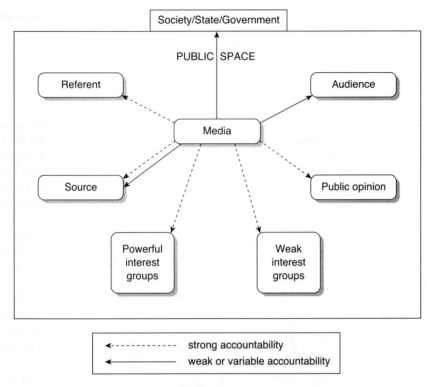

FIGURE 15.1   LINES OF ACCOUNTABILITY (FROM MCQUAIL, 1994)

Accountability

1. To the public:

    I.   Truthfulness of information;
    II.   Clarity of information;
    III.   Defence of public rights;
    IV.   Responsibilities as creators of public opinion.

2. To the sources and referents:

    V.   Gathering and presenting information;
    VI.   Integrity of the source.

3. To the state:

    VII.   Respect for state institutions.

4. To the employers:

    VIII.   Loyalty to the employer.

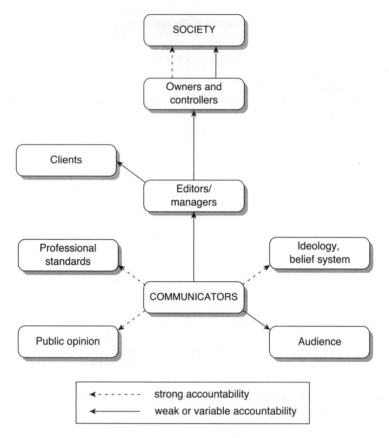

FIGURE 15.2   INTRA-MEDIA ACCOUNTABILITY RELATIONS (FROM MCQUAIL, 1994)

Professional Identity

5. Protection of the integrity of journalists:

    IX.   General rights and prohibitions;
    X.   Protection from public powers;
    XI.   Protection from employers and advertisers.

6. Protection of the unity of the profession:

    XII. Protection of the status of journalism;
    XIII. Protection of the solidarity within the profession.

Under these 13 categories, 61 specific principles of journalistic ethics were identified.

The most common functions

The comparison was based on identifying the presence or absence of the 61 principles in each of the 31 codes. When calculating this it turns out that the most common

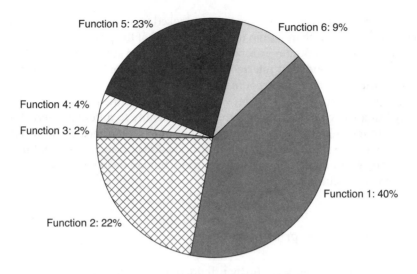

FUNCTION 1: Showing accountability to the *public*
FUNCTION 2: Showing accountability to the *sources* and *referents*
FUNCTION 3: Showing accountability to the *state*
FUNCTION 4: Showing accountability to the *employers*
FUNCTION 5: Protecting journalists' *professional integrity*
FUNCTION 6: Protecting the *status* and *unity* of the profession

FIGURE 15.3   THE FUNCTIONS OF THE EUROPEAN CODES

functions of the European codes are: accountability to the public (function 1), account-ability to the sources and the referents (function 2) and the protection of journalists' professional integrity (function 5). The principles corresponding to these three func-tions cover 85 percent of all the principles in the national codes studied.

Most of the national codes examined stay in this division of three more or three less common functions. Only in the codes of Bulgaria, France, Hungary and Iceland is the emphasis among the functions clearly different. The Bulgarian, French and Hungarian codes differ by putting more emphasis on pro-tection of the status and unity of journalism (function 6) than on protection of the integrity of the profession (function 5). In the Icelandic code the principles answering to functions 1, 5 and 6 get equal emphasis; more than the sources and referents (function 2). All these differences 'get crooked' into the direction of function 6, none of the national codes emphasizing functions 3 or 4. The general coverage of the six functions is illustrated in Figure 15.3.

As Figure 15.3 shows, most of the national codes place a clear emphasis on the principles showing accountability to the different regulatory groups of journalism. Functions 1–4 cover 67 percent of all the principles of the 31 national codes studied, whereas the principles stressing the protection of journalists' professional identity (see the two main functions of the codes) get only 33 percent coverage.

This shows – at least in principle – that the European journalists mainly base their professional activities on their accountability to the public and to other regulatory groups. This could mean that if/when journalism is accused of irresponsibility, the reasons for this must be looked for elsewhere in the institution of journalism rather than within the ethical values of the profession. If this is the case, a creation of common European media ethics (as suggested in the Resolution and Recommendation referred to in the Introduction) would probably not make journalism any more accountable.

Taking the actual dissatisfaction with journalism on the part of the public in many European countries, the fact that accountability to different external regulatory groups of journalism is emphasized so much could mean that the ethical codes have little significance in real terms. They may contain beautiful phrases about the rights of the public and the sources – but are mere words which do not get put into practice.

The most common principles

The six function classes were further divided into 13 categories. Their coverage in the national codes is illustrated in Table 15.2.

As Table 15.2 shows, the codes of the Italian, Slovak and Slovenian journalists have the widest variety of ethical principles – they include principles corresponding to all 13 categories. The categories stressing truthfulness of information (I), integrity of the source (VI) and general integrity of the journalist (IX) get complete national support. Only the categories emphasizing respect for state institutions (VII) and protection of the solidarity of the journalistic profession (XIII) get support from less than two-thirds of the 31 national codes.

On the level of the individual principles there are quite a few differences between the codes. The classification scheme used in the examination comprised 61 different ethical principles gathered from the national codes overall. None of those principles were present in every one of the codes. Ten principles were present in 75 percent or more, and 24 in more than half of the codes. In the following the principles common to more than half of the European codes are listed in the order of their frequency. After the principle its coverage is presented both in percentages and in absolute numbers in parentheses.

		%
1.	Truthfulness, honesty, accuracy of information (category I)	90 (28)
2.	Correction of errors (I)	90 (28)
3.	Prohibition of discrimination on the basis of race/ethnicity/religion (IV)	87 (27)
4.	Respect for privacy (VI)	87 (27)
5.	Prohibition of accepting bribes or any other benefits (IX)	87 (27)
6.	Fair means in gathering the information (V)	84 (26)
7.	Prohibition of allowing any outsider to have influence on the journalistic work (IX)	84 (26)
8.	Prohibition of discrimination on the basis of sex/social class, etc. (IV)	81 (25)
9.	Freedom of expression, speech, comment, criticism (III)	74 (23)

TABLE 15.2 COVERAGE OF THE 13 CATEGORIES IN THE NATIONAL CODES

Code by	I	II	III	IV	V	VI	VII	VIII	IX	X	XI	XII	XIII	Total
1. Austria	X	–	X	X	X	X	–	–	X	–	–	X	–	7
2. Belgium	X	X	X	X	–	X	–	–	X	X	X	–	–	8
3. Bulgaria	X	X	X	X	X	X	–	X	X	–	X	X	X	11
4. Catalonia	X	X	X	X	X	X	–	X	X	X	X	X	–	11
5. Croatia	X	–	X	X	X	X	X	X	X	X	X	X	X	12
6. Czech Republic	X	X	X	X	X	X	X	X	X	X	–	X	X	12
7. Denmark	X	X	X	X	X	X	–	–	X	–	X	–	–	8
8. Finland	X	X	X	X	X	X	–	X	X	X	X	–	X	11
9. France	X	X	–	X	X	X	–	X	X	X	–	X	X	10
10. Germany	X	X	X	X	X	X	X	X	X	–	X	X	–	11
11. Greece	X	–	X	X	–	X	X	X	X	X	–	X	–	9
12. Hungary	X	–	X	X	X	X	X	X	X	X	X	X	X	11
13. Iceland	X	X	–	X	X	X	–	X	X	X	X	X	X	11
14. Ireland	X	X	X	X	X	X	–	X	X	X	X	X	–	11
15. Italy	X	X	X	X	X	X	X	X	X	X	X	X	X	13
16. Latvia	X	X	X	X	X	X	X	–	X	X	X	–	X	11
17. Luxembourg	X	X	X	–	X	X	–	–	X	–	X	–	–	8
18. Malta	X	X	X	X	X	X	–	X	X	X	X	X	X	12
19. Netherlands	X	X	X	X	X	X	X	X	X	X	–	X	X	12
20. Norway	X	X	X	X	X	X	–	X	X	X	X	X	–	11
21. Poland	X	X	X	X	X	X	–	–	X	–	X	X	–	9
22. Portugal	X	X	X	X	X	X	–	X	X	–	X	–	X	10
23. Russia	X	X	–	X	X	X	X	X	X	X	X	X	X	12
24. Slovak Republic	X	X	X	X	X	X	X	X	X	X	X	X	X	13
25. Slovenia	X	X	X	X	X	X	X	X	X	X	X	X	X	13
26. Spain	X	X	X	X	X	X	–	X	X	X	X	X	X	12
27. Sweden	X	X	X	X	X	X	X	X	X	–	X	–	X	11
28. Switzerland	X	X	X	–	X	X	–	X	X	X	X	X	X	11
29. Turkey	X	X	X	X	X	X	–	X	X	–	X	X	–	9
30. UK I	X	X	X	X	X	X	–	X	X	X	X	X	–	11
31. UK II	X	X	–	X	X	X	–	X	X	X	–	X	–	9
Total	31	27	26	29	29	31	12	25	31	22	25	24	18	

I. Truthfulness of information.
II. Clarity of information.
III. Defence of public's rights.
IV. Responsibilities as creators of public opinion.
V. Gathering and presenting information.
VI. Integrity of the source.
VII. Respect for the state institutions.
VIII. Loyalty to the employer.

IX. Rights and prohibitions protecting journalists' integrity.
X. Protection from public powers.
XI. Protection from employers and advertisers.
XII. Protection of the status and unity of journalism.
XIII. Protection of the solidarity within the profession.

10.	Professional secrecy (VI)	74 (23)
11.	Prohibition to misuse journalistic position in order to acquire personal benefit (VIII)	68 (21)
12.	Coverage of the headlines in the text (I)	65 (20)
13.	Separation of facts and opinions/assumptions (II)	65 (20)
14.	Prohibition of selection and misrepresentation (II)	65 (20)
15.	Respect of copyright and laws of citation (V)	65 (20)

16.	Special consideration in reporting crimes, accidents, etc. (VI)	61 (19)
17.	Checking the facts and the sources (I)	58 (18)
18.	Prohibition of slander, libel, unfounded accusations (V)	58 (18)
19.	Presumption of innocence (VI)	58 (18)
20.	Conscience clause (XI)	58 (18)
21.	Separation of advertisements and editorial material (XI)	58 (18)
22.	Responsibility over everything reported (IV)	55 (17)
23.	Right to free criticism (IX)	52 (16)
24.	Fight against censorship (X)	52 (16)

Occasions 31: 100%

Thus the most common principles in the European codes emphasize different aspects of truthfulness, the need to protect the integrity and independence of journalists, the responsibility of journalists in forming public opinion, fair means in the gathering and presentation of information, protection of the rights of sources and referents, and the freedom to express and communicate ideas and information without hindrance.

These most common themes of the codes correspond well with the earlier studies on codes of ethics in an international perspective. Thomas W. Cooper (1989) distinguishes between three major areas of worldwide concern within the field of media ethics. First, the 'quest for truth' appears, according to him, in all the written codes in the world in one form or another. The second common to them all is the 'desire for responsibility' among communicators: the need for accountability and justice in reporting. The third common area Cooper finds is the 'call for free expression': the demand that information is allowed to flow free from censorship or other outside pressure (Cooper, 1989: 20–1).

Lars Bruun (1979) and J. Clement Jones (1980) also find themes such as truthfulness and objectivity, professional integrity and integrity of the source, as well as equality (prohibition of discrimination on the basis of race, etc.) to be the most common among the different codes of ethics around the world (Bruun, 1979: 27–45; Jones, 1980: 52–3). [...]

The adopters and contents of the codes

One could imagine that the codes adopted exclusively by the journalists themselves would put more emphasis on the protection and the rights of the journalists than the other codes. It could also be assumed that in the codes adopted by the publishers and journalists in conjunction, the principles regarding accountability to the employers would be stressed more than in other codes. And as for the codes adopted by the press councils, it should be the principles stressing the rights of the public and sources which receive greatest emphasis, due to the function of the press councils in dealing with complaints from the public.

However, there does not seem to be any clear connection between the adopting bodies and the contents of the codes. Only the codes adopted by press councils seem to correlate with their adopters: all five codes (the Austrian, British II,

German, Luxembourg and Turkish) having a greater number of principles stressing accountability to the public and sources than average. As for the codes adopted by journalists themselves, and by publishers and journalists together, there is no or only limited connection between the contents of the code and its adopting body. Explanations for the differences between the national codes must thus be looked for elsewhere, for instance in the state and status of journalism, and in the social, cultural and political factors of the given societies.

Towards more responsible codes?

The codes seem to have changed somewhat in the course of time. This is revealed when 13 of the code texts are compared to their earlier versions according to a comparative study on the Conference of Security and Cooperation in Europe (CSCE) countries' ethical codes made by Pauli Juusela (1991).

In most of the cases, the number of principles has increased. The principles that have increased the most are those banning bribes or any outside influence on journalistic work, and the principles stressing copyright. Also the demands for the right to reply, presumption of innocence and prohibition of praising/inciting violence have clearly increased in the codes of the 13 countries. Principles protecting the professional integrity of journalists (function 5) and showing accountability to the public (function 1) have increased the most. The fact that the principles stressing bribes and other outside influences have increased is understandable, taking the growing media concentration and commercialization into consideration. The increased significance of the right to reply, the presumption of innocence and the principles fighting violence might refer to the sensationalism, or, together with copyright, also to the internationalization and the ethical problems caused by new technologies.

Only a few principles have disappeared from the 13 codes. Types of principles that have decreased are those calling for contribution to peace and professional secrecy, stressing accountability to the public (function 1), to the sources and referents (function 2), and protecting journalists' professional integrity (function 5).

According to Hifzi Topuz (1989), the tendency of the ethical principles has been towards more responsibility and international understanding.

> We witness the birth of a new generation of ethical principles. It is no longer the matter of a mere defining of classical principles such as objectivity, truthfulness, ban of plagiarism ... but of the principles aimed at contributing to the development of human rights, securing the respect for a variety of cultures, philosophical and ideological convictions, defending peace and security, avoiding aggression and war propaganda ..., and contributing towards international understanding. (Topuz, 1989: 267)

Kaarle Nordenstreng has also had similar visions about 'internationalizing codes of ethics (see Nordenstreng, 1992: 190–2). Their thoughts get some – though rather weak – support on the basis of the 13 European codes studied.

The possibility of European ethics?

At the beginning of this article a question concerning the possibility of European media ethics was posed. Is there, then, enough basis for a common code in the national codes; do they express similar norms and values, similar ideals of good journalism?

Since there are so many differences among the individual principles of the 31 codes studied, this possibility can only be found on the basis of some principles – or rather themes of principles. The question is how much 'cross-national support' do the principles/themes need in order to be possible ingredients for a European code?

The first criterion would naturally be complete support, hence in order for a principle to be a possible ingredient for a European code, it should be present in all the national, European codes of ethics. But, since there is not a single principle common to all codes this criterion does not take us very far.

Another possible criterion could be – in accordance with the majority principle – that the given principles have to be present in most (more than 50%) of the national codes. Can it thus be postulated that the 24 most common principles listed above are possible ingredients for a European code? Does the fact that they are missing in some – or even in 46 percent of the codes – create a problem?

Not necessarily. When some principles are missing from a code, it does not have to mean they are not regarded as significant by those adopting that code. It might be so, but it can also be that the rights or duties of the missing principles are taken for granted, or that they are considered to be covered by some other principle. For instance, the principle of truthfulness can in some codes also include ideas of objectivity, essentiality, diversity and plurality of information, etc., which are separately mentioned in many other codes. The fact that some codes are already considerably shorter (Austrian, Belgian or Greek) than others (German or Finnish) suggests this.

It is also significant how great/severe the differences between the codes actually are. Are the missing principles along the same lines as the clauses that do exist in the code, or are they in contradiction/opposition to them? It is worth taking into account the aim of the European code. Should it only be a copy of the national codes, or should it also bring something new with it? It would seem logical that a European code should be something more than just a sum of the national codes.

Hence I suggest that if a national code that is lacking a certain principle of those 24 principles common to most of the codes, has some other principle(s) covering the same theme (the same category), and/or if the missing principle is not in contradiction with the other principles of the code, the absence of this principle does not create a problem for the prospects of a European code. The coverage of the 13 categories in the national codes is presented in Table 15.2 (see above).

As can be seen in the table, all but two (VII and XIII) of the 13 categories find support in at least two-thirds of the codes. This strengthens the relevance of the principles representing these categories being ingredients of a European code. Most of these principles also serve the three functions that were found to be the most common ones in the national codes (1: accountability to the public, 2: accountability to the sources and referents, 5: protection of the journalists' professional integrity). All except one of the 24 principles common to more than half of the codes correspond to these categories. They could thus go to make up a European code, which could – and should – contain at least the following themes:

- Truthfulness in gathering and reporting information;
- Freedom of expression and comment, defence of these rights;
- Equality by not discriminating anyone on the basis of his or her race, ethnicity or religion, sex, social class, profession, handicap or any other personal characteristics;
- Fairness by using only straightforward means in the gathering of information;
- Respect for the sources and referents and their integrity; for the copyright and laws of citation;
- Independence/integrity by refusing bribes or any other outside influences on the work, by demanding the conscience clause.

These themes represent the most common functions manifested in the national codes of ethics. In addition, they are actually present in more than half of the national codes. A common European code based on these themes should therefore be consistent with the values and norms of European journalists as expressed in their respective codes of ethics.

Note

1. My thesis was supervised by Professor Kaarle Nordenstreng and Lecturer Ari Heinonen at the University of Tampere, Finland. The topic was chosen whilst studying at the University of Amsterdam (through ERASMUS student mobility programme) under Professor Denis McQuail.

References

Alanen, Antti (1979) 'Journalistien eettiset säännöt ja kansainvälinen oikeus' (The International Law and the Ethical Codes of Journalists), MA thesis, University of Tampere, Finland.
Bruun, Lars (ed.) (1979) *Professional Codes in Journalism*. Prague: International Organization of Journalists.
Cooper, Thomas W. (1989) 'Global Universals: In Search of a Common Ground', pp. 20–39 in T.W. Cooper et al. (eds), *Communication Ethics and Global Change*. New York: Longman.
Council of Europe (1993) 'The Ethics of Journalism', report of the Committee on Culture and Education, Strasbourg.
Harris, Nigel G.E. (1992) 'Codes of Conduct for Journalists', pp. 62–76 in A. Belsey and R. Chadwick (eds), *Ethical Issues in Journalism and Media*. London: Routledge.
Heinonen, Ari (1995) *Vahtikoiran Omatunto. Journalismin itsesäätely ja toimittajat* (The Conscience of a Watchdog. Self-regulation of Journalism and Journalists). Tampere: University of Tampere.

Jones, Clement J. (1980) *Mass Media Codes of Ethics and Councils*. Paris: UNESCO Reports and Papers on Mass Communication.

Juusela, Pauli (1991) *Journalistic Codes of Ethics of the CSCE-countries. An Examination*. Tampere: University of Tampere.

Leppänen, Harri (1977) 'Journalisten kansalliset ja kansainväliset ammatilliset säännöstöt' (The National and International Codes of Journalists), MA thesis, University of Tampere, Finland.

McQuail, Denis (1994) Lecture on 'Media Accountability', University of Amsterdam, 17 March.

Nissen Kruuse, Helle (1993) 'Denmark', pp. 22–55 in Grellier Berlins, and H. Nissen Kruuse (eds), *Les droits et les devoirs des journalistes dans les douze pays de l'Union Européenne*. Paris: Centre de Formation et de Perfectionnement des journalistes.

Nordenstreng, Kaarle (ed.) (1992) *Kansainvälinen Journalistietiikka* (International Ethics of Journalism). Helsinki: Yliopistopaino.

Sonninen, Päivi and Tiina Laitila (1995) 'Press Councils in Europe', survey for WAPC Conference in Helsinki. Forthcoming in the report series of the Department of Journalism and Mass Communication, University of Tampere, December.

Topuz, Hifzi (1989) 'Summary of Rights and Responsibilities', pp. 261–7 in Kaarle Nordenstreng and Hifzi Topuz (eds), *Journalist: Status, Rights and Responsibilities*. Prague: International Organization of Journalists.

16 'Infosuasion' in European Newspapers: A Case Study on the War in Kosovo

Rossella Savarese

From a theoretical point of view, persuasive communication[1] can be portrayed schematically as a diagonal line on a graph with two orthogonal axes: one of the axes being 'interactive communication' while the other is that of 'transactional communication' (Jowett and O'Donnell, 1992). While the purpose of the first is the interaction between people independent of the cognitive content (emotive participation), the aim of transactional communication is to give access to information (Brown and Yule, 1983). In fact, the two forms are always interwoven and each communication is accompanied by both a content aspect and one of relation (Watzlavick et al., 1967).

However, persuasive communication uses interactive communication for a very definite purpose: to influence the interlocutor's attitude to the content in the direction established by the speaker. It may use both verbal and non-verbal language to achieve its aim (Savarese, 1995). On a verbal level, traditional figures of speech, narrative structure and other persuasive techniques are used unconsciously or otherwise to persuade the audience on a specific point of view.

Of all the different forms of mass media, television is the one that acts most on the emotive aspects of persuasion because it uses various and different signals (iconic, verbal and kinaesthetic) and reaches the recipient using two principal sensory channels, those of sight and sound. For this reason television is considered as being the most persuasive and insidious means of communication ever. The persuasive capability of television has grown with the advent of 'neotelevisione'. The concept of 'neotelevisione' was first put forward by Eco (1983). Eco took up Williams's (1974) idea of television's flux. Among the principal characteristics of 'neotelevisione' he described are: the supremacy of contact with respect to the referential function; the evidence of the enunciation verified by the news reader when he or she looks directly into the camera, the announcer's machine; the unclear relationship between information and fiction, inasmuch as events are organized for the purpose of television broadcasting.

In the 1980s, a new type of television programme was established, in which information and entertainment are mixed together, so as to influence not only on a cognitive level but also on an emotive one. Altheide (1991) has defined this kind of format as 'infotainment'.

Source: *EJC* (2000), vol. 15, no. 3: 363–381.

Competition with television has forced newspapers to develop a new way of communicating that gets people's attention and emotive involvement. The circular relationship between the printed press and television led several researchers to speak of a 'media logic', as early as the beginning of the 1970s (Altheide and Snow, 1979). In confirmation of this idea, one can recall the complete graphic transformation that many western newspapers underwent in the 1980s, which started with the launch of the American newspaper *USA Today*. This process climaxed with the introduction of four-colour printing in the daily press (Savarese, 1991). This contributed to an increase in the persuasive aspect of journalistic communication in general. The object of this study is therefore to look at journalistic discourse as a form of persuasive communication.

In analogy with the concept of 'infotainment' we have coined the term 'infosuasion', i.e. mixed and persuasive information. It is a fact that simply reporting someone else's point of view can have a persuasive effect if it is not offset by different points of view. The 'infosuasion' hypothesis, however, goes even further and considers as elements of persuasive language not only the explicitly reported opinions but also the use of figures of speech, already used in ancient rhetoric, modern propaganda techniques and narrative structure itself. Such persuasive techniques are used either deliberately or unwittingly to convince the public of a certain point of view (for or against something) without being explicit, and are part of journalistic routine. A restrictive interpretation of persuasion and of the way in which it acts in terms of language would in fact ultimately leave the media with a wide-ranging freedom and a restrictive conception of objectivity (Tuchman, 1972). In other words, a restrictive interpretation of the concept of persuasion would endorse a formal, rather than a substantial, conception of objectivity.

The aim of this article is to evaluate the type of information produced by European newspapers during the war in Kosovo. It specifically looks at the ways of communicating used in newspapers in France, Spain, Italy, the UK and Germany, before and during the first days of NATO's aerial operations.

NATO's armed intervention against Milosevic's government in spring 1999 is an extremely interesting case study both for the enormous amount of western press coverage and because of the similar analysis done during the crisis in the Persian Gulf (Savarese, 1992). During this earlier event, the US-led coalition intervened with military force against Iraq, which had invaded Kuwait.

On the strength of the results of the previous case study, it has been possible to apply some of the same hypotheses to the crisis in Kosovo. In particular, we look at the idea that a 'media logic' is a common denominator among the biggest and most well-known daily European newspapers with regard to their selection, production and diffusion of news.

Methodology

The investigation was conducted on newspaper articles, in their twofold dimension as testis and as textum. The testis refers to the significance of a text as testimony, the consolidation of an event. The textum relates to its internal structure. This looks at the way in which a text is produced, starting with its framework and ending up with its narrative scheme.[2]

In this study the analysis of the textum concentrated on singling out figures of speech[3] and the use of persuasive techniques. These techniques were selected in a previous research project using the extensive literature on the subject (Savarese, 1995).

The techniques can be divided into two groups. The first group contains techniques based on gestures and speech. These originate in the speeches made in the Roman forum. These techniques, typical of the rhetorical approach to persuasion, are based on language and on the credibility and fame of their source. Moreover, some of these strategies consist in a single communicative act such as a single word.

The second group contains those techniques that go further than the explicit use of speech and gestures. Often the real message is implicit, if not completely concealed. All possible forms of communication (verbal, non-verbal and paraverbal) are employed. They are part of a persuasive strategy which consists of more than one communicative act.[4]

Moreover, the analysis of the textum examines the narrative structure of each article (report or comment), using Greimas's (1983) method (to determine the heroes, the missions, etc.). This method is an elaboration of Russian formalists' narratology, which enables one to adapt the narratological scheme of any text that contains a sequence of events. In fact, according to narratology, telling a story means narrating the transformations which during an event make one situation turn into another. Following Greimas's method these transformations happen at different stages.

In general, in every narrative there is only one hero and one anti-hero. Friends and enemies on the other hand can be numerous, as can be the value objects. We limited our research to finding the most important of these: friends, enemies, value objects. It is also necessary to underline the fact that following Greimas's methodology, narrative roles are not necessarily filled by humans but can also be attributed to abstract or inanimate objects.

Following this method an analysis schedule consisting of a series of multiple choice answers was prepared and tested on different daily newspapers by five analysts, who were all mother-tongue graduates. The interpretation of the articles according to the schedule is without doubt more reliable if the reader-analyst shares the same cultural background as the model reader and author. Even after taking this into account, the actual analysis began after an initial preparation period of three weeks of pretesting and discussion.

The strategy used to analyse data follows both the usual paths taken in descriptive statistical analysis and the method perfected by Lebart et al. (1977) known as 'multiple correspondence analysis' (MCA). This instrument enables the contemporaneous elaboration of a large number of qualitative variables after they have been converted into quantitative variables.[5] The aim of MCA is to analyse the structure of the associations among the various modalities of the variables observed using a questionnaire as a function of latent variables or factors underlying the data. In other words, MCA allows the structure underlying the observed phenomena to be identified, grouping the data together as in factorial analysis.

In order to interpret the modalities correctly, it is necessary to analyse the relationship in terms of relative contributions, as each modality plays a part in structuring the phenomenon. The relationship among modalities is actually represented as a distance between points in three-dimensional space. The sum of the contributions is equal to one. The points making the greatest contribution are thus selected. In other words, the modalities with the highest contribution are thus more significant as regards comprehension of the aspects characterizing the phenomenon. The 'weight' of the modalities is thus a significant synthetic indicator.

Another advantage of adopting this method is that of being able to use a graphic representation of the data on an X-Y axis and in this way to be able to see straight away the typical aspects of the phenomena being studied.

Sample and hypotheses

The sample of 10 daily newspapers used in this project included those considered quality papers and with the biggest circulations. Two newspapers from each country (France, the UK, Italy, Spain and Germany) were selected, one known as being conservative and the other as being liberal. The conservative papers we chose were *Le Figaro, The Times, Il Corriere della Sera, ABC* and *Die Welt*. As examples of the liberal press, we chose: *Le Monde, The Guardian, La Repubblica, El Pais* and *Frankfurter Rundschau*.

All articles published between 17 and 29 March were selected (897 articles). The schedule used to analyse these articles contained 150 multiple choice answers.

In spite of the differences between each individual newspaper, the European press studied had many points in common – typical of what has been called the 'media logic' (Altheide and Snow, 1979). Indicators of this logic include the coverage of the news and the way in which it is presented. Articles dedicated to a particular event follow a characteristic course which depends on the importance of the event and that of the people involved. By carefully choosing the words, images and type faces, the European press uses various dramatic forms in its presentation of events. The news media also use narrative structures, which are typical in fiction, to relate facts.

Moreover, the press expresses a position either for or against the event, both directly or by quoting the opinions of others. Sometimes the use of both more traditional and more recent persuasive techniques conceals these opinions. In this way the press, inasmuch as it declares itself to be objective, influences the formation of what Lippmann (1922) termed as the 'pseudo-environment' of the reader and therefore acts on his or her opinions.

Therefore the research was performed with a view to verifying the following hypotheses, starting from the consideration that the perspective of the article can be deduced by looking both at the words written by the author and the quotes included in the text:

Hypothesis 1.1: Press coverage followed the phases already examined in previous studies, with a 'downpour' of articles occurring once the armed intervention began.

Hypothesis 1.2: The most important perspectives were those about NATO and armed operations in Kosovo (as being necessary, unavoidable, successful and so on).

Hypothesis 1.3: During the week before the beginning of armed operations and the week following, the press prepared public opinion by inviting it to accept the idea of bombing, even without authorization of the UN.

Hypothesis 1.4: The description of events is often based on a process of simplification (e.g. Milosevic = Serbia) and on dichotomous frameworks (for example hero/anti-hero, friend/enemy), according to Greimas's method.

Hypothesis 2: The press 'dramatizes' events using language rich in figures of speech: alliteration, calembour, quotation, euphemism, metaphor, metonymy, oxymoron, simile.

Hypothesis 3: Using the techniques of persuasion adopted in military and political propaganda, like 'name calling', the press tries to build up social images of the characters involved, e.g. the 'monster' Milosevic.

Hypothesis 4: An important aspect of the process of dramatization is the use of non-verbal components (images and layout) to underline and focus people's attention on the emotive aspect of what is happening.

The findings

Media logic

Looking at the coverage during the week before NATO intervention commenced, there are very few articles dedicated to the argument in the daily newspapers in our sample. The data collected were divided into two subperiods (17–22 and 23–29 March). In the first period, 179 articles were published (20 percent of the total), while 718 were published during the second period (80 percent).

A huge increase in the number of articles commenced on 24 March, the day before the first aerial bombing. This is in line with the curve of growing attention found in our earlier research project done on the Persian Gulf crisis, in particular with the stage defined as the 'downpour' (Savarese, 1993: 56). In first place is *Il Corriere della Sera* with two news articles, one comment, a photograph and a cartoon on the front page and nine news articles, two comment pieces, 13 photographs and two graphics in the inside pages.

The other Italian newspaper, *La Repubblica*, contained a news article, two comment pieces and a cartoon strip on the front page. On the inside pages there were six news articles, one comment, 14 photographs and two graphics.

Each of the British newspapers dedicated two articles and a photograph to Kosovo on their front pages, and *The Times* went as far as seven articles on the inside pages. *El Pais* had two articles on the aerial attacks on its front page, one comment piece, two in-depth articles and 14 news items. The articles were accompanied by graphics on the deployment of armed forces and two photographs.

The German dailies and *Le Figaro* each had one article on the front page and five pieces on the inside pages. *Le Figaro* published one photo on the front page and another on the inside pages as did *Die Welt. Frankfurter Rundschau* had a cartoon on the front page and a photo on the inside.

Il Corriere della Sera was the most assiduous, with 142 items during the period between 17 and 29 March inclusive. *La Repubblica* followed with 126 articles.

For and against

The use of arms in Serbia was one of the principal arguments in the public debate. Initially, public opinion was not prepared for discussion on aerial intervention. The news media had given little importance to the negotiations taking place at Rambouillet or the risk posed by Milosevic's despotism. During the first weeks of the conflict many opinion polls were carried out to evaluate the public's attitude. One such poll was carried out by the Archivo Disarmo in Rome and the Trieste company SWG on a sample of 1007 individuals between 15 and 25 April (that is, three weeks from the beginning of intervention). It showed that informed citizens, i.e. those that read a daily paper at least twice a week, were more favourable towards the conflict (48 percent) than those not informed (28 percent).

One area of the schedule used in this study is dedicated to the analysis of the positions held explicitly by both the people quoted and the author and to what motivated them to take a particular position. The following figures are expressed as percentages of the total sample of articles.

The motivations behind the positions people adopted were deduced from a sample of articles and public debates. The necessity for intervention has been graduated into five levels: 'unavoidable', 'indispensable', 'necessary', 'not indispensable' and 'avoidable'. Given that there is often more than one opinion, the schedule took multiple answers into account. In order to facilitate interpretation of the role of the press in supporting or criticizing favourable attitudes to intervention, a portion of the analysis sheet was dedicated to the positions and reasons explicitly stated by the persons quoted and by the authors of the articles. Cross-checking the responses separately produces a clearer picture and it is possible to ascertain whether the positions are quantitatively balanced.

Furthermore, the collected data have been divided into two subperiods: the week preceding the first air attack and the one following it. During the first period some 179 articles were published, or 20 percent of the total, and 718 in the second.

The proportion of favourable opinions towards armed intervention, i.e. considered 'unavoidable', is 26 percent (6 percent in the first week and 20 percent in the second), whereas 23 percent do not feel it was 'unavoidable'.

The number of articles expressing intervention to be 'indispensable', opined by people other than the author of the article, amounts to 11 percent (of which 9 percent are during the second period). The number of articles wherein intervention is expressed as 'necessary' amounts to 31 percent (23 percent in the second period), while 11 percent express it as unnecessary. While 24 percent consider it to be legitimate even without the UN's authorization, only 2.3 percent feel that it is effective and 0.7 percent that it will be resolved rapidly.

In comparison, 11.6 percent consider aerial attacks to be 'avoidable' (9.6 percent during the second week), 3 percent consider attacks as being 'not indispensable' (2.7 percent during the second period), 5.8 percent as being unnecessary. Moreover, 3.8 percent consider that the intervention is not succeeding, 2 percent that it is rather slow and 8.5 percent that it is ineffective. These data could be used as evidence of the fact that the debate was being raised and played through on a basis of decidedly favourable positions.

The percentages show that there is an intermediate area (11.6 percent) where no definite position has been adopted. This can be put into context by looking at the type of article and the type of event that the author talks about but it is also due to the fact that during the first week nobody believed in armed intervention. When opinions are evident, the position held in general is that aerial bombing is necessary and legitimate even without UN authorization.

It is interesting to see how rarely, on the whole, journalists express their point of view[6] explicitly, preferring to quote the ideas of others or to publish comments made by persons beyond the editorial office. By looking at the same variables, the percentage of 'no response' varies between 57 percent and 81 percent. Only 3 percent of those who signed their articles (against 10 percent of those who did not) feel that intervention is 'indispensable', while 17 percent consider it to be 'inevitable' and 12 percent 'necessary'. Almost nobody (2 percent) imagines it to be an overall success and even fewer to be effective (0.3 percent) or rapid (0.3 percent), even though 8 percent consider it legitimate even without the UN's authorization.

In short, during this period the European press approved of, or at least justified, NATO intervention, even when there were consistent doubts as to its effectiveness and legitimacy. The intervention was considered favourably because it was held to be necessary and unavoidable.

The most frequently mentioned reasons behind this justification are the necessity to stop the genocide and Milosevic's refusal to sign the treaty of Rambouillet. In both Italian newspapers the need to keep to the agreements made with NATO are underlined.

The reasons against intervention include the possible strengthening of Milosevic's position, reprisals by both the army and the Serb armed groups against the Kosovars, and the internal dissent in the respective countries in which the paper is published. *Le Monde* is one of the newspapers taking politicians' reactions most into account, and which most often quotes the politicians and comments on the consequences for internal affairs. Among the reasons for dissent are again lack of approval by the parliaments in the countries involved and the fact that aerial intervention may not be effective without ground troops.

Persuasive techniques in the newspapers

In the 897 articles considered, the use of persuasive techniques is found 425 times (that is in every other article). The techniques most used are: 'name calling', 'credibility of the source', 'band wagon' and 'guilt technique'.

'Name calling'[7] appears 114 times, followed by the 'transfer technique'[8] which appears 55 times, as does 'cognitive dissonance'.[9] Many also use the 'guilt technique'[10] (36 times) and 'factoids'[11] (23 times). 'Name calling' is nowhere as heavy or as frequent as it is in the Italian newspapers, where Milosevic is often compared to Hitler and Saddam Hussein. *Il Corriere della Sera* refers to him as the 'butcher', the Saddam of the Balkans, 'the last Stalin' and the 'monster without a heart'. One unusual metaphor refers to him as 'Milosevic, the fossil', as 'an example of political conservation that should be consigned to the scientists'.[12] Of the French newspapers *Le Monde* makes most use of persuasive techniques. 'Transfer' is used to compare Serbia's situation with that of Kosovo ('The West doesn't want to replay the Bosnian film again') and the NATO bombings with the German bombs during the Second World War. In this way there is a reminder of the sentiments already felt on other occasions which are implicitly transferred to feelings on Kosovo. *Le Monde* uses 'name calling' both for NATO and for Clinton, defined, respectively, through metaphor as 'the international police' and 'the American policeman'. *Le Figaro* often employs the 'credibility of the source' technique, using articles written by commentators and intellectuals more often than those by house journalists, who are sometimes quite explicit about the limits of the intervention.

The 'guilt technique' is often used in *Frankfurter Rundschau*. In fact this German daily has to deal with the fact that there are two irreconcilable positions within Germany. On the one hand, there is the pacifist stance, which is prevalent in the younger generations, motivated by a strong sense of collective guilt that stems from the two World Wars, and because they had not wanted to 'see the holocaust' (this is a phrase used in the *Frankfurter Rundaschau* and possibly refers to a process of psychological repression with regard to the holocaust). On the other hand, there is the opposite perspective – that it is precisely for this reason that Germans cannot ignore the genocide in Kosovo. The dilemma is resolved in the newspaper by voicing both opinions using the 'guilt technique' and that of 'transfer': guilt if one does not take action against Milosevic, who is defined using a typical example of 'name calling', 'a new Hitler', while, at the same time, contemporary history is recalled. After the departure of the first German Tornados from the bases at Piacenza, the newspaper reminds people of 6 September 1941, the day on which Hitler's pilots attacked Yugoslavia dropping bombs on Belgrade. By doing so the newspaper makes people relive the feelings of guilt for the original aggression and transfers it to Belgrade in the 1990s under NATO's missiles. Both points of view are expressed both by the author and in the quotes in the articles.

Die Welt, on the other hand, alludes to these problems, but dedicates itself to considerations like the 'great abilities' of the German pilots, as remembered by British RAF veterans. NATO's position is often represented and its intervention without a UN mandate is justified in order to avoid a 'humanitarian catastrophe'.

According to the German newspaper, if NATO did not intervene Kosovo would be subjugated by the Serbian armed forces, burning houses, killing people and provoking a new wave of refugees. Furthermore, NATO would lose its authority as an organ of political and military security, putting the stability of Europe in great danger.

The Spanish newspapers stand in contrast to these papers: here there is only a limited use of persuasive techniques in non-significant percentages.

Figures of speech

With regard to the figures of speech used in the language of the headlines, one can say that *El Pais* and the French newspapers tend to use referential expressions. The German newspapers, even if their headlines do not scream out, make ample use of the age-old tradition of alliteration. *Die Welt*, for example, titles a commentary 'Bauern und Bomben', that is 'Farmers and Bombs'; but farmers only get a brief mention in the article at the beginning, probably only to support the alliteration used. *Frankfurter Rundschau* writes 'Die Maenner mit den Muetzen ruecken' for 'The Men with Balaclavas are Advancing', the alliteration in this case raises interest but has nothing to do with what is written in the article.

The headlines in *The Guardian* are particularly effective in their use of metaphors, for example in the case of 'Civilians Escape While the Serb Forces put Kosovo to the Torch' and 'Europe Faces the Spectre of Ground Warfare'. Every now and then *The Times* relaxes its style by using metaphor and metonymy, like 'The Serbs Continue with Their Scorched Earth Strategy' or 'Belgrade Calls its Fathers to Arms'.

Il Corriere della Sera uses a lot of quotations, like 'Clinton says "We can't allow another genocide"'; 'Blair warns that "There's no more space for optimism"'; 'Chirac explains that "There are no alternatives but the use of force"', 'Clinton "We must avoid a catastrophe", "Our action will be morally right"'.

Layout

Finally, the European press dramatizes events through the use of images that serve to move and inspire pity in the reader. Sometimes the images emphasize the news even if they are not coherent with the text. On 22 March both *The Times* and *The Guardian* published the same picture of refugees escaping on a tractor. Another photo that figured in the Italian press was that of heavy artillery, primed for action. On 25 March some of the foreign newspapers published on their front pages the picture of an aeroplane taken from the front, so that it was possible to see the whole of its wingspan.

Although Italian dailies mirrored the others in the use of persuasive techniques, they distinguished themselves for their graphic abilities. During the 'hot' days *La Repubblica* in particular published large colour photographs on the front page and used a lot of graphics on the inside pages, illustrating the military operations with maps and models of the aeroplanes.

Analysis of the groups

As the graphic representation of the MCA became illegible owing to the large number of variables considered, a cluster analysis (Jambu and Leboux, 1983) was performed on the more significant factorial axes identified by MCA.

As is known, each cluster represents a group identified according to the greater relative weight taken on by several modalities contained in it. In other words, the various groups are defined by means of the relations between the modalities with the greatest weight.[13] This also explains why the same newspaper may be found in different groups.

Five distinct groups that characterize the press's behaviour have emerged. *El Pais* and *ABC* were in the first group, while *Die Welt, Frankfurter Rundschau, La Repubblica, Le Monde* and *Le Figaro* were in the second, *Il Corriere della Sera* and *The Guardian* were in the third, only *Il Corriere della Sera* was in the fourth, and finally in the fifth, *The Times* and *The Guardian*.

El Pais, ABC

The first group is characterized by a well-outlined narrative scheme, in which the hero is played by NATO (weight of the modality is 6.5 percent) and the anti-hero (enemy) by Milosevic (5 percent). The mission was recognized as being that of guaranteeing international safety/security (3 percent), and the value objects for the hero were first human rights (7.7 percent), followed by human life (6.8 percent), independence (4.7 percent) and political independence (3.7 percent).

The dispatcher (to use the linguistic term) of the mission is yet again NATO with the weight of the modality amounting to 7.8 percent. The aerial bombings on Serbia by NATO constitute the sanction (6.9 percent) for the anti-hero's behaviour.

Neither figures of speech nor persuasive techniques characterize this group. In both these newspapers the authors of the articles (15.4 percent) express favourable opinions towards aerial intervention by NATO. The authors consider intervention as unavoidable (16.5 percent), as necessary (8.1 percent) and as legitimate (6.8 percent). To a minor extent, other positions appear in which the authors declare themselves to be against intervention, believing it to be avoidable (5.4 percent).

Moving on to the opinions expressed by the persons that appear in the articles, one can see that they are in general also favourable towards intervention, with percentages that oscillate from 5.5 percent to 3.2 percent. Intervention is considered as being unavoidable, with the weight of the modality being 10.4 percent, and legitimate, with the weight of the modality being 3.8 percent. Even in this case it is possible to find contrary opinions, which believe that intervention is avoidable (4.5 percent).

It is important to underline that the group is characterized by being in favour of intervention. It is considered legitimate even without UN authorization (weight of the modality, 15.37 percent), necessary, unavoidable and indispensable in order to guarantee international security, which is being threatened by the Balkans crisis (13.85 percent), and because Serbia has not accepted the conditions of Rambouillet (7.9 percent). Furthermore, it is deemed necessary to stop armed aggression on those who cannot defend themselves (5.9 percent).

Intervention is considered as likely to succeed due to the superiority of NATO's military equipment (3.69 percent). Where, on the contrary, intervention is considered as not indispensable, unnecessary or avoidable, it is because the Serbs are the victims of Albanian separatists (the Democratic League of Kosovo, or LCK, and the Kosovo Liberation Army, or KLA) and other ethnic groups (5.65 percent).

The data show that international organizations (17.73 percent), armed forces (16.65 percent) – Spanish forces in particular (2.76 percent) or from other NATO countries (2.84 percent) – civilians (15.68 percent) and representatives or politicians from NATO countries (2.70 percent) appear most frequently in the headlines. The language used is generally assertive (5.45 percent) and full-page headline weight is 3.56 percent on the identification of the group.

Il Corriere della Sera

This Italian daily distinguishes itself from all the other newspapers examined in several specific ways. From a statistical point of view it constitutes a group unto itself.

The newspaper distinguishes itself because it does not resemble the others either in terms of narrative structure, persuasive techniques or figures of speech. Unlike the other papers, it dedicates little space to opinions for or against intervention in Kosovo.

Where the issue is discussed, arguments against intervention have a higher modality weight than arguments for. Many of those expressing an opinion are afraid that the action is being inflicted on an unarmed population and feel that the blame lies equally with both sides and that the people from Kosovo are not being threatened. For the majority of the authors of these articles the bombings are neither legitimate nor effective. The opinions of various different journalists tend to even out. The articles are not in general characterized by the figures of hero or anti-hero as they are in the Spanish press.

In the headlines the UN, the Organisation for Security and Co-Operation in Europe, the refugees, the armed forces, the politicians and the Serbian civilians are mentioned most often.

The Italian newspaper reappears in another group together with *The Guardian*.

Il Corriere della Sera and The Guardian

Il Corriere della Sera and The Guardian form a separate group because they express a balanced position. First, the authors of the articles, even when their own personal opinion with regard to intervention is being expressed explicitly, do not use the same terms as the other newspapers in their arguments. In particular, they do not make judgements on the necessity, the rapidity, the legitimacy or the effectiveness of the mission, and nor do they consider it as being unavoidable, indispensable, or destined to be victorious. In fact, all these variables have an effect on the weight of the modality from 12.9 percent to 10.1 percent. Many doubt the necessity, the speed, the legitimacy or the effectiveness of the mission (weight of the modality about 13 percent). On the other hand, some consider it as being unavoidable, indispensable or destined to succeed (average weight of the modality, 12 percent).

Furthermore, neither paper considers intervention as an issue of victory because the majority of those involved are against Serbia (11.2 percent), or are of the belief that it is legitimate regardless of the lack of a UN mandate because the aim is to get help to the people of Kosovo (9.5 percent), or are in favour of giving a lesson to those who violate human rights (9.5 percent), or consider the problem lies in the UN being blocked by certain members' vetoes (9.3 percent). Intervention is not considered to be necessary, unavoidable or indispensable to guarantee the international security which the situation in the Balkans threatens (8.5 percent), or to put on a show of force to the bellicose people in the region (8.9 percent), or to block the construction of a Greater Serbia at the expense of others (8.4 percent), or because the peace negotiations at Rambouillet were left off.

The Times and The Guardian

This group is characterized by a balancing of opinions. Half the authors of the articles, although not necessarily journalists, declare themselves to be against intervention in as much as they believe that the operation is not (in this order) successful, or rapid, or effective, or necessary, or indispensable. The other half declares itself to be in favour of action for those same reasons (weight of the modality between 21.60 percent and 19.79 percent). Even the opinions quoted in the articles are balanced.

Those against action feel that the Serbs have their roots in Kosovo and are therefore defending their rights and that the conflict will worsen because Russia and China will become actively involved in the fighting on the Serbian side. However, it is also preferable to use diplomacy in these situations. Those in favour emphasize the fact that human rights have been violated, that Milosevic is authoritarian and that the UN has been blocked by vetoes (from 19.43 percent to 10.36 percent).

The characters of both hero and anti-hero are well delineated. The former's main value objects are democracy, equality, liberty, independence and cultural independence. The latter's are authoritarianism, justice, peace and nationalism.

In British newspapers the narrative scheme usually presents itself as the following. NATO is the dispatcher, with the help of Blair and Clinton, and the mission is that of humanitarian help to the people of Kosovo, entrusted to pilots from different allied nations, who are the heroes against Milosevic, who, ignoring the threats, continues with ethnic cleansing.

Persuasive techniques and rhetoric are found in this group and the main type of figure of speech used in the headlines is the metaphor.

Die Welt, Frankfurter Rundschau, La Repubblica, Le Monde and Le Figaro

The factor common to all these dailies is a very clear, though very simple narrative scheme, in which the heroes tend to be the political figures of the country in which the newspaper was published. The weight of the hero in the determination of the group is almost 10 percent. The politicians from countries that belong to the Atlantic pact are sometimes seen as helpers or friends, and sometimes as hinderers or enemies. Seldom does NATO assume the role of anti-hero, but Milosevic was generally assigned that role. The hero's principal value is that of political and cultural freedom, which contributes around 20 percent in influencing the structure of the axes. Peace follows some way behind, while the anti-hero's object is tradition. The weakest weight of the modality was that of the mission, only one could be found: the defence of Serbian territory. Among the persuasive techniques that characterize this group is 'name calling' (6.9 percent). The most used figures of speech are alliteration (weight of the modality 6 percent) and quotation (5 percent). The most common type of article in these newspapers is the news report with in-depth explanation (3.7 percent).

Moreover, this group is not characterized by journalists' opinions on the mission; though there is a certain agreement over the fact that it is indispensable (a weight of the modality of 2.7 percent) and effective (2.5 percent). In conclusion, these newspapers are less explicit when taking a position for or against intervention and in the communication of this position to others. It is clear that a lot of attention is given to politicians.

Conclusions

The empirical evidence seems to confirm the working hypotheses: in the case of both 'infosuasion' and media logic. The inevitable differences among the dailies do not detract from the overall trends.

As far as media logic is concerned, the coverage of the event was similar in all the newspapers examined: only a few articles during the first week, followed by a shower of articles starting 24 March. This is in line with the curve of growing attention found during the Persian Gulf crisis. During this phase, defined as a 'downpour', the articles were accompanied by photographs and/or cartoons, with large photographs on the front pages.

The European press dramatizes events through the use of images that have the effect of moving and inspiring pity in the reader. Sometimes the images emphasize the news even if they are not coherent with the text.

Unlike the press during the Gulf War, journalists, in general, preferred not to express explicitly their own personal opinions. In spite of this, they took up a positive stance towards NATO's decisions, by quoting others, like *Il Corriere della Sera*. Even the newspapers that presented a balance of opinions, like *The Times* and *The Guardian*, ended up by representing a very schematic reality and in general presented a positive image of NATO.

This was made possible through the use of figures of speech and other persuasive techniques, and by giving articles a narrative scheme. The most frequently used persuasive techniques were 'name calling', 'transfer technique', 'cognitive dissonance', 'guilt technique' and 'factoids'. This supports the 'infosuasion' hypothesis, which was found also in terms of the use of figures of speech: the most commonly used were alliteration, typical of the two German dailies, and metaphor and quotation, used frequently in the Italian daily *Il Corriere della Sera*.

A narrative structure in which one of the NATO governments or politicians was depicted as the hero and Milosevic as anti-hero also characterized dailies like *ABC* and *El Pais*, which only rarely used persuasive techniques or figures of speech.

As a final point, there were no differences observed between liberal and conservative newspapers.

Notes

The research reported in this article was carried out in collaboration with the Archivo Disarmo of Rome. The author would like to thank Professor Luigi D'Ambra, who carried out the statistical analysis.

1. Studies on persuasion have a long history, with roots in the rhetorical approach; however, they were taken up again at the beginning of the 20th century to enable an examination of political and military propaganda.
2. Text analysis belongs to contemporary linguistics.
3. Alliteration, calembour (punning), euphemism (e.g. using the expression 'collateral'), metaphor, metonymy, oxymoron, simile (e.g. Belgrade is like Dresden, Serbia = new Vietnam, Milosevic = Saddam; this use of similes is part of the technique of 'name calling').
4. In this case the persuasive techniques most used are: 'name calling', 'credibility of the source', 'band wagon' and 'guilt technique', which belong to both groups.
5. Classical methods of statistical elaboration, which use cross-referenced tables of variable elements inserted into a questionnaire, enable one to only partially analyse the results of an investigation of this type. Such an analytical approach considers only partially the variables, generally two by two, where tables can sometimes foresee thousands. These methods constitute approaches that, other than the difficulty in choosing variables, present difficulties in the combination of information gathered from the tables, with the result that a lot of valuable information on a subject is not used.
6. For a clearer idea of each individual newspaper see the following analysis of the groups.
7. Where one labels a person or an idea negatively without first examining the evidence.
8. 'Transfer technique' refers to the transfer of the subject's opinion about an accepted situation to that which the propagandist is interested in promoting.
9. This technique is used to create incoherence between each of the reader's cognitions.

10. Inducing guilty feelings produces surrender: for example by saying that if no action is taken against Serbia, the West will have more than 100,000 refugees on its conscience.
11. Facts that have not been verified or proven, but used as if true. The use of factoids is easy to identify because they are not accompanied by the references needed to recognize them among known events or to be able to verify them.
12. In other words, Milosevic's policies are so out of date that they should be analysed like an archaeological find.
13. From now on each percentage is to be referred to as the 'weight'.

References

Altheide, D. and D. Snow (1979) *Media Logic*. London and Beverly Hills, CA: Sage.

Altheide, D.L. (1991) *Media Worlds in the Postjournalism Era*. New York: Aldyne de Gruyter.

Brown, G. and G. Yule (1983) *Discourse Analysis*. Cambridge: Cambridge University Press.

Eco, U. (1983) 'TV: la trasparenza perduta', *Sette anni di desiderio*. Milan: Bompiani.

Greimas, A.J. (1983) *Du Sense II, Essais sémiotiques*. Paris: Editions du Seuil.

Jambu, M. and M.O. Leboux (1983) *Cluster Analysis and Data Analysis*. Amsterdam: North Holland.

Jowett, G.S. and V. O'Donnell (1992) *Propaganda and Persuasion*. London: Sage.

Lebart, L., A. Morineau and N. Tabard (1977) *Technique de la description statistique. Methodes et logiciels pour l'analyse de grands tableaux*. Paris: Dunod Ed.

Lippmann, W. (1922) *Public Opinion*. New York: Free Press.

Savarese, R. (1991) 'Grafica quotidiana', pp. 183–203 in M. Bonfantini (ed.), *Le semiotiche speciali*. Naples: Esi.

Savarese, R. (1992) *Guerre intelligenti: Stampa, radio, tv dalla Crimea alla Somalia*. Milan: F. Angeli.

Savarese, R. (1993) 'The European Press and Saladin the Fierce', *European Journal of Communication* 8: 53–75.

Savarese, R. (1995) *L'Americanizzazione della politica in Italia*. Milan: F. Angeli.

Tuchman, G. (1972) 'Objectivity as Strategic Ritual', *American Journal of Sociology* 77: 660–80.

Watzlavick, P., J.H. Beavin and D.D. Jackson (1967) *Pragmatics of Human Communication*. New York: W.H. Norton.

Williams, R. (1974) *Television: Technology and Cultural Form*. London: Routledge.

17 News Production in Contemporary Russia: Practices of Power

Olessia Koltsova

Key problems in the studies of post-Communist media

Why study power practices in Russian news production? Although the issue of media control both before and after the collapse of the Soviet Union has generated a large body of literature, it has usually had a single focus. What has mostly attracted the attention of scholars from the 'West'[1] is the question of the development of press freedom (or, as one of my western colleagues put it more succinctly, 'does Russian government still pressure the media?').

This question is important, but the way it is asked indicates at least three western clichés about the post-Communist media (often borrowed by 'eastern' scholars who tend to ascribe to western research a higher symbolic status). First, in many cases these media are (implicitly) examined through the prism of traditional normative discourse of press freedom, although other approaches have been successfully applied both to western and 'Third World' media.[2] Second, applied to post-Communist media, 'freedom' usually means freedom from government control, though obviously there exist other ways of conceptualizing freedom and power, as is illustrated in some detail later in the article.

Third, such statements as the one about the Russian government 'still pressuring the media' betray the existence of a common though usually silent assumption that western governments have ceased to do so. Colin Sparks (Sparks and Reading, 1998) is one of the few scholars who also points out the existence of similar assumptions. He reproaches his colleagues for permanent, explicit and implicit comparisons of fully manipulated 'Communist' media with an idealized system of western 'free' media, that itself has hardly ever existed in reality.

However, in a non-comparative perspective many western scholars often criticize domestic media. For example, while straightforward pressure and open conflict are not widely known in the West, analysis of media content has made the existence of influence apparent (Herman and Chomsky, 1988). This has given the scholars a ground to conclude that explicit exercise of power by the US government must be substituted by mechanisms of domination. Thus (in general) a wide range of power relations in western news production has been studied with a variety of approaches drawing a polyphonic picture of multiform social influences experienced by media-makers.

Source: *EJC* (1998), vol. 16, no. 3: 315–335.

Strangely enough, when it comes to post-Communist media, the scope of academic enquiry has been predominantly narrowed to normative theories of democracy, often merged with the theory of modernization. Though the latter may not be used explicitly, it enters the analysis of non-western media in a more latent way. Modernization theory implies that all societies move (or should move) along the same trajectory: from inferior (premodern, precapitalist, authoritarian) to superior (modern, capitalist, democratic). So, with or without reference to the notion of modernization, the role of post-Communist media is usually evaluated according to their ability to promote this unitary course of development – this applies, for example, to a most comprehensive account of Russian television production and control over it by E. Mickiewicz (1997). Sometimes media are even expected to *want* to become independent from normatively undesirable forms of control (political, economic) and to subject themselves to normatively approved forms (legal, control by public opinion).

The main problem with this approach is that it tends to substitute descriptive or explanatory concepts by prescriptive categories, which weakens analysis of *any* society – either 'eastern' or 'western'. In the beginning of the 1990s it led to 'developmentalist' and 'transitional' hopes for rapid post-Communist westernization that never came true. Later studies are more realistic. Ivan Zassoursky's book (1999) is one of the pioneers among the few Russian monographs on post-Soviet media, though most of them are still more narrative than analytical. Contrary to Zassoursky, Slavko Splichal's sophisticated study (1994) evaluates the recent development of Eastern European media within an openly normative framework, but prescriptive and descriptive elements are carefully divorced. Splichal also criticizes some elements of western theories often taken for granted by many 'eastern' scholars (for example, 'market idealism').

Several recent works have been critical of unconscious normativism in post-Communist media studies as well (Downing, 1996; Sparks and Reading, 1998). Downing convincingly demonstrates the irrelevance of the concepts of public sphere and civil society for any description of post-Communist societies and shows the limitations of political economy. Instead, he characterizes the situation in the Russian media as 'competitive pluralism of power' (Downing, 1996: 145).

Colin Sparks – whose critical approach has been already mentioned – similarly notes that the struggle between different power centres may explain the development of post-Communist media much better than any normative approach (Sparks and Reading, 1998). Sparks is the first to list some of these powers for Eastern Europe. He describes four types of agents: politicians, business people, media organizations' authorities and their employees (Sparks and Reading, 1998: 137). [...]

The idea of power as a unifying concept

Thus to integrate various kinds of power relations into one empirical study it is necessary to unite the aforementioned related areas into a consistent approach. Different scholars have used such words as 'influence', 'power' and 'control' quite differently, sometimes not clarifying them at all. In various studies one can find everything from Marxist domination (in Shoemaker's scheme it would occupy the 'ideology' level) to structural-functionalist control (at the 'extra-media' level) to Berger and Luckmann's constructivist understanding of knowledge production (the 'routines' level).

In an empirical study this diversity, valuable in itself, has to be reduced in order to avoid eclecticism. For my purpose, an approach to power should bear at least two features: it should be able to include different social influences (not only the government) and be applicable to the fluid character of contemporary Russian society. An insight for a unifying concept of power can be found in some ideas of Michel de Certeau (1984) and his rethinking of Michel Foucault – a tradition that to my knowledge has never been used to theorize media production.

The main novelty of Foucault's works is that he was the first to treat power as (1) 'something that is rather exercised than possessed' (de Certeau, 1984: 26), that is as practice, and as (2) something not solely repressive, but productive as well. This is what de Certeau directly borrows from Foucault, but, unlike the latter, he gives more attention to agents of practices, especially 'weak' ones whose role in power relations is often invisible, yet very important. According to de Certeau, Foucault (1977) only examined the practices of production of power, while de Certeau looks at how power might be assimilated, accepted or resisted.

Using these ideas as a starting point, I understand power as practice. By practices of power – my major unit of analysis – I mean typical actions of imposing agents' will, restrictive or productive, to media producers or directly to the final media product. Thus, for the purpose of my research I reduce media production to a system of interactions between individuals or groups who possess certain resources that in turn shape their practices. My study suggests three most important resources: (1) access to violence/enforcement, (2) economic capital and (3) information resource. Access to creation of rules (4) (that in de Certeau's terms discriminates between weak and strong agents) is also a very important resource, though of a slightly different nature. Based on various combinations of these resources, the following ideal types of power agents may be discerned: 'state' agents (resources 1–4); other, i.e. 'illegitimate' sources of violence (1); advertisers (2, 3); owners (2, 4) and sources of information (3). In practice, agents may also possess different combinations of resources, as well as form temporary alliances and constant teams with holders of other resources. The reasons for exclusion of audience from the list of agents is addressed in one of the following sections.

Unlike audiences, news producers – from rank-and-file reporters to media executives – are active players of the game and possess their special resources: privileged access to media production (an institutional resource) and a monopoly of certain skills (professional). This opposes them to all the rest as 'internal' agents to 'external' ones, following the Shoemaker–Reese distinction. However, this externality is nothing more than a necessity to act through media workers in order to influence the final product; despite it, 'external' agents are hardly less constitutive for news production than the journalists themselves. The boundaries between media organizations and their environment are blurred, and real people often form teams across them, as well as divide into competing groups within their institutions. To my knowledge, this may apply even to stable, 'western' societies.

The fluid character of institutions in Russia seems to make my accent on agency and practice (vs structures) especially relevant. Values are unclear and rules are predominantly informal, individuals identify themselves with their institutions very loosely, and act counter to institutional interests; agents make choices in an atmosphere of uncertainty and relatively low predictability; their decisions are situational and their strategies are short-term. It is an open question whether these are temporary traits of a transforming society, or constant traits specific to Russia, if specific at all. Of course, all societies and their media systems possess some degree of fluidity; the question is, when the fluidity is significant enough to consider a given society a different case. These questions cannot be settled here; next I argue that the proposed model fits the Russian media better than either normative or purely institutional approaches.

Empirical base of the study

The empirical material that was collected for the current study also suggests that conclusions presented here may apply to news (mostly on television), while broader generalizations would demand further study. Moreover, the currently available sources on Russian television news (both primary and secondary) are very heterogeneous and cover some power agents and their practices much better than others. That is why my study is more narrowly framed than, for example, the work of Shoemaker and Reese, who could rely on hundreds of research studies.

The most important source of my data is participant observation in the St Petersburg affiliates of two national television channels, one private and one state owned. The observation is documented in field notes and 23 interviews, and was supplemented with visits to other channels. These data produce a full and detailed ('thick') description of the practices of rank-and-file television news producers in St Petersburg; secondary sources have provided information on other regions, and it seems to agree with my observations. A most important source here is the 'Monitoring' archive of the Glasnost Defence Foundation. Since 1996 it has collected annually from 700 to 1200 cases of conflicts related to the mass media throughout Russia, which are reported by volunteers and presented as one-paragraph stories (see Glasnost Defence Foundation, 1997a, 1998a, 1998b, 1999a, 2000).

The peculiarities of economic influence

To classify practices of influence, it is convenient to take the Shoemaker–Reese scheme as a starting point. The most abstract level of influence – the ideological – suggests that a system of values shared in any given society is structured to serve the interests of a power elite. However, when it comes to the question of *how* this occurs, one inevitably has to go down to lower levels and look at extra-media practices of influence and at media routines.

Practices at the extra-media level in Russia are marked by the most dramatic change since the Soviet period: a relatively unified agent of control (the Party-State) has split into a number of competing actors. The most significant among them were listed earlier.

The most heated public discussion in Russia in the early post-Communist years has been centred around economic agents (owners and advertisers). Their influence has surfaced after the abolition of preliminary censorship. Censorship had been the major mechanism of control in the Soviet period and that is why it had been seen as the only obstacle to freedom (although, of course, the Soviet system of control included an economic component, but this was 'hidden' behind its administrative exterior). Thus, since economic influence has come as an unpleasant surprise, it has been described in largely negative terms. This attitude resembles that of those European countries in which private television was introduced relatively late, for example, France.

To describe specific traits of Russian media ownership, it is useful to introduce a distinction between 'internal' and 'external' owners, the latter meaning individuals or groups whose major interests lie outside media business. In the West, when ownership is external to a media organization, it is usually in the hands of the state. Private ownership is mostly internal; it means that owners possess media outlets only, have no interests outside the media industry and thus do not use media as a vehicle for promotion of those interests. Influence patterns within these two formats have been widely studied: e.g. Schlesinger (1987) on government control, and Tunstall and Palmer (1991) on business control. By contrast, cases of external private ownership (like General Electric and NBC) are less well studied.

In Russia, however, nearly all media, including private ones, are owned externally, and the majority of them are unprofitable. Because Russian business and political elites are extremely interdependent, both see media first of all as weapons to gain political capital – a vital resource that later can be converted into all other forms of capital outside the media domain.

Let us consider an example of Boris Berezovsky, who until recently was an influential media mogul backing the first national television channel and a well-known entrepreneur, in particular engaged in automobile sales. Obviously, he was interested in a favourable legislative climate and privileges for his primary business. Two basic strategies of approaching the federal authorities are available to a media backer like him: either offering them the loyalty of your media outlet in exchange for favours, or 'media blackmailing', that is threat of refusing to be loyal. There is no legally proven evidence on whether Berezovsky was using one or both of these strategies, but some consequences of his successful lobbyism are well known. High taxes for imported automobiles gave an enormous advantage to Berezovsky's firm Logovaz in selling outdated domestic cars. Ironically, this measure, seemingly aimed at protection of domestic products, was combined with privileges given to Logovaz to import the most luxurious western car models.

Seeing their media outlets as instruments for non-media goals, such owners are not always interested in the profitability of their media business, and often choose obedience of media people at the cost of temporary financial losses. However, what differentiates this situation from the previous Soviet regime is that various power groups compete in their struggle for resources, thus providing some pluralism of interpretations that sometimes grows into fierce 'information wars'. To get an idea of the tenseness of these wars one has to remember just what has been at stake in Russia in the 1990s: a huge sector of state property has been put forward for privatization, and it was the government who was deciding on the rules of this game.

Restricting some aspects of media content, owners in Russia, like any power centre, open new possibilities for the media as well, first of all the possibility to survive. This serves the interests of both top media executives and rank-and-file employees. It explains why numerous unprofitable Russian media, instead of merging into bigger entities and realizing economies of scale by shrinking their staff, prefer searching for additional funding from external owners. Thus unprofitability of the Russian media seems to be both cause and consequence of external ownership.

In this situation, it is not surprising that owner control is most often legitimized by journalists (though they admit that in theory it is not desirable). To 'work for the company's policy' is considered normal and even a mark of professionalism. This was confirmed by all of my respondents. It is not by chance that the Glasnost Defence Foundation monitoring reports contain so few conflicts with economic actors (about 10 percent in 1998); such monitoring, collecting the cases of open rivalry, is not able to flag latent conflicts and contradictions.

While rank-and-file journalists often do not recognize this control as control, news editors can feel the owner's influence more clearly. They claim they have regular talks with their bosses that provide general guidelines for news policy (for example, lists of taboo topics/persons), and the rest has to be divined from a knowledge of the larger political situation. This knowledge, apart from watching television, is gained through informal interaction with different elites. News editors may also receive telephone calls concerning particular events or persons. For example, in one city the municipal authority owned a television company and prohibited coverage of the visit of the leader of a competing political party.

Advertisers' control is more readily regarded as illegitimate, though its existence is very often frankly acknowledged as an inevitable evil. In Moscow, where the advertising business has been developing rapidly, this control is mediated by audience research firms, and the number of commercials on the air is directly dependent on ratings, despite low levels of trust to these ratings (Koneva, 1998). Outside Moscow and in St Petersburg in particular, the advertising market is more chaotic (especially after the crisis of 1998) and is only loosely connected to any ratings. Each programme is on the air as long as it can find funding (Pushkarskaya, 1998). This leads to fragmentation of media organizations (when nearly every programme is registered as a separate medium), and to a large amount of hidden advertisement – stories favourable to and paid by the source, but presented as news. In one of the newsrooms under study, there was a newscast schedule on the wall on which 'hidden' commercials were openly marked with the word *zakaz* (story by order). Though advertiser pressure is not unknown in the West, it is usually exercised through contract allocation and seems to be initiated mainly by the advertisers themselves, not volunteered by media organizations.

In Russia, the search for *zakaz* stories is usually reciprocal: media organizations need money and various organizations need to be publicized more effectively than by explicit commercials. If a firm can organize an event that looks newsworthy, it is very likely that its aim to have the story aired will be satisfied. What is more, if a firm is considered rich enough to pay, then it is quite unlikely that it will get on the air without paying, even if its event meets journalistic criteria of newsworthiness. A reporter told me how once shortly before Christmas he was trying to make an entertaining story about a famous craftsman who worked at a factory for New Year tree decorations. The director of the factory said he would permit it only if the whole enterprise could be advertised in the story. The news editor, in turn, demanded payment for *zakaz*; the director refused, and the story was killed.

The amount of payment varies greatly from Moscow to the regions, from television to newspapers, and from 'retail' to 'wholesale'. Media organizations often have elaborate tariff systems for such services. Some fraction of the proceeds is usually given to the journalist who produces the story. Rank-and-file journalists generally do not like to produce such stories and try to avoid them, but open refusal is rare, since persistence may end in dismissal.

High production costs also force media organizations to go one step further – to hand over production to advertisers (thus openly stretching the process of media production beyond the journalistic community). For example, in St Petersburg, a computer trading firm produces an information and entertainment programme about computers – and, concurrently, about itself. In Moscow, one of the leading universities makes a game show for high school students, and the winners are accepted at the university without taking entrance exams. Both the jury and the anchor of the show are university professors.

However, trying to maximize control over production, media producers are not always willing to participate in such collaboration. A typical tactic of resistance – which has not always been successful – is to change or combine different sponsors/advertisers on which a media organization is dependent (Fossato and Kachkaeva, 1998; Belin, 1997). When it comes to negotiations, a frequent tactic is rhetoric of presenting 'objectivity' as a commodity that can be exchanged for high ratings and that therefore should be favoured by economic actors.

State influences without the 'state'

A second group of strategies of external influence is exercised by state executives and legislators, including elected bodies, the administration, the police, state-owned education and medical care organizations, in short, everyone who has access to deficit public resources. These resources give power to solve private problems when used outside the prescribed way of implementation. Although all those actors belong to the state institutionally, 'the state' cannot be seen as a unified actor. 'State' actors tend to form temporary alliances among themselves and with external agents and pursue their short-term group interests rather than the interests of 'the state'. The case of the struggle for the nationwide relay system belonging to St Petersburg Channel 5 in 1997 especially clearly shows how various 'parts' of the state were competing with one another. Among the most important rivals were: the state Duma upper chamber (representing regional elites), Moscow's mayor, the St Petersburg governor and the state-owned Moscow-based national channel RTR, backed by the Vice-Minister of Culture.

Thus absence of a unified centre of oppressive power may be found not only in countries traditionally referred to as democratic, but, for instance, in Russia, though the nature of this phenomenon is different. In western societies, the state usually manages to enforce the fulfilment of rules effectively, and its various 'parts' interact more or less within these rules. In Russia, power groups emerge informally, exceeding the boundaries of the state as an institution, and struggle in a loosely regulated situation.

A typical negative strategy of the 'state' agents is selective use of sanctions: while many violate the rules, only media failing to show loyalty are punished. The most recent case is NTV – the only private national channel and one of the few media organizations that was aiming at western-style internal ownership (that is, at selling objective news as commodity). While all national channels had comparable debts, repayment was demanded only from the non-obedient NTV.

State agents may use any available institutional resources to influence media: the tax police, fire and sanitary control organizations, the customs agency, etc. Often a local administration makes media organizations rent their buildings from it and then switches off water, electricity, increases rent, etc. (Glasnost Defence Foundation, 1997a: 353). This is possible because most real estate is state-owned and buying an office is too expensive for small businesses. State officers, along with other agents, also use the strategy of bringing legal suits in court against media organizations, usually on defamation grounds. The purpose of such suits is mainly not financial compensation, but increasing the media organizations' costs in producing unfavourable information.

Positive strategies, apart from monetary bribery, can be described as barter and other kinds of exchange. They include giving personal privileges (free resort trips, etc.), and using the aforementioned organizations, but 'constructively': absence of oversight visits, quick resolution of custom and visa difficulties, help with law-enforcement problems. Professional privileges are also given, for instance, access to closed sources of information and communication channels (Glasnost Defence Foundation, 1997b: 11).

When these relations are shaped as an open exchange, they are closer to barter. But often a service (medical care, registration, etc.) is given to a journalist as an act of 'friendship' or 'assistance', and the conditions of reciprocal service (time, amount, content) are not discussed. Then a return service is theoretically not necessary, but it is expected as gratitude, otherwise the 'friendship' will founder.

Barter also characterizes many relationships between journalists and their sources. These kind of relations are addressed later.

Other external influences

A last practice, open violence, is less usual than others. Journalists perish mainly in the war zones (Chechnya, for example), or in accidents whose connection with journalists' professional activity is questionable. A little short of that, violence or its threat are used both by criminals and by 'power' ministries (police, secret service, the military). My respondents complained that *bratki* (rank and file mafia members) do not let them shoot certain scenes, threatening to take or damage their cameras or just to create 'trouble' for them. Exactly the same is often done by the police, but they can also take journalists to the police station (Glasnost Defence Foundation, 1997a: 355). Both criminal and state actors are also not unfamiliar with blackmail and telephone threats.

All these practices are not used by one type of actor exclusively; actors make alliances and thus may have access to a whole range of strategies. In their book *Press Control Around the World*, Jane Curry and Joan Dassin enumerate many of these practices as typical of nearly all countries (Curry and Dassin, 1982); so it is not practices, but their combinations that are unique. It may be argued that no one switches off the electricity in US media offices to pressure them. That is true, but this does not necessarily ensure that American media have more autonomy. As has been already noted, absence of open conflict may indicate successful hegemony (here we come back to the level of ideology).

Ironically, the concept of hegemony does not work very well for Russia. For hegemony, a relatively unified centre of power and a consensus over basic values are needed. As already mentioned, neither is found in contemporary Russia. No matter how much media may be controlled by fragmented groups, public opinion polls show deep cleavages on core issues (Bocharova and Kim, 2000).[3] Confusion about values, first, increases the role of individual decisions and, second, replaces value-based choices with actions that are often driven by a cost-benefit analysis. This is more clearly seen at the intra-media level, but before turning to this, it is appropriate to consider why the audience has been called a 'quasi-agent'.

It is true that the appeal to the audience's interest is widely used by all players to legitimize their activity, but this does not mean that the audience is a real player. Neither viewers nor readers have direct influence on the media; most often they do not contact journalists. Rather, it is their image that participates in the game. As a respondent put it, the audience 'is a myth which a journalist invents for himself', and a myth is something that can be defined and redefined more easily than a relationship with a real actor. Even when measured through ratings, the audience has a status in decision-makers' minds which is closer to that of values, rules and habits than to actual individuals.

Media executives as power mediators

It is impossible to talk about the intra-media level apart from other levels. The routines of rank-and-file journalists consist mostly of their interactions with sources, while media executives serve as mediators of all other outside pressures concealed within 'organizational' control. However, reporters preserve some degree of autonomy from their bosses. It is because their labour is connected with symbolic production, that they cannot be precisely controlled. I witnessed some cases in which journalists managed to successfully negotiate with their bosses.

Once I watched a dispute between an anchor of a state national television programme with her editor, who wanted to cut out a negative part of a story about Chechen refugee children – in that case the major reason was the lack of time. 'You can't make a story completely rosy,' the anchor said, 'because when another channel makes it black, people say that they are telling the truth and you are lying.' The negative part was kept. Even when the topic and the 'accents' are imposed on journalists from above, they still choose the interviewees, the 'picture' and the composition creating the relative importance of topics by their ordering in a story.

Of course, another mechanism of control often works when open pressure is seemingly absent – recruitment of employees who are selected so that the ongoing relation with them is built on trust. A news editor once said in an interview that, although he is supposed to read all the materials before airing them, he often signs them without scrutiny because he is confident of his people's consciousness. He noted: 'all anchors are grown-ups, all sane … an inner censor is sitting inside them; everybody understands that something can be said, something not: do not swear on the air'.

This note about swearing is very typical, and reflects the fact that journalists feel themselves subject first to the control of professional standards or organizational routines. Imposition of a topic, idea, timing, style, etc. is usually attributed to this form of influence. Though superficial observation would confirm this, the role of the control of routines should not be overestimated. In reality, journalists often do not know their bosses' full motivation (very much like each boss does not know for sure what is going on in the higher layers of the hierarchy, ending with equally disconnected political elites). Journalists make guesses about the processes going on at higher levels on the basis of negotiations with their editors and – as everyone of us – from watching television programmes. Thus political control is 'installed' into the control of routines and is lost in it. It is not specific to Russia, but the available data suggest that American journalists are even less conscious of this device, maybe because of lack of open conflict.

In Russia, at the state television company under study, the bosses' political motives sometimes were spoken of openly. In general, journalists in both state and private television companies are aware of political control and see it as inevitable; they seem to be more inclined than their American colleagues to acknowledge the constructed character of their products. They very seldom use the notion of 'objectivity', and comment on the freedom of press only when asked: they see it as a western myth that westerners themselves recollect only when they 'start teaching [them] democracy'. So, in addition to economic control, journalists legitimize political control ('a journalist sells their skill to make stories just as a surgeon sells their skill to perform operations'). One of the respondents told me that he would never work for Communist leader

Zyuganov, but 'on a more vague level – Luzhkov, Gorbachev – I don't care'. This awareness of external control and cognizant adaptation to it are typical of my respondents. It allows one to assume that Russian journalists are more controlled than dominated, while their American colleagues may be more dominated than controlled. This may change in Russia as the system equilibrates.

Journalists and their sources: negotiation and conflict

The second type of power agents with whom journalists most often interact are sources of information. Journalists have more power resources in this rela-tionship. Media and their sources are mutually dependent: media producers impose their format and, in general, the necessity to 'mediatize'; sources try to define content, often successfully, using their monopoly of certain knowledge (or newsworthiness). This interdependence leads to informal cooperation and com-promise. This is characteristic of mass media in all societies, but, in Russia, coop-eration is especially intertwined with exchange relations – for example, when in *zakaz* stories a 'source' is a hidden advertiser. Open bribes are more and more prevalent at the level of media organizations than with individual journalists because management tries to gain control over this source of income.

Individual journalists more often shape their relations with sources as 'help', and problem-solving occurs without money being involved. Appropriate accents are given to news stories for transportation of furniture or dental treatment, for instance – whatever a source can provide. If the return service is delayed, these rela-tions are not recognized as exchange. In general, they are most often described as problems experienced by other media organizations. Tariffs on hidden advertise-ment are named in reference to other companies (according to available sources they vary from US$100 to 2000 per story, depending on the size of audience, while the average income in Russia is, very roughly, equivalent to US$100 a month).

Thus the exchange relations between journalists and their sources may be seen as a continuum of practices with increasing legitimacy: from story-making for money on the one extreme to compromising in exchange only for those resources necessary for journalists' professional activity, e.g. for access to information.

In their well-known study of news sources, Ericson et al. (1989) underscore the consensus that dominates journalist–source relations. That might be true for stable systems, where interactions have become habitual, but not for Russia. In Russia, sources as autonomous actors have emerged only recently, while during the Soviet period the major tensions were between media producers and censors, who mediated journalist–source relations. Furthermore, conflict seems to be inherent in these relations in general, and derives from different interests of the actors: information in which sources are interested is not journalistically valuable, and vice versa. Both sides try to maximize their power. Journalists treat their sources according to these sources' degree of power. For example, a two-hour wait for a minister at an airport was taken by journalists as normal, while a one-hour tardi-ness of a press secretary from a museum caused a journalist to become indignant and threaten to cancel the story if 'they can't manage it normally'.

Although creating a hierarchy of sources is not impossible, often their power is unstable and has to be assessed separately in each situation, on the basis of incomplete information. One of the most indicative (and verifiable) examples is connected with my own journalistic investigation (though it was during my participant observation at a newspaper editorial office, not in television). I was threatened on the phone by an NGO representative whom I was going to interview. I told my boss that I had no idea if this person had enough power to act on his threats, and if this 'NGO' might be just a cover for criminal activities. I asked to take my name off the publication, but my boss decided the threat was not dangerous and published it (which happily was not followed by any harmful consequences). Later my respondents confirmed that such indeterminate situations were typical.

Both journalists and sources are active in their game. Journalists elaborate and maintain a network of permanent sources, they initiate searches for new ones, they check one source against another, use informal connections – in short, they implement the entire range of instruments known to their colleagues worldwide. However, sources have some resources which are not typical in western countries. For example, there are many different degrees of secrecy of documents and places, whose lists are relatively easily expanded both legally and semi-legally (Glasnost Defence Foundation, 1998b: 70). During my research, reporters were denied the right to film a blown-up gas container; the reasoning was that the enterprise where the accident took place was 'classified', even though journalists were not going to show these secret objects. The institutional position of sources gives them multiform possibilities to invent various other methods for concealing information. For example, once during my observation journalists approached custom officials for basic information about a man suspected of smuggling. He had been arrested at the Russian border the day before. The officials first denied the mere fact of the arrest and a few hours later refused to give any details, insisting that their investigation was not completed. Such practices are encouraged by less elaborate legislation (in comparison with western countries) and by differences in cultural-normative traditions.

On the other hand, the fluidity of all structures, including legislation and corporate solidarity, results in both easier leaks and more possibilities for illegal management of information by journalists (both in terms of access and publication). One of my respondents told me how he, before his departure for the first Chechen war, was advised to buy several issues of *Playboy* magazine. These were then presented to soldiers at the check-posts, and in some cases the gifts quickly solved the problem of access to restricted battle zones. If that did not help, the journalist offered soldiers the unique opportunity to call home from his mobile phone (which was more expensive). This story shows how journalists may informally expand the sphere of their autonomy, and such tactics cannot be traced by formal institutional analysis.

An alternative strategy to concealing unfavourable information is the persistent supply of favourable information, which pre-empts and sidelines journalists' independent investigation. Information produced by press services and public relations offices of different institutions has its pros and cons for journalists. It is easily accessible but does not fully fit their criteria of newsworthiness.

But in the current situation of economic weakness in Russian media, the pluses of such information outweigh the minuses.

Not only journalistic investigation, but any search for a topic costs a lot, especially on television. My experimental investigation at a newspaper took about six weeks, I made a dozen trips to various organizations, about 60 telephone calls, and, as mentioned, was threatened. The honorarium I got was roughly enough to buy a pair of boots. Thus the most frequent methods to block investigation in Russia now resemble western PR: in most cases, it is enough to flood editorial offices with positive information about yourself, sometimes coupled with negative data on your competitors, and you do not need restrictive sanctions too often.

Moving towards this technique of influence is a general trend in sources' behaviour. Their very first autonomous actions after official abolition of censorship were mere imitations of old Soviet methods, that is direct administrative orders. The problem now was that this did not work, because sources had no resources to mandate the fulfilment of their orders. So they switched to the strategy of concealing information from reporters and refusing to speak on air. This strategy had its own disadvantage: when your voice is not presented in the media, it is very likely to be replaced by the voice of your rival. This was the major reason why the Russian government lost the information war in the first Chechen campaign. Banning access to information through the federal military provoked journalists to use Chechen sources, who were more than willing to provide their own version of reality. It should be added that the government had no clear information policy in general, it made no preparations for the campaign and seemed to try the Afghanistan scenario again.

In the second war, the change in strategy was dramatic, and reflected a broad change in sources' attitude towards the media. This time the government (more exactly, Mr Putin) had a consistent policy, which was active construction of an official version of events in Chechnya, and setting conditions for its dissemination through the media. For instance, the government press centre has borrowed the idea of pools from the Gulf War, and it is hard to get information except from them – first of all, because the war zone is not safe (for more details on Chechnya, see Koltsova, 2000).

On the whole, the development of relations between reporters and their sources can be characterized as mutual learning. Journalists are acquiring skills of working with information in new conditions, and information sources, including political actors, are learning new manipulative tactics. Sources, particularly government sources, are moving from preliminary censorship, to concealing unfavourable information, to imposing favourable information on media producers. However, each time the situation seems to quieten down, a new conflict emerges, reshuffling actors and reshaping their balance of power.

Conclusion

The format of an academic article does not allow for a more detailed account of power relations in Russian news production. However, this brief description based on the concept of power as practice is enough to support some conclusions. First, it has shown that all agents, including media producers, possess some resources and thus can exercise power. This means that complex power relations in news production are not unidirectional, and that the production itself does not take place exclusively within the journalistic community (contradicting normative visions of journalism as 'independent' activity).

Second, practice-oriented approaches are very helpful in studying rapidly transforming societies (such as Russia in the 1990s), where formal institutional analysis has little explanatory capacity. In Russia, old power relations have suddenly collapsed, while 'new' ones are still not routinized and thus have become highly visible to the actors. This leads not only to explicit forms of control and conflict, but also to greater reflexivity of all social actors, their general awareness of various mechanisms of power and pragmatic use of them.

One of the major limitations of the suggested approach is that power defined as practice can hardly be quantified, and thus the overall distribution of power between the actors cannot be 'calculated'. But it is questionable whether any other approach is able to answer this question, especially in cases of transforming societies.

As an end note, when this article was being prepared for publication, my forecast of the possibility of a new open conflict came true. The dramatic story of NTV, the only national channel not controlled by the new Russian government, found its end in what de facto meant its shutting down. This event starts a new epoch in the history of post-Soviet media and, I am afraid, makes the media landscape described in my article a part of Russia's past.

Notes

This research was supported by the Moscow Public Scientific Foundation and the European University at St Petersburg, Russia. I would also like to thank Dr Volkov, Professor Downing, Professor Nordenstreng and Professor Mickiewicz for academic advice during my research and critical comments on the drafts of this article.

1. Understanding the conventional character of the notion of the West and its possible antonyms, I shall apply this word to countries traditionally referred to as 'developed' and 'democratic', that is Western Europe and North America.
2. 'New audience research' based on various cultural approaches (e.g. Lull, 1988) has made media studies of the 'Third World' much richer than those of the former 'Second World'.
3. For example, during the last three years they showed constant disagreement about Russia's preferable path of development: western-type – 'capitalist/democratic' (from 47 to 39 percent at various times) – Soviet-type (21–25 percent), or a unique way (17–25 percent).

References

Belin, Laura (1997) 'Politicization and Self-Censorship in the Russian Media', paper presented at the national conference of the American Association for the Advancement of Slavic Studies, Seattle, WA; available at website of Radio Free Europe/Radio Liberty, Inc.: www.rferl.org/nca/special/rumedia4/index.html

Bocharova, Oksana and Natalia Kim (2000) 'Rossia i Zapad – Obschnost ili Otchuzhdenie?' [Russia and the West – Commonality or Alienation?], report of the Russian Centre for Public Opinion Research (VCIOM), 14 April; available at: www.polit.ru

Curry, Jane L. and Joan R. Dassin (eds) (1982) *Press Control Around the World*. New York: Praeger.

De Certeau, Michel (1984) *The Practice of Everyday Life*. Berkeley, Los Angeles and London: University of California Press.

Downing, John (1996) *Internationalizing Media Theory: Transition, Power, Culture: Reflections on Media in Russia, Poland and Hungary, 1980–95*. London: Sage.

Ericson, Richard V., Patricia M. Baranek and Janet B.L. Chan (1989) *Negotiating Control: A Study of News Sources*. Toronto: University of Toronto Press.

Fossato, Floriana and Anna Kachkaeva (1998) 'Russian Media Empires I, II, III, IV', special report available at website of Radio Free Europe/Radio Liberty, Inc.: www.rferl.org/nca/special/rumedia4/index.html

Foucault, Michel (1977) *Discipline and Punish: The Birth of the Prison*. New York: Pantheon.

Glasnost Defence Foundation (1997a) *Pressa na Territorii Rossii: Konflikti I Pravonarushenia* [Press in Russian Federation: Conflicts and Law Violations]. Moscow: Prava Cheloveka.

Glasnost Defence Foundation (1997b) *Zhurnalist v Poiskah Informatsii* [Journalist Searching for Information]. Moscow: Prava Cheloveka.

Glasnost Defence Foundation (1998a, 1999a, 2000) databases available at: www.gdf.ru

Glasnost Defence Foundation (1998b) *Yezhegodnik Fonda Zaschiti Glasnosti (Otchet za 1997 god)* [Annual Report of the Glasnost Defence Foundation for 1997]. Moscow: Prava Cheloveka.

Glasnost Defence Foundation (1999b) *Zakoni I Praktika Sredstv Massovoi Informatsii v Stranah SNG I Baltii* [Media Legislation and Practice in the CIS and Baltic Countries]. Moscow: Galeria.

Herman, Edward S. and Noam Chomsky (1988) *Manufacturing Consent: The Political Economy of the Mass Media*. New York: Random House.

Koltsova, Olessia (2000) 'Change in the Coverage of the Chechen Wars: Reasons and Consequences', *Javnost/The Public* 7(4): 39–54.

Koneva, Elena (1998) 'Tsena Reitinga' [The Price of Rating], *Sreda* 4–5: 17–23.

Lull, James (ed.) (1988) *World Families Watch Television*. Newbury Park, CA: Sage.

Mickiewicz, Ellen (1997) *Changing Channels: Television and the Struggle for Power in Russia*. New York: Oxford University Press.

Pushkarskaya, Anna (1998) 'Mif o Kulturnoi Stolitse Trebuyet Deneg' [The Myth about the Cultural Capital Demands Money], *Sreda* 6: 20–4.

Schlesinger, Philip (1987) *Putting 'Reality' Together. BBC News*, 2nd edn. London: Routledge.

Sparks, Colin and Anna Reading (1998) *Communism, Capitalism and the Mass Media*. London: Sage.

Splichal, Slavko (1994) *Media Beyond Socialism. Theory and Practice in East-Central Europe*. Boulder, CO: Westview Press.

Tunstall, Jeremy and Michael Palmer (1991) *Media Moguls*. London: Routledge.

Zassoursky Ivan (1999) *Mass Media Vtoroi Respubliki* [Mass Media of the Second Republic]. Moscow: Moscow University Press.

Section Five

Media Culture

European Soap Operas: The Diversification of a Genre

Tamar Liebes and Sonia Livingstone

Why analyse European soap operas?

How does Europe preserve its cultural diversity vis-a-vis the swamping of imported, mainly American, globally diffused, soap operas? The first massive influx of American television during the 1980s has already stirred the worried European film and television producers to consider seriously how to rise to the challenge. *Dallas*, the American prime-time soap, immensely popular in Europe, became the symbol of what was then labelled 'American cultural imperialism' or Americanization (Mancini and Swanson, 1996), terms which may better be replaced by the more neutral 'globalization' or even audiovisual 'modernization' (Schrøder and Skovmand, 1992). 'Europe fights back' was the spirited slogan (Silj, 1988) which called for the local production of European family series in order to combat the threat of television capitulating to Americanization.

But the result on the screens was disappointing. True, France delivered its answer to *Dallas* in the form of *Châteauvallon*, a best-seller which transferred the dynastic family from Texas to a French provincial town, and changed the characters from oil moguls into the more cultured occupation of publishers. But it took only a car accident involving its main star for the show to collapse. Germany's *Lindenstrasse* is another case in point. Explicitly modelled on the British example of *Coronation Street*, it has nevertheless been influenced by the American formula, focusing less on community issues and more on illicit sex and romance.

Source: *EJC* (1998), vol. 13, no. 2: 147–180.

A decade and a half later, there is a common perception that the soap opera form has proved so successful in winning large audiences that as a specifically American form it is taking over from many others, and that soaps are spreading around the world to the possible detriment of more 'serious' or local or public service oriented materials (Schiller, 1992). Of course, defenders of the soap opera (including many feminist academic researchers as well as a sizeable audience) might not judge this trend such a bad thing. What surprised us, when deciding to explore this spread of soap operas specifically within the European context, was that this common perception appears to be mistaken: most European countries produce only a few soaps, and some, for example France and Italy, produce none at all.[1] Moreover, of those produced domestically, many are not simply local versions of an American format.

Our focus in this article is not on the import of soaps made elsewhere but on the production of local soaps. In this respect we classify countries roughly into three groups: the big producers (Great Britain, Germany), those countries producing one or a few soaps (Greece, the Netherlands, Scandinavia) and those who produce none (France, Italy, Spain). Of course there are always exceptions, and there have been various attempts by different countries at different times (e.g. Spain introduced a new soap – *Medico de familia* – in 1996, and Italy has a series of short serials – modelled on the first, best-selling, *Edera* – of the telenovella form). […]

A related concern has to do with the new salience of the issue of cultural identity in Europe. With the growing economic integration of the European Union, and, in parallel, the ethnic and cultural segmentation within national states (not only the extreme case of the former Yugoslavia but also in Belgium, Spain and the UK) – there is a new urgency in dealing with matters of national identity. How do the multiple member states, and ethnic and cultural communities within these states, preserve their own language, art and history? One possible, though not 'purist' answer is producing home-soaps. As Québecois journalist, Denise Bombardier (1985), has stated, 'if we could have a soap, we would have a nation'.

The focus of this article is the examination of the diversity and evolution of soap opera forms in Europe. In so doing, we aim to broaden the range of soap operas which researchers consider, for the focus on the 'canon' (comprising predominantly American, and perhaps also British, soap operas) reinforces the impression that it is the American form which is predominant everywhere. Indeed, in an earlier article we contrasted the British and American traditions of soap opera, arguing that their differences are sufficiently great to justify dividing them into two different subgenres (Liebes and Livingstone, 1992). British soaps (e.g. *Coronation Street*) typically present separate, distinct families, all living in one community, characterized by multipersonal and 'vertical' (intergenerational) encounters. There are many links between families, and 'organic solidarity' in the community. The network of American soaps consists of a system of destabilized dyadic relationships, in which the balance is always collapsing, and has to be repaired by destroying another balance. The families are intermixed by a thick web of marriage and romance which undermines the family structure. The focus of the American soaps on romantic couples means that they are unigenerational – stretching to include parents of grown-up characters, as long as they may participate in the game of romance – with few or no babies,[2] children or old women (e.g. *The Young and the Restless*).

These subgenres represent everyday life – particularly women's lives – very differently. The British soaps opt for motherhood, with various mother figures at hand daily. When genetic mothers are in trouble, surrogate mothers often step in. American female soap characters, on the other hand, are concerned mainly with romance, and both career and motherhood are subordinated to the importance of this. The differences between the soaps in the two cultures were interpreted in light of (1) the choice of the US commercial networks to recycle romantic myths while British television, drawing on social realism, sometimes emerges as too self-consciously, paternalistically pedagogic, and (2) the different social ethos whereby American society, which sees itself as open, individualist, non class based, and where everyone is allowed to believe they are upwardly mobile, may be juxtaposed with the relatively rigid British class structure (Hoggart, 1957; Williams, 1974).

But the picture is more complex. First, two distinct varieties of American soap opera exist, the daytime and prime-time. Second, none of these forms are close to the major soap opera form of the telenovella, strong both in South America and most of Southern Europe.[3] Using similar analytic methods to before (Liebes and Livingstone, 1992, 1994), our present concern is to broaden the analysis of soap opera by surveying European forms of the genre. For this, we suggest at the outset that three main prototypical forms or models can be applied to the soap operas of different countries.

Dynastic

This model focuses on one powerful family, with some satellite outsiders – connected by romance, marriage or rivalry – on its periphery. Some have a parallel, interconnected, 'downstairs' network.

Community

A number of equal, separate, middle- and working-class, multi-generational families (including single-parent ones), and single characters, mostly not romantically connected, all living within one geographical neighbourhood and belonging to one community.

Dyadic

A destabilized network of a number of young, densely interconnected, mostly unigenerational, interchanging couples, with past, present and future romantic ties, continually absorbed in the process of reinventing kinship relations.

As argued elsewhere (Liebes and Livingstone, 1992), the American prime-time soap operas appear to fit the dynastic model, and the kinship chart for *Dallas* is reproduced here to illustrate the main features of this model. Similarly, the American daytime soap operas are structured according to the dyadic model. Lastly, the community model was identified through the kinship structure of the British soap operas, *Coronation Street* and *EastEnders*.

These three prototypical forms or models have in some instances evolved historically through the direct imitation of a programme produced elsewhere (for example, *The Bold and the Beautiful* served as basis for *Brightness*, and *Coronation Street* was the source for *Lindenstrasse*). In other cases, the model represents an analytic category which attempts to characterize parallel developments in soap opera forms across different countries. More work on the origins of soaps in each country is needed to establish the patterns of diffusion, deliberate or otherwise, and to identify why certain forms appear to fit and be successful in the cultural contexts of different countries.

Research orientation and method

The present analysis is not intended as a complete study of the meanings of European soap operas. Many of the conclusions which emerge from a textual analysis must remain provisional until followed through in an audience study. However, our approach starts with the assumption that texts constrain audiences and that the right balance has to be found between the recognition that audiences are active and the acknowledgement of the restrictions imposed on this activity by the text.

In order to study locally made soaps in Europe, we have devised a new methodological approach modelled on 'ethnographic observation' which we applied to the life world in the soap opera (Liebes and Livingstone, 1994). We believe that it makes sense to study social relations and cultural identity in soaps by examining the ways in which the society within the soap functions on the micro-level. By labelling our approach 'ethnographic', we want to emphasize that we start from charting the network of family and romantic relationships as the social context of the soap world in order not to impose our own (paradigmatic or syntagmatic) analytical categories. Moreover, as the story evolves through interactions, and is involved with relationships, the appropriate way to observe characters is within the context of these relationships, focusing on the rules according to which certain ties are allowed, approved of, punished, taken for granted (or combinations thereof) within the kinship structure of the soap opera. Our ethnographic approach does not regard the society portrayed in the soap opera as mimetic, as a realistic portrayal of the society in front of the screen. Rather, we analyse the characters, narratives and situations of the soap opera as they are established and evolve over the lengthy course of a programme's own history, in order to reveal the agenda of concerns, values and metanarratives of the soap opera. Based on what audience researchers have learned of soap opera audiences in terms of their viewing resources, motivations and contexts (Herzog, 1944; Liebes and Katz, 1993; Livingstone, 1998; Press, 1991), this agenda of concerns, values and metanarratives may be seen as indicative of the agenda of the society which watches the soap opera. In short, while any simple mapping of the soap world on to 'real world' is to be avoided, media texts of diverse genres have always been read as revealing the society which produces and views them.

In our own viewing of selected episodes of European-made soaps we were accompanied by informants who were fans of 'their' soap and who belong to the soap-producing country.[4] As long-term viewers, these informants supplied us with expert knowledge on the world of the soap operas and enriched the study by adding their 'national' perspective to the interpretation. Our point in emphasizing an ethnographic approach is to stress the importance of conducting this analysis in terms of the generic and programme context, and, especially important for long-running serials like soap operas, in terms of the web of intergenerational and intragenerational relations of blood and romance, together with the meanings that these relations generate over the duration of the serial and which are familiar to its typically long-term viewers. In this way, the meanings analysed are not imposed a priori on to the text, as is the case with much formal content analysis aimed at testing particular theoretical positions, but meanings are revealed, bottom-up, through a detailed immersion in the text. The advantage of a comparative approach is that if texts reveal something of the society in which they are successful, then questions of local or global culture may be addressed through textual analysis, provided one conducts an analysis of multiple national soap operas using a common research methodology.

Our ethnographic approach also differs from attempts of more thematic textual analyses of soap operas. These focus on the syntagmatic aspect of the evolving drama rather than on the paradigmatic, demographic structure (Allen, 1985). These types of studies deal with the motifs of soaps and with the meaning of the form and format of the genre. Cultural sociologists analyse the attributes of the normative framework, asking about the transformation of the Horatio Alger myth in American soaps, or about reflection of modern vs postmodern ethics (Mander, 1983; Arlen, 1980). More literary scholars examine the characteristics of narratives that do not end and the message inherent in a balance built on an endless sequence of unsolved crises (Thorborn, 1982; Braudy, 1982). Others look at the structure of digressions, slow speed, the 'openness' and segmentation of the multiple, never-ending, subplots, in an effort to answer questions concerning the source of dramatic tension,[5] the relationship between structure and ideology (Fiske, 1987) and between structure and the 'constitution' of viewers (Modleski, 1982). Our own analysis of the way in which the form positions the viewers (Livingstone and Liebes, 1995) points to the socialization of the American soap opera to popularized, psychoanalytic (anti-feminist) notions by the recycling of the oedipal myth.

Our approach to the study of the texts of soap operas attempts to map the social structures represented in the genre. How do the social networks of soaps compare cross-culturally? Are there national differences? We start by charting the kinship structures of the two most successful soap operas in each of several European countries. Our comparisons attempted, insofar as proved practical, to

TABLE 18.1   THE MOST POPULAR LOCAL SOAP OPERAS IN EACH OF FIVE EUROPEAN
COUNTRIES (1990–5)

Country	Title	Duration (yrs)	Freq./ week	Channel	Time
Germany	*Lindenstrasse*	12	1	ARD (Public)	18.40–19.30
Germany	*Gute Zeiten, Schlechte Zeiten*	5	5	RTL	19.40–20.15
Netherlands	*Onderweg Naar Morgen*	2	5	Nederland 2 (Public)	19.00–19.30
Netherlands	*Goede Tijden, Slechte Tijden*	6	5	RTL4 (Cable TV)	20.00–20.30
Greece	*The Brightness*	6	5	ANT1 (Private)	19.45–20.30
Greece	*Goodmorning Life*	2	5	ANT1 (Private)	18.40–19.10
Britain	*Coronation Street*	37	3	ITV	19.30–20.00
Britain	*EastEnders*	12	3	BBC1	19.30–20.00
Sweden	*Redereit*	5	1	SVT1 (Public)	20.00–20.45
Sweden	*Tre Kronor*		1	TV4	20.00–20.45

include soaps from Northern and Southern Europe and from large and small countries. A successful soap is thus defined as one which has a relatively long history and high ratings. In order to qualify for our list, a series had to be among the two most popular family serials made locally between 1990 and 1995. While we surveyed the domestic soap operas in a number of countries, only Britain, Germany, Sweden, the Netherlands and Greece had at least two successful soaps at the time (see Table 18.1).[6] We also viewed soaps from a number of other countries.[7]

Collecting the data was more problematic than we expected because, like Silj and his colleagues 10 years earlier (Silj, 1988), we had to compromise with almost unreconcilable differences in the realities of shared definition and production. First, despite various attempts to define the genre, there is no common definition of the soap opera shared across Europe (Mohr and O'Donnell, 1996). Nonetheless, we discovered that, for example, Denmark and Norway had only produced one series, that France did not produce any, that Italy had produced three relatively short-run telenovellas, and that Greece had two successful soaps running, produced and written (Vargas-style) by the same person. Looking more closely, it was in fact rather difficult to establish whether the French produce soaps, for it would seem that the French pattern is rather the production of romantic teenage comedies in serial form (Pasquier, 1994). For each country we attempted to consult with media academics about their national series and serials, but it was notable that they disagreed among themselves over what counted as a soap opera.

Second, it was difficult to assemble comparable data as, for example, audience data on the genre (e.g. collected by the European Audiovisual Observatory) carry no distinctions between imported and home-produced programmes. We included two soap formats – long-term, 'never-ending' ones, and 'telenovellas' or 'maxi-mini' series which may be between 30 and 100 episodes (Mohr and O'Donnell, 1996).[8]

Despite these difficulties, however, it was generally possible to identify the two most popular soap operas in a number of countries. Thus in Germany, the two most popular soaps were *Lindenstrasse*, viewed by some 8.17 million per episode (11.8%) (Akyuz, 1994) and *Gute Zeiten, Schlechte Zeiten*, with an audience

TABLE 18.2 THREE MODELS FOR A COMPARATIVE ANALYSIS OF SOAP OPERAS (WITH EXAMPLES)

	Dynastic	Communitarian	Dyadic
America	Dallas		Bold and the Beautiful
	Dynasty		As the World Turns
Britain		Coronation Street	
		EastEnders	
Germany	Die Schwarzwaldklinik	Lindenstrasse	Gute Zeiten, Schlechte Zeiten
Netherlands			Onderweg Naar Morgen
			Goede Tijden, Slechte Tijden
Sweden	Redereit	Tre Kronen	
Denmark		Landsbeyen	
Norway		I de Beste Familier	
Greece	Brightness		
	Goodmorning Life		

of approximately 3.91 million (5.5%) per episode (source: ZDF – Medienforschung, Germany, 1995). In the Netherlands, some 555,000 (4.0%) watch *Onderweg Naar Morgen*, while the most popular soap opera, *Goede Tijden, Slechte Tijden*, is viewed by 1.7 million (12.3%) (source: NOS Hilversum, Audience Research, the Netherlands, 1995). Similarly, in Sweden, the popular *Redereit* is watched by some 2.2 million per week with a slightly smaller audience of 1.8 million watching *Tre Kronor* (O'Donnell, 1996a). And in Britain, some 31 percent of the population (16.5 million) watch *Coronation Street*, and a similar 32 percent (17 million) watch *EastEnders* (source: BARB/AGB).

Following the viewing of those soaps for which sufficient information was available, we adopted the anthropological model of analysing cultures by mapping the relationships of blood, marriage and romance among the long-term characters in each programme. The resulting kinship charts were then analysed in terms of the structure of family (extended/nuclear), of community (relationships among families) and relationships between generations (mother/daughter, mother/son) (Liebes and Livingstone, 1992). Having constructed the kinship charts for different countries, we offer a preliminary categorization of the soap operas in terms of the three main models (dynastic, community, dyadic) outlined above (see Table 18.2).

The European soap-producing cultures may be divided into 'single-pattern' countries, and 'multiple-pattern' ones. The two relatively prolific producers – Britain and Germany – represent these two types, with Britain's specialization in community soaps and Germany trying its hand in all three patterns. On a smaller scale, Greece and Italy opt for the dynastic family model, Denmark and Norway and Sweden produce some community soaps in rural settings (albeit less cohesive communities than the British), with Sweden also following the dynastic pattern. Meanwhile the soaps made in the Netherlands appear to adopt the pattern of interchanging dyadic couples. One wonders how accidental this pattern is: could a dynastic or dyadic form work in Britain (in fact, attempts thus far have proved failures); could Greece succeed with a community soap?

Looking across European countries, how does their adoption of particular models reflect the cultural contexts and/or institutional structures of broadcasting? Our initial assumption that there are substantial differences because soaps are difficult to export turned out to be unsupported, as many soaps travel well, and represent a considerable export market in certain cases (Cunningham and Jacka, 1994; Mowlana, 1990; Rogers and Antola, 1985). A close look at the different soap operas suggests that both the choice of a particular soap opera model and the way in which each pattern is elaborated is likely to be dependent on the different cultural settings in which it is produced. Thus we turn to an examination of the characteristics of the three soap opera models – dynastic, community and dyadic, according to the broad cultural parameters of (1) power structures, (2) social locus and (3) gender relations (see also Liebes and Livingstone, forthcoming). Undoubtedly the 'choice' of a soap opera model has consequences for the representation of power, social locus and gender in the life world of the soap, in turn offering different national audiences particular versions of 'everyday life'. Inevitably, such an examination requires a relatively detailed account of the characters and narratives in each soap: we outline these below, attempting to draw out the key features which reveal the national characteristics of each domestic soap opera.

The dynastic model

In this model, the patriarchal family network is the most conservative form in terms of power structure, family and gender relations. Divided into two subtypes – the godfather, and the honourable patriarch (business or professional) – they invoke somewhat different types of involvement, drama and moral codes. The godfather family of the Greek and Italian variants represent cultural variations on the mafia-chief story, turned into a television series (Mander, 1983). These families fill the whole screen, have enough power to organize the world around them (by bribery, extortion, etc.), and economic power is translated into political power. They provide an escape to the world in which crooks may be admired in spite of their immoral actions because they are successful, or because the blame falls on a corrupt society in which the only way to succeed is to have the backing of a mafia-style family.

The second type of dynastic model is seen in the honourable patriarchal families of *Die Schwarzwaldklinik* (not shown here as no longer in production) and *Redereit*. These are less glamorous, on a smaller scale, with more claim to 'realistic' representation. Unlike the godfather model, corruption here is not celebrated and may be controlled. The patriarch is upright and responsible, burdened by having to manage a network of professionals, less totally dependent (and dependable) than family and servants. Brinkman and Dahl'en operate within some constraints from an external social world and have to contend with its rules. The dramatic tension in this type emerges from the struggles over authority. Can the patriarch impose his will within the family and exercise power over the workers in the family company?

[B]oth dynastic types [...] have relations between masters and employees (connected through romantic relations); both have three generations linked through a strong hierarchical structure. In both, the mother of the dynasty is dead, the second generation's siblings compete for inheriting the family power, flirt with servants and employees and marry heirs of rival dynasties.

Power structure

Godfather and patriarch soaps take for granted an unshakeable class structure in which the glamorous, larger than life dynasty is the only one worth looking at, both for escaping into a dream world and, at the same time, for 'proving' that the rich and powerful are unhappy. Interestingly 'taking class for granted' has different manifestations in the various cultures. The Greek *Brightness* and the Italian *Edera* show no American-style guilt about exposing the servants' network and acknowledging inequality and, on the other hand, personalize and humanize the servants, finding it acceptable to have downstairs characters who take part in the plot, even making it a route for mobility. The patriarchal families *Die Schwarzwaldklinik* and *Redereit* prefer to ignore the existence of servants in the household, implying a certain cultural unease about class structure. The British in the original *Upstairs/Downstairs*, chose to tell parallel stories of masters and servants (whereas *Coronation Street* and *EastEnders* stay within one, working-class context, pretending that this is the world).

Social loci

In all patriarchal soaps men commute between home and work and there is a mutual invasion of the two realms, so that each is used for gaining points in the other. The clear division of labour, according to which women run the home and the men rule the real world from their steel and glass offices, is predominantly maintained in *Brightness* and *Edera*. Mothers and wives have jobs, businesses, even careers, but are seen mainly at home, worrying about romance and motherhood.

In *Die Schwarzwaldklinik* and *Redereit* the workplace, with its network of professionals, achieves a relative autonomy by introducing another parallel network of characters – that of the family company's employees. Although doctors and nurses who work in the clinic in *Die Schwarzwaldklinik* and the shipping line workers of *Redereit* are dependent on the family, they provide another physical and social locus for the entanglements of the plot. True, the clinic and the boat are where patriarchal family men may exercise their power, but the employees are not just the patriarchs' trusty followers but are given a life of their own in the series. The women of *Die Schwarzwaldklinik* appear (mostly as subordinates) in the workplace, and they have to choose between advancing as professionals in the clinic and marrying the patriarch. In *Redereit*, 'commuting' takes place between home, office and boat. Mothers stay at home but the dynasty's daughters work in the shipping line. The patriarch's workplace is transformed from the sleek locus of power manoeuvres to the more recognizable reality of a professional or business setting.

Gender relations

As in the American model, wives sometimes have a profession or work (e.g. Virna of *Brightness*; Brinkman's women are nurses, even doctors; Edera sells clothes) but they are not allowed a career or real power (in *Die Schwarzwaldklinik* Christa, for example, has to leave Brinkman's life and the soap when she decides to specialize, Reider Dahl'en's granddaughter, who becomes the head of *Redereit*, remains totally dependent on her grandfather and adviser). Their access to power is still measured by their ability to deliver (beauty or baby) to their husbands (Liebes and Katz, 1993).

In terms of acceptable sexual mores, the asymmetry between the sexes is far more blatant than, say, in the classic dynastic soap, *Dallas*. While the broader circle of characters are distributed rather equally between JR and Sue Ellen, the entourage of 'old friends' around the central couple of Yagos and his (second) wife Virna consists mostly of a trail of (past and present) women lovers of Yagos. Moreover, as men are assumed to be polygamous in nature, their illicit affairs are often not kept clandestine. Yagos is portrayed as a good husband although his wife Virna knows him to be frequently unfaithful. The rules of sexual behaviour in *Brightness* and in *Edera* also prioritize men far beyond their given biological advantages. Two patterns of love relationships – in which men initiate, and act, and women pay the consequences – stand out as different from *Dallas*, to the extent to which this latter pattern allows men to exercise violence towards women without being punished. On the one hand, there is a proliferation of men's 'pure', unrequited love of a woman and, at the other extreme, the same men may rape the women they love, or kill their foetus when a baby is undesirable. As rape is seen as a masculine privilege it is not punished.[9]

The community model

Community soaps open up the closed, self-sufficient structure of an overpowering *Dallas*-type family to include a whole neighbourhood of ordinary families. The all-embracing, hierarchical, dynastic dream world is substituted with a community in which loves, betrayals and reconciliations are part of the struggle through recognizable daily routines, coloured by more or less pedestrian hardships of sickness, unemployment and teenage drug habits. Britain, as stated above, has the longest tradition of community soaps celebrating the life of working-class urban people. Whereas in the 1990s some small beginnings have been made in Scandinavian countries to produce soaps which portray their own rural communities (Denmark and Norway with *Landsbeyen* and *I de Beste Familier* respectively), the most established, long-term production of a community soap in Europe is the German *Lindenstrasse*, which has been running, partly in parallel with *Die Schwarzwaldklinik*, since the mid-1980s.[10] Not surprisingly, in spite of the professed intention of its producer, *Lindenstrasse* turned out to be quite different from its British inspiration.

Power structure

European community soaps all attempt to overcome social conflicts and class differences by offering an idealized or nostalgic vision of living together. The British tradition of community soap is proudly working class (with *Brookside* as a more middle-class exception). The harmonious, all-embracing neighbourhood acts as a cosy environment in which the restrictions on upward mobility are not noticeable as both success and failure drive characters out of the neighbourhood and the soap. *Lindenstrasse*, Germany's community soap opera, is about middle-class people, although there are many lower middle-class characters, and most women work as secretaries, waitresses or nurses.

Nostalgia for a *gemeinschaft* in Denmark's *Lansbeyen* stresses the value of the country and to a traditional community of farmers who have to rely on each other to weather daily hardships and economic slavery to the banks. Directed at an older audience, as is *Coronation Street*, the rural community of *Landsbeyen* is another form of nostalgia – for life in the country and for working the land. In the modern world of capitalism and materialism, it tells us that the good old values of hard work and loyalty to friends are lost. The villain in this almost Ibsen-like drama is the new bank manager, originally a boy from the village, who left with a grudge, made good and comes back to avenge himself.

Social loci

In all European community soap operas characters struggle through domestic and work problems both at home and at work, and they work mostly within the community. People meet in the common public places. In *Coronation Street*, these are the pub, the garage, the greengrocer's, the newspaper shop and the launderette; among the gloomier public spaces of *Landsbeyen*, the bank is a prominent symbol of threat; in the street, central to *Lindenstrasse*, we are introduced to the cafe, the doctor's clinic, the flower shop, the bench in the park and the Italian and Greek restaurants. Fewer chores, more leisure.

Gender relations

A look at the relationships between couples shows that women are stronger in the British community. Like *Coronation Street*, the families of *Lindenstrasse* are mostly of two generations – characters in their twenties with middle-aged parents. Unlike *Coronation Street*, it is a common (but acceptable) scandal for older men to have affairs with much younger women, often going on to marry them (as in the case of Brinkman in *Die Schwarzwaldklinik*). During the episodes we reviewed it was the 50-year-old Kurt Sperling who was having an affair with Iffi, his son Momo's girlfriend, while the two teenagers were bringing up their (perhaps his) child. Other cases in the history of the soap include Hans Breimer, who divorced his wife Helga because he was having an affair with the younger Anna Ziegler, whom he then married, Andy Zenke (Iffi's father, married to the much younger Gabi), and the 55-year-old Dr Dressler, who had two children from a former marriage and is married to the 30-year-old Tanja.

In *Coronation Street*, while characters break up, have affairs and remarry, romance and marriage usually stays within the same generation. Moreover, there are a number of older single women who are active and independent and take part in the story. In *Lindenstrasse* most women are young; the few older ones, such as Else King, who, with Onkel Franz, provides the moments of comic relief, and Helga Beimer ('fat, not nice or attractive', according to our informant, 'was the boss in the house when she and Hans were married') are ridiculed, even hated. The one exception is Amelie Von Der Marwitz, sixty-ish, aristocratic and the 'fairy godmother' of Lisa, who has no real mother. Our informant adds that her money comes 'from having had relations with wealthy men', and she is now single. Interestingly, though *Lindenstrasse* provides a middle-class environment, Eva Sperling (Kurt Sperling's wife) is the only woman who has a profession but (as in the American daytime soaps) she is not shown in her professional surroundings and the story-line presents her as weaker than her unemployed husband. Gender patterns seem to indicate a segregation between networks of buddies, and (to a lesser extent) of women friends, who feel much better with same-sex than with opposite-sex contacts.

The dyadic model

Interchanging couples constitutes a type of soap which is destabilized in three ways. First, it operates by characters constantly exchanging places within the framework of intragenerational and intergenerational relations, with characters perpetually experimenting with new intimate partners. Second, the structure of those relationships is changed as characters experiment with new forms of partnership (from heterosexual to homosexual, from a dyad to a triad). Third, the biological structure itself is constantly reinvented as characters keep trying to resurrect a 'real' (and maybe stable) lost family, and relationships have to be redefined as familiar characters emerge as biological blood relations. This type of soap both redefines family and community, and brings about the destruction of each as a stable environment and framework for the story.

This pattern is represented in our sample by the German *Gute Zeiten, Schlechte Zeiten* and the Dutch *Goede Tijden, Slechte Tijden*[11] and *Onderweg Naar Morgen*. While this subgenre draws heavily on melodrama – no social realism here – it goes one step beyond the classical American daytime soaps, which do feature interchangeable couples but keep the dependence of the young generation on powerful patriarchal moguls. (Less family-centred soaps such as *Melrose Place* and *Beverly Hills* may be a closer variant.)

Power structure

As in the community (and unlike the patriarchal) soap, the status of characters of changing couples is equal and interchangeable. The older generation is demoted from power. This type of soap is mostly one-generational, about young couples, with a few middle-aged characters of the parent generation[12] who participate in the romantic game but have lost their authority. The motivating force is individual fulfilment, not the continuation of the dynasty. The holding, stable framing of community has also disappeared as characters are metaphorical orphans and do not belong to families or to communities.

Social loci

The network of changing couples may be casually organized around a bar (as in the case of *Gute Zeiten, Schlechte Zeiten*) or a cafe (run by Jan Reitsema in *Onderweg Naar Morgen*) frequented by protagonists or, as in the case of *Goede Tijden*, around a person – in this case, an ex-high school teacher, a postmodern surrogate mother, whom a number of the young people have studied with at high school.

Gender relations

As nobody can be sure of their lovers, all relationships are in constant conflict, often accompanied by extreme violence. The stable, sometimes boring, harmony of the community gives way to high melodrama. It is not uncommon for a lover or a spouse to attempt to kill their mate[13] and, in the spirit of postmodern lifestyle, everything goes and characters may go to prison only to return to the soap untainted. Thus, paradoxically, the world in which both genders dedicate their lives to seeking happiness and true love is filled with distrust and fear of the person who is supposedly the closest to them. Violence in these soaps lies therefore within the most intimate circle and constitutes the deepest anxieties (Cavell, 1981). Not surprisingly, as romance fails it is not uncommon for people to have mental breakdowns and end up in a religious sect or in mental hospital. The chaotic, casual interchanging of couples, the deep mistrust of the credibility and durability of human emotions and the (paradoxical) quest for durable relationships lead characters to trespass traditionally accepted boundaries. Every boundary becomes a challenge. There is no respect for generational differences or for accepted family taboos.

Incestuous love occurs sometimes knowingly, in other cases innocently.[14] Sex or romance override professional relationships (between patient and therapist), and work relations between bosses and employees. Traditional forms of intimacy are also unsatisfying. These include perverse forms such as women falling in love with men who come to molest or kill them.[15] Heterosexual love has to be weighed against homosexual love (recall the lesbian relationship of Laura). The idea of couples is put into question not only by the constant exchange of mates but by trying out new forms, such as menage a trois.

Listening to our informants, it seems that these constant exchanges and experiments are extremely casual affairs: 'Vera recently fell in love with a man', recounts one fan of *Gute Zeiten, Schlechte Zeiten*, 'she wanted to go round the world with him on holiday but when Clemens [her husband] shows up in the airport to give her something, she makes her decision to go back to her husband.' But though characters act in a way which puts their lives in total jeopardy, these acts are accompanied by what would seem outdated, intense, often violent emotions of possessiveness, jealousy and suspicion which move the story along. Melodrama is intensified not only by threatened and actual crime, but also by a lot of disappearing and reappearing, looking for one's 'real' mother or father, and trying to discover one's sexual identity.

Conclusions

The soap opera: a diversity of subgenres

Despite the common assumption that European television is undergoing, willingly or not, a process of Americanization, we have argued that detailed examination of the diversity of soap operas around Europe reveals that the soap opera is not simply an American genre which is being imported – either directly, or by adapting formats and conventions – into Europe. While undoubtedly American (and Latin American and Australian) soap operas prove highly popular when imported into Europe, we have shown that Britain, Scandinavia and Northern Europe, and, to a lesser extent, Southern Europe, have developed three distinctive subtypes of the genre – the community soap, the dynastic soap and the dyadic soap. Of these, only the last owes much to the American daytime soap opera and an institutional analysis of cross-national export and production would doubtless reveal a story which might fairly be labelled 'Americanisation' (Mancini and Swanson, 1996). Following the analysis of *Dallas*'s success offered by Liebes and Katz (1993), we suggest that both America and Europe sustain, at various times, various examples of the dynastic model because the patriarchal and primordial themes which structure social relations in these soap operas draw on common and fundamental themes in western culture. In these cases, therefore, it is inappropriate to argue that influence flows from America towards Europe, even though it may be true historically that the overwhelming success of *Dallas* prompted the development of this version of the genre in other countries. Lastly, the community subgenre – the most distinctively European of the three forms – would seem to be associated with a strong public broadcasting tradition, for it comes to prominence, typically among the top rated programmes for the country, in Britain, Germany and Scandinavia. Whether this form could be made to succeed in France, Italy or Greece is unknown: while there are many successful formats available for import across national boundaries, certain choices are made, and these surely reveal the cultural assumptions and audience expectations of a particular nation.

How should the apparent success of different forms or subgenres of the soap opera in different countries be explained? We offer the possibility here that a social-anthropological perspective which links family structures and ideological systems may prove useful. For example, how should we explain the choice of the dynastic type in the first locally made productions in Germany (*Schwarzwaldklinik*) and in Sweden (*Redereit*)? Emmanuel Todd (1985) analyses the type of family relations (between fathers and sons and between husbands and wives) which characterizes different European countries. Distinguishing between authoritarian and individualist family types, he suggests that Germany and Sweden belong in the authoritarian type, as inheritance is customarily unequal (that is, one son only inherits and married sons continue cohabiting with their parents). The Anglo-Saxon world, on the other hand, with equal inheritance and no cohabitation, is characterized by Todd as individualist. If one accepts this mapping of family structures and cultural assumptions, then the further link to the conditions for production and reception of different subgenres of the soap opera within different European countries is relatively straightforward.

In addition to considering the possible connections between the soap opera world and the everyday culture of the audience, we suggest further that each of the three subgenres creates a particular communicative relationship with the viewers. Frye (1957; see also Chesebro, 1987) distinguishes among dramatic genres by the way in which they establish relations between viewer and text. Five types of communicative relationships – ironic, mimetic, leader oriented, romantic and mythic – are derived from the characterization of the main characters' intelligence and capacity to control the environment in comparison with those of the viewers. Analysing the European subgenres of the soap opera according to Frye's scheme, we find that community soaps are mainly mimetic (positioning the viewers with characters 'like us' on both dimensions), with some ironic elements (characters whom we may feel superior to). Dynastic soaps are either romantic, with leaders of a superior *level* of intelligence and capacity to control the surroundings (recall the Swedish or German serials), or mythic, with leaders who are superior in *kind* on both counts (the Greek soaps, faithful followers of *Dynasty* and *Dallas*). Dyadic soaps, seemingly mimetic, go through mythic transformations, in which (lost and existing) characters are found or rediscovered as owning special powers.

The moral economy (Morley and Silverstone, 1990) of the soap opera is connected with the kind of relationship it establishes with its viewers. The more mimetic the subgenre – the less it escapes from the dilemmas of daily life – the more it is socially responsible. Thus, the community subgenre is always socially responsible. The dynastic soap may take one of two forms, depending on whether it is anchored in a broader social reality, and dominated by a socially responsible patriarch (Sweden, Germany) or situated in a fantasy world, and dominated by a power-crazy rogue (Greece; see Mander, 1983). The dyadic is never socially responsible, as it is in search of a new, as yet undiscovered, moral code.

While both the patriarchal soaps and the community soaps operate within a structure of power relations that they take for granted, the community soaps have been produced in the spirit of public broadcasting, indicating certain pedagogic aims. Thus, unlike the patriarchal dynastic type which is supposed only to appeal to the viewers' fantasy, here we may examine the kinship structure in terms of the social message they are consciously seeking to transmit, i.e. what issues are intentionally problematized, and, in parallel, what these soaps take for granted. In other words, we were interested in how they constitute a type of public forum for debating social issues. We regard the kinship network as the static, taken for granted, hegemonic elements, and thematic analysis as complementing the picture by revealing the extent and patterns of openness to change.

Within this gender and class context, what social problems do community soaps in British and German cultures address? Both have unemployed characters, teenage drug taking, sexual harassment and battered wives. Both soaps make attempts to deal with the issue of xenophobia and racism.[16] *Lindenstrasse* transmits two messages regarding immigrants on the street. One is the explicit statement of the immigrants themselves that they would prefer to go home. The second, implicit in the story, is that violence of neo-Nazis against immigrants is exercised by misguided, harmless youngsters, and is basically under control.[17] *Coronation Street* did not at this point have any foreign inhabitants.[18] While both communities are harmonious, and in control of violence, it does threaten. Our tentative observation (which has to be confirmed) is that in *Coronation Street* violence is mostly external, anonymous and arbitrary.[19] In *Lindenstrasse* there is more violence from within.[20]

The postmodern future?

Both the community and dynastic types offer stable patterns of social relations, and hence an image of a stable society. Two main forms of stability are represented, one based on generational hierarchy, the other based on social class. With regard to the production of soap operas in Europe, it seems that the community and dynastic forms are the two most commonly adopted. The community model, as noted above, is more often associated with public service tradition, the latter seems to fit with the cultural preoccupations of the countries which produce them. Or, more accurately, one might say that the dynastic form, based on hierarchical power relations of one form or another, allows space for the expression of particular sociocultural concerns, where these differ across nations, in a manner not so readily permitted by the dyadic form of soap opera, in which individualistic longings take over. Thus *Redereit* struggles with issues of ecology, town planning and workers' rights (all invading the grand designs of the dynastic family), while *Die Schwarzwaldklinik* addresses such issues as the limits of patriarchy and the meaning of 'countryside' in the German tradition (Kreutzner and Seiter, 1995).

In the dyadic form, the absence of cultural content is the point. This form, we suggest, lacks stability. Hence the primordial quest for blood relations. While this type makes no attempt to debate social issues, in its pursuit of viewers (and ratings) it harps on the despair of too much freedom and too little trust that goes with the modern and postmodern loss of a sense of place. In a destabilized social environment, where families have disappeared, no biological ties may be relied on as 'real', as new ones keep cropping up, romantic dyads are precarious, as no emotional ties are sustained for long (nor is it believed to be possible); seeking 'real', enduring ties becomes a major concern for the characters, taking the form of a quest for the most primordial biological relations – a parent, a sibling, a son. The sources of melodrama reside in the turmoil of losing and finding transient lovers, and in losing and finding 'genuine' blood ties. Thus, new experimental lifestyles, which transcend the family, and primordial longings which precede it, operate side by side in the pursuit of happiness, creating chaotic kinship patterns. In other words, the invention of a cohort of 'self-imagined orphans', who go on not only with the losing battle of securing their own romantic relationships, but also with trying to reinvent (or reconstruct) the biological ties they rejected, has jeopardized the structure of kinship itself, put it into constant flux, and (having all but destroyed it) attempts to recreate it by trying out various options of dyadic relationships, and various candidates for 'blood' relatives. In effect, then, this dyadic form is less expressive of any particular cultural environment; insofar as this form is coming to represent the global form of the soap opera, this makes it increasingly difficult for nationally produced soap operas to reflect the cultural concerns of their country.

From the beginning of the 1990s, the trend of both community soaps and dynastic soaps seems to be developing in the direction of the increasing success of the dyadic form. Thus, *Die Schwarzwaldklinik* and *Châteauvallon*, both dynastic forms, have ended. New soap operas are either dyadic or combine dynastic and dyadic. Older soap operas, rooted in either community or dynastic forms, such as *EastEnders*, *Coronation Street* and *Lindenstrasse*, may be said to be moving increasingly in the direction of the dyadic. Thus while European soap operas have traditionally become established by expressing, in various ways, significant national cultural concerns, this has depended upon incorporating both formal and content features of the genre. Thus, the move away from culturally specific contents towards a more 'empty form' may be seen to threaten cultural expression through the soap opera.

More optimistically, it may be that where the broadcasting capability exists, countries may produce soap operas on more than one model. For example, in Germany, both the community and dyadic models exist; and in the new Greek soap operas, again, one fits the dyadic model, the other the dynastic. The exceptions may require national explanations. As discussed in Liebes and Livingstone (1994), British soaps are always community soaps, and attempts to produce dyadic models have not succeeded. In the Netherlands, both main soaps are dyadic: this may reflect a combination of factors in the broadcasting system, first as a country with no tradition of local soap opera production, and second as a country which, because of its size and geographic location, has a tradition of receiving programmes from multi-channel cable channels, from diverse countries in Europe and America. The preference for local soaps over imported ones wherever these exist (Silj, 1988) suggests that local production remains worth pursuing for both economic and cultural reasons.

Notes

The authors would like to acknowledge financial support from the EC 'Human Capital and Mobility' Programme (awarded to Liebes and Livingstone at the European Gender Research Laboratory, LSE). They would also like to thank Shelley Anderson, Charlotte Martin, Sarit Moldovan, Nina Nissel and Tsfira Grebelsky for research assistance, together with those colleagues in Europe who kindly answered our questions about European soap operas, including Christina Apostolidi and Maria Ralli (on Greece), Millie Buonanno (on Italy), Carmelo Garitonandia (on Spain), Dominique Pasquier (on France), Sven Ross and Runar Woldt (on Sweden) and Hugh O'Donnell (on European soaps in general).

1. In the forever-open issue of what series may qualify as soaps we have decided to adopt the definition of the genre commonly assumed, if not made explicit, within the research literature: a programme which continues endlessly (not a finite number of episodes culminating in a conclusion), featuring at least two generations, concerned with the daily lives of the characters, with no single hero figure, and reliant more on dialogue than action. We therefore excluded such offshoots or kin-genres as romantic comedies and teenage series, which, while sharing a number of features with soaps, are constructed on other forms of social networks or which make viewers laugh as much as they make them cry or which adopt a linear narrative which progresses towards a closure. These deserve a separate study.

2. The *idea* of babies, however, does play a central part in the plot, mostly as pawns in the exchange between the sexes. Women often use a baby, real, false or expected, for improving their position, but babies hardly ever appear on the screen.

3. We arrived at the three forms in two stages. First, we found it useful to label the basic structure of the networks of the American vs the British subgenre as 'dyadic' and 'community'. Second, when we observed the networks of other soap-producing countries in Europe, we found that some clearly conformed to one of our two categories, albeit within a specific cultural context (i.e. the community of *Lindenstrasse*), while others adopted the network of one dynastic family.

4. These informants were recruited by advertising for soap fans among European students in London.

5. In each scene rather than in the overall plot-line, which is expected and never ending at the same time (Thorburn, 1982).

6. France and Spain did not produce any soaps, although Spain did subsequently produce a popular soap in 1996. Among the European states only Germany is a prolific producer which may be compared to Britain.

7. We are extremely grateful to our colleagues across Europe who recorded and supplied tapes, provided reprints in the various languages, and themselves assisted in interpreting the cultural meanings of European-made soaps.

8. A third category, in terms of target audience, are the 'minority' soaps such as Catalan (in Spain), Gaelic (Ireland) and Flemish (Belgium). These are made specifically for a regional audience, or, in other cases, as a means of preserving a local language or dialect.

9. Thus, for example, Demitris, who rapes Elvira, ends up marrying her mother, while Elvira keeps her baby.

10. It is somewhat ironic that *Die Schwarzwaldklinik*, itself strong on German cultural connotations, was aimed at being exported overseas, and succeeded in doing so, while *Lindenstrasse*, modelled on the very British *Coronation Street* and *EastEnders*, had been intended only for home consumption (Silj, 1988).

11. Both, according to Mohr and O'Donnell (1996), based on a long defunct Australian soap *The Restless Years*, with Dutch scripts produced after the first two seasons and developed independently in both cultures.

12. Such as Laura, in *Goede Tijden*, who has an affair with Sten, her son's best friend.
13. In *Goede Tijden* it happened to Helen, everybody's surrogate mother whose lover Koen tried to kill her, and to Robert, who was pushed through a mirror by his wife Laura; in *Onderweg Naar Morgen* Frank was pushed down the stairs by (as it turned out) his wife Daphne; in *Gute Zeiten, Schlechte Zeiten* the man who goes out with Saskia plans to murder her.
14. Two examples: Renco in *Goede Tijden* falls in love with Diane, who turns out to be his half-sister, and so does Pim, in *Onderweg Naar Morgen*.
15. Such as Saskia of *Gute Zeiten, Schlechte Zeiten* falling in love with a man who was trying to murder her, or Tina (in the same soap) breaking off with her lover Tom because she falls in love with an extortionist kidnapper.
16. While no immigrants then lived on *Coronation Street*, two immigrant families lived on *Lindenstrasse* – the Pavaroties, who own an Italian restaurant, and the Sarikakis, who own a Greek restaurant.
17. Seeing Olli, *Lindenstrasse's* neo-Nazi, as a basically decent guy, who had suffered from lack of love as a child, and deserves a second chance, is shared by the viewer and by Lisa Hoffmeister, a young teenager – blond, spiritual, orphaned. Lisa, the gentlest, kindest, most innocently beautiful Cinderella believes in Olli against the advice of older people, making him the hero of the one 'pure' love story of the soap.
18. The exception, which ended tragically, was Deirdre's marriage to Samia, a Moroccan who was under threat of being deported. Samia's kidney was found compatible with the kidney of Deirdre's daughter Tracy, who suffered the consequences of a drug addiction. After Samia donated this kidney he was the victim of a racial attack and died. The story is beautifully pedagogic, as it demonstrates that human blood is identical everywhere, and the spirit of generosity and self-sacrifice as well as brutal hatred is not the property of one's own community.
19. Samia, as recounted, was killed by hooligans. Gail's husband Brian is stabbed to death, Vicki's parents are killed in a car crash.
20. In addition to the violence of the two neo-Nazis against foreigners, there are violent husbands – Olaf King, who attempted to rape his wife (and caused her death), and Anna Ziegler's first husband, who beat her up.

References

Akyuz, G. (1994) 'Soaps Make a Clean Sweep', *TV World* June: 16–22.
Allen, R.C. (1985) *Speaking of Soap Operas*. Chapel Hill: University of North Carolina Press.
Allen, R.C. (ed.) (1995) *To Be Continued …: Soap Operas Around the World*. London: Routledge.
Arlen, M. (1980) *Camera Age: Essays on Television*, pp. 38–50. New York: Fearrar, Strauss and Giroux.
Bombardier, D. (1985) 'Television as Instrument of Cultural Identity: The Case of Quebec', pp. 177–82 in E.M. Rogers and F. Balle (eds), *The Media Revolution in American and Western Europe*. Norwood, NJ: Ablex.
Braudy, L. (1982) 'Popular Culture and Personal Time', *The Yale Review* 71: 41: 481–8.
Cavell, S. (1981) *Pursuits of Happiness: The Hollywood Comedy of Remarriage*. Cambridge, MA: Cambridge University Press.
Chesebro, J.W. (1987) 'Communication, Values, and Popular Television Series – a Four Year Assessment', pp. 8–46 in H. Newcomb (ed.), *Television: The Critical View*, 4th edn. New York: Oxford University Press.
Cunningham, S. and E. Jacka (1994) 'Neighbourly Relations? Cross-cultural Reception Analysis and Australian Soaps in Britain', *Cultural Studies* 8(3): 509–26.
Fiske, J. (1987) *Television Culture*. London: Methuen.
Frye, N. (1957) *Anatomy of Criticism*. Princeton, NJ: Princeton University Press.
Hagedorn, R. (1995) 'Doubtless to be Continued: A Brief History of Serial Narrative', pp. 27–48 in R.C. Allen (ed.), *To Be Continued …: Soap Operas Around the World*. London: Routledge.
Herzog, H. (1944) 'What Do We Really Know about Daytime Serial Listeners?', pp. 3–33 in P. Lazarsfeld and F. Stanton (eds), *Radio Research*. New York: Duell, Sloan and Pearce.

Hoggart, R. (1957) *The Uses of Literacy*. London: Chatto & Windus.

Kreutzner, G. and E. Seiter (1995) 'Not all "Soaps" are Created Equal: Towards a Cross-cultural Criticism of Television Serials', pp. 234–55 in R.C. Allen (ed.), *To Be Continued …: Soap Operas Around the World*. London: Routledge.

Liebes, T. and E. Katz (1993) *The Export of Meaning*. Cambridge: Polity Press.

Liebes, T. and S.M. Livingstone (1992) 'Mothers and Lovers: Managing Women's Role Conflicts in American and British Soap Operas', pp. 94–120 in J.G. Blumler, J.M. McLeod and K.E. Rosengren (eds), *Communication and Culture Across Space and Time: Prospects of Comparative Analysis*. Newbury Park, CA: Sage.

Liebes, T. and S.M. Livingstone (1994) 'The Structure of Family and Romantic Ties in the Soap Opera: An Ethnographic Approach to the Cultural Framing of Primordiality', *Communication Research* 21: 717–41.

Liebes, T. and S.M. Livingstone (forthcoming) 'Gender Relations in European Soap Operas: A Comparative Analysis', manuscript in preparation.

Livingstone, S. (1998) *Making Sense of Television: The Psychology of Audience Interpretation*. 2nd edition. London: Routledge.

Livingstone, S. and T. Liebes (1995) 'Where Have all the Mothers Gone? Soap Opera's Replaying of the Oedipal Story', *Critical Studies in Mass Communication* 12: 155–75.

Mancini, P. and D.L. Swanson (1996) 'Politics, Media, and Modern Democracy: Introduction', pp. 1–26 in D.L. Swanson and P. Mancini (eds), *Politics, Media, and Modern Democracy: An International Study of Innovations in Electoral Campaigning and their Consequences*. New York: Praeger.

Mander, M. (1983) 'Dallas: The Mythology of Crime and the Moral Occult', *Journal of Popular Culture* 17: 44–8.

Modleski, T. (1982) *Loving with a Vengeance*. New York: Methuen.

Mohr, P.J. and H. O'Donnell (1996) 'The Rise and Rise of Soap Operas in Europe', *The Scottish Communication Association Journal* 2: 34–70.

Morley, D. and R. Silverstone (1990) 'Domestic Communications: Technologies and Meanings', *Media, Culture and Society* 12(1): 31–55.

Mowlana, H. (1990) 'Japanese Programs on Iranian Television: A Study in International Flow of Information', paper presented at the 17th World Congress of the International Association for Mass Communication Researchers, Yugoslavia.

O'Donnell, H. (1996a) 'People's Home to Home and Away: The Growth and Development of Soap Opera in Sweden', *Irish Communication Review* 6: 56–68.

O'Donnell, H. (1996b) 'From a Manichean Universe to the Kitchen Sink: The Telenovella in the Iberian Peninsula', *International Journal of Iberian Studies* 9(1): 7–18.

Pasquier, D. (1994) 'Hélène et les Garçons: éducation sentimentale', manuscript, ESPRIT.

Press, A. (1991) *Women Watching Television*. Philadelphia: University of Pennsylvania Press.

Rogers, E.M. and L. Antola (1985) 'Telenovelas: A Latin American Success Story', *Journal of Communication* 35(4): 24–35.

Schiller, H.I. (1992) *Mass Communication: An American Empire*. Boulder, CO: Westview Press.

Schrøder, K.C. and M. Skovmand (1992) 'Introduction', pp. 1–21 in M. Skovmand and K.C. Schrøder (eds), *Media Cultures: Reappraising Transnational Media*. London: Routledge.

Silj, A. (1988) *East of Dallas: The European Challenge to American Television*. London: British Film Institute.

Thorburn, D. (1982) 'Television Melodrama', pp. 529–46 in H. Newcomb (ed.), *Television: The Critical View*. New York: Oxford University Press.

Todd, E. (1985) *The Explanation of Ideology: Family Structures and Social Systems*. Oxford: Basil Blackwell.

Tracey, M. (1985) 'The Poisoned Chalice? International Television and the Idea of Dominance', *Dedalus* 114(4): 17–56.

Tracey, M. (1988) 'Popular Culture and the Economics of the Global Village', *Intermedia* 16(2): 8–25.

Williams, R. (1974) *Television: Technology and Cultural Form*. London: Fontana.

Gendering the Internet: Claims, Controversies and Cultures

Liesbet van Zoonen

Internet is a contested medium as far as its social cultural meanings and significance are concerned. A core issue in the debate is the meaning of the Internet for gender: how does gender influence Internet communication, contents and use, and – the other way around – how do Internet communication, contents and use impact upon gender? In the terms common to cultural studies of technology, what is at stake is the *mutual shaping* of gender and the Internet (see van Oost, 1995). The Internet arose in the early 1960s out of the collaboration of American universities and the Pentagon (see Naughton, 1999). It thus has its roots in the so-called military–industrial complex, which according to many feminist critics inevitably constitutes it as a medium deeply embedded in masculine codes and values (see van Zoonen, 1992).

In recent years, however, other feminist authors have reclaimed the Internet as a technology close to the core qualities of femininity (e.g. Spender, 1995). Yet other, cyberfeminist authors contend that it enables a transgression of the dichotomous categories of male and female, constructing transgender or even genderless human identities and relations (e.g. Braidotti, 1996). This article discusses these three claims on the gender codes of the Internet, and shows that interpretations of the Internet as masculine, feminine or even transgender are based on limited conceptualizations of both gender and technology. An alternative analysis based on particular use cultures of the Internet in everyday life shows how both technology and gender are multidimensional processes that are articulated in complex and contradictory ways which escape straightforward gender definitions. To begin with, I briefly review the gender codes of the Internet's enabling technologies: the telephone and the computer.

Gender codes of enabling technologies

At the end of the 19th century the telephone appeared in American society. The technology was still in its infancy: one needed operators to connect calls, there were still few subscribers, there were more party lines than private lines and competition between telephone companies was fierce (Fischer, 1992). It was in

Source: *EJC* (2002), vol. 17, no. 1: 5–23.

that situation that one of the independent telephone companies in Indiana called a hearing of the Indiana Public Service Commission about acceptable uses of the telephone. The company objected to women's uses of the telephone in particular: women talked for long periods on the telephone about supposedly trivial matters and this was not what the medium was meant for, so the company claimed (Rakow, 1988). The telephone had indeed been propagated by the burgeoning industry as a medium for practical management and household purposes; businessmen were the first target groups. Exhibits, telephone vendors and advertisements in trade journals all claimed that the telephone would 'increase efficiency, save time, and impress customers' (Fischer, 1992: 66). As far as women were addressed in this early period, the business of the household was emphasized: 'the telephone could help the affluent household manager to accomplish her task' (Fischer, 1992: 67). Many women, however, had a completely different appreciation of the new medium and used it for 'social purposes': keeping in touch with family and friends, exchanging personal experiences and the latest community news, and – in the more rural areas – using it as a companion in lonely times. Industry leaders and professionals objected to such uses of the telephone. They considered chatting on the telephone as 'one more female foolishness' (Fischer, 1992: 231). In trade journals and advertisements 'talkative women and their frivolous electrical conversations about inconsequential personal subjects were contrasted with the efficient task-oriented, worldly talk of business and professional men' (Marvin, 1988: 23). Complaints were issued in newspapers about 'women's habits of talking on the phone for "futile motives"' (Martin, 1988: 96). [...]

Nowadays it is hard to imagine the telephone as anything else then a medium to maintain social contact. It is therefore not a far-fetched conclusion to say that 'women subscribers were largely responsible for the development of a culture of the telephone' (Martin, 1991: 171, quoted in Fischer, 1992: 236), as we know it today.

The gender codes of the computer emerged quite differently and turn the light to another historical scene, set in mid-19th-century, upperclass England. At a dinner party hosted by Mary Somerville, a woman whose mathematical work was used at Cambridge, one of the people attending was Charles Babbage who played a leading role in the scientific and technical development of the period. Nowadays he is credited with having developed the first calculator and the first blueprint for a computer. At the dinner party, he told his audience about a machine he had built – the Difference Engine – which was capable of making various calculations and tables. Among the attentive listeners were Lady Byron and her 18-year-old daughter, Ada. Lady Byron was a gifted mathematician herself and known in high society as the Princess of Parallelograms. Her daughter definitively inherited her intellectual gifts and had at the age of 13 produced a design for a flying machine. Ada and her mother were fascinated by Babbage's ideas and went to see the Difference Engine in his studio. One of the observers of that scene remembers 'Miss Byron, young as she was, understood its workings, and saw the great beauty of its invention' (Moore, 1977: 44, quoted in Plant, 1998: 47). [...]

Ada became an outspoken advocate of Babbage's invention. She translated an Italian paper about the Engine and added her own extensive notes to it, which were three times longer than the original text. The notes contained a set of instructions for how to use the Engine. Nowadays we would consider such instructions to be a computer program and for that reason Ada has been credited with being the first computer programmer in history. 'Ada understood the potential power of a computing machine such as envisioned by Babbage – one that had internal memory, could make choices and repeat instructions – and she foresaw its application in mathematical computation, artificial intelligence and even computer music' (Freeman, 1996). Babbage's Analytical Engine and Ada's work on it disappeared from the public eye until 1937, when his unpublished notebooks were discovered. Ada's contribution to computer history has been acknowledged by various sources, most notably the American Defence Department which named its primary programming language, ADA, after her.

We can consider the telephone and the computer as respectively the mother and the father of the Internet, the global network of computers that came into being in the early to mid-1960s. The child is some 40 years old then but its gender is still undecided. Starting out as the masculine technology associated with the military–industrial complex, it has in recent years been reclaimed as a typical expression of femininity, by feminists and market researchers alike (van Zoonen, 2001a). It might even escape these categories and produce completely new transgender or even genderless codes of human identity and communication. In the following sections I discuss these claims in more detail.[1]

Gender codes and the Internet: femininity

Several highly reputed feminist scholars have claimed that the Internet is a woman's medium. This belief has become so widespread and largely undisputed that long-time feminist critic of technology Ellen Balka (1997) recently exclaimed: 'Where have all the feminist technology critics gone?' She argues that earlier critical views on information technologies have given way to an optimism that is seduced by the radical potential of the World Wide Web. Dale Spender (1995), for instance, made an early feminist claim on the Internet as a medium especially relevant for individual and collective networking of women, and also for other subordinated groups, for that matter. Sherry Turkle, professor in the sociology of science at the MIT and author of an influential book on the construction of identities through Internet communication (Turkle, 1995), claims that one needs an ethic of community, consensus and communication on the Internet and this is what she thinks women in particular are good at (quoted in Jenkins, 1999: 332). Similarly, Sadie Plant (1998), acclaimed in the British press as the most radical 'techno theorist' of the day, sees femininity to be the core element of network technology, which she considers to build on women's relation to weaving. Other authors have compared the experience of the Net, the immersion of its user in its textual, visual and virtual realities, to that of the foetus in the womb. Internet experience is considered analogous to the secure and unconstrained experience of the maternal matrix that offers an escape from the constraints of the body (Smelik, 2000).

Side-stepping for a moment the gender essentialism contained in such views and looking at the pragmatic effects of such arguments, we can see how authors like Spender, Turkle and Plant are working towards a redefinition of the Internet from the exclusively masculine domain born out of the American military–industrial–academic complex towards its feminine antithesis of peaceful communication and experimentation. Thinking back on the history of the telephone, for instance, and the way women had to fight their way into its acceptable use (Martin, 1991), thinking of the masculine culture that still encapsulates the computer, thinking more generally of the way technology has been made masculine throughout its history (Oldenziel, 1999), one can recognize the relevance of such a project of redefinition.

Feminist authors who claim the Internet to be a woman's medium find themselves in an unexpected and unsolicited alliance with Internet marketing researchers. They too claim the Internet to be a 'woman's world' (VODW, 1999) and female users of the World Wide Web are thought to be distinct in their goals and online behaviour. Several marketing studies claim to show women are more interested than men in personal interaction and support (e.g. email, chat groups and forums). They seek to build a personal relation with a site and feel strongly connected to online communities. In a trend report conducted for the German women's magazine *Freundin* (translation: *Girl Friend*), it is argued that womanhood offers many opportunities nowadays and very few disadvantages, new technologies like the Internet make life easier, enhance the possibilities for communication and offer new possibilities for consumption: 'The new media enlarge women's horizons and scope of action. Women will shape the nature of the Net economy' (Wipperman, 2000). At present, marketing research constructs women as communicative consumers for whom the Internet provides opportunities never had before. This picture is so convincing that many e-commerce strategies are built on it: the American portal women.com, for instance, offers not only an enormous amount of online content (over 90,000 pages) on traditional women's concerns but also forums and chatline possibilities on a variety of traditionally gendered topics.

Gender codes and the Internet: masculinity

Only 10 years ago, the dominant feminist vision on new information and communication technologies (ICTs) was that they were male dominated. Structural, social-psychological and cultural factors rooted in a patriarchal society were all seen to prevent women from gaining access to ICTs, both as producers and as users (see van Zoonen, 1992). The claims of the Internet being a technology true and close to women and femininity might thus come as a surprise since the structural, social-psychological and cultural factors that explained women's reticence towards ICTs in the early 1990s have not changed dramatically yet. Looking at the actor networks, texts, representations and communicative practices on the Internet there is little reason to think it provides a whole new gender context in comparison with earlier ICTs.

The so-called 'actor network' of human and technical actors involved in the development of the Internet as a technology is almost 100 percent male. In John Naughton's (1999) brief history of the Internet only one woman is found, Nicola Pellow, who was involved in the development of HTML in the 1980s.[2] Male dominance in ICT research and development is not likely to change. On the contrary, the number of women studying and working in the sector in the US has fallen from 30 percent in 1989 to 15 percent in 1999 (Nua, 1998) and similar downward trends have been noted in Europe. The image of the IT sector turns out to be a strong prohibitive factor for women who associate IT work with long working hours, unsociable male colleagues and a male chauvinist culture. Evidence of the latter can be seen, for instance, in a recent discussion in the hacker community about the role of women. In hacker news network, editor Eric Parker describes women in the hacker community as 'scene whores':

> They are a real threat. They waste our time, ruin friendships, cause chaos between hackers, and generally ruin periods of our life. A sure sign after being compromised by a scene whore, after they are done with you, is when you go to talk to friends you have neglected during the period compromise, and they say 'Welcome back, we missed you.' (Parker, 2000)

As this quote shows, in terms of texts, representations and communicative practices the Internet is also not simply a women's haven. Although there are few systematic analyses of the representations and constructions of gender on the Internet, there is enough evidence about (child) pornography, right-wing extremism, sexual harassment, flaming and other unpleasantness to disclaim any utopian vision of the Internet as an unproblematic feminine environment. It is telling that an important women's movement on the net, that of the web-grrls, had to name itself 'grrls', instead of 'girls' because searching on the net for 'girls' mainly produces sex sites and very little relevant material for women (Sherman, 1998). An important source on gender patterns in online communication comes from computer-mediated communication (CMC) studies. Email, chat boxes, news groups, discussion lists are all examples of CMC. Several researchers have analysed the communicative practices in CMC, finding feminine discourse in groups dominated by women: apologetic, consensual and communicative language patterns are typical for them. Masculine discourse occurs in male groups; it is found to be factual, action oriented, impersonal, argumentative, sometimes rude and aggressive. Masculine discourse is seen in most mixed-gender groups as well, making it difficult if not impossible for women to participate fully in such groups (for an overview, see Postmes et al., 2000).

There seems thus as much evidence for the claim that the Internet is masculine and a male world, as there is for the claim that it is feminine and a female world. There is yet another claim to the gender of the Internet, and that is that it has no gender, or better that it is a gender laboratory, a playground for experimenting with gender symbols and identity, a space to escape from the dichotomy of gender and the boundaries produced by physical bodies.

Gender codes and the Internet: cyberfeminism

Cyberfeminism is a term for a variety of academic and artistic practices that centre around and in the Internet, and other new technologies. Some authors even have it that 'after years of post-structuralist theoretical arrogance, philosophy lags behind art and fiction in the difficult struggle to keep up with today's world' (Braidotti, 1996). Whether art or philosophy is the motor, cyberfeminism is the current version of one of the key feminist essentials to connect theory with practice. The year 1997 even witnessed the beginning of Cyberfeminist International during the renowned art fair Documenta in Kassel, Germany. Cyberfeminism is very much in debate but has some defining common features. Transgender politics or gender bending is one of them, referring to the possibilities that the new technologies offer to escape from bodily gender definitions and construct new gender identities, or even genderless identities. Technophilia is another defining factor of cyberfeminism, accepting and celebrating the fact that technology is no longer an external factor to the human body but has become an integral part of it. Donna Haraway's writing on cyborgs offers the almost canonical frame of reference here, the cyborg being 'a cybernetic organism, a fusion of the organic and the technical forged in particular, historical, cultural practices' (Haraway, 1997: 51). Thinking of pacemakers, hearing aids and even glasses, cyborgs are completely ordinary as well as the subject of science fiction such as *Robocop* and *Total Recall*.

Cyberfeminism on the Internet is found among others in the so-called Multi User Dungeons (MUDs). MUDs have attracted the attention of many feminist authors and seem to have become paradigmatic for the Internet as a laboratory for gender. MUDs are text-based, virtual games which may have the different purposes of seeking adventure and killing monsters, of socializing with others and building new communities. They also offer a tool for teaching by constructing virtual classrooms. One usually does not access a MUD through the World Wide Web, but links up through Telnet. When logging on for the first time, one chooses a name for the character one wants to be and keeps that name for the duration of the game, which can – in fact – go on for years. It is precisely this choice of identity at the beginning of the game that the MUD reputation of being a laboratory for gender experiments comes from. Women play as men, men operate as women, others choose multiple identities like Laurel and Hardy, or try what it means to operate as an 'it'. Sherry Turkle's (1995) book *Life on the Screen: Identity in the Age of the Internet* offers the most extensive account of gender experience in the MUDs, concluding that MUDs provide a postmodern utopian space in which existing social boundaries and dichotomies cease to have relevance. In the words of Turkle: 'MUDs are proving grounds for an action based philosophical practice that can serve as a form of consciousness raising about gender issues' (Turkle, 1995: 214).

Whereas life in the MUDs challenges gender identities, other forms of cyberfeminism undermine existing gender symbols and representations in different ways. Parody and irony are the postmodern stylistic devices used to construct typical cyber varieties of gender, that are neither traditional nor feminist. It is expressed in its terminology of geekgrrls, bitches, riotgrrls, guerilla grrls and other cybergrrls, terms which indicate an escape both from traditional gender relations and from common feminist practice. Ladendorf (2000) shows how their sites use images of the female body from the 1950s, the ultimate decade of traditional gender patterns, and other icons and stylistic devices of pop culture to construct a new particular cyberculture of womanhood. Their sites contain a rich variety of gender challenges and contestations popular among young women. As a result of the latter, some of them have been taken over by commercial entrepreneurs, which has modified their vanguard character (van den Boomen, 1997).

Gender and technology: multidimensional concepts

The Internet is thus claimed as feminine, masculine and as beyond gender. The easy solution to these contradictions would be to say that the Internet is so vast and complex that all three positions are true and exist easily alongside each other. And for one part, it is indeed as simple as that. However, we do need to complicate that other part in order to make sense of the varied and contradictory articulations of gender and the Internet. One thing that is striking if we recapitulate the feminine, masculine and transgender features of the Internet, is that in all three claims different dimensions of gender are used as decisive evidence. In gender theory gender is understood as referring to three dimensions: social structures which relegate women and men to different social positions, individual identities and experience of what it means to be a woman or a man, and symbolic organization of society in which several dualities like nature/culture, private/public, leisure/work, coincide with female/male. The claims that the Internet is a masculine domain are strongly supported by the fact that the overwhelming majority of actors in design and production are male – an argument which evokes gender as social dimension – and that texts, representations and communicative practices are masculine – a claim that is built on the symbolic dimensions of gender. Gender as identity does not appear in the picture here, which leads to a well-known dilemma in the research on women working in the communication industries, namely that their participation and positive experience can only be explained by assuming masculine identities in them (van Zoonen, 1988, 1994). Similarly, the claim that the Internet is feminine is built on a limited conceptualization of gender, in particular on gender as identity. The Internet's supposed femininity is said to be located in the communicative, consensual and community-building aspects, features which are thought by feminist and marketing researchers alike to be constitutive parts of feminine identities. Such an understanding, however, ignores the social fact of male-dominated actor networks, and the symbolic reconstructions of traditional gender on the levels of texts and representations. Cyberfeminism, finally, in its aims to undermine the concept of gender in all its dimensions all together, operates particularly at the level of representations, and is much less concerned with social actors or individual identities.

When it comes to understanding technology, masculine, feminine and transgender conceptualizations of the Internet differ in their understanding of where gender is located in the circuit of culture that constitutes the Internet. I borrow the idea of technology as constituted in a circuit of culture from Du Gay et al. (1997), who use the Sony Walkman as a case study of the way meanings of technological artefacts emerge. Five cultural processes are identified – representation, identity, production, consumption and regulation – which when applied to the Internet raise questions as to how the Internet is represented and which representations it carries, what social identities are associated with it, how it is produced and consumed, and what mechanisms regulate its distribution and use. In a study of the mutual shaping of gender and the magnetron, Cynthia Cockburn and Susan Ormrod (1993) have used a similar approach defining mutual shaping as taking place in a sequence of moments in the life trajectory, or the biography of a techno-logical artefact, which runs from design, development, production and marketing, to distribution, sales, use and domestication. Thinking back once again to the claims of the Internet being respectively feminine, masculine and beyond gender, we can see that these claims are in fact all built on a partial understanding of the Internet as a socially constructed technology. The claims for masculinity are located in the moments of design, development and production, and in the moments of representation. The claims for femininity are mainly located in the moments of marketing, distribution and use, whereas cyberfeminism manifests itself foremost in moments of representation.

Mutual shaping

What then would be an alternative approach to the mutual shaping of gender and the Internet which takes into account the different dimensions of gender as well as the circuit of culture that constitutes the Internet? The theoretical issue behind that question concerns how social meanings of technology come into being, and whether there is a decisive moment in the circuit of culture that is particularly rel-evant in relation to the gendering of technology. Histories of technologies all seem to point in the direction of the moments of usage that may be the most important in the development of social meanings. Thinking back on the history of the tele-phone, it was the usage of women that turned the technology into a sociable instrument. Thinking back on the history of the computer, the early and key pres-ence of Ada Lovelace in research and development did not result in the construc-tion of the computer as feminine. The history of the radio suggests that its initial two-way interactive nature, providing communicative possibilities much like today's Internet, disappeared under pressure of usage patterns in the family which turned the radio into a passive receiving practice (Moores, 1988). Television's history shows similarly its adaptation to circumstances of use in the family (van Zoonen and Wieten, 1994). Silverstone and Hirsch (1992), in their studies of domestic technologies, have coined such adaptations as a process of domesti-cation in which technologies are incorporated into the routines of daily life. Domestication is not a smooth linear process, but has – especially at the early stages of the introduction of a technology – the nature of a struggle for meaning, a process of framing which even after meanings have become more solid and consensual, is never finished and always under contestation. Other authors use other concepts for the same process: Ruth Schwartz Cowan (1987), for instance, speaks of the consumption junction in which technologies acquire meanings, and Everett Rogers (1983) has referred to the everyday use of technology in terms of the reinvention of technology.

These studies all suggest that the decisive moment in the circuit of culture is in the moment of consumption, when technologies are domesticated in everyday lives. In these everyday lives gender appears in its three dimensions simultaneously; whereas social structures, individual identities and symbolic representations of gender may be analytically distinguished, in the concrete social practices of the everyday they work inextricably together in their interpellation and positioning of women and men. How these three dimensions come into play in concrete everyday situations was the object of an exploratory qualitative study we conducted among 24 young Dutch couples, between 20 and 30 years old, living together without children. In-depth interviews were held and transcribed about the uses and interpretations of various ICTs in their households, with particular attention to their uses of the Internet. The analysis followed an accumulation of analytic procedures, analogous to techniques proposed by Strauss and Corbin (1990) to develop 'grounded' theory. Each conversation fragment in the interview was first represented as a unique proposition. As a second step in the analysis, these propositions were then clustered according to similarities in content. Finally the interviews were considered in terms of discursive styles characterizing the specific interactions between the couples.[3] The outcomes show how specific family relations result in different articulations of gender and the Internet, which – in their turn – inspire new rituals and relations within the household. The dimensions of gender that come to the fore in this process appear to vary across households, resulting in the reconstruction of four kinds of articulations which we labelled as traditional, deliberative, individualized and reversed IT cultures in the household.

Articulating gender and the Internet in everyday life

The various ways in which gender and the Internet appeared to be articulated in the 24 households we studied, could be summarized as four 'media cultures': First, there is a fairly straightforward *traditional* culture in which computer and the Internet are considered to be the domain of the male partner in the household. He uses them most often, knows most about it and is highly interested in these new technologies. In the most extreme cases, he monopolizes the computer and the Internet:

> *Man:* Actually I work alone on it. Occasionally Ingrid would like to send a mail or so, but we do that together. She will tell me what has to be in it, and then I will do the actual sending. She has become more interested in the Internet. Before she didn't pay any attention to the computer, but now once in a while she likes to send a mail, or look up some information, for the holidays or so.

Woman: Well, as he says, I don't use it very often. I don't understand much of it yet. I think if I knew more about it, I would use it more as well. Now I always need Norman's help, to mail and stuff. That is because my work does not involve computers, his does.

In this interview fragment we see how the social position of one of the partners (he works with computers, she doesn't) translates into a traditional culture at home around the computer and the Internet. Thus the social dimension of gender comes into play here, normalizing and legitimizing the specific media culture of these two partners and coding the Internet and PC at a symbolic level as male territory in the household. Most couples whose computer and Internet use could be typified in these traditional terms, recognized the traditional nature of their use, but did not consider it very problematic. That might testify to a relatively neat fit between the social, symbolic and individual (identity) dimension of gender, although the acknowledgement of the traditional nature of these arrangements also shows that this arrangement is no longer self-evident. What is further striking in this fragment is that the Internet has drawn the woman to the computer, negotiating the former exclusively male codes of the PC.

In other cases, the media culture could be typified as *deliberative*: the partners negotiate about the use of the PC and the Internet, and also consider them to be a subject of common concern:

Woman: I like the PC best for the Internet applications. You do too, don't you Marc?
Man: Yes, some e-mail as well.
Woman: And to look up things for the holidays, or about living or gardening and stuff.
Man: It is about the same for me, sometimes some random clicking and surfing, but the novelty has worn off a bit and now we don't use it that frequently anymore.

This interview fragment shows clearly how PC and Internet use are instrumental in constructing a sense of togetherness among the partners ('*we* don't use it that frequently anymore'), instead of them being the domain of the male partner as in more traditional use cultures. The collective identity as a couple overwrites in this case the individual (gender) identities of the partners. A deliberative use culture is simplified because most couples in this study identified the PC and the Internet with work or school-related tasks. That makes their use relatively easy to prioritize: work or studies take precedence over surfing or gaming. Notwithstanding the gender neutrality of such a priority, it turns out to be male biased in the context of Dutch households where – even among young couples – men are the main or primary providers:

Woman: He usually has more important things to do on it than I have, I only want to [go on the] Internet a bit. So he goes first and I will do something else.

When the partners have equal careers, there is greater potential conflict about PC and Internet use. However, most couples then look for practical solutions. An extra PC or laptop is bought or brought in from work. The media culture than changes from a deliberative into an *individualized* culture:

> Man: She is writing her thesis at the moment and if she is really busy with it, I'll take a laptop home from work.

In such individualized cultures gender as a factor that regulates the access to and use of the PC and Internet at home disappears into the background. Gender as a factor in the individual use and interpretations of the PC and Internet, as a dimension of the user's gender identity does remain relevant, but is no longer constructed in interaction with the partner.

In two extraordinary cases, women took the lead in PC and Internet use: they were the most important users and also the ones to make the decisions. In both cases, however, the male partners appeared to have jobs in which they worked with computers all day. Not wanting to spend their leisure time in such a way, the home PC and the Internet became available to the female partners, both at the time of the interview immersed in writing their final theses:

> Man: I work with computers all day and really don't want to go home to stare at that screen once again.
> Woman: And I am writing my thesis at present, so really need to be able to work on it full time.

In these two cases, we see how the social position of the partners can also result in a reversal of the traditional use culture around the PC and the Internet, which indicates that even one, single dimension of gender, i.e. the social one, does not result in a univocal articulation of the technology.

The four use cultures vary as to how gender and the Internet are mutually shaped. It is tempting to conclude that in three out of the four cultures, male usage offers the main explanation for the specific articulations we found: in a traditional culture the male partner claims the PC and the Internet as his domain, while in the reversed culture it is the lack of a claim by the male partner which enables women to dominate the PC and Internet. In addition, in the deliberative culture negotiation disappears as soon as one of the partners can occupy the PC and the Internet because of work or school requirements. This systematically favours the partner with the highest income, most of the time – especially in Dutch gender relations – the man. Only in the individualized use culture, in which both partners use their own appliances, does the male grip on the PC and the Internet use seem to dissolve. Although such a conclusion is partly warranted, it is insufficient in its denial of the active role that women play in the construction of the PC and the Internet as male. Women's distance from the computer is not only the result of processes of exclusion, but can also be interpreted as part of a conscious gender strategy. Turkle (1988) has shown how women use their reticence towards computers as evidence of their true identity as a woman. After all, an interest or even a passion for computers does not align well with traditional understandings of femininity. Gray (1992) has concluded similarly that women sometimes use their technical inabilities to make their husbands take up their share of domestic duties. If they showed technical capacities themselves, they feared they would be confronted with even more work, now related to the domestic technologies. Turkle's and Gray's observations are further indicators of the complex, situational and relational character of the articulations of gender and the Internet.

Conclusion

The interviews have shown the complexity of articulations of gender and the Internet at the micro-level of everyday lives. Nevertheless, at the macro-level of social discourse there are rather univocal claims about the Internet being masculine, feminine or transgender. These claims do have their value as part of the social struggle about the meaning of the Internet: the claim of it being feminine redefines technology as a domain appropriate for women; the observations of it being masculine puts oppressive and sexist practices on and behind the Net on political and social agendas; and cyberfeminism challenges us to move beyond the dual categories of gender. In analytical terms, however, these three claims fall short because of their limited conceptualization of gender and their insufficient approach of technology. Instead, we proposed a multidimensional understanding of the mutual shaping of gender and technology, in which it is claimed that in the end the social meanings of the Internet will emerge from particular contexts and practices of usage. We have seen from the brief discussion of the interviews that the mutual shaping that takes place in the domestication of the Internet in households of young heterosexual couples tends to frame it in traditional gender terms. Especially in its connection to the PC, our results show the Internet being taken up as an extension of male territory in the household. This does not necessarily lead to the exclusion of women since men are also seen to consciously leave the PC to their partners. Neither are women passive partners in this process. They actively take part in interactions which constitute their respective gender identities with regard to use of the PC and Internet.

Like every academic study, this one has its particular location in time but for two reasons the longevity of the analysis presented here may be briefer than usual with academic work. The use of the Internet at present takes place mainly through the PC and it is particularly the masculine codes of the PC that resound in the everyday use cultures we found around Internet use. In the future, however, the Internet is expected to be an ordinary extension of each and every communication technology – television, (mobile) telephone, radio, etc. – and even of most other domestic technologies from refrigerator to microwave and washing machine. Each of these appliances have their own gendered uses and gender codes which will result in new and different articulations of gender with the Internet. Second, the individualization of media use in the household can be expected to increase. Many households at present have two television sets and a mobile phone for each family member. It is only a matter of time before this trend extends to a multiple presence of PCs and Internet access, making Internet use in everyday life much more individual than we found in the current interviews. Such individualization may yet again change the articulations of gender and Internet and disconnect them from the interaction between partners.

Notes

1. I have also discussed these claims in van Zoonen (2001a).
2. The author himself went to some trouble to find more women in Internet history but could not find them. Email exchange, 1999; and see www.briefhistory.com
3. This procedure has been applied successfully in other work on the use of ICTs, e.g. van Zoonen (2001b), van Zoonen and Aalberts (forthcoming).

References

Balka, E. (1997) *Computer Networking: Spinsters on the Web. Resources for Research and Action.* Ottawa: CRIAW/ICREF.

Braidotti, R. (1996) 'Cyberfeminism with a Difference'; available at: www.let.uu.nl/women's_studies/rosi/cyberfem.htm (consulted 23 May 2001).

Cockburn, C. and S. Ormrod (1993) *Gender and Technology in the Making.* London: Sage.

Du Gay, P., S. Hall, L. Janes, H. Mackay and K. Negus (1997) *Doing Cultural Studies: The Story of the Sony Walkman.* London: Sage.

Fischer, C. (1992) *America Calling: A Social History of the Telephone to 1940.* Berkeley: University of California Press.

Freeman, E. (1996) 'Ada and the Analytical Engine', *Educom Review.* March/April.

Gray, A. (1992) *Video Playtime. The Gendering of a Leisure Technology.* London: Routledge.

Haraway, D. (1997) *Modest_Witness@Second_Millennium. Female Man Meets Onco Mouse.* London: Routledge.

Jenkins, H. (1999) 'Voices From the Combat Zone: Game Grrlz Talk Back', pp. 328–41 in J. Cassels and H. Jenkins (eds), *From Barbie to Mortal Kombat: Gender and Computer Games.* Cambridge, MA: MIT Press.

Ladendorf, M. (2000) 'Pin-Ups and Grrls. The Pictures of Grrlzines', paper presented at the Crossroads in Cultural Studies Conference, Birmingham.

Martin, M. (1988) ' "Rulers of the Wires"? Women's Contribution to the Structure of Communication', *Journal of Communication Inquiry* 12(2): 89–103.

Martin, M. (1991) *Hello Central: Gender, Technology and Culture in the Formation of the Telephone System.* Montreal: McGill/Queen's University Press.

Marvin, C. (1988) *When Old Technologies Were New.* New York: Oxford University Press.

Moores, S. (1988) 'The Box on the Dresser: Memoirs of Early Radio and Everyday Life', *Media, Culture & Society* 10(1): 23–40.

Naughton, J. (1999) *A Brief History of the Future: The Origins of the Internet.* London: Weidenfeld and Nicolson.

Nua (1998) 'It's an Image Thing', Nua Internet Surveys; available at: www.nua.ie/surveys/?f=VS&art_id=886595295&rel=true (consulted 28 April 2000).

Oldenziel, R. (1999) *Making Technology Masculine.* Amsterdam: Amsterdam University Press.

Parker, E. (2000) http://www.projectgamma.com/news/archive/2000/january/0110100-1539.shtml

Plant, S. (1998) *Zeros and Ones: Digital Women and the New Technoculture.* London: Fourth Estate.

Postmes, T. (2000) 'Social Psychological Approaches to ICT'; available at: www.infodrome.nl

Rakow, L. (1988) 'Women and the Telephone: The Gendering of a Communications Technology', pp. 207–29 in C. Kramarae (ed.), *Technology and Women's Voices: Keeping in Touch*. New York: Routledge and Kegan Paul.

Rogers, E. (1983) *The Diffusion of Innovations*. New York: Free Press.

Schwartz Cowan, R. (1987) 'The Consumption Junction: A Proposal for Research Strategies in the Sociology of Technology', in W. Bijker, T. Hughes and T. Pinch (eds), *The Social Construction of Technological Systems*. Cambridge, MA: MIT Press.

Sherman, A. (1998) *Cybergrrl: A Woman's Guide to the World Wide Web*. New York: Ballantine Books.

Silverstone, R. and E. Hirsch (eds) (1992) *Consuming Technologies: Media and Information in Domestic Spaces*. London: Routledge.

Smelik, A. (2000) 'Die virtuele matrix. Het lichaam in cyberpunkfilms', *Tijdschrift voor Genderstudies* 3(4): 4–13.

Spender, D. (1995) *Nattering on the Net: Women, Power and Cyberspace*. North Melbourne: Spinifex Press.

Strauss, A. and J. Corbin (1990) *Qualitative Data Analysis*. Beverly Hills, CA: Sage.

Turkle, S. (1988) 'Computational Reticence: Why Women Fear the Intimate Machine', pp. 41–61 in C. Kramarae (ed.), *Technology and Women's Voices*. London: Routledge.

Turkle, S. (1995) *Life on the Screen: Identity in the Age of the Internet*. New York: Simon and Schuster.

Van den Boomen, M. (1997) 'Grrls en bitches: postfeministische e-zines', *Lover* 24(3): 8–10.

Van Oost, E. (1995) 'Over vrouwelijke en mannelijke dingen', in M. Brouns, M. Verloo and M. Grunell (eds), *Vrouwenstudies in de jaren negentig. Een kennismaking vanuit verschillende disciplines*. Bussum: Coutinho.

Van Zoonen, L. (1988) 'Rethinking Women and the News', *European Journal of Communication* 3(1): 35–53.

Van Zoonen, L. (1992) 'Feminist Theory and Information Technology', *Media, Culture & Society* 14(1): 9–31.

Van Zoonen, L. (1994) *Feminist Media Studies*. London: Sage.

Van Zoonen, L. (2001a) 'Feminist Internet Studies', *Feminist Media Studies* 1(1): 67–72.

Van Zoonen, L. (2001b) 'Een computer kan niet knuffelen. De betekenis van internet voor communicatie en identiteit' [A Computer Cannot Give You a Hug: Rethinking Communication and Identity Through the Internet], pp. 71–90 in H. Bouwman (ed.), *Communicatie in de informatiesamenleving* [Communication in the Information Society]. Utrecht: Lemma.

Van Zoonen, L. and C. Aalberts (forthcoming) 'The Uses of Interactive Television in the Everyday Lives of Young Couples', in M. Consalvo (ed.), *Women and Everyday Uses of the Internet: Agency and Identity*. New York: Peter Lang.

Van Zoonen, L. and J. Wieten (1994) 'It Wasn't Exactly a Miracle: The Introduction of Television in the Netherlands', *Media, Culture & Society* 17(3): 641–60.

VODW (1999) 'Internet: It's a Woman's World', VODW Making Waves New York; available at: www.vodw.com/makingwaves/ (consulted 28 April 2000).

Wipperman, P. (2000) *Millenium Frauen.com. Weibliche Strategien für das digitale Zeitalter*. Trendbüro Hamburg/freundin Verlag Gmbh.

Lifestyle Segmentation: From Attitudes, Interests and Opinions, to Values, Aesthetic Styles, Life Visions and Media Preferences

Patrick Vyncke

Introduction

An organization that decides to operate in some market – whether consumer, industrial, re-seller or government – must recognize that it normally cannot equally serve all the customers in that market. These customers may be too numerous, too widely scattered and especially too heterogeneous in their needs and wants. Recognizing that those heterogeneous markets are actually made up of a number of smaller homogeneous submarkets, Smith (1956) introduced the concept of market segmentation – the process of dividing the total market into several relatively homogeneous groups with similar product or service interests, with similar needs and desires. From then on, market segmentation became the core concept of fine-tuned target marketing and communication campaigns.

Of course, many criteria can be used to assign potential customers to homogeneous groups. Commonly, these variables are grouped into three general categories (e.g. Gunter and Furnham, 1992: 4):

- *Product-specific, behavioural attribute segmentations* classify consumers focusing upon their purchase behaviour within the relevant product category or the benefits the consumer expects to derive from a product category.
- *General, physical attribute segmentations* of consumers, which use such easily observable criteria as geographic, demographic or socioeconomic variables to create homogeneous target markets.
- *General, psychological attribute segmentations,* which utilize profiles of consumers developed either from standardized personality inventories or, more recently, from lifestyle analyses. This kind of segmentation is often called 'psychographics'.

Source: *EJC* (2002), vol. 17, no. 4: 445–463.

Of course, in the end, the target group needs to be profiled on all three descriptive levels. However, in this article we focus on psychographics, and especially on lifestyles as a targeting criterion, because these data are of most value for communication managers. Indeed, since different brands within a product category are often hard to distinguish in terms of physical product attributes, many advertisers now profile their brand on rather psychological dimensions (Biel, 1992). Or, as Hornik (1989) points out, the basic premise of psychographics is that the more we know about people's lifestyle, the more effectively we can communicate with them. Correspondingly, research by Chiagouris (1991) has shown that marketing communication is more effective when end-user lifestyle profiles are understood and reflected in the content of the message. This means that lifestyle research is of capital interest for communication managers to 'visualize' their audiences more effectively.

Psychographics

Psychographics was a term first introduced by Demby (1974), putting together 'psychology', and 'demographics'. He felt the need to put more psychological flesh on the purely geodemographic bones, to add the richness of the social and behavioural sciences to demographics, in order to enhance understanding of consumer behaviour, and to develop more adequate advertising strategies. Indeed, demographic segmentations provide relatively hollow classifications of consumers, which reveal nothing about the motives underlying their consumption decisions.

Now, the first wave of psychographic research was mainly rooted in personality profiles. The most frequently used scale for measuring general aspects of personality as a way to define homogeneous submarkets is Edward's Personal Preference Schedule. Many other personality traits have been used to try to segment markets, and even today some scholars keep this line of research alive (see, for example, Wolburg and Pokrywczynski, 2001).

In general, however, these studies, being plagued with consistently low and even inconsistent correlations with consumer behaviour, have been disappointing and failed to satisfy marketers' needs. One of the main reasons probably was due to the fact that this research used standardized personality tests originally developed in clinical (read: for purposes of medical diagnostics) or academic (read: based on populations of students) contexts (Gunter and Furnham, 1992: 27, 33, 40).

In a second wave of psychographic research, the personality concept was replaced with the concept of 'lifestyle' (introduced by Lazer, 1963). Today, lifestyle is usually defined as the patterns in which people live and spend their time and money (Kaynak and Kara, 2001: 458). Chaney (1996: 4) defines lifestyles as 'patterns of action that differentiate people. ... Lifestyles therefore help to make sense of what people do, and why they do it, and what doing it means to them and others.' Today, the lifestyle concept has become so central, and the personality concept so marginal to psychographic research, that the latter is currently equated with lifestyle research (see, for example, Hawkins et al., 1995: 328; Kahle and Chiagouris, 1997: x).

In general, lifestyle research is based on extensive surveys using appropriate quantitative methods. Again, we can distinguish different waves of research.

The AIO approach

At first, lifestyles were researched using large sets of AIO items. AIO refers to measures of activities, interests and opinions. Thus, authors such as Peter and Olson (1994: 463) define 'lifestyle' as 'the manner in which people conduct their lives, including activities, interests, and opinions'. Activities are manifest actions (work, hobbies, social events, vacation, entertainment, clubs, community, shopping, sports, etc.). Interest in some objects, events or topics (family, home, job, community, recreation, fashion, food, media, achievements, etc.) is the degree of excitement that accompanies both special and continuing attention to it. Finally, opinions are descriptive beliefs (of oneself, social issues, politics, business, economics, education, products, future, culture, etc.) (Plummer, 1974). For some examples of typical AIO statements, see, for example, Ewing et al. (2001) and Kaynak and Kara (2001). Three typical statements could be:

- I often listen to popular music (activity);
- I am very interested in the latest fashion trends (interest);
- A woman's place is in the home (opinion).

Often very large batteries of AIO items were used. For example, Wells and Tigert (1971) formulated 300 AIO items, while Cosmas (1982) used a questionnaire containing 250 AIO items.

The value systems approach

In a second wave of research, the value concept came to replace this very extensive and burdensome AIO approach. Values are commonly defined as desirable, trans-situational goals, varying in importance, that serve as guiding principles in people's lives.

The most important instrument for measuring values is the Rokeach Value Survey (Rokeach, 1973). His inventory comprises 18 values:

- A comfortable life;
- An exciting life;
- A sense of accomplishment;
- A world at peace;
- A world of beauty;
- Equality;

- Family security;
- Freedom;
- Happiness;
- Inner harmony;
- Mature love;
- National security;
- Pleasure;
- Salvation;
- Self-respect;
- Social recognition;
- True friendship;
- Wisdom.

A shorter and more easily implemented instrument is the List of Values (LOV), suggested by Kahle (1983), including only nine values. Another important scale for assessing value systems was developed by Schwartz and Bilsky (1990) and later modified by Schwartz (1992) (see Struch et al. [2002: 27] for the complete inventory developed by Schwartz, comprising 56 values).

Now, values are of particular interest because values may affect a wide spectrum of behaviour across many situations (Seligman et al., 1996). Indeed, individuals' value priorities are part of their basic worldviews (Struch et al., 2002: 16). Therefore, values are also important lifestyle determinants. As Gunter and Furnham (1992: 70) point out: 'Lifestyles are defined as patterns in which people live and spend their time and money. They are primarily functions of consumers' values.' Solomon (1994: 621) even defines lifestyle as an exhibited 'set of shared values'. Moreover, values are broader in scope than attitudes or the types of variables contained in AIO measures. They transcend specific situations (Grunert-Beckmann and Askegaard, 1997: 164). Finally, value inventories in general often only contain a handful of values, instead of 200 or 300 AIO items.

This led researchers of the second wave of lifestyle research to use value batteries as input for their questionnaires, which proved to be much more elegant and fundamental than the AIO approach.

Now, looking at the most often used inventory, the one developed by Rokeach, one must say that this inventory cannot go without considerable criticism (although one cannot doubt the importance of Rokeach as a scientist of values). First, there is the supposed universality of these values. As Ness and Stith (1984: 235) point out: 'It can be concluded that the Rokeach values are basically American middle-class values.' Second, and more importantly, there is a lack of a strong theoretical and/or empirical base underpinning his inventories. Rokeach combined a literature study, the ideas of some 30 psychology students and the values as reported by some 100 adult respondents living in Lansing (Michigan) and to whom was explained what values are. This suggests that intuition played a far more important role than theory or empirical research in constructing the value inventory. The random character of his inventory was clearly illustrated by Jones et al. (1978), who found that the Rokeach values hardly represent one-third of the values people spontaneously put forward in empirical research.

Anyway, these criticisms made us engage in a rather compelling project: developing a value inventory ourselves, in order to use this for studying lifestyles.

Developing the value questionnaire

To develop a new value inventory, we followed two different approaches, complementing one another.

First, we took a quota sample of the Flemish population between 18 and 65 years old ($N = 236$). Each was asked to formulate some 20 desires. This provided us with a set of 4312 desires. Now, these desires can be regarded as expressions of underlying personal values. Values being very abstract, desires being very concrete, people find it easier to formulate desires than to express their values. Analysing these desires could thus lead us to a new value inventory. Using qualitative content analysis, we arrived at an inventory of 27 values.

A second approach started with 80 students formulating all kinds of possible values. This yielded a list of 981 values. Again, using qualitative content analysis, this list was reduced to a set of 124 values. These were then administered to a quota sample of the Flemish population between 18 and 65 years old ($N = 672$). Factor analysis (alpha factoring and oblimin rotation) yielded 26 factors (global values) explaining 66 percent of variance.

The results of both research projects were then merged, which led us to a value inventory of 35 values, including such things as:

- Being respected and appreciated by others;
- Wisdom;
- Joy and pleasure, having fun in life;
- Leading a simple and modest life;
- Good health, being healthy;
- Safety, living in a safe world;

and so on. The complete questionnaire is available upon request from the author. In the final questionnaire, respondents were asked to indicate on a seven-point scale how important each value was in their lives.

However, we did not take the value concept as our sole way of constructing a lifestyle typology. We added two different approaches, without, however, returning to the burdensome, extremely ad hoc and very intuitive AIO approach.

Adding the concept of life visions

The value concept being very broad and general, we wanted to add a second section that was more concrete and specific, something which had to do with societal trends, the general issues that underlie AIO constructs, the way people 'look at life'. We call this 'life visions'. Life visions then can be defined as the perspective people take on some major issues in life. We drew up a list of 20 items that could be understood as major points of attention in contemporary western culture, including such things as health, beauty, male/female identities, work/money/time considerations, the use of leisure, partner relations, family relations, friends, culture, politics, economics and science.

Then, for each item, we formulated two polarized visions. For instance, for 'male/female identities', the corresponding statements were:

- Men and women are fundamentally equal. The roles society prescribes for them should be abandoned.
- Men and women are fundamentally different. Therefore, society must permit men to act as a true male and women to act as a true female.

Again, the complete questionnaire is available upon request. Respondents were then asked to indicate on a seven-point scale how strongly they agreed either with the vision on the left or with the vision on the right of the seven-point scale (cf. a semantic differential).

Contrary to this 'content-oriented' part of the questionnaire, we added a third section which has more to do with 'form-oriented' things.

Adding the concept of aesthetic styles

Many authors have argued that we live in a postmodern society. Although postmodernism is a vague enough concept, some definitions of postmodernism stress the aestheticization of everyday life (e.g. Featherstone, 1991: 65–82). Of course, this aestheticization has profound implications for consumer culture.

Therefore, we wanted to add a section on aesthetic styles to our questionnaire. The point of departure was that style preferences are perhaps most visible in four 'product' categories: clothing, cars, houses and house interiors. For each of those categories, we assembled 30 different and diverse pictures. Then 25 respondents – 11 males and 14 females, twelve aged between 18 and 30, six between 31 and 45, and seven between 46 and 60 – were asked to perform a natural grouping task. Natural grouping is a research technique where respondents are asked to form 'natural' groups of stimuli, that is to group stimuli (here pictures of clothing, cars, houses and house interiors) that have something in common according to the feelings of the respondents. The results are then coded in (4 × 25) similarity matrices. Through multidimensional scaling, one can then produce two-dimensional scatterplots, showing which pictures 'naturally' group together. We then asked the respondents to provide proper style labels for each group of stimuli. For clothing, cars, houses and house interiors, this procedure resulted each time in seven different aesthetic styles.

In the final questionnaire, each of these 28 styles were visualized by two photographs and then presented to the respondents. They were asked to rate each style on a seven-point scale according to how appealing they found each of these styles, i.e. according to their personal taste. Again, the complete pictorial questionnaire is available upon request from the author.

Adding media preferences, product categories and demographics

Now, since our aim is a lifestyle typology relevant for predicting individual differences across a wide variety of behaviour, we included four product categories in our questionnaire: cars (a classic product), tourism (a service), political parties (a non-commercial product) and media. For both cars, tourism and political parties, a set of potential attributes or benefits was developed:

- *Cars*: 14 attributes, including safety, design, powerful engine, reliability, etc.;
- *Tourism*: 14 attributes of the ideal holiday, including warm and sunny climate, cultural infrastructure, luxurious, romantic, etc.;
- *Political parties*: 15 potential elements of party programmes, including: job opportunities for everyone, lowering taxes on labour, raising pensions, fighting unemployment, aiding the Third World, etc.

The media section focused on television, films and magazines:

- *Television*: 16 programme categories;
- *Films*: 12 'movie ingredients', including romance, adventure, hard action, humour, etc.;
- *Magazines*: 14 categories of magazines, including male, female, television, general information, fashion, sports, cars, etc.

The appealing power of each of these product attributes or benefits and each of these media categories was scored on a seven-point scale.

Finally, we added a section on demographics, asking the respondents for their sex, age, social class and stage of life.

Segmenting the market

The questionnaire was administered to a quota sample of the Flemish population ($N = 995$). In order to group these 995 respondents into more or less homogeneous lifestyle segments, we conducted a cluster analysis (which is, in marketing research, the dominant method for market segmentation). We selected a two-stage approach combining both hierarchical and non-hierarchical clustering methods (Punj and Stewart, 1983; Fournier et al., 1992: 331). Initial solutions, using Ward's hierarchical method, provided a preliminary indication of the total number of clusters. The final cluster solution was then identified using the Quick Cluster K-Means procedure. Here we identified a range of solutions (from five to ten clusters) and chose the solution where (1) there were as many segments as possible, but no small segments of less than 5 percent, and (2) the number of clusters was justified by the results obtained through Ward's method.

Remarkably, for values (V), life visions (L), aesthetic styles (A) and a combination of those three categories of variables (V-L-A), this yielded a seven-cluster

TABLE 20.1 SIZE (PERCENTAGES) OF THE DIFFERENT TYPES/MARKET SEGMENTS IN EACH OF THE DIFFERENT LIFESTYLE TYPOLOGIES

Type	Values	Life visions	Aesthetic styles	Overall V–L–A
Type 1	10.3	8.9	14.7	17.8
Type 2	8.8	14.8	17.6	20.5
Type 3	19.2	18.7	16.9	10.9
Type 4	24.2	14.2	9.5	16.1
Type 5	13.2	16.3	10.3	12.6
Type 6	14.5	11.6	15.6	13.4
Type 7	9.8	15.5	15.2	8.8
Total N = 995	100.0	100.0	100.0	100.0

TABLE 20.2 THE GLOBAL LIFESTYLE TYPOLOGY, INCLUDING VALUES (V), LIFE VISIONS (L), AESTHETIC STYLES (A) AND MEDIA PREFERENCES (M)

Type	Global V–L–A–M
Type 1	12.7
Type 2	13.2
Type 3	12.2
Type 4	12.1
Type 5	8.8
Type 6	17.6
Type 7	9.4
Type 8	14.1
Total N = 995	100.0

solution. Table 20.1 shows the size of the different segments in each lifestyle typology.

Next, we set out to analyse the performance of the different lifestyle typologies in four different markets (cars, tourism, political parties and media), and compare their discriminative power to that of classic demographic variables. However – before we turn to the research results in the next paragraph – we developed one more typology, using the same clustering procedure but including not only values, life visions and aesthetic style preferences, but also media variables (preferences for the 16 television programme categories, the 12 film ingredients and the 14 magazine categories, mentioned earlier). This resulted in again a very balanced typology of eight different lifestyles (see Table 20.2).

A comparison in different markets

Frank et al. (1972) and Wells (1975) concluded that the predictive validity of lifestyle with respect to purchase behaviour can be substantially better than that of general observable segmentation bases, such as geographic, demographic or socioeconomic variables. How do our typologies perform? To test the significant differences among the clusters on product attribute importance, a one-way ANOVA was performed (Kaynak and Kara, 2001: 468, Kahle et al., 1992: 347).

The next table summarizes our findings, by indicating how many product attributes (total = 85) proved to be significant (respectively at the .05 and the .01 level) or not, within the different product categories and in total. The overall lifestyle typology (V-L-A) combines values, life visions and aesthetic style preferences. The global lifestyle typology (V-L-A-M) combines values, life visions, aesthetic style preferences and media preferences. The demographic variables are sex, age (three segments: 18–30 years old, 31–45 years old and 46–65 years old), social groups (highest, high, low, lowest) and (nine) stages of life (from 'young – living with their parents' to 'elderly parents – most children have left home').

Table 20.3 reads as follows: if we look at the product category 'cars', we find, for example, that the consumer typology based on the values dimension results on all 14 car benefits in significant differences below the .01 level, while a segmentation based on the sex of the consumer only results in such significant differences on seven attributes, besides three attributes that score at the .05 level of significance and four attributes yielding no significant differences.

Notice that all psychographic segmentations perform extremely well compared to the much weaker performance of demographic and socioeconomic segmentations (which yield much larger numbers of nonsignificance), and this in all markets analysed here. The lowest number of significant differences is provided by the social class concept. One can refer here to the debates over 'the death of class' and so on, but this would take us too far from our subject.

To further distinguish the discriminative power of the different psychographic lifestyle typologies developed here, we also computed measures of association between the different typologies and the respective product attributes or benefits. Since we are combining nominal and interval data here, we chose to calculate eta (with the cluster variable as independent and the benefit measure as dependent variable). To summarize our findings, we calculated an averaged eta (over all benefits or attributes) for all markets under scrutiny, and compared the different cluster typologies on how they perform (see Table 20.4). One demographic variable – sex (which was one of the relatively better performing demographic variables in Table 20.3) – was included for reasons of comparison.

First, notice that of the three single-dimension typologies, the value typology performs better than the typologies based on either life visions or aesthetic style preferences (which both yield similar results). Moreover, adding life visions and aesthetic style preferences to the value-based research instrument, in order to create the overall V-L-A typology, hardly raises the average eta-value of the typology based on values alone. In 1978, Clawson and Vinson suggested that values perhaps equal or surpass the contribution of other major psychographic constructs in understanding consumer behaviour. Nevertheless, for communication strategists, adding life visions and aesthetic styles to the value dimension of course increases the richness of the lifestyle profiles obtained.

Second, notice that adding a section on media preferences to develop the global V-L-A-M typology *does* improve the average eta-value of the overall V-L-A typology

TABLE 20.3 OVERVIEW OF THE PERFORMANCE OF DIFFERENT LIFESTYLE AND DEMOGRAPHIC SEGMENTATION SYSTEMS IN DIFFERENT MARKETS

Product category	Values	Life visions	Aesthetic styles	Overall V–L–A	Global (V–L–A–M)	Sex	Age	Social group	Stage of life
Television									
NS	–	5	3	–	I	5	2	8	4
< .05	–	–	I	2	–	2	4	5	3
< .01	16	II	12	14	15	9	10	3	9
N = 16	16	16	16	16	16	16	16	16	16
Films									
NS	I	2	I	–	–	2	5	II	4
< .05	–	I	I	I	I	–	–	I	3
< .01	II	9	10	II	II	10	7	–	5
N = 12	12	12	12	12	12	12	12	12	12
Magazines									
NS	–	I	I	I	–	I	6	9	6
< .05	2	–	I	–	I	I	3	3	3
< .01	12	13	12	13	13	12	5	2	5
N = 14	14	14	14	14	14	14	14	14	14
Cars									
NS	–	–	–	–	–	4	I	13	2
< .05	–	I	–	–	–	3	3	I	I
< .01	14	13	14	14	14	7	10	–	II
N = 14	14	14	14	14	14	14	14	14	14
Tourism									
NS	–	I	I	–	–	4	2	II	3
< .05	I	2	–	–	–	4	2	2	–
< .01	13	II	13	14	14	6	10	I	II
N = 14	14	14	14	14	14	14	14	14	14
Political parties									
NS	–	–	I	–	–	5	3	12	6
< .05	I	–	–	–	–	–	–	–	–
< .01	14	15	14	15	15	10	12	3	9
N = 15	15	15	15	15	15	15	15	15	15
Total									
NS	I	9	7	I	I	21	19	64	25
< .05	4	4	3	3	2	10	12	12	10
< .01	80	72	75	81	82	54	54	9	50
N = 85	85	85	85	85	85	85	85	85	85

NS: not significant.

substantially. This suggests the fruitfulness and even necessity of including a section on media preferences in developing a lifestyle questionnaire. Moreover, this section can yield very useful data for the media planning decisions the communication manager has to make.

Third, notice the difference between the selected media markets and non-media markets. In the three non-media markets, the five different lifestyle typologies all clearly outperform the classic demographic segmentation based

TABLE 20.4 COMPARISON OF ETA-VALUES OF THE DIFFERENT LIFESTYLE TYPOLOGIES IN DIFFERENT MARKETS

Product category	Values	Life visions	Aesthetic styles	Overall V–L–A	Global V–L–A–M	Sex
Television Average Eta	.204	.176	.166	.207	.355	.146
Films Average Eta	.208	.185	.179	.221	.353	.182
Magazines Average Eta	.219	.200	.180	.222	.492	.350
Subtotal media Average Eta	.210	.186	.174	.216	.400	.224
Cars Average Eta	.319	.251	.273	.318	.348	.113
Tourism Average Eta	.292	.245	.234	.289	.333	.098
Political parties Average Eta	.317	.282	.235	.320	.349	.109
Subtotal cars, tourism, political parties Average Eta	.309	.260	.247	.309	.343	.106
Total all product categories Average Eta	.260	.224	.211	.263	.371	.165

on sex (which results in only very low eta-values). In the media markets, this is clearly much less the case, with sex even outperforming the lifestyle segmentations in the submarket of magazines. That only the global V-L-A-M typology performs extremely well in media markets needs not surprise us, since the corresponding media variables are included in the set of variables used to develop the typology itself. Research results may be somewhat misleading here.

Summary

Lifestyle research emerged from the recognition that important demographic distinctions simply do not exist in many product categories and even where they do, one cannot intelligently decide how to attract any particular market segment unless one knows why the distinctions exist. In order to attract and motivate a particular group of consumers through communication campaigns, one must gain insight into their psychological profile, i.e. their lifestyle.

Our research results suggest that it is possible to develop robust and balanced general lifestyle typologies (using either values, life visions or aesthetic style preferences alone, or in combination) that can be used by communication and marketing managers for strategic segmentation decisions across very different markets. These lifestyle typologies often outperform classic demographic and socioeconomic segmentation variables in terms of product benefit or attribute evaluation. A global typology, combining sections on values, life visions, aesthetic style preferences and media preferences, not only provides the richest data (for communication strategists, creatives and media planners), but also yields the best discriminative performance compared to other lifestyle segmentation methods.

Discussion

However, a general problem with lifestyle typologies has to do with questions of reliability and validity (for an extensive discussion, see Gunter and Furnham, 1992: 91–7). The main points of criticism are:

- *The methods used are purely inductive and not guided by theory.* Often, the items used in lifestyle questionnaires are based on common sense reasoning and implicit experience in carrying out market research. However, inasmuch as we have been basing ourselves on the value concept, it must be said that this is a concept very well grounded in both general social theory (mainly due to Rokeach) and in the theory of consumer behaviour (mainly due to the work of Reynolds, Gutman and Olson). Moreover, for both the value concept and the newer concepts of life visions and aesthetic preferences our inventories are based on considerable exploratory research.
- *The explanatory value of lifestyle types or dimensions concerning consumer behaviour is low and not well documented.* When it has been attempted to relate purchase data and lifestyle data in such a way that the amount of variance in the former explained by the latter can be ascertained, the amount of variance explained has often been very modest, sometimes even below the variance explained by demographic variables alone (Wells and Tigert, 1971). As Wells (1975) put it in a review article: 'Stated as correlation coefficients these relationships appear shockingly small – frequently in the .1 or .2 range, seldom higher than .3 or .4.' Notice that our research instrument clearly yields better results, with average (!) eta-values at the .35 level.

Our option for dimensions (values, life visions, aesthetic style and media preferences) that are more reflective of lasting personal characteristics and behaviours, compared to the more variable and superficial AIO items, certainly improves the reliability of the research instrument. However, much more research needs to be done.

Indeed, we do recognize that the project of developing value inventories, life visions and aesthetic style preferences remains a subjective enterprise. Therefore, it would be interesting to see what other researchers, following a similar approach, would come up with. Equally interesting would be research exploring other markets than the ones under scrutiny here.

Nevertheless, some authors claim that the use of psychographics or lifestyle research remains even today one of the least understood but potentially most powerful approaches in market and communication research (see, for example, Gunter and Furnham, 1992: 30; Heath, 1995; Wolburg and Pokrywczynski, 2001). We hope that this article may contribute to a better understanding and a renewed interest in these little researched lifestyle dimensions.

References

Biel, A.L. (1992) 'How Brand Image Drives Brand Equity', *Journal of Advertising Research* November/December: 6–12.

Chaney, D. (1996) *Lifestyles*. London: Routledge.

Chiagouris, L.G. (1991) 'The Personal Dynamics of the Decision Maker', PhD dissertation, The City University of New York, Baruch Graduate School of Business.

Clawson, D.J. and D.E. Vinson (1978) 'Human Values: An Historical and Interdisciplinary Analysis', pp. 396–402 in H.K. Hunt (ed.), *Advances in Consumer Research*. Vol. 5. Ann Arbor, MI: Association for Consumer Research.

Cosmas, S.C. (1982) 'Life Styles and Consumption Patterns', *Journal of Consumer Research* 8: 453–5.

Demby, E. (1974) 'Psychographics and from Where it Came', pp. 9–30 in W.D. Wells (ed.), *Life Style and Psychographics*. Chicago, IL: American Marketing Association.

Ewing, M.T., T.M. Pinto and G.N. Soutar (2001) 'Agency–Client Chemistry: Demographic and Psychographic Influences', *International Journal of Advertising* 20: 169–87.

Feathertone, M. (1991) *Consumer Culture and Postmodernism*. London: Sage.

Fournier, S., D. Antes and G. Beaumier (1992), 'Nine Consumption Lifestyles', *Advances in Consumer Research* 19: 329–37.

Frank, R.E., W.F. Massy and Y. Wind (1972) *Market Segmentation*. Englewood Cliffs, NJ: Prentice-Hall.

Grunert-Beckmann, S.C. and S. Askegaard (1997) 'Seeing With the Mind's Eye: On the Use of Pictorial Stimuli in Values and Lifestyle Research', pp. 161–81 in L.R. Kahle and L. Chiagouris (eds), *Values, Lifestyles, and Psychographics*. Mahwah, NJ: Lawrence Erlbaum.

Gunter, B. and A. Furnham (1992) *Consumer Profiles: An Introduction to Psychographics*. London: Routledge.

Hawkins, D.I., R.J. Best and K.A. Coney (1995) *Consumer Behavior: Implications for Marketing Strategy*. Chicago, IL: Irwin.

Heath, R.P. (1995) 'Psychographics: Qu'est-ce que c'est?', *American Demographics* 11.

Hornik, J. (1989) 'A Temporal and Lifestyle Typology to Model Consumers' Smoking Behavior', *Advances in Consumer Research* 16: 44–50.

Jones, A., J. Sensenig and R. Ashmore (1978) 'Systems of Values and their Multidimensional Representations', *Multivariate Behavioural Research* 13: 255–70.

Kahle, L.R. (ed.) (1983) *Social Values and Social Change: Adaptation to Life in America*. New York: Praeger.

Kahle, L.R. and L. Chiagouris (eds) (1997) *Values, Lifestyles, and Psychographics*. Mahwah, NJ: Lawrence Erlbaum.

Kahle, L.R., R. Liu and H. Watkins (1992) 'Psychographic Variation across United States Geographic Regions', *Advances in Consumer Research* 19: 346–52.

Kaynak, E. and A. Kara (2001) 'An Examination of the Relationship among Consumer Lifestyles, Ethnocentrism, Knowledge Structures, Attitudes and Behavioural Tendencies: A Comparative Study in Two CIS States', *International Journal of Advertising* 20(4): 457–82.

Lazer, W. (1963) 'Lifestyle Concepts and Marketing', pp. 243–52 in S. Greysser (ed.), *Toward Scientific Marketing*. Chicago, IL: American Marketing Association.

Ness, T.E. and M.T. Stith (1984) 'Middle-Class Values in Blacks and Whites', pp. 231–7 in R.E. Pitts and A.G. Woodside (eds), *Personal Values and Consumer Psychology*. Lexington, MA: Heath and Co.

Peter, J.P. and J.C. Olson (1994) *Understanding Consumer Behavior*. Burr Ridge, IL: Irwin.

Plummer, J.T. (1974) 'The Concept of Life Style Segmentation', *Journal of Marketing* 38: 33–7.

Punj, G. and D.W. Stewart (1983) 'Cluster Analysis in Marketing Research: Review and Suggestions for Application', *Journal of Marketing Research* 20: 134–48.

Reynolds, T.J. and J. Gutman (1988) 'Laddering Theory, Method, Analysis, and Interpretation', *Journal of Advertising Research* 28: 1–34.

Rokeach, M. (1973) *The Nature of Human Values*. New York: Free Press.

Schwartz, S. (1992) 'Universals in the Content and Structure of Values: Theoretical Advances and Empirical Tests in 20 Countries', pp. 1–65 in M.P. Zanna (ed.), *Advances in Experimental Social Psychology*. New York: Academic Press.

Schwartz, S. and W. Bilsky (1990) 'Towards a Universal Psychological Structure of Human Values', *Journal of Personality and Social Psychology* 53: 550–62.

Seligman, C., J.M. Olson and M.P. Zanna (eds) (1996) *Values: The Ontario Symposium*, Vol. 8. Hillsdale, NJ: Lawrence Erlbaum.

Smith, W. (1956) 'Product Differentation and Market Segmentation as Alternative Marketing Strategies', *Journal of Marketing* 21: 3–8.

Solomon, M.R. (1994) *Consumer Behavior: Buying, Having, Being*. Boston, MA: Allyn and Bacon.

Struch, N., S.H. Schwartz and W.A. van der Kloot (2002) 'Meanings of Basic Values for Women and Men: A Cross-Cultural Analysis', *Personality and Social Psychology Bulletin* 28(1): 16–28.

Wells, W.D. (1975) 'Psychographics: A Critical Review', *Journal of Marketing Research* 12: 196–213.

Wells, W.D. and D. Tigert (1971) 'Activities, Interests and Opinions', *Journal of Advertising Research* 11: 27–35.

Wolburg, J.M. and J. Pokrywczynski (2001) 'A Psychographic Analysis of Generation Y College Students', *Journal of Advertising Research* 41(5): 33–50.

21

Consumer Culture, Islam and the Politics of Lifestyle: Fashion for Veiling in Contemporary Turkey

Bariş Kiliçbay and Mutlu Binark

Introduction: the Turkish modernization project and the construction of a collective identity

Since the late 1980s, Turkey's economic structure has been reformed in parallel with the integration process into the global market economy. The adoption of the principles of a market economy has influenced individuals and their ways of self-definition within everyday life. Simultaneously, as a consequence of a homogenized national culture and national identity – two projects of Kemalist ideology, which the nation-state has been based on since the establishment of the Turkish Republic in 1923 – the problem of the representation of 'the others' has come about. Two tensions have arisen from discussions on the representation of the marginalized 'others'. The necessity to define the centre and the periphery has stimulated the first tension, while the second tension is a result of seeking control mechanisms to strengthen the nation-state ideology, which conceives secularism as one of its founding principles. Turkish secularism is not an equivalent of the Anglo-Saxon conceptualization of secularism, which includes 'the separation of the church and the state'. In Turkey, secularism is rather interpreted as the regulation and the administration of religious practices and institutions by the nation-state and its agent, the General Directorate of Religious Affairs. Since the foundation of the Turkish Republic, this interpretation of secularism has been called in the Turkish Constitution *laicism*, following the French model, but also differing from it (Göle, 1997: 64–5). We refer to the Turkish Republic's interpretation of secularism as 'didactic secularism', and define it as moralistic and pedagogical, and also as a controlling and teaching mechanism, which conceives secularism as a western lifestyle.

We also argue that Turkish modernization, conceptualized as a project of social engineering, resulted both in the homogenization and the absorption of different identities within the monocultural identity. Only the use of the Turkish language was allowed in public institutions, and there was to be only one single

Source: *EJC* (2002), vol. 17, no. 4: 495–511.

national identity; in order to orientate every citizen, their duties and their obligations towards the Turkish Republic. The end result of these disciplinary techniques, in the attempt to forge a collective identity, was the removal of different identities/social movements from the public sphere. Therefore, from the early 1920s to the present, local bourgeoisie and religious sects have been located at the periphery by the nation-state's elites, which include military officers, bureaucrats and Kemalist intellectuals (Mardin, 1973). For the sake of the regime, as Kevin Robins (1996: 70) states, 'the conditions of diversity and pluralism necessary to democratic life were stifled from the beginning'. The difference between the modernization *process* in the West and the modernization *project* in Turkey must be emphasized (Göle, 1996).

Since the early 1990s, local bourgeoisie and religious sects have gained an opportunity to intervene in the established meanings and positions of the centre and the periphery. This is a result of the development of an Islamic bourgeoisie with middle-sized investments ranging from textiles to the automotive industries, from the food sector to the media industry. It is possible that the Welfare Party (Refah Partisi), representing political Islam in the Grand National Assembly of the Turkish Republic, has also accelerated this process. When the Welfare Party came into power at a municipal level in 1994, and took part in the coalition government from January 1995 to February 1998, political Islam became more visible. Furthermore, both the mainstream and Islamist media have helped to bring political Islam into the public sphere. Also raising political Islam's public presence have been demonstrations such as the 'headscarf protest', which was initiated by the demand by some Muslim women to be allowed to cover their heads according to the Islamic principle while attending public schools, universities and working in public institutes (Göle, 1997: 62).[1]

This new visibility has popularized Islam in the cultural realm in several ways. The most important aspects of this popularization are twofold. On the one hand, the emergence of the Islamist media and on the other, the rise of new consumption patterns. The Islamist media includes newspapers, periodicals, literature, including some best-sellers, movies and radio and television programmes that enable the voice of the Islamic other. The new consumption patterns include new leisure-time activities for Islamic communities, such as tourism and fashion. For instance, Kanal 7, Samanyolu TV, Işik TV and to some extent TGRT are both nationwide and transnational Islamist television channels (see Binark and Çelikcan, 2000; Öncü, 2000); Akra FM, Dünya FM, Radyo Arifan are some of the popular Islamist radio channels; and Islamist newspapers include *Zaman*, *Yeni Şafak*, *Vakit* and *Milli Gazete*.

Shifting meanings of the practice of veiling

Religious and traditional meaning

In Turkey, the practice of veiling is generally discussed in two contexts. First, the practice indicates the 'primary and pure meaning' based on Islamic principles with reference to the Koran, the essential and divine source of Islamic thought, and the Sunna through the Hadith, the secondary and worldly source generated from the commentaries of the Prophet Muhammed. They suggest the necessity of covering the female body to conceal it from the male gaze, as a sign of adherence to the Islamic faith and belief (El Guindi, 1999: 55–7). In this first meaning, the scarf, often in pastel or austere colours, covers the head and half the shoulder. In Turkey, this first meaning is evident in the traditional mode of dress favoured by housemaids and many peasant women (Norton, 1997: 167; Ilyasoğlu, 1994: 107). This first meaning is usually symbolized in the use of a 'headscarf' (*başxörtüsü*), which is defined in the latest edition of the dictionary of the Turkish Language Institute as 'a covering, made of muslin or silk that women wrap round their heads to cover their hair'. Until the mid-1980s, the word 'headscarf' only carried the first meaning, which eventually came to be seen as the symbol of popular religiosity in Turkey (Subaşı, 2000).

Political meaning

In the second context, the practice of veiling is considered a powerful symbol of 'political Islam', seeking representation in the public sphere through the idealization of veiled women. According to some Islamist intellectuals, the question of identification either with the West or with Islam is closely linked to the veiling issue. They argue that when women today decide whether or not to wear a veil, they are not simply selecting a form of dress, rather they are locating themselves in one of these worlds: the West, or Islam. Hence, they insist on women's wearing the veil as an obligation, and as a true way to practise Islamic principles in everyday life. We could interpret political Islam's insistence on the practice of veiling as using political symbolism to challenge the nation-state's ideology and its conceptualization of civilized identity in Turkey. The second meaning of veiling, in contrast to the first, is generally seen in urban areas, such as in Istanbul, Ankara and Konya (Göle, 1997: 73). In this second, political meaning, the word *türban* describes how to cover the head, hair, neck and shoulders carefully. In the course of time, the practice of veiling came to mean that 'the Islamic woman' should conceal the rest of her body completely as well as the head and the shoulders. Hence, Muslim women have begun to wear long coats and a modern *türban*, instead of a headscarf, which together come to signify the practice of veiling (*tesettür*). This second meaning represents something beyond an attachment to Islam as a religion, rather addressing Islamism as a political movement, known to many sources – especially in the West – as 'Islamic fundamentalism' or 'Islamic revivalism'.

A new meaning: consumption context

We claim that a new meaning could be attributed to the practice of veiling, that is the articulation of a religious practice to the consumption culture. In Turkey, since the early 1990s, the rise of what could be called a 'fashion for veiling' is a result of this articulation process. We argue that the practice of veiling is inseparable from consumption, commodity, even pleasure patterns, and is stimulated by global and local trends of the market economy. Following these trends, some of the clothing companies in Turkey offer various veiling models and styles to women belonging to urban middle and upper classes who are compelled to or who willingly chose to dress according to Islamic principles.

While political Islam empowers and promotes the return of Muslim actors, ethics and aesthetics to the public sphere, the lifestyles of Muslim actors are correspondingly changing due to their encounter with modernized lifestyles. New social divisions are occurring among Islamic communities. Therefore, as Göle points out, the representation of the Islamic other in the public sphere is very complex, and there is a compound relationship between the identity politics of Islamic communities and the global forces of consumerism and of market economics (Göle, 1997: 74–7).[2] Since the 1990s, with the aim of presenting alternative consumption strategies to the westernized and dominant ones, new consumption practices are being developed by the newly formed Islamic middle classes (Göle, 2000: 94), such as Islamic fashion and the Islamization of urban ways of life like patronizing restaurants, supermarkets and hotels. For instance, there is a luxury hotel, the *Caprice*, which is very is popular among these new middle classes. Its name is in French and the word itself is not in line with Islamic ethics and aesthetics.[3] It is located on the western coast of Turkey and offers summer holidays that conform with Islamic principles, such as separate beaches for men and women and respect for the praying hours. Leisure is 'Islamicized' but in line with the market system, and as a consequence, the lifestyles of Muslim subjects are transformed. In other words, the subjects of the periphery are assimilated into the centre. Muslim women are at the core of all these alterations, because of the shifting meaning of the practice of veiling. Fashion shows and new designs for veiling targeting urban middle-class Muslim women are indicators of this new meaning, a consumption context to the practice of veiling, which promotes the habit of purchasing.

Islamic women's magazines

In the early 1980s, Turkey saw an increase in the number of Islamic newspapers and periodicals being published, and following the abolition of the state monopoly on broadcasting in the early 1990s, a whole range of Islamist audiovisual media came on air, adding a new dimension to this scene throughout the 1990s. When one focuses on Islamist media in Turkey, it is common to neglect the presence of Islamic women's magazines, which show the more intimate face and the everyday life perspective of the 1980s phenomenon, political Islam. Few researchers have analysed Islamic women's magazines in Turkey specifically (see Arat, 1995; Acar, 1995; Alankuş-Kural, 1995; Demir, 1998; Sallan Gül and Gül, 2000). They have generally focused on the discourse of these magazines in the context of the representation of female sexuality, the social visibility of Muslim women, the participation of women in the public sphere, women's movements and the construction of the Islamic other. We think that a consumer culture based perspective has been lacking from previous works. Questioning the mechanism through which the practices of veiling have been articulated within consumer culture led us to the analysis of the discourses of the news and articles on fashion that appeared in these magazines, and the emergence of a 'fashion for veiling' in the fashion advertisements. This phenomenon is only visible in the Islamic women's magazines and in Islamic fashion catalogues. The mainstream media in Turkey, which is dominantly liberal and supportive of Kemalist ideology, regards the fashion for veiling as an 'exotic' phenomenon and covers Islamic fashion shows as tabloid news.

The oldest Islamic women's magazines are *Kadin ve Aile* (Woman and Family) and *Mektup* (Letter); both were established in 1985. The subtitle of *Kadin ve Aile* is: 'Monthly home magazine', while *Mektup* has a more slogan-type subtitle: 'From women's pen for everyone including men and women'. The third magazine is called *Bizim Aile* (Our Family) and it was published between 1988 and 1989. Its subtitle is simply: 'Monthly women's magazine'. Later this magazine changed its title to *Yeni Bizim Aile* (The New 'Our Family'). *Kadin Kimliği* (Woman's Identity) is the newest of all, being published since 1995 and it has a much more unusual subtitle: 'A different perspective on life'. The Kemalist modernization project conceived women as the symbol of modernization and encouraged women's magazines to offer Turkish women new and modern lifestyles. Similarly, Islamist discourse, following the symbolization of the women as holders of the veil, has targeted women from various Islamic communities in Turkey through Islamic women's magazines. These Muslim women, who have been idealized as 'the fighters for religion', have been important actors in the popularization of political Islam in the attempt to penetrate both the private and public spheres. These magazines generally take a critical position against the modern capitalist system and consumer society, which are seen as consequences of western civilization. More common subjects like clothing, health issues and childcare are treated from the Islamic point of view. Fashion as a practice of the consumption culture is criticized as an anti-Islamic ideology in the articles and by the leading journalists who write for the magazines such as Cihan Aktaş and Emine Şenlikoğlu. But in contrast to these articles, the advertisements appearing in these magazines invite the readers to be consumers in the fashion for veiling. The articulation of a consumption culture is a somewhat unavoidable result of the inclusion of the Islamic bourgeoisie into the various areas of social and everyday life.

The analysis of the articles, interviews and the advertisements published in the Islamist women's magazines shows the dominance of a discourse which denies the fashion phenomenon. The reason for this is inevitably the argument that fashion is contrary to Islamic principles, which forbid waste (*israf*) of any kind; and that fashion is the result of an imposed lifestyle of modern capitalist societies. The relation between women and fashion as represented in the Islamic women's magazines is important and problematic in the sense that it shows the conflict between a lifestyle according to Islamic principles and a modern capitalist lifestyle. The articles published in these magazines discuss the fashion phenomenon from an intellectual and Islamic point of view, while the advertisements introduce the products of the fashion for veiling, which are one of the visible aspects of consumerism experienced by the Islamic middle class as a symbolic capital. The results of this contradiction can be followed in special issues devoted to discussions about fashion.[4] A considerable number of articles published in these special issues are written by famous Islamist intellectuals, whose discussions on political Islam, civil society and Islamist feminism are well known. The dominant approach of these articles is to invite the Islamic bourgeoisie to an experience of consumerism within the limits of Islamic principles.

A general review of all the articles, interviews and news published in the Islamic women's magazines allows us to conclude that fashion as a whole and particularly the fashion for veiling are discussed from a negative perspective. The writers are aware that the capitalist system is powerful enough to assimilate religious institutions, ethics and the aesthetics of Islam into consumption, which is thereby considered a threat to the Islamic lifestyle. While the Islamic intellectuals writing in these magazines have a reservation concerning fashion and while other articles show a stronger rejection of the entire capitalist system; the advertisements and the news in these magazines prove the ongoing articulation process of the Islamic faith into the consumer culture. The major reason for the denial of the capitalist production system by Islamic thought is based on the importance of sustenance (*rızık*). In Islam, economic activity is seen as sustenance rather than production. That is why 'waste' is the essential concept setting constraints on consumption. With the 1980s, new economic activities appropriate to Islamic principles have been developed and some members of Islamic communities have started to appear in these activities. One of the results of this was the discovery of three important concepts by Muslim investors, which are fashion, brand and profit. Abdurrahman Arslan points out how the name *Tekbir*, which indicates the magnificence of Allah, is now used commercially as the brand name for an Islamic clothing company and has lost its original sense (Arslan, 2000: 162–3).

Indeed, fashion is not only considered a threat to Islamic lifestyle in women's magazines, but also in Islamist literature. There are plenty of books devoted to this subject such as Abdurrahman Kasapoğlu's (1994) *Kadın, Modernizm ve Örtünme* (Women, Modernity and Veiling), Aysel Zeynep's (1997) *Kadının Tercihi* (The Choice of Woman) and famous Islamist woman author Cihan Aktaş's two-volume study of women's clothing, titled *Tanzimattan Günümüze Kılık, Kıyafet ve İktidar* (Clothing and Power from the Tanzimat Reformation to the Present) (1990) and *Mahremiyetin Tükenişi* (The Decline of Intimacy) (1995). In this literature, fashion is defined as 'a basis for sexual deviance' (Kasapoğlu, 1994: 83); 'exhibitionism and consumerism' (Zeynep, 1997: 45–9); and 'an indication of a loss of intimacy' (Aktaş, 1995: 12–13). Particularly, Aktaş criticizes the fashion for veiling because it indicates the surrender of the religion and its practices to the capitalist consumption culture (Aktaş, 1995: 194). As a result of the fashion for veiling, according to Aktaş, veiled women are relocated in depoliticized positions, and gradually become consumers, who act within the 'system' (Aktaş, 1995: 194). Moreover, these women try to legitimize their consumption thus: 'up to now *they* consumed, now *we* do'. In conclusion, Aktaş claims that the transformation of Islamic communities, particularly women, towards the articulation of consumption culture is a reflection of an 'American dream' of the Islamic bourgeoisie (Aktaş, 1995: 195). Sociologist Ümit Meriç, describing clothing, uses the following analogy. According to Meriç, clothing, therefore veiling, unlike fashion, is not humankind's second skin, but rather is 'home' (Meriç, 1987: 33, 36). Some Islamist authors even try to advise women how to avoid the seduction of the fashion for veiling. They claim if one loses one's dignity, it is because of fashion. Therefore, they suggest women should not display their body. They define fashion as forcing a nation to lose its roots, its ethics and its primary objectives (Ormanlar, 1999: 86). As discussed earlier, Islamic discourse generally equates fashion and the fashion for veiling with a loss of religious faith and Islamic principles.[5]

The Fashion for veiling[6]

History

The analysis of the advertisements in the Islamist women's magazines points to the shifting meaning of the practice of veiling, as we have previously discussed. The progress of the fashion advertisements indicates the existence of two phases: the first phase coincides with the period when clothing companies discovered a potential market for veiled women. The absence within the advertisements of some essential terms and concepts of the fashion industry typifies this period. The majority of the companies preferred to announce their names, distribution addresses and the types of products they sold. For instance, the advertisement titled 'Tesettürde Hayrun Nisa Giyim' (*Bizim Aile*, 1991), gives information about items available to customers. The advertisement itself does not contain any written information about the practice of veiling, but the illustration of the female in the advert depicts the ideal customer of this clothing company (Figure 21.1). In another advertisement for 'Tesettürlü Ceran Manifatura' (*Mektup*, February 1990) religious messages are introduced, such as 'veiling is not a tradition, but, a law of Allah'. In this advertisement it is also emphasized that the clothing company aims to serve 'Muslim sisters'. Referring to the practice of veiling and its political meaning, this advertisement uses exclusively illustrations of females, drawn in black clothes and without faces. The text of the advertisement, while insisting on the political meaning of veiling, refers also to a search for quality and variety; thus the advertisement invites female customers to buy.

The major characteristic of these first phase advertisements is the use of illustrations in which the female face is generally not pictured, instead of photographs. The absence of faces might be a result of the Islamic prohibitions concerning women, or a denial of female sexuality in order to conceal 'intimate' female bodies from the male gaze. This first phase dates back to the late 1980s, and the first fashion show for veiling products organized by the Tekbir Clothing Company marks its conclusion. The owner of the Tekbir Clothing Company, Mustafa Karaduman, in one of his interviews with Islamic women's magazines, tried to legitimize his fashion shows. 'In this fashion show', he said, 'our goal is to

TESETTÜRDE
HAYRUN NISA
GiYiM

- Abaye
- Harmane
- Manto
- Gömlek
- Pardesu
- Eşarp

- Bluz
- Elbise
- Çamaşir
- Etek
- Çorap
- Ipek Eşarp

Turgut Yurtgan

Tel: 354 24 58
Çarşi Camii Pasaji No: 7
Pendik/ISTANBUL

FIGURE 21.1

represent the practice of veiling in the best way … we do not intend to reduce the practice of veiling to an instrument of fashion. Indeed, our aim is to use fashion as an instrument of *tesettür*. That is to say, we are trying to orient the masses to practise *tesettür*' (*Yeni Bizim Aile*, July 1992: 9–11).

The second phase of the fashion for veiling is characterized by the concern with creating marketing strategies such as brands and images. Photographs of models are used in the majority of the advertisements and the images are reinforced by texts which invite the consumers to be different from others. But this difference is closely linked with an appurtenance of a community, which is the intersection of religion and fashion. As it is widely accepted that the construction of identity is a complex and ongoing negotiation, while one uses all the material and cultural determinants to locate oneself in a suitable/desirable location, one also uses items of consumption such as clothing, popular music, leisure-time activities. Through the advertisements for the fashion for veiling, the women of Islamic communities are invited to relocate their identities in terms of differentiation from women who practise veiling as tradition and those who do not practise veiling.

Analysis

Eight fashion catalogues for the year 1998–9 for some of the major Islamic clothing companies in Turkey such as Tekbir Clothing, Sitare Clothing, the Setre Collection and Hilye Textiles were also analysed to identify their characteristics and similarities. We particularly focused on the cover pages of the catalogues due to their function of drawing consumers' attention (McCracken, 1993: 14–15). Additionally, visual codes, the use of space, *mise-en-scène*, the use of brand names, different models, introductory texts and slogans are analysed.

The brand names of the companies are generally linked to a foreign word, either English or French, and some are completely in English, like Mode Ziynet, the Hilye Collection, High Generation, and The Fashion of Woman to 2000 Years [*sic*]. The use of foreign words implies that Islamic clothing companies regard fashion as a western practice following general Turkish marketing trends. It is common in Turkey to name products and companies by foreign words in order to render customers a symbolic gratification that creates an illusion of a reinforcement of their social status. This branding strategy indicates that the ideal customer will be affiliated with the symbolic value derived from the consumption. As David Chaney (1996) puts it, the customer through the brands of the goods reveals taste and cultural capital. The brand no longer indicates the material nature of the object; it is rather a sign of the social nature of the object (Bourdieu, 1993).

Jennifer Craick argues that in non-western cultures clothing is seen both as a necessity to cover the body and an expression of spirituality, religiosity within the art form (Craick, 1994: 18). She claims that in non-western cultures the term 'fashion' is rarely referred to; as a consequence western researchers consider the clothing in those cultures to be timeless and unchanging (Craick, 1994: 19). Contrary to this argument, we reveal that a fashion for veiling exists, and the accentuation of the brand name with western words provides customers with a symbolic modernity even though they prefer to remain within the limits of Islamic principles.

Two styles of veiling appear in these catalogues. The first style is derived from the experience of political Islam, in which the face is covered in a different style from the traditional headscarfs. The second style shows the variety of new models of veiling throughout the products presented in the catalogues. It is sometimes possible to see a part of the hair and the skirts may be shorter than normal. For instance, in a page in a Hilye catalogue (see Figure 21.2), the product presented is relatively modern in style. The model is posing in a traditional street, she is using a mobile phone indicating the offer of a modern lifestyle to women who veil. When the customer sees this, the preferred reading might be an articulation of a 'naive' religious practice as a way of life within the modern consumer society. While in the first two meanings of veiling that we previously discussed, namely the pure and the political meanings, the woman's body is concealed, the images in these catalogues expose the woman's body. Thus, women are not only invited to consume, but they also become objects of consumption. Furthermore, the texts of the fashion catalogues[7] invite customers to purchase quality and sophistication. For instance in Setre Tesettur's 1998 Spring–Summer catalogue, the definition of fashion is expressed thus: 'an expectation of uniqueness', supplied by Setre Tesettur through its clothes and promise of quality. The company claims that 'Setre introduces women to quality and to elegance'. In the same catalogue the word 'Setre' is described as 'a limitless world where dreams come true within the borders of veiling'. Ironically, the emphasis on the dreamlike characteristic of the practice of veiling as opposed to the customers' religious expectations reveals the 'hybrid meaning' of the practice in which Islamic codes lose their original context.

FIGURE 21.2

Another feature of these catalogues is the presence of various status symbols such as mobile phones and camcorders, for example in the Sitare and Hilye catalogues. The models are photographed with symbols of modernity. Consequently, these catalogues offer symbolic gratification to the consumer and thus associate their products with socially desired values. Furthermore, veiled women purchase these veiling products in order to be different from other female members of their Islamic community and from the rest of the society. However, the accessories used in the photographs of the models connect the veiled women to the consumption patterns of modern capitalist society.

The clothes themselves vary from a simple headscarf to complicated suits. Some clothes are for daily use, including business suits. Some of them are smart

FIGURE 21.3

nightwear. Business suits include jackets and trousers; the models wearing these clothes are photographed in offices. Smart dresses have an orientalistic connotation; they create an 'imaginary' oriental setting. While these clothes conceal a woman's body, they also expose it by using oriental elements; thus the reading of female sexuality is mediated (see Figure 21.3). Contrary to the business clothes photographed in modern public spaces, orientalistic clothes are placed in exotic settings. Finally, in some catalogues, clothes have names such as Selen Abiye, Ubeyda Afkan, Kudret Abiye Takim, which are specifically women's names that generally carry a religious connotation (see Figure 21.4). Naming one of the items of clothes Fazilet Pardesü is a pun on the name of a pro-Islamic party, Fazilet Partisi (Virtue Party), which was represented in the National Assembly.[8]

FIGURE 21.4

Concluding remarks

Our analysis shows that the Islamic discourses on veiling as a religious practice are not as coherent as they claim to be, and that the practice of veiling does not have a singular meaning. Turkey's experience of modernization, which has lasted since the early 19th century, has considerably affected the Islamic movement and its conceptualization in daily life. We think that the meanings and the context of the practice of veiling are subject to constant change. We argue that Turkish Muslim women use the veil in multiple ways according to their relation to the practice of veiling either as a purely religious or a traditional practice, as a political symbol, as a symbol of status, as a marker of difference or as a new form of consumption. A woman who wears the veil refuses to be included in the dominant definition of modernity and civilization. On the one hand, she experiences a feeling of being 'privileged' and of being different from the others; on the other hand, she reproduces the new meaning of veiling, which in this article is defined as the consumption context of the practice of veiling.

Notes

We would like to thank Stuart Duckworth, Lawrence Raw and Emine Onaran İncirlioğlu for their valuable comments. An earlier version of this article was presented in the Third International Crossroads in Cultural Studies Conference, 21–25 June 2000, Birmingham, UK.

1. Following the military takeover on 12 September 1980, a 'Dress and Appearance Regulation' was issued. This regulation prohibits employees while on duty in public agencies and institutes from wearing, in the case of men, moustaches, beards or long hair; and in the case of women, mini-skirts, low-necked dresses and headscarves. The regulation applies to students as well as civil servants. Therefore, the Muslim women's movement in the mid-1980s targeted this prohibition and attempted to gain public sympathy towards the use of the 'headscarf' in public institutions despite the Kemalist rule.
2. In addition to media and leisure-time activities, since the 1990s Islamist communities have gradually gained an interest in the food sector and opened chain stores like Beğendik and Yimpaş in metropolitan areas; and invested in the automotive industry and its subsectors, founding JETPA Ltd. and Kombassan Ltd. The Islamist bourgeoisie has also invested in bank-like monetary activities such as Faisal Finans, Ihlas Finans, Al-baraka Turk, Kuveyt-Turk, where customers are supposed to share the profits not 'the interest' in accordance with Islamic trading principles.
3. Unlike the names of many other hotels or holiday resorts owned by Muslim companies, which denote an Islamic way of life (see Öncü, 2000).
4. The titles of these special issues are for example: 'Fashion and Veiling' (*Yeni Bizim Aile*, July 1992, October 1994), 'What Fashion Has Taken Away From Us' (*Kadın ve Aile*, February 1986), 'Muslim Women and Fashion' (*Kadın ve Aile*, May 1991) and 'Veiling and Women' (*Kadın ve Aile*, November 1997).
5. There has been a discussion recently among Islamist authors about the fashion for veiling. The 24 July issue of *Yeni Şafak*, an Islamic newspaper, covers the summer 2001 fashion show organized by Tekbir Clothing and the clothes are introduced as follows: 'three pieces are "in", one piece is "out"; abstract designs for the scarf are "in", designs with flowers are "out"; long jackets are "in"', etc. The popular colours for veiling are also mentioned. Although the traditional colour is 'green', in summer 2001, the popular colour for veiling will be 'red', which was a very popular colour in 2001 fashion all around the world. However, this kind of news coverage is severely criticized by Demet Tezcan, woman journalist for *Akit*, a pro-Islamist newspaper, in the following headline: 'Degeneration Is In, Veiling Practice Is Out' (cited in *Milliyet*, 5 August 2001: 17). Tezcan claims that the news coverage of the fashion for veiling by *Yeni Şafak* is similar to the tabloid newspapers, and she adds that due to the emergence of the fashion for veiling and its seductive invitation to Islamic subjects to consume, in the future there will be no real Islamic subject left.
6. We use the term 'fashion for veiling' in a double sense. The first meaning refers to the fact that carrying a veil is a matter of fashion and the term also means fashion as applied to the actual veils and clothes.
7. The texts of the fashion catalogues are often placed in between the images and give hints about the new meaning of the practice of veiling, and guide the customer to recognize the brand name of the product by using common fashion terminology.
8. The current owner of the Tekbir Clothing Company, Cafer Karaduman, explains they are influenced by the political agenda while naming their products (see *Tempo*, No. 619, 1999: 56).

References

Acar, F. (1995) 'Women and Islam in Turkey', pp. 46–65 in Ş. Tekeli (ed.), *Women in Modern Turkish Society: A Reader*. London: Zed Books.

Aktaş, C. (1990) *Tanzimattan Günümüze Kılık, Kıyafet ve Iktidar*. Istanbul: Nehir.

Aktaş, C. (1995) *Mahremiyetin Tukenişi*. Istanbul: Nehir.

Alankuş-Kural, S. (1995) 'Türkiye'de Alternatif Kamular ve Islamcı Kadınlar', *Toplum ve Bilim* 67: 76–110.

Arat, Y. (1995) 'Feminism and Islam: Considerations on the Journal *Kadın ve Aile* Turkey', pp. 66–78 in Ş. Tekeli (ed.), *Women in Modern Turkish Society: A Reader*. London: Zed Books.

Arslan, A. (2000) *Modern Dünyada Müslümanlar*. Istanbul: Iletisxim.

Binark, M. and P. Çelikcan (2000) 'Border Crossings in a Multi-Channel TV. Environment: The Discourse of the Islamic Other in Turkey', *Iletişim* 5: 71–92.

Bourdieu, P. (1993) *Sociology in Question*. London: Sage.

Chaney, D. (1996) *Lifestyles*. London: Routledge.

Craick, J. (1994) *The Face of Fashion: Cultural Studies in Fashion*. London: Routledge.

Demir, H. (1998) *İslamcı Kadının Aynadaki Sureti*. Istanbul: Sel.

El Guindi, F. (1999) 'Veiling Resistance', *Fashion Theory* 3(1): 51–80.

Göle, N. (1996) *The Forbidden Modern: Civilization and Veiling*. Ann Arbor: University of Michigan Press.

Göle, N. (1997) 'The Gendered Nature of the Public Sphere', *Public Culture* 10(1): 61–81.

Göle, N. (2000) 'Snapshots of Islamic Modernities', *Daedalus* 129(1): 91–117.

Ilyasoglu, A. (1994) *Örtülü Kimlik*. Istanbul: Metis.

Kasapoğlu, A. (1994) *Kadın, Modernizm ve Örtünme*. Konya: Esra.

McCracken, E. (1993) *Decoding Women's Magazines*. London: Macmillan.

Mardin, S. (1973) 'Center and Periphery Relations: A Key to Turkish Politics', *Daedalus* Winter: 169–90.

Meriç, Ü. (1987) 'Sosyolojik Açıdan Kılık-Kıyafet ve İslam'da Örtünme', pp. 29–37 in I. Kurt (ed.), *İslam'da Kılık-Kıyafet ve Örtünme*. İstanbul: İslami İlimler Araştirma Vakfi Yay1nlar1.

Norton, J. (1997) 'Faith and Fashion in Turkey', pp. 149–77 in N. Lindisfarne-Tapper and B. Ingham (eds), *Languages of Dress in the Middle East*. London: Curzon Press.

Öncü, A. (2000) 'The Banal and the Subversive: Politics of Language on Turkish Television', *European Journal of Cultural Studies* 3(3): 296–318.

Ormanlar, C. (1999) 'Giyim Kuşam Modaları', pp. 42–91 in O. Baydar and D. Ozkan (eds), *75. Yılında Değişen İnsan: Cumhuriyet Modaları*. Istanbul: Tarih Vakfi.

Robins, K. (1996) 'Interrupting Identities: Turkey/Europe', pp. 61–86 in S. Hall and P. du Gay (eds), *Questions of Cultural Identity*. London: Sage.

Sallan Gül, S. and H. Gül (2000) 'The Question of Women in Islamic Revivalism in Turkey: A Review of the Islamic Press', *Current Sociology* 48(2): 1–26.

Subaşı, N. (2000) '80'li Yıllarda Örtünmenin Anlamı', *Islamiyat*: 3(2): 61–70.

Zeynep, A. (1997) *Kadının Tercihi*. Istanbul: Denge.

Index